EKNATH EASWARAN

Born into an ancient matrilineal Hindu family in Kerala
state, South India, Eknath Easwaran regards his mother's
mother as his spiritual teacher. She taught him by her
selfless example how to find complete fulfillment in the
family context.

Easwaran was chairman of the English department
of a well-known Indian university when he came to the
U.S. on the Fulbright exchange program. Here, as in India, his humor and humanness soon made him a teacher
of enormous appeal. In 1960 he established the Blue
Mountain Center of Meditation in Berkeley, California—
"to move," as he puts it, "from education for degrees to
education for living." As the Center's director, he continues to teach meditation in the greater San Francisco
Bay Area to those who want to lead active, spiritually
fulfilling lives in the midst of family, friends, and society.

Easwaran brings to this volume a rare combination
of literary skill, scholarship, and spiritual wisdom. His
Sanskrit comes from one of the purest traditions in India,
and for almost twenty years he followed a successful
career as a writer, lecturer, and teacher of English literature. But it is essentially the stamp of personal experience
that makes Easwaran's presentation of the spiritual life
so effective. In this book, without metaphysics or philosophy, he illustrates the practicality of the Bhagavad
Gita with familiar anecdotes from daily living.

दिवि सूर्यसहस्रस्य भवेद्युगपदुत्थिता । यदि भाः सदृशी सा स्याद्भासस्तस्य महात्मनः ॥१२॥

If a thousand suns were to rise at the same time, the blaze of their light would resemble a little the supreme splendor of the Lord.
—BHAGAVAD GITA I I : I 2

THE BHAGAVAD GITA
FOR DAILY LIVING, VOLUME 2

Like a Thousand Suns

BY EKNATH EASWARAN

NILGIRI PRESS

©1979 by The Blue Mountain Center of Meditation
Eleventh printing February 2005
All rights reserved. Printed in the United States of America
I S B N : *cloth,* 0–915132–04–4; *paper,* 0–915132–18–4

The Blue Mountain Center of Meditation, founded
in Berkeley California in 1961 by Eknath Easwaran,
publishes books on how to lead the spiritual life in the
home and the community. For information please write
to Nilgiri Press, Box 256, Tomales, California 94971.
On the Web at www.nilgiri.org

This volume has been published simultaneously in a
hardcover edition under the title *The Bhagavad Gita
for Daily Living, Chapters 7 through 12*

Library of Congress Cataloging in Publication Data
will be found on the last page of this book.

Table of Contents

To my Teacher
EKNATH CHIPPU KUNCHI AMMAL
my Grandmother & my Playmate

The Unity of Life

The Bhagavad Gita is the most practical of the Hindu scriptures. Some of its poetry is so magnificent that I have seldom seen its equal in any other language, but to me, the Gita is only secondarily a great work of art. Its primary value, which cuts across all barriers of time, culture, and religious background, lies in showing us how to make a work of art out of our own lives.

It is the essence of the mystical experience to enter into the depths of consciousness and discover that none of us is separate from the rest of life. All creation is part of one infinite Reality—or, in more personal language, all of us are one. This is the theme of this volume, which presents the middle six chapters of the Gita. The Lord of Love, by whatever name—Christ or Sri Krishna, Allah or Adonai or the Divine Mother—dwells in every creature as our real Self.

In India, this realization has been part of a common spiritual heritage for thousands of years, fed by the personal experience of mystics from most of the world's major religions. Hinduism and Buddhism, of course, originated there; Islam and Zoroastrianism have contributed to its culture for several centuries. Jewish communities in South India date from before the Christian era; and Christianity arrived in Kerala state, where I was born, long before it reached most of Europe—in fact, according to Church tradition, the Gospel was brought to India by the Apostle Thomas himself in the first century A.D. Indians are used to being surrounded by many paths to God, and I don't think any people are more catholic in accepting truth in whatever religion they find it.

Against this background, there is a story about a missionary school being inspected by one of the church officials. These inspections could come at any time, and the inspector—who, of course, was usually not Indian—had the privilege of stepping unannounced into any classroom, playing the teacher, and asking whatever question he liked. In this story, an inspector steps in on an English class and says—in English—"Let me ask you three questions: One, what does God know? Two, what can he do? Three, where is he to be found?"

Most of the village children were taken by surprise: after all, it is hard enough to discuss theology in your own language, let alone in somebody else's. But there was one little fellow at the back who really knew his spiritual heritage. He stood up and said politely, "Sir, may I ask *you* three questions?"

The examiner was a good sport, so he said yes. And the boy asked: "What does God *not* know? What can he not do? Where is he not?"

It is a simple reply, but it says a great deal. To the mystic, it is absurd to say there is no God. He is our life, our very Self; how can we deny him? Only when we think that God is something outside us is it possible to say that God does not exist.

A few years ago I remember a columnist describing his family's trip to Europe. While they were driving through France, the children kept complaining, "Dad, when are we going to see Europe?" It is much like that with God. If you want to see the Lord, the mystics say, just look around you; what else is there? "Open your eyes," says Hugh of St. Victor; "the world is full of God."

The Sufis have a vivid image for this. The Lord, they say, is the Showman, but he is also the show. In Sanskrit he is *Mahāmāyī*, the Cosmic Magician, who has cast the illusion of separateness over all the universe. P. T. Barnum may have been proud of the "greatest show on earth," but the earth itself is only a small part of the vast show that is the Lord's. So the Hindu scriptures do not talk about God creating the world; they say that he *became* the world. It is not something different from him; it is a form which he has put on.

In our āshram, our spiritual community, we have three boys living with us who are under the age of four, and every day I have to ask them what they are. One day it is an elephant; the next, a fox or rabbit or raccoon. As one of them says, "When I see an animal, I *be* it." He comes over in the morning and announces, "I'm a baby elephant!" I pretend to be Uncle Elephant, twisting my trunk and wiggling my broad ears—and then he suddenly says, "Now I'm a mouse!" And everything changes; he becomes a mouse. Yet the mouse is not somebody else; it is always the same little boy.

This is how it is with the Lord. He is eternal, formless Reality, yet in his play he has put on a cosmic form, which the Buddhists call *Dharmakaya:* the universe itself. Galaxies, black holes, quasars, the very fabric of space and time—all are part of the Cosmic Magician's display. "There is nothing that exists separate from me," the Lord says in the Gita. "The entire universe is suspended from me as my necklace of jewels."

In Sanskrit, the Lord as Sri Krishna is called *Vistharah,* 'he who has expanded himself'—much in the language of modern cosmology, which describes an expanding universe. Yet in the same breath he is called *Sthāvarasthānuh,* 'he who is completely still.' This is the paradox; he is both. When we look through the eyes of duality, we see a world of phenomena, of constant change—matter and energy, time and death, creation and destruction. But when we look through the eye of unity—as Jesus says, "when our eye is single"—we see that all this is only surface appearance. The restlessness, the change, the duality were in our vision; beneath that appearance there is only the changeless Reality we call God.

One of the appealing implications of this is that it pulls the rug out from the disputes between religion and science. The underlying assumption in these disputes is that God and the world are separate—that we are here and the Lord is out there. It is not only scientists who make this mistake; it is made in the name of religion too. Yet both science and religion are talking about the same thing, as I try to show abundantly in the chapters that follow. I have no particular interest in the philosophy behind these traditional disagreements. But it is a matter of utmost concern to all of us that scientific inquiry proceed hand in hand with spiritual awareness. Without this awareness, we are liable to violate the unity of life everywhere we go, in everything we do.

Scientific knowledge, in other words, is knowledge of separate parts of life. Spiritual knowledge—"wisdom" is a better word—is knowledge of the whole. Scientific knowledge means knowing facts; spiritual wisdom means knowing how to live. A man may be an excellent astronomer, but if he comes home in the evening and loses patience with his children, he is showing his ignorance of life's unity. A woman may be a first-rate physician, but if she is selfish, she has not yet realized that all of us are one. Because life is whole, everything in it is interconnected; everything we do affects the rest. If we live in harmony, everything benefits a little, from our own lives through the rest of the biosphere. But if we violate the unity of existence, everything suffers—our family, our society, and our own health and happiness.

Today, because of the impact of ecology, we are accustomed to this idea that all things in nature are connected. But to judge from our behavior, I think very few of us realize that the same unity applies to life at every level. The implications are very practical. For one, it means that I cannot find my happiness at your expense. If I try, it is not only you who will suffer, I will suffer too. If I am hostile, *I* will get asthma or peptic ulcer; if I am resentful, *I* will get high blood pressure. More than that, if I try to make money at the expense of the environment, all of us are going to suffer—I have to breathe the air and drink the water too. On the other hand, if I live for the welfare of the whole, my own individual welfare is included in that. If I am patient, everyone near me benefits—including me. I will be more relaxed, more secure, better able to weather the storm and stress that is an inescapable part of living.

The unity of life is an unalterable law, the central law of existence. We cannot break it; we can only break ourselves against it. This is our greatest source of suffering, and to me there is nothing more grievous than to see every day how this law is being flouted—by nations, by families, by individuals, everywhere. After thousands of years of evolution we should be beginning to understand the basis of living: nobody can attain fulfillment separately. For all of us, our destiny is one and indivisible.

This is why we need a commentary on the world's great scriptures that addresses itself to daily living. The Gita strikes the same note at the beginning of this volume. It is not enough to have a poetic awareness of unity. It is not enough to have *jnāna,* the direct realization that life is one. In these troubled times, it is essential that we also strive for *vijnāna*—the skillful capacity to apply spiritual understanding to bridge divisions in the home, heal wounds in the minds of individuals, bring together estranged communities, put out the flames of violence, and banish the menace of nuclear war that threatens life today.

Sometimes I hear the mistaken notion that to be spiritual we should withdraw from the world—hide ourselves in a cave and put up a sign saying, "Meditating. Do Not Disturb." The message of the Gita is just the opposite: heal the divisions within yourself and throw yourself into service of others without any thought of profit or prestige for yourself. It is not necessary to preach at others or force them to follow particular ideas. If we try to live out the unity of existence where we are—in our homes, at our jobs—the influence of our lives cannot help spreading to others in proportion to our spiritual growth.

So it should not be surprising that after all the illustrations about galaxies and quasars, the climax of this volume is the chapter entitled "The Way of Love." This is what unity means when translated into daily living. Most of us think of love as a one-to-one relationship. But the mystics tell us, "Don't ever be satisfied with just loving two or three people, with loving only now and then. Learn to make the whole world your own." As the Buddha puts it, when we realize the unity of life, we shall love and protect every creature on earth as a mother loves and protects her only child.

This is a complete transformation of consciousness. The medieval mystic Ruysbroek, when some students asked him for a motto, said, *"Vos estis tam sancti sicut vultis"*: you are as holy as you want to be. I would add, in the same way, we are as happy as we want to be, or as selfless, or as secure—just as, conversely, we are as hostile as we want to be, as selfish, as lonely. The choice in all this is up to us, and the tool for exercising choice is meditation.

Since "meditation" can refer to so many practices today, I think it will be helpful here to summarize the eight-step program for spiritual living which I have found effective in my own life. These steps are elaborated more fully throughout the pages that follow.

1. *Meditation.* The heart of this program is meditation—half an hour every morning, as early as is convenient. Do not increase this period; if you want to meditate more, have half an hour in the evening also, preferably at the very end of the day.

Set aside a room in your home to be used only for meditation and spiritual reading. After a while that room will become associated with meditation in your mind, so that simply entering it will have a calming effect. If you cannot spare a room, have a particular corner. But whichever you choose, keep your meditation place clean, well ventilated, and reasonably austere.

Sit in a straight-backed chair or on the floor and gently close your eyes. If you sit on the floor, you may need to support your back lightly against a wall. You should be comfortable enough to forget your body, but not so comfortable that you become drowsy.

Whatever position you choose, be sure to keep your head, neck, and spinal column erect in a straight line. As concentration deepens, the nervous system relaxes and you may begin to fall asleep. It is important to resist this tendency right from the beginning, by drawing yourself up and away from your back support until the wave of sleep has passed.

Then, in your mind, go *slowly* through a passage from the scriptures or the great mystics. I usually recommend the Prayer of St. Francis of Assisi:

> *Lord, make me an instrument of thy peace.*
> *Where there is hatred, let me sow love;*
> *Where there is injury, pardon;*
> *Where there is doubt, faith;*
> *Where there is despair, hope;*

Where there is darkness, light;
Where there is sadness, joy.

O Divine Master, grant that I may not so much seek
To be consoled as to console,
To be understood as to understand,
To be loved as to love;
For it is in giving that we receive,
It is in pardoning that we are pardoned,
It is in dying [to self] that we are born to eternal life.

Do not follow any association of ideas or try to think about the passage. If you are giving your attention to the words, the meaning *has* to sink in. When distractions come, do not resist them, but try to give more and more attention to the words of the passage. If your mind strays from the passage completely, bring it back gently to the beginning and start again.

When you reach the end of the passage, you may use it again and again until you have memorized others. It is helpful to have a wide variety of passages for meditation, drawn from all the world's major traditions. I recommend chapters two and twelve of the Bhagavad Gita, the Lord's Prayer, the Twenty-third Psalm, the Beatitudes, and the first chapter of the Dhammapada of the Buddha. I have also translated some of the Upanishads for use in meditation. Whatever you choose, the passage should be positive and practical, chosen from a major scripture or a mystic of the highest stature.

The secret of meditation is simple: you become what you meditate on. When you use the Prayer of St. Francis every day in meditation, you are driving the words deep into your consciousness. Eventually they become an integral part of your personality, which means that they will find constant expression in what you do, what you say, and even what you think.

2. *Repetition of the Mantram.* A mantram is a powerful spiritual formula which, when repeated silently in the mind, has the capacity to transform consciousness. There is nothing magical about this. It is simply a matter of practice, as all of us can verify for ourselves.

Every religious tradition has a mantram, often more than one. For Christians, the name of Jesus itself is a powerful mantram; Catholics also use *Hail Mary* or *Ave Maria*. Jews may use *Barukh attah Adonai;* Muslims use the name of Allah or *Allahu akbar*. Probably the oldest Buddhist mantram is *Om mani padme hum*. And in Hinduism, among many choices, I recommend *Rāma, Rāma,* which was Mahatma Gandhi's mantram, or the longer mantram used by my own spiritual teacher, my Grandmother:

> *Haré Rāma Haré Rāma*
> *Rāma Rāma Haré Haré*
> *Haré Krishna Haré Krishna*
> *Krishna Krishna Haré Haré*

Select a mantram that appeals to you deeply. Then, once you have chosen, do not change your mantram again. Otherwise, as Sri Ramakrishna puts it, you will be like a man digging little holes in many places; you will never go deep enough to find water.

Repeat your mantram silently whenever you get the chance: while walking, while waiting, while doing mechanical chores like washing dishes, and especially when you are falling asleep. You will find that this is not mindless repetition; the mantram will help to keep you relaxed and alert. Whenever you are angry or afraid, nervous or worried or resentful, repeat the mantram until the agitation subsides. The mantram works to steady the mind, and all these emotions are power running against you which the mantram can harness and put to work.

3. *Slowing Down*. Hurry makes for tension, insecurity, inefficiency, and superficial living. To guard against hurrying through the day, start your day early and simplify your life so that you do not try to fill each day with more than you can do. When you find yourself beginning to speed up, repeat the mantram to help you to slow down.

It is important here not to confuse slowness with sloth, which breeds carelessness, procrastination, and general inefficiency. In slowing down we should attend meticulously to details, giving our very best even to the smallest undertaking.

4. *One-pointedness*. Doing more than one thing at a time divides attention and fragments consciousness. When we try to read and eat at the same time, for example, part of our mind is on what we are reading and part on what we are eating; we are not getting the most from either activity. Similarly, when talking with someone, give him or her your full attention. These are little things, but all together they help to unify consciousness and deepen concentration.

Everything we do should be worthy of our full attention. When the mind is one-pointed it will be secure, free from tension, and capable of the concentration that is the mark of genius in any field.

5. *Training the Senses*. In the food we eat, the books and magazines we read, the movies we see, all of us are subject to the dictatorship of rigid likes and dislikes. To free ourselves from this conditioning, we need to learn to change our likes and dislikes freely when it is for the welfare of those around us as well as our own.

6. *Putting Others First*. When we dwell on ourselves, we build a wall between ourselves and others. Those who keep thinking about *their* needs, *their* wants, *their* plans, *their* ideas cannot help being lonely and insecure. The simple but effective technique I suggest is to learn to put other people first within the circle of your family and friends, where there is already a basis of love on which to build. When husband and wife try to put each other first, for example, they are not only moving closer to each other. They are removing the barriers of their ego-prison, which deepens their relationships with everyone else as well.

7. *Readings in World Mysticism*. We are so immersed these days in what the mass media offer that it is very helpful to give half an hour or so each day to reading the scriptures and the writings of the great mystics of all religions. Just before bedtime, after evening meditation, is a particularly good time, because the thoughts you fall asleep in will be with you throughout the night.

8. *Satsang* (association with spiritually oriented people). When trying to change our life, we need the support of others with a similar

goal. If you have friends who are meditating along the lines suggested here, you can get together regularly to share a meal, meditate, and perhaps read and discuss this commentary on the Gita or other spiritual works. Share your times of entertainment, too; relaxation is an important part of spiritual living. Who has ever seen a mystic with a sour face?

By practicing this eightfold program sincerely and systematically, as I can testify from my own small experience, it is possible for every one of us to realize the unity of life. This is the purpose for which we have been born, and though it is called by different names in different religions—*moksha, nirvana,* illumination, entering the Promised Land or the kingdom of heaven within—it is all the same supreme discovery, nothing less than which will ever fill the void in our hearts.

There is a Sufi story which illustrates this. One day a man gave coins to four travelers he met on the road. The first, a Persian, said, "Let's spend this on *angur*." The second, an Arab, objected, "I don't want *angur;* I want *inab*." "What's *inab*?" said the Greek. "What's *angur*? What we need on a hot day like this is *stafilia*." And the fourth, a Turk, insisted, "Friends, be still; the thing to buy is *uzum*."

The man who had given them the coins laughed and interrupted their bickering. "I can understand all of you," he said. "Give me back the money and I'll get you something you'll all be happy with." He took them to the bazaar, found the fruit stall, and bought them the grapes for which they had all been asking.

The Bhagavad Gita for Daily Living

Wisdom from Realization

श्री भगवानुवाच
मय्यासक्तमनाः पार्थ योगं युञ्जन्मदाश्रयः ।
असंशयं समग्रं मां यथा ज्ञास्यसि तच्छृणु ॥१॥

SRI KRISHNA:

*1. With your mind intent on Me, Arjuna, discipline
yourself with the practice of yoga. Depend on Me
completely. Listen, and I will dispel all your doubts;
you will come to know Me fully and be united
with Me.*

We are dropping into the middle of a long conversation between
Arjuna, a prince in ancient India, and Sri Krishna, Arjuna's charioteer and spiritual teacher, who represents the Lord, present in the
hearts of us all. This is not an external conversation; it is very much
internal. Arjuna is every man and every woman, and in the Bhagavad Gita we have slipped into his heart to listen in on a dialogue
between two levels of our own consciousness. The voice we recognize belongs to the surface level of awareness—intelligent and well-
intentioned, but full of doubts about the meaning of life and how we
ought to live. The other voice, so full of wisdom, is the voice of our
real Self, the Lord of Love, whether we call him Sri Krishna or the
Christ, Allah or the Buddha or the Divine Mother.

As long as we are living for ourselves, dwelling on our own separate needs and problems, we cannot help identifying with our ap-
parent self. It is very much like wearing a mask too long, so long
that we think we are the mask and forget who we really are. But
through the practice of meditation and its allied disciplines, all of us

can learn to take off this mask and discover beneath it our real Self, called the Ātman in Sanskrit, who is the source of all love, all security, all wisdom, and all joy.

In 1960, when I first began teaching meditation in the United States, these ideas were still very new. In those days, if you told someone you were interested in meditation, you had to be prepared to face a certain amount of laughter. Later, when I offered a credit course on meditation on the University of California campus in Berkeley—probably the first course of its kind to be offered by an American university—it drew about six hundred people and thirteen dogs. Now meditation is in the air, and I think the idea must be familiar to everyone in this country. Yet I think there is still no more maligned word in any language than the word *yoga,* with which Sri Krishna opens this chapter. Yoga is not exercises or physical postures; it is not a religion; it is not art or archery or music or dance. It is a body of dynamic disciplines which can be practiced by anyone, from any religious tradition or from no tradition at all, to enable us to remove this mask of separateness and learn to identify ourselves completely with our real Self.

Every spiritual tradition has its own formulation of these disciplines, but though they may differ in name and detail—the Sermon on the Mount, the Noble Eightfold Path, the Eight Limbs of Yoga—there is no difference between them when it comes to the actual practice and their effect on daily living. In my own life, I have found a set of eight steps to be tremendously effective in leading the spiritual life in the modern world. I have listed these steps in the Introduction, and everything I say is with an eye to how they can be applied.

The heart of this program is meditation, which Patanjali, a great spiritual teacher in ancient India, divides conveniently into three stages: *dhārana, dhyāna,* and *samādhi.* Patanjali's exposition is so precise and so free from dogma that I don't think it can ever be improved on in these qualities. But it is written in a kind of lecture note style, in the expectation that other teachers will elaborate on these notes in their own way on the basis of their experience. So instead of quoting Patanjali, let me tell you from my own experience what these three stages in meditation amount to in their impact on daily living.

In the first stage of meditation, called *dhārana,* we make an astonishing experiential discovery: we are not the body. It is not an intellectual discovery, it is an experiential discovery, and the first time we hear this statement it doesn't make sense at all. If this body is not us, what is it? This is the question I was always asked after my talks, and I have developed all sorts of ways to convey what this experience of dhārana means.

For one, this body of mine is very much like a jacket. I have a brown jacket with a Nehru collar, made in India, which has served me very well; I take good care of it, and I expect it to last me at least another five years. In just the same way, this body of mine is another brown jacket, made in South India and impeccably tailored to my requirements by a master tailor, whose label is right inside. This jacket has to last me much longer than the other, so I am very careful with it; I give it the right amounts of nutritious food and exercise and keep it clean inside as well as out. But just like my Nehru jacket, this body-jacket will someday become too worn to serve me well, and having made this discovery that I am not my body, when death comes I will be able to set it aside too, with no more tears than I would shed when I give my Nehru jacket to the Salvation Army.

In this discovery that you are not your body, you discover simultaneously that others are not their bodies either. The consequences of this are far-reaching. For one, you no longer see people as white or black, yellow or red or brown; you see people just like yourself wearing different-colored jackets. The whole question of race or skin color becomes absurd: black is beautiful, white is beautiful, and of course brown is beautiful too.

Secondly, when you no longer identify others with their bodies, you will be able to see them as people instead. It lifts an immense burden from your relationships with the opposite sex. No matter what the media try to tell us, I don't think anything is more certain to disrupt a relationship than treating the other person as a physical object. On the physical level, all of us are separate, and it is the very nature of physical attraction to change with the passage of time. On the other hand, nothing is more certain to deepen a relationship than concern for the other person's real welfare, which we can see clearly only when we cease identifying people with the body-jackets they wear.

Another way I sometimes look at my body is as a compact little car, built for service. It doesn't guzzle a lot of gas; I can park it anywhere; nobody notices it at all. But it is the car; I have to be the driver. I don't let it pick me up in the middle of the night and take me off to some casino; it has to go where I choose to drive it. As St. Francis put it, speaking of his body, "This is Brother Ass. I will wash him, I will feed him, but I am going to ride on him; he is not going to ride on me."

The practical implication is that in this stage of meditation, we gain some measure of control over problems at the physical level. Many of our problems have a physical component, even if their roots are in the mind, and in dhārana we learn to have some say in things that used to be compulsive. Overeating, for example, is not really a physical problem; it can be solved only in the mind. But if you have a problem with overeating, it is a tremendous help to be able to tell your hand what to do. I have friends with this problem who sometimes come to me and confess, "I can't believe I ate the whole thing." I can understand this kind of craving easily, but what used to puzzle me was, even if we want something terribly, why should we have to put our hand out and put it into our mouth? If we know we shouldn't eat it, we should be able to sit on our hands and that would be the end of the matter. But when I mentioned this to my friends they would just reply, "I couldn't help myself. Some unseen power took over my hand and put the whole lemon meringue pie into it." This kind of eating is compulsive, which means there is very little enjoyment in it. But in dhārana, as we begin not to identify with the body, our whole perspective on eating changes; we begin to have some say in what we put into our mouths.

The second stage of meditation is called *dhyāna*, from which the Japanese get their word for meditation, *zen*. In this stage we make an even more astonishing experiential discovery: we are not the mind either. When I used to say this in my classes on meditation on the Berkeley campus, there would be groans from the back of the lecture hall. "First he says I'm not my body; now he tells me I'm not my mind." And they would ask, "Then what *is* the mind?" My answer is that just as the body is the external instrument we use in life, the mind is the internal instrument. If the human body is like the body of a car, the mind is very much like the engine. It is capable of tremendous power, but most of us spend so much time on the appearance of the body of the car that we don't get around to opening up the hood to see if the engine is still there. It *is* there, but in order to get it running properly, it is essential not to think that we are a part of it. And once we get this perspective in dhyāna, we can lie down on our backs on our little meditation trolleys, just as mechanics in garages do, get under the mind, and say, "Oh, yes, that old resentment; there's a little screw over there that's too tight." Then we make the necessary adjustments and the problem is gone.

In other words, emotional problems like depression and insecurity are only mechanical difficulties with our engine, the mind, which means that every one of them can be solved. The implications of this are tremendous. Most of us go through life thinking that we can never be different from what we are. We may like it, more often we may dislike it, but we cannot get rid of the liabilities with which we have been born or which we have acquired in growing up. As long as we think that we are the body and the mind, this is true. But just as in the first stage of meditation we see that it is possible to change any physical habit, in the second stage of meditation we gain the capacity to change any emotional habit, to transform insecurity into security, rigidity into flexibility, hostility into compassion, hatred into love.

The secret of this transformation is breathtakingly simple: we become what we meditate on. There is a story in ancient India about a sculptor who was so gifted that his statues almost seemed to come to life out of the stone. Once, lost in admiration over his stone elephants, one of his students asked, "How do you do this? These elephants are more real than real elephants are; you can almost hear them trumpeting." And the sculptor replied, "There's no secret to it. I just go and get a big block of stone, set it up in my studio, and study it very carefully. Then I take my hammers and chisels and slowly, over a number of years, I chip away everything that is not elephant."

When I see a person sitting quietly with eyes closed, giving all his attention to the Prayer of St. Francis, I like to think of this great sculptor, studying his big block of stone with such intense concentration that he really can see the elephant coming to life within: the trunk, and the big ears, and those keen, absurdly small eyes. *We* see only a block of stone, but for the sculptor, the elephant is already right there inside, struggling to be released. This is very much what we do in meditation, only instead of an elephant, it is the Ātman who is imprisoned within us. In meditation, each of us is in a life sculpture class in which we are both the sculptor and the rock. Almost four billion big, shapeless rocks—no wonder we are sometimes uncomfortable with ourselves or think the world is ugly. But a mystic like St. Francis might say, "Of course, the rock *is* shapeless; no one would deny that. But look within, with intense concentration, and you can see the halo and the harp."

In meditation we give the mind a shining model and study it very carefully every morning and every evening until it is printed on our hearts. Then, throughout the rest of the day, we go along chipping away at everything that is not Self. It takes many years, but in the end, the great mystics of all religions tell us, every bit of anger, fear, and greed can be removed from our consciousness, so that our whole life becomes a flawless work of art. This is the third stage of meditation, called *samādhi*. Samādhi really is not a stage at all, but a stupendous realization in which all the barriers of separateness fall. Then there are no walls between the conscious and unconscious, no walls between you and others; your consciousness is completely integrated, from the attic to the cellar. When this happens, Patanjali says in one of the grandest understatements in mystical literature, you see yourself as you really are: the Ātman, the Self, who dwells in the hearts of us all.

Most of us cannot even glimpse how miraculous this transformation is until we try to achieve it ourselves. Then we shall see why the mystics tell us there is no greater challenge on earth than the challenge of Self-realization. The Compassionate Buddha puts it beautifully in one simple word: *patisotagāmi*, "going against the current"—the current of all our conditioning, in how we act, how we speak, and even how we think.

In my village in Kerala state, South India, when the sky was a solid wash of water and the river was swollen from the monsoon rains, we boys liked to jump into the river and swim to the other side, not with the current—anyone could do that—but against it. It wasn't just that the current was fierce; the river would be full of branches and all sorts of other debris, so that even if you had good, strong arms and a lot of stamina, there was the danger of being drowned. That was the challenge of it. It might take an hour to get across, and there were very few who could reach the other side exactly opposite the point from which they left. Most of us would end up a few hundred yards downstream. But there were one or two—we used to admire them tremendously—who were such strong swimmers that they could make it straight across. It required strong muscles, powerful lungs, a lot of endurance, and—most of all—an indomitable will.

That is just the kind of spirit you need in meditation. When a flood of anger is sweeping over you with monsoon swiftness, that's no time to let yourself be carried away. As Jesus might say, "Anyone can do that." Swim against it; that's what it means to live. You will find your arms almost breaking, your endurance stretched to the limit, but you'll find there is such satisfaction in the achievement that nothing easier will seem worthy of your effort again. That is why the spiritual life appeals so deeply to the young and adventurous. It is only when you take on this challenge and begin to understand the extent of it, the daring and the courage and the resolute, dauntless spirit it requires, that you can look at St. Teresa of Ávila or Sri Ramakrishna and see that this is someone who has climbed the Himālayas of the spirit, who has stood on Mount Everest and seen the entire cosmos aflame with the glory of God.

Can you see from this what Sri Krishna means when he says in this verse, "Depend on Me completely"? No one in the world is so self-reliant as those who have realized God, just because they have put all their faith in the Lord within. When the mystics talk about God, when they refer to the Lord or the Divine Mother, they are not talking about somebody outside us, floating in space somewhere between Uranus and Neptune; they are talking about the Self, the Ātman, who is nearer to us than the body is, dearer to us than our life. In samādhi, when all the barriers between us and the Self fall, there are no more doubts about the meaning of life, no more vacillations, no more sense of inadequacy or insecurity. We become part of an infinite force of love that can never perish, and all the resources of the Lord within flow into our lives to be harnessed for the welfare of the whole.

ज्ञानं तेऽहं सविज्ञानमिदं वक्ष्याम्यशेषतः ।
यज्ज्ञात्वा नेह भूयोऽन्यज्ज्ञातव्यमवशिष्यते ॥२॥

2. I will give you both jnāna and vijnāna—spiritual wisdom and the capacity to apply it to daily living. When both these are realized, there is nothing more you need to know.

Once, while the Compassionate Buddha was camping in a shimshapā grove with his disciples, one of the more philosophical among them was asking him all kinds of abstract questions—whether or not there is a God, whether or not there is an immortal soul, whether the universe had a beginning and will have an end. In reply, the Buddha is said to have picked a few leaves from a shimshapā tree and asked, "Are there more leaves in my hand or on this tree?"

Everybody agreed, "Of course, there are many more leaves on the tree than the Blessed One has in his hand."

"Similarly," the Buddha replied, "there is much more in my consciousness than you can see, much more than you can grasp, much more than you can use. What I give you is only what you need to free yourself from the conditioning in life that is the cause of all your sorrow."

That is the sense in which Sri Krishna tells us here, "I will give you *jnāna* and *vijnāna;* that is all you need to know." It is not that there is not more to know; it is that these two together are the key to the art of living.

According to Shankara, an eighth-century Indian mystic and one of the greatest spiritual authorities of any age, jnāna is spiritual knowledge and vijnāna is spiritual experience. Spiritual knowledge is not intellectual knowledge; it is direct experiential knowledge of the unity of life. As Sri Ramakrishna, the great saint of nineteenth-century Bengal, puts it, it is knowing for oneself that God dwells in all beings, which is the discovery we make in the climax of meditation called samādhi. But what is vijnāna, "spiritual experience"? Sri Ramakrishna goes on to tell us in his inimitable way, "He who has only heard of milk is ignorant. He who has seen milk has jnāna. But he who has drunk milk and been strengthened by it has attained vijnāna."

This interpretation can be made even more practical to meet the needs of the world today. In the light of my own small experience, I would say that jnāna is spiritual wisdom and vijnāna is the capacity to apply this wisdom in daily living. Jnāna is knowledge of timeless truths; vijnāna is putting this knowledge into action—to solve problems, to deepen personal relationships, and to show those around us how to wake up from this dream of separateness in which virtually everyone is caught today. Vijnāna, in other words, is "inside" knowledge. Once you have realized the unity of life and begin to live it out, you begin to see into the heart of life. It's very much like being taken into a family; you're on such close terms with the head of the house that everything is opened to you. Here you are on such intimate terms with the Source of life that all you have to do is knock at the door of a problem and it will open, so that you know both its cause and its cure.

There is nothing mysterious about this capacity; it is simply a matter of wisdom and will. When, after many years of meditation, you attain the realization that all life is one, you will find it impossible to think or act like a separate creature again. You will not be able to exploit anyone, or discriminate against anyone, or do anything that is at the expense of life; and you will never forget that the welfare of each of us can only be found in the welfare of all. But to solve the grave problems that are making life impossible today—violence in the streets, environmental pollution, loneliness, the breakdown of the family and of personal relationships—it is not enough just to live in constant awareness of this unity. For that you need vijnāna, the skillful capacity to apply this awareness of unity to heal the deep divisions in people's hearts and minds and to bring them together in trust and harmony.

You don't get this skill overnight; it comes with the overwhelming desire to help. When, after many years, you have succeeded in freeing yourself from all the things that people suffer from, you will not be able to sit by and let others go on suffering; you will have to come up with solutions that are of immediate value to everyone. Not only that, it must all be very skillfully and attractively done. You can't just say, "Here, now, stop competing with each other; don't you know that husband and wife are one?" You have to offer a more desirable alternative, and package it attractively in your own life so that people can look at you and say, "Oh, yes, *now* I see; that's what it means for two people to complete each other. I want to be like that too." With some of these problems this may take years. But you won't take no for an answer; you just will not rest until all these problems are solved. Your desire, your concentration, is so intense that it can penetrate into the heart of the matter. You will be able to see below symptoms to the underlying cause and come up with a creative solution.

In other words, this is a skill that flows naturally from the intimate realization that all of us are one. Once this realization comes, with your eyes you will still see people around you as different—different names, different faces, different hair styles, different ways of thinking and acting—but in your heart you will never forget for an instant that there is no real separation between you and others at all. When you talk to your friend Jessica, you will *be* Jessica. You will be able to put yourself in her shoes and see the world through her eyes, which means that you will understand her completely. You will be incapable of judging her, because you will see how any problems she has have evolved. But you *will* be able to help her, because you will not be caught in her perspective; you will have the vantage point of your own experience from which to extend a hand.

Once you reach this state, there is no possibility of misunderstanding in personal relationships. I'm not saying there will not be differences of opinion, there will be. But in my experience it is not 'differences of opinon that disrupt relationships; it is lack of faith, lack of love. When you have jnāna, you will trust Jessica completely. You will know that she is incapable of doing anything that can harm you, and that her deepest need is to love and be loved. And when you have vijnāna, you will find all kinds of little ways to express your trust and draw your friend Jessica to you, no matter how different your views might be on inflation or French novels or the causes of the First World War. That is why I said that vijnāna is "inside" knowledge. You don't stand around outside a problem the way you do when you meet someone at church on Sunday; you get right inside, into the kitchen, and see it as it is at home.

This doesn't apply just to your own relationships; it applies to every human problem. If you have vijnāna, wherever you go you will be a peacemaker—as Jesus puts it, "a child of God." Wherever there are differences of opinion, no matter how serious, you will be able to slip behind the lines on each side and see things through their eyes, probably better than they can see for themselves. From your perspective you *will* see the problems, but you will also see the underlying unity in which the welfare of both sides is included. Both sides can come to see the other's point of view, and when this happens, though it may take a lot of work, it is only a matter of time before you can find a point of view that is common to all.

I can give you a small example of this from my own experience. It's not something that happened after I had become established in meditation, either; it took place at the very beginning of my teaching career in India, when relations between Hindus and Muslims were particularly strained. Even in the college where I was teaching, where tempers were not yet so inflamed, Hindu and Muslim students had begun to isolate themselves in groups on opposite sides of the room and refuse to speak to each other. All this used to hurt me deeply. As I said, I still had a long way to go in my meditation, but from my association with my Grandmother I already had some

awareness of the unity of life, and it grieved me deeply to think that
our campus might become divided into warring camps.

Now, it happened that one of my closest friends on the faculty
was a Muslim, and a devout Muslim at that. He and I had gone
to graduate school together, where we were inseparable, and it
had never occurred to us that there was anything in our two backgrounds that put us in opposite camps.

After we graduated we went separate ways, and we lost track of
each other. Then, after a few years, I was posted to a beautiful campus in central India. On the long train journey from Kerala I was
wondering where I was going to stay, because suitable rooms are
not readily available in small college towns in India. But when I got
down from the tonga, the horse-drawn carriage, my Muslim friend
just walked up from nowhere with a big grin on his face. "Come
on," he said. "You're coming home with me. What are you looking
so dumbfounded about?" That was the kind of bond we had; it
wasn't something that could be broken by communal quarrels that
had nothing to do with religion at all.

So when Hindu–Muslim antagonism began to disrupt our class-
rooms, instead of criticizing one community or the other, my friend
and I quietly went to share the home of a Muslim aristocrat who
had gone on pilgrimage to Mecca. It wasn't a deliberate effort; it
just came about naturally, without planning, out of the depth of our
concern. At first our students couldn't believe that we could live
peacefully under the same roof. People kept telling us, "It's an extremely dangerous situation; both of you will be hurt." Neither of
us were very brave. But we put our heads together and said, "If we
are going to get hurt, we might as well get hurt together."

What was important was that we hadn't done this as some political gesture. Everyone knew we were the very best of friends, and yet
both very deeply in love with the heritage of our different faiths. So
though people criticized us sharply, they were watching us very
closely to see how we held up. And gradually, as our friendship only
deepened, our students began to feel a little ashamed. One by one,
some of our bolder students began sitting next to each other again.
Then they began to talk to each other, and finally they were laugh-

ing and working together just as they had before. It opened our eyes to how just two little people trying to practice the unity of life can change the direction of a whole community. That is vijñāna, and there is no art more essential to daily living today.

In later chapters, Sri Krishna will show how this art can be developed through the practice of meditation. First, however, he will tell Arjuna more about the unity of life.

मनुष्याणां सहस्रेषु कश्चिद्यतति सिद्धये ।
यततामपि सिद्धानां कश्चिन्मां वेत्ति तत्त्वतः ॥३॥

3. One person in many thousands may seek perfection, yet of these only a few reach the goal and come to realize Me.

Many years ago, before the Blue Mountain Center of Meditation was even founded, I gave a series of talks on the Upanishads and the Bhagavad Gita in a little bookstore in San Francisco. In those days very few people had heard of meditation, and if you told someone he was not the body, he might just call the police. So I used to introduce topics like this very gradually, and in a public lecture I never gave instruction in meditation at all. But this particular audience was quite responsive. Many of them were from the "beat generation," and when I told them they were never born and would never die they wouldn't even bat an eye. I began to get the idea that they could take to meditation, and finally, toward the end of the series, I gave them the instructions you will find summarized in the Introduction and suggested that we all close our eyes and give it a try for just ten minutes. When I opened my eyes, there were only three people in that room: me, my wife, and the store owner.

Many people have read about mysticism, many have attended lectures on meditation, but few have the daring to lead the spiritual life. The majority will admit, "We concede the validity of spiritual living, but we are not prepared to pay the price."

Meditation is dull, hard work; I would be the first to admit it. To continue to practice meditation day in and day out requires real depth of desire and commitment. This should not be surprising; after all, to attain excellence in anything we have to work at it morning, noon, and night. The outstanding tennis player thinks tennis, eats tennis, and dreams tennis. The members of his family never worry about him, because they always know where to find him—on the tennis court. An Olympic swimming champion doesn't go for her workout to the Richmond Plunge once a week on a Sunday afternoon; she swims for hours every day. Whether it is in swimming or tennis or meditation, mastery does not come from dabbling.

Today it is a rare person who can give himself or herself completely to a great purpose. Granted, there are many who are prepared to give themselves to a not-so-worthy cause. But even these are to be preferred to people who sit on the fence until, as some wit said, the wood finally enters their soul. Those who vacillate achieve nothing in life. They go out by the same door they came in, and the Hindu and Buddhist scriptures add that such people keep coming in and going out again and again, until the door falls off its hinges. It is good to have consuming enthusiasm, especially sustained enthusiasm that motivates you to give your best; but it is better still to have it for the right purpose. Look at our films, our folk art festivals and rock concerts, and see what talent is lavished on an embroidered shirt or on a guitar or a piece of pottery. Some of these people have tremendous potential and the capacity to subordinate everything in life to a single purpose. When they take to meditation, they can go far.

In spite of our best efforts, however, there will be times in meditation when we find ourselves in a difficult predicament—times when the senses defy us, when self-will goes on a rampage. Then it is that an experienced, skillful spiritual teacher can come to our rescue. The spiritual journey is long and full of peril. It is fortunate that we are not able to enter the depths of consciousness in meditation until we have already gone some distance towards our goal. The seabed of consciousness is a vast, uncharted domain, full of mountains and canyons where selfish passions roam like monsters in the darkness.

If we do not have a map of this world showing what to avoid and how to make the return trip, we can become completely lost. This is why it is essential to have the guidance of someone who has made the journey before us and who knows how to avoid the pitfalls we can encounter on the way.

Once, on a drive in the country, my wife and I somehow managed to back our car into a particularly awkward position with the axle over a rock, so that we could go neither forward nor backward. Three strong young fellows who happened to be walking by stopped and tried to help, but they only succeeded in getting the car more completely wedged in. Finally a friend called a nearby service station to bring a tow truck, and in less than fifteen minutes we were able to drive away. That is the kind of service a spiritual teacher performs. A good spiritual teacher is like a tow truck driver who is on call twenty-four hours a day, and one of the hooks in his vast assortment is just the right size for us. When we get ourselves stuck in meditation and find we can't go forward or back, he pulls us forward just enough to get us free. Then, the moment we can move again, he removes the tow chain and lets us go forward again on our own.

भूमिरापोऽनलो वायुः खं मनो बुद्धिरेव च ।
अहंकार इतीयं मे भिन्ना प्रकृतिरष्टधा ॥४॥

*4. Earth, water, fire, air, ether, mind,
intellect, and ego—these are the eight divisions
of my prakriti.*

Now, as he promised, the Lord begins to reveal to Arjuna his real nature.

This verse always makes me think of a market scene in village India. When a housewife wants to buy curry powder, she goes to the marketplace and finds a stall which has all the basic spices in separate pots. The merchant takes a large banana leaf and puts the spices on it as they are selected: a bit of turmeric, a pinch of chili powder, some cardamom, pepper, and coriander, and maybe a little garlic. Then he puts them all together, wraps up the packet, and ties a strand of fiber from the banana leaf around it so the housewife can carry it home.

This is very much like what the Lord does with *prakriti,* which is the basic stuff of which the universe is created. I like to imagine Sri Krishna going to his cosmic marketplace and picking out just the right pair of brown eyes, the right ears, mouth, and other organs—even the right mind, with just the right weakness for classical literature—wrapping them all up in a beautiful brown skin for protection from the tropical sun of India, and calling it this body. Even to the biologist, that is all the body really is: a compact package of chemical components, which when I was going to school used to be worth less than two dollars. By now, because of inflation, that two dollars may be more like five, but that has nothing to do with the value of you or me. We are not this packet of chemicals; the body is only a house for our real Self.

In this verse and the one which follows, Sri Krishna is explaining the vital distinction between what the Sanskrit scriptures call *prakriti* and *Purusha.* Purusha is eternal spirit, the Ātman or Self, beyond all change and limitation. Everything else, everything that is subject to change, belongs to the realm of prakriti, the world of birth, decay, and death. The body, of course, is part of prakriti; made up of the five elements, it was assembled in the process called birth and will one day be resolved back into its constituents in the change called death. We like to think of the body as relatively stable, but this is because our vision is so limited. If we could see more deeply, we would see that every cell of the body is in a state of constant change. It is just the same with the mind. If we could perceive our thoughts more clearly—as we gradually learn to do through the practice of meditation—we would see that our interior world, too, is in a constant state of change. So prakriti includes not only the material world of matter and energy, but emotion, thought, and ego as well. All these came together when our body was born, and all will go their separate ways again at the time of death.

The Katha Upanishad describes prakriti in terms of a chariot drawn by horses straining at the bit:

> Know the Self as lord of the chariot,
> The body as the chariot indeed,
> The discriminating intellect as
> The charioteer, and the mind as the reins.
> The senses, say the wise, are the horses;
> Selfish desires are the roads they travel.
> When the Self is confused, they point out,
> With the body, senses, and mind, he seems
> To enjoy pleasure and suffer sorrow.

To use more contemporary language, I sometimes describe this body of mine as a rented car, which I leased at birth and which I would like to return with as few dents, rattles, and broken parts as possible when the lease is up. Discrimination—*buddhi,* the discriminating intellect—is the driver of this car. He has special instructions from the Boss not to exceed the speed limit or grind the gears, to make sure it gets regular checkups, and to use the best gasoline and oil so that the engine will last a long time. But he is only the chauffeur; it is I who decide where to go.

Unfortunately, however, most of us do not realize that this car needs a careful driver, and we let it take us wherever it likes—to the bar, or Reno, or one of these "disaster" films, or wherever the senses tell us that joy is being given away to all. This, of course, takes quite a lot of gas, and with all these side trips we slowly use up our supply of fuel until finally we run out completely. Soon it is time for us to return the car to the rental agency without even having realized there is a destination to reach. It is only when we no longer let our energy and vitality leak out in activities which take us nowhere that we will be able to reach the journey's end.

The day we take to meditation, we begin the long process of breaking through our obsessive identification with the body. At first this may produce a cry of protest. The senses will complain that they are being starved; the body will tell us that all the fun has gone out of life; the mind will complain that it's restless and doesn't want to quiet down. It is like trying to train a dog when you have always let him chase cars, sleep on the couch, and run about freely all night. Just the other day, for example, someone was telling me how he had managed for a week to keep to three nutritious meals a day until he happened to walk by a Danish bakery and got sucked in by some mysterious power. So we shouldn't get angry with the palate for not knowing about vitamins and trace elements and amino acids; we haven't educated it along these lines. If we could have a private talk about nutrition with the palate, it would say, "Nutrition? Never heard of it. George Briggs? Jean Mayer? Never heard of them. Ask me about Marco Polo, without whom we wouldn't have ice cream; I can tell you about him."

In the spiritual life, it is especially important to eat fresh, nutritious food, have daily physical exercise, and get the right amount of sleep every night. If we set ourselves up as stoics, eating only soy grits and sleeping on the bare floor, we will only ruin our health and deprive ourselves of the strength we need for serving others. Instead we need to train the senses by making wise choices. One of the most noticeable benefits of meditation is the growing capacity to turn a deaf ear to the clamor of the senses when they demand wrong food, cigarettes, alcohol, or other things to which they have become addicted. When we have a great purpose that we are eager to achieve and the powerful tool of meditation with which to achieve it, it is only a matter of time before even the most tenacious addiction will lose its power over us. Hundreds of people who have been meditating with me have given up smoking, drinking, and drugging. I don't criticize them when they come to me, and I don't insist that they change their ways in order to start meditating. I know that once they take to meditation these old habits will get up and leave of their own accord, because in meditation we gradually lose our obsessive identification with the body, senses, and mind.

Actually, training the senses is not a physical problem; it is a mental problem. When I first began to speak in this country about the world within the mind, scientists used to tell me, "We don't understand all this talk about a 'world within.' Our instruments can't measure it." To talk about a world without and a world within, as if these were two places we could identify in an atlas of the universe, is to create an artificial division. What we call external and internal are part of one continuous whole. Health, for example, is not maintained just by following certain physical rules; there are also mental and spiritual rules which we must follow. Illness is not only caused by harmful bacteria and viruses, but by destructive passions and negative states of mind. If we cannot control our competitiveness, it may lead to ulcers; if we cannot control deep-seated resentments, we may end up victims of severe breathing disorders like asthma.

Hindu and Buddhist spiritual psychology accounts for this by pointing out that the mind is no less a part of prakriti than matter is. Thoughts are things, even though we cannot hold them in our hands or see them with our eyes. This is very different from our usual view. Usually we consider thoughts as immaterial, so we are not aware of how a fleeting thought can affect us. If I throw a beach ball at you, it won't hurt much; in five minutes you will have forgotten about it. But if I say something harsh to you, you will not be able to forget that thought; you will take it home in your mind, have nightmares about it, and wake up oppressed the next morning. We all know from personal experience how a harsh comment from a parent or a friend can rankle in our consciousness for years. This is the immense power of thoughts.

The intellect is also classified as an aspect of prakriti, for intellectual knowledge too is subject to change. When I was a boy, I used to run home after school every day to tell my Grandmother and mother what I had learned. Once, I remember, I told my mother they had taught us something quite astonishing—that the earth is round. She laughed until tears came to her eyes. Even years later she was still telling her friends with great amusement, "He's a professor of English; he writes for the newspapers; he gives talks over All India Radio—but he still believes the earth is round." When I was a boy, of course, I tried to convince her that those who know about geography would say that her idea of a flat earth was a dinosaur. But it is not impossible that in the next century some geophysicist may discover that the earth is not spherical either, but is constantly changing in shape. This is the nature of intellectual knowledge; it is always subject to revision because it describes a relative, changing world that is limited by space, time, and circumstance.

Lastly, the ego itself is classed as prakriti, because it has no more permanence than the thoughts or emotions it claims to own. The implications of this are tremendous. If our thoughts and emotions are constantly changing, what we call our personality must be constantly changing too. We like to think of ourselves as always the same person, yet as Somerset Maugham points out, most of us are a bundle of endless contradictions, behaving differently to different people innumerable times every day. Yet through all these inconsistencies, there is something deep within us whispering that we are the same person from day to day. The Gita would say, very reassuringly, "Yes, you *are* the same. The problem is that this fickle collection of thoughts and desires is not you; it is just a mask with which you've come to identify. Underneath that mask is your real Self, which is beyond all change."

अपरेयमितस्त्वन्यां प्रकृतिं विद्धि मे पराम् ।
जीवभूतां महाबाहो ययेदं धार्यते जगत् ॥५॥

*5. Beyond this prakriti I have another, higher
nature, Arjuna; it supports the whole universe and
is the source of life in all beings.*

When I first came to this country and was still growing used to American English, I remember being driven to some engagement or other by a young woman who suddenly turned to me and exclaimed, "I'm out of water!" I was really alarmed; I thought perhaps she had some rare disease in which all the vital fluids dry up. But instead of going to a hospital, she pulled into a gas station. Only then did I realize that she didn't mean herself; she meant her car.

When we are asked to identify ourselves, most of us pull out our driver's license and list our vital statistics or launch into a discussion of our personality. It is very much like thinking we are the car we drive. This is not our real identity; this is the limited, egocentric, ever-changing mask which lies within the realm of prakriti. Our real personality, called *Purusha* in the Sanskrit scriptures, is infinite, immortal, and immutable.

Shankara, the great spiritual teacher of ancient India, has given us a profound principle called *adhyāropa* to explain why we make the colossal mistake of identifying ourselves with what is subject to change and death. Scholars usually translate *adhyāropa* as the "theory of superimposition," which sounds rather forbidding until we realize how it applies in our own lives. According to this principle, each of us confuses his or her limited, mortal ego and the real, immortal Self. This is what we do when we say "I am five foot seven" or "I like to ski"; we are looking at prakriti—the body and mind—and imagining we see Purusha instead. As long as this confusion clouds our minds, we can never see life as it is; we have to look at everything through this narrow little ego-slit we think is us: Sagittarius, thirty-five years old, slightly more open-minded than most of the people we know, with a weakness for spinach crepes and a slight tendency to begrudge opinions different from our own.

Of course, we are not just confused about our own identity, we are also confused about the identity of everyone else. Each of us has certain needs and expectations which we tend to project, or "superimpose," onto those around us. It's as if we had taken our own needs and expectations and shaped them into plastic molds with eyes, ears, a nose, and a mouth. We carry these molds around with us and try to put them on our parents, our partner, our children, our friends, everybody. Then, of course, we expect people to behave exactly like the mold we have imposed on them. In India we have a beautiful marriage ceremony in which bride and groom each place a garland of flowers around the other's neck. It signifies marriage so deeply that in my mother tongue you have only to say "So-and-so was garlanded the other day"; everyone will understand you mean a wedding. Actually, in most marriages all over the world, what really happens is that in place of garlands, the bride and groom use their adhyāropa molds. They stand facing one another, raise their molds, and pull them down over their partners, folding over an ear and pushing the nose to one side until each is squeezed into the other's image of what he or she should be like. Most of us, in fact, carry around an extensive collection of molds like this that we have accumulated over the years, and when we meet someone we hurry to our private collection, select a mold, and mentally cram him into it. When our unsuspecting friend goes on acting the way he is used to, we become outraged because he is ruining our mold. Then we wonder why our relationship is falling apart. Shankara would answer that the estrangement has nothing to do with our friend; the problem is what we have imposed on him.

To repair our relationships, we have to stop playing this game of adhyāropa and put a padlock on the mold-room door. There is only one way to do this, and that is to break out of the mold we have imposed on ourselves. This is not at all a pleasant task. The prospect of pulling apart someone else's mold isn't too distressing; what we find heartrending is breaking open our own mold, which we are absolutely convinced is just right. It may take years, but if we can even get a glimpse of ourselves as we really are, not separate from anyone but a part of the whole, the mold will crack. When we have learned to translate this insight into our daily living, the mold will be in a hundred pieces at our feet, and with it all the molds we once imposed on others. Then we will see ourselves, and others as well, as we really are: the Ātman or Purusha, who is pure, perfect, and immortal.

एतद्योनीनि भूतानि सर्वाणीत्युपधारय ।
अहं कृत्स्रस्य जगतः प्रभवः प्रलयस्तथा ॥६॥
मत्तः परतरं नान्यत्किंचिदस्ति धनंजय ।
मयि सर्वमिदं प्रोतं सूत्रे मणिगणा इव ॥७॥

*6. In these two aspects of my nature is the womb
of all creation. The birth and dissolution of the entire
universe take place in Me.
7. There is nothing which exists separate from Me,
Arjuna. The entire universe is suspended from Me as
my necklace of jewels.*

In India when you go to see a film they usually fill out the program by showing what we call a "trailer," in which the highlights of the coming films are all run together so that you have something to which you can look forward. These next few verses are like that; they are a kind of preview of what is to come in the following chapters. Sri Krishna is stirring up Arjuna's love for him until finally, in chapters eleven and twelve, Arjuna will beg to see the Lord's real nature and be united with him forever.

Here the Lord begins by giving us a glimpse of the vastness of his glory. Everything in the cosmos, he tells Arjuna, takes its rise from him, and one day it will be dissolved back into him again. This is not a matter of the Lord standing *here* and creating something *over there;* Sri Krishna is trying to explain in these verses that the ever-changing world of time and space, matter and energy called prakriti, and the changeless Reality which underlies that world, are simply two aspects of his divine nature. Spinoza, the seventeenth-century Dutch mystic, calls this the finite world resting on the bosom of the Infinite, as if the universe were just the restless surface of the infinite, motionless expanse of God. Ramdas, the delightful mystic of South India whom my wife and I had the blessing of meeting some years ago, puts it simply when he says, "The world *is* God." This is the great truth that will be developed throughout this volume of the Gita: the Lord is everywhere, in everything, for those who open their eyes to see. In the next few chapters Sri Krishna will go into the mysteries of his real nature, how he creates, pervades, supports, and dissolves the cosmos. Now, to whet Arjuna's enthusiasm, he just mentions casually that this whole vast universe, with all its galaxies and forms of life, is no more than a necklace adorning his dark neck.

Recently I have been looking into a few books on astronomy to see the backdrop against which these insights of the Bhagavad Gita are set. The sweep and majesty of it can take our breath away. Now, for example, we take space travel for granted, and every schoolchild probably knows that it takes a ray of light just one second to reach us from the moon. It makes me feel very comfortable; I can look up at the moon and think, "Just one second! You might as well live next door." If we could ride a beam of light, we could get here from the moon before we even had a chance to say where we were going; that's how fast light travels. Yet even at that rate it would take us eight minutes to get from here to the sun, ninety-three million miles away. It should make us pause to think. Ninety-three million miles isn't exactly next door—until we back up a little. Even at the speed of light—about 5,878 billion miles a year—we would be riding that light beam for four whole years before we came to the nearest star. That gives us the units our sun must be thinking in; for him, "next door" means four light-years, which is already more than we can comprehend. For the sun, a long voyage is something like crossing the Milky Way, a vast galaxy of stars and incandescent gases one hundred thousand light-years across, where Mr. Sun is tucked away in a little corner towards the outside edge. It isn't possible even to imagine a distance like that. Yet the Milky Way is just one of the countless galaxies our modern instruments have detected in the starry sky. If we could back up still further, we would see these vast galaxies sprinkled by the millions across incomprehensible stretches of empty space, each just a single jewel in the necklace of the Lord.

Astronomers have become quite humble about all this. They no longer talk about the universe as it is; they say, "This is what we know about the *observable* universe; what's beyond that we just can't say." They tell us there are stellar objects billions of times brighter than our sun and "black holes" into which billions of tons of matter disappear without a trace; and when we ask how all this can be, even the most hard-boiled of astronomers will just shrug and answer, "We don't know." And Sri Krishna smiles mischievously as if to say, "Keep on going. Even if you could travel till the end of time, you would never find a place where I am not, or reach the limit of my creation."

I read about these things and I am not lost in wonder, I am *found* in wonder. One of the books I have been reading is by Sir Fred Hoyle, a brilliant British astronomer whom I like very much. Sir Fred seems to have been working recently with an Indian astronomer, because when I read one of these astounding statements and then look down at the footnote I see it is attributed to Sir Fred Hoyle and Jayant Vishnu Narlikar. It always makes me smile, because Vishnu is one of Sri Krishna's names. He is the Author of all these wonders, and whenever I run into that little footnote I glance up at the picture of him above my bed. His body is a deep blue like the monsoon sky or a stormy night, above his forehead he wears a peacock feather, shimmering with all the colors of the universe, and in place of the traditional necklace I see bright galaxies and quasars and black holes like dark, lustrous gems strung in garlands about his neck. I look at him and think, "Is it true? You really did all this?" And he just smiles as if to say, "Read on; that's only the beginning."

रसोऽहमप्सु कौन्तेय प्रभास्मि शशिसूर्ययो: ।
प्रणव: सर्ववेदेषु शब्द: खे पौरुषं नृषु ॥८॥

*8. Arjuna, I am the taste of pure water and
the radiance of the sun and moon. I am the sacred
word and the sound heard in air, and the courage
of human beings.*

Now Sri Krishna startles us: he is not only the infinitely vast; he is the essence in every created thing. In India, where the sun can get terribly hot and the monsoon rains literally make the difference between life and death for millions of living creatures, water is precious every day of the year. In summer, one of the services my ancestral family used to perform was to keep huge earthen pots of water in the outer courtyard so that travelers in the hot sun could quench their thirst without anyone ever asking who or why. In this kind of heat school begins early in the morning so as to let out early in the afternoon, and when I was a boy, as soon as school was out, we all used to run back to the village to play soccer together for hours. After even a little of this, running constantly in the heat of an Indian afternoon, every pore of your body is crying out for water; and when it was time to go home we would throw ourselves on those huge pots and drink them almost dry. Nothing could have tasted better to us than that water did after hours of playing soccer in the sun, and if Sri Krishna could have got my ear then he would have whispered, "Do you know what's so satisfying in that water? It's *me*."

The Compassionate Buddha must have had a village like ours in mind when he called the ego's fierce cravings for personal satisfaction *tanhā,* the kind of burning thirst that will not let us rest until it has been satisfied. No earthly waters can satisfy this thirst. Our need for fulfillment is infinite, and as long as we think we are the body and try to find satisfaction in things that come and go, we are only going to get more and more parched. That is the point of the story of Jesus and the woman of Samaria, whom Jesus asks for a drink of water. When she questions him because he is a Jew, he replies: "Whoever drinks of this water shall thirst again, but whoever drinks of the water I give him shall never thirst; the water that I give him shall be in him a well of water springing up into everlasting life."

Then Sri Krishna adds, a bit playfully, "When you were quenching your thirst on those hot days, I wasn't just in the water you drank; I was also the blazing radiance of the sun." It is not just beautiful poetry; it's a simple statement of fact, though one which is very difficult to comprehend. The Sanskrit scriptures tell us that just as the moon reflects the light of the sun, the sun only reflects the light of the Self, from which all forms of energy come. If our vision were not so drastically limited, physicists tell us, we could look beneath the illusion of solid forms to see the whole of creation as a dance of light, from which elements and substances emerge and to which they return. This pure energy is the light which is the source of all the light we see. The Katha Upanishad says:

> There shines not the sun, neither moon nor star,
> Nor flash of lightning, nor fire lit on earth.
> The Self is the light reflected by all.
> He shining, everything shines after him.

Similarly, just as the Lord is the Light in all forms of light, he is the Sound that underlies all sounds. In the Hindu scriptures this sound is said to be approximated by the sacred syllable *Om*—or, as it is sometimes pronounced, *Aum.* This is not a physical sound, so it cannot be heard by the ear. But after many years of meditation, when your concentration is so deep that you are no longer aware of the cars on the road or the birds outside your window, this sound may sometimes be heard reverberating throughout consciousness.

In the Hindu and Buddhist traditions, *Om* is often repeated as part of a mantram or spiritual formula. But the use of such formulas is not confined to Hinduism and Buddhism; it plays an important part in all the world's great mystical traditions, usually in connection with the Holy Name. In Christianity, for example, the name of Jesus is one of the most powerful of mantrams. In Jewish mysticism, we have similar formulas in *Barukh attah Adonai* and the Shema—"Hear, O Israel; the Lord thy God, the Lord is one." Muslim mystics repeat the name of Allah or a formula like the *Bismillāh:* "In the name of God, the Merciful, the Compassionate." One of the oldest Buddhist mantrams is *Om mani padme hum,* referring to the Self as the "jewel in the lotus of the heart." And the most common Hindu mantram is simply *Rāma, Rāma,* calling on the Lord within us as the source of all joy. In all these traditions, we are urged to choose one mantram and then repeat it over and over again whenever we have an opportunity. It sounds simple, but these formulas carry tremendous power. Over a period of years, they can transform everything negative in our consciousness into what is positive: anger into sympathy, impatience into patience, hostility into love.

After many years of japam, the mantram becomes an integral part of consciousness. In Sanskrit this is called *ajapajapa,* 'japam without japam.' The person who becomes established in this state carries the Lord with him wherever he goes. Sri Ramakrishna says that such a person is like an office worker who retires on his pension after many years of working with the company: he doesn't have to work any more, but he still receives his check every month in the mail for all the years of work he has done before. Similarly, after many years of making an effort to repeat the mantram, it becomes as much a part of you as your breathing or the beat of your heart. Then you don't have to work at it; you don't have to think about it; it will go on unceasingly of itself.

पुण्यो गन्धः पृथिव्यां च तेजश्चास्मि विभावसौ ।
जीवनं सर्वभूतेषु तपश्चास्मि तपस्विषु ॥९॥

*9. I am the sweet fragrance in the earth and
the heat in fire; I am the life in every creature,
and the effort of the spiritual aspirant.*

To appreciate this verse fully you have to experience the onset of
the monsoon season in a tropical country like India, when the
ground has been parched for months by the burning sun. It isn't
just the villager with his little rice field that waits almost breathlessly for rain; the food supply of the whole Indian subcontinent depends on the monsoon. Everybody waits for the dark clouds to
gather on the horizon, and as the day gets close, no matter what you
are doing, you always have one ear open for the first sweet clap of
thunder proclaiming the advent of rain. You can almost hear the
earth panting for water. Then, the great Sanskrit poets say, there is
no fragrance so satisfying as Mother Earth's when the rain clouds
finally break and pour heavy rain on her dried, burnt soil; it delights
the senses and soothes the mind and spirit. Sri Krishna says, "As
the earth gives a deep sigh of joy and gratitude when the monsoon
waters slake her thirst, so the longings of all those who have been
parched for lasting joy and unshakable security are fulfilled by
union with Me."

Calling our little planet Mother Earth is a beautiful way of expressing the unity of life, for every aspect of life on earth is part of
an interrelated whole. Not only can we not raze a rain forest in the
Amazon basin without affecting the lives of the millions of creatures who live there; that rain forest in Brazil influences long-range
climatic patterns as far away as India. And when the monsoon rains
of India fall into the ocean instead of on the continent, leaving the
croplands barren—as they are now beginning to do, through just
such pillage—it means suffering to Mother Earth and all her children, not only in India but in Russia and America, too.

That is why I say it is not enough simply to have jnāna, the knowledge of life's unity; we have to learn to apply this knowledge to the problems of daily living. In the case of the environment, this means learning to be trustees for all the earth's resources. We would never dream of throwing old beer cans into our bathtub, yet many people do not think twice about tossing their cans into a river or dumping tons of garbage into the ocean. If our house has faulty plumbing or a leaking roof, we can always call the repairman or figure out a way of solving the problem ourselves. But the poor creatures of the earth have no say in the condition of their home. All they can do is suffer in silence until you and I, their trustees, realize what we are doing and clean up the mess we have created.

In clear, simple language the Lord is telling us that all life is sacred: *jīvanam sarvabhūteshu,* 'I am the life in every creature.' It's not just a philosophical statement. When I go out in the morning and see all these quail scurrying around outside our meditation hall, I *do* see them as quail, but only with my eyes, with my intellect. With the little spiritual awareness that has come to me from my Grandmother, I see that the power that makes them scurry and peck is the power of the Lord; their very life is the divine energy that moves us all. That is why we should not kill. This is the way to show respect for life—by not injuring any being, because the Lord is present in every creature on the face of the earth. When I walk down the lane to our home there are usually cows and calves grazing on both sides of the road, and on summer evenings the calves frolic about playing games that look very much like those our boys and girls play. The mother cows mutter among themselves while their little ones romp, and to my ears their *maa, maa* becomes *am-mama,* which in my mother tongue means uncle. They are telling their children, "Hey, there goes your uncle, who is helping to save your life."

The other two key words here are *tapas* and *tejas,* 'heat' and 'brilliance'—not just of an external fire but also of the fire within. This is an image you see often in the annals of mysticism all over the world, and probably no one has used it more beautifully than St. John of the Cross:

O fire that burns to purify,
O wound that brings love of the Lord,
Whose soft hand and tender caress
Reveals new life, cancels all debts,
And, slaying, grants eternal life.

This inner fire is not a figure of speech; it is associated with the rise of an immense source of energy called *kundalinī* in Sanskrit. Kundalinī is the power behind the process of evolution. By virtue of our being human, each of us has a vast amount of this energy, but very few ever learn to harness it. As long as we are living for ourselves we have no access to kundalinī, though we can get a glimpse of its power in the tremendous drive of sex. But when, through the practice of meditation, we begin to harness our personal desires for the sake of a higher goal, kundalinī slowly gets released into daily living. We find ourselves more patient and more cheerful; things that used to rankle in our consciousness for weeks now no longer bother us; we have more energy for giving to others, and a greater ability to understand the problems around us and come up with a lasting solution. And when some old attachment comes and wants us to dance to its tune—to smoke this, or sniff that, or buy this, or nibble at that—we can turn our backs on it. All these are signs of kundalinī rising, and when this power is completely harnessed, as in great mystics like Mahatma Gandhi or St. Francis, it can transform every negative factor in the personality into a positive force. This is why the Hindu mystics say that in meditation you can take your evolution into your own hands: by getting hold of kundalinī, you can learn to go beyond all biological conditioning.

Of course, it isn't at all easy to turn your back on a strong desire; often it is quite painful. It's very much like learning to use a stiff arm again. When your arm has been cramped and twisted into a rigid position, even the slightest little movement becomes painful. Yet you have to learn to move it in order to regain the use of your arm. There *is* suffering in this, as there so often is in any kind of growth. This suffering, this painful effort, is *tapas,* and it should be a source of great consolation to remember that whenever you choose to go against some self-centered desire for the sake of spiritual growth, the Lord says here, "I am your effort; I am your suffering; I come to life in your will."

बीजं मां सर्वभूतानां विद्धि पार्थ सनातनम् ।
बुद्धिर्बुद्धिमतामस्मि तेजस्तेजस्विनामहम् ॥ १० ॥

10. O Pārtha, my eternal seed is to be found in every creature. I am the power of discrimination in those who are intelligent, and the glory of the heroic.

The Lord is the seed of creativity in every being. Meister Eckhart uses the same image when he says that the seed of God is in everyone. Just as pear seeds grow into pear trees and apple seeds grow into apple trees, so this God-seed within us will grow into a God-tree of love and service if we nourish it and protect it from weeds.

These days, I am glad to say, more and more people seem to be growing their own vegetables. I'm told there are even office buildings that offer little plots to their workers to make a cooperative garden. This is a very encouraging movement, but though it is good to know how to raise your own food in your backyard, it is much more important to know how to cultivate the God-seed in your heart. If you want to grow tomatoes, you buy some seeds and plant them in your garden. But what would you think of someone who looks out the window the next morning, can't see a single tomato, and phones the store to complain that their merchandise is bad? It would require a great deal of patience on the part of the storekeeper to explain that tomato seeds don't produce tomatoes overnight, and that the seeds need just the right conditions before they will germinate and grow. It is very much the same with the God-seed; we need to nurture it carefully if we want it to grow and bear fruit.

Fortunately, however, this seed is indestructible. It does not need to be planted on a particular calendar date, for it is already within us. In the depths of the Dakota winter, at ten degrees below zero, the God-seed can thrive; in the heat of Death Valley it can still flourish. No matter what our past has been, no matter how many mistakes we have made, the God-seed is still intact. When at last we begin to search for it we discover it is covered with weeds—weeds of fear and anger and giant thistles of greed that try to choke out everything else. But once we take to meditation and start making all the little choices that strengthen it every day, the weeds begin to wither and droop, and finally they fall to enrich the soil where the God-seed has begun to grow.

In Sanskrit, all the little choices we make in weeding out this inner garden are ascribed to *buddhi,* 'discrimination' or 'intelligence.' Buddhi is the precious capacity to discriminate between what is pleasant for the moment and what is fufilling always. In the chariot image from the Katha Upanishad a few verses earlier, buddhi is the charioteer; when it takes its directions from the Ātman or Self, it can guide us intelligently down even the most dangerous road. Today, surrounded by a bewildering array of attitudes and life-styles and models of behavior, most of which promise just the opposite of what they deliver, we need this capacity to make wise choices every moment just to keep from being swept away.

Buddhi and the will—the capacity to see clearly what is wise and the capacity to translate that insight into action—go hand in hand. So this verse is very much like the last; Sri Krishna says, "Whenever you make an intelligent decision, even if it is unpleasant at the time, I am the wisdom in your choice." Once you begin to taste the freedom of this, you will find a certain fierce joy in choosing something of lasting benefit over what you crave right now. But for a long, long time, these choices are never easy, for they go against the very grain of our conditioning. It takes real courage and endurance to go on making such choices day in and day out, and that is why even climbing the Himālayas or venturing into space would seem tame to a great mystic like Gandhiji or St. Teresa. So the Lord returns to this word *tejas* again: "If you have the courage to take to this challenge, *I* will be your courage."

Do you see the insight these verses give us into the nature of God? It's not as if the Lord were something outside us, in a given place at a given time; he is right within, in our will, in our determination, whenever we are giving our very best to achieve the goal of life. As a Sufi mystic puts it, he is the life of our life, nearer to us than our body is; throughout creation he is the principle of creativity itself. One astronomer I have been reading recently calls it cowardly to conclude that God created the universe just because we cannot comprehend the conditions of its creation. He is still thinking of someone outside, holding court beyond the Andromeda galaxy; he hasn't glimpsed that all this *is* God, and wherever there is light, or beauty, or excellence in anything, we are seeing a little more of His glory.

बलं बलवतां चाहं कामरागविवर्जितम् ।
धर्माविरुद्धो भूतेषु कामोऽस्मि भरतर्षभ ॥११॥

11. In those who are strong, I am strength, free
from passion and selfish attachment. I am desire itself,
if that desire is in harmony with the purpose of life.

Often over the years I have met people who amazed me with some of their physical exploits. They could run very fast, or jump very far, or lift immense weights, or dive from great heights into shallow pools in the river that runs by our village in Kerala. It always used to surprise me to see how many of these people, endowed with uncommon physical capacities, would just go to pieces when faced with some emotional crisis. Gradually, as I began to observe my Granny, I came to understand that real strength has nothing to do with developing a set of muscles that is the envy of Muscle Beach. Strength is endurance, resilience, stamina, the capacity to face everything life sends you squarely and turn it into an opportunity.

This kind of strength can only come from self-control. During the struggle for Indian independence Gandhiji used to ask us over and over again, "What kind of strength does it take to retaliate, to lash back at others?" Retaliation simply means that the person is out of control, and if you watch someone who gets angry easily, you will see that he or she is vulnerable to any little impulse that comes along. But when you can rein in your passions and hold them in check, you have enormous power at your fingertips to harness for the welfare of all.

When I was learning English in my little village school, we used to encounter the phrase "a bull in a china shop." It didn't mean much to us, since we had never even seen china, much less a china shop. We used to eat off fresh banana leaves, which make perfect plates for curry dishes; and after a meal, instead of washing the dishes, we would feed them all to the cows, to whom banana leaves are like ice cream. So our English teacher, who was my uncle, would explain it in terms of a mad elephant. *That* we understood. An elephant is one of the most powerful of creatures; no animal except perhaps a tiger would even dream of attacking an elephant, and even the tiger has to resort to a sneak attack by lying in wait on the branch of a tree and jumping on the elephant's head. Usually this giant of a creature is, as the Bible puts it, "slow to wrath." But there is a peculiar condition called *must*—fortunately rare—in which the elephant will suddenly go into a rage and run amuck, tearing up everything that gets in its way. It is a terrible sight, and the moment they hear cries of "mad elephant!" everyone in the village will run for cover. Anger is like that; it is immense power that is running amuck and striking out at anyone who gets in its way. But when that same power, instead of running amuck, is doing something constructive, it is no longer anger; it is immense strength. It is much the same with other nearly uncontrollable emotions, too. Fear, for example, is as great a source of power as anger; and an obsessive desire, especially for pleasure or power, is a real Niagara. It takes a lot of endurance to turn your back on a powerful emotion or an obsessive, self-centered desire, but when you can do this, Sri Krishna says, "that endurance, that strength, is me."

Then, as if reading the look in Arjuna's eyes, the Lord adds: "But if that desire is *not* self-centered, I am that desire too." This is the real artistry of the Gita. You don't have to give up all desires to be strong; you just have to give up all selfish desires. For example, when you have food that strengthens the body, especially when it is cooked and served with love and eaten in the company of family or friends, you don't need to pass it up just because you like the taste of it. The Lord would say, "Dig in; I am in that desire too."

I am very much like my Grandmother in this respect. When there was a feast coming I don't think she ever thought about the food before or after; but while she was eating I have never seen anyone enjoy a meal more. At our āshram, whenever there is a special occasion, whether it be Jewish or Christian, Hindu or Muslim, we really have a feast. And when someone comes in and puts a steaming platter of blintzes on the table, we don't turn our eyes away and say, "We can't eat blintzes; they're not mentioned in the scriptures." We sit down, repeat the mantram, and polish them off.

On the other hand, you can't expect Sri Krishna to be present in, say, Puerto Rican rum, which you drink when you can't solve a problem. There the way to celebrate is to ignore the rum and solve the problem; then, if you still want to celebrate, ask for another problem and solve that one too.

The question in all these matters is, are you doing this for yourself or for others? You can't go to a wedding and have lentil soup and ice water when everyone around you is having quiche and champagne; it makes people feel a little sour. So when I go to the wedding of one of our friends, I have champagne too. Once in a way I have two glasses, one for the bride and one for the groom, and if afterwards a little poetry comes out, a speech from Shakespeare or a few lines by Shelley, I don't mind at all; it's part of the occasion. Once I went to a wedding where sparkling cider was served instead of champagne, and nothing came out but prose.

It is much the same with the other legitimate pleasures of life; they all can have a place in spiritual living. Though I lead a very busy life, I still find time to go swimming with my wife and friends, or follow championship tennis, or attend a concert of South Indian devotional music or a movie of Satyajit Ray's. In fact, I go to our local repertory theater so regularly that when we went to see *Hamlet* the other day I couldn't help nudging Christine and whispering, "That's not Hamlet; that's last month's Bluntschli in *Arms and the Man.*" In other words, we don't need to turn our backs on the innocent delights of life to be spiritual. We can participate fully in life as long as we are trying our best to put those around us first.

ये चैव सात्त्विका भावा राजसास्तामसाश्च ये ।
मत्त एवेति तान्विद्धि न त्वहं तेषु ते मयि ॥१२॥
त्रिभिर्गुणमयैर्भावैरेभिः सर्वमिदं जगत् ।
मोहितं नाभिजानाति मामेभ्यः परमव्ययम् ॥१३॥

*12. The states of sattva, rajas, and tamas come
from Me. They are in Me, but I am not in them.
13. These three gunas deceive the world, so
people fail to look beyond them to Me, supreme
and imperishable.*

According to the Sanskrit scriptures, the universe evolved out of a
state of undifferentiated consciousness, in which there was not a
trace of separate existence. The world was a thought lying unex-
pressed in the consciousness of the Lord, as the impressions of our
waking and dreaming states lie latent in the mind when we rest in
dreamless sleep. In their usual vivid way, some of these scriptures
picture this unimaginable state as the Lord—Vishnu, 'he who pervades everything,' of whom our own Sri Krishna is an incarnation—
lying fast asleep on his favorite bed, the endless serpent Ananta, in
the cosmic sea. There is very little to disturb the scene. Not only is
there no light, there is nothing else: the sea is Vishnu, Ananta is
Vishnu, everything is Vishnu. Then, it is said, the Lord begins to
dream. The dream is our own world, called Māyā in Sanskrit, and
the substance of this dream is the three qualities called *gunas: sattva, rajas,* and *tamas,* which may be roughly translated as law, energy, and inertia. At the time of creation the gunas begin to interact
with each other, and out of this interaction, step by step, the world
of prakriti evolves.

We can see these three forces at work in our own evolution as human beings, too. Although each of us has some measure of sattva,
rajas, and tamas, usually there is one of the three which dominates
our character. Those who are overcome by inertia and lethargy,
who procrastinate and give up easily, are under the sway of tamas.
They may as well be statues; you could put them on a pedestal and
come back after a month to find they had not moved a hair's

breadth. But it is more positive to look on tamas as frozen power, latent drive which has been kept in a deep freeze of disuse for so long that it has turned into a block of ice. Through the practice of meditation, this glacier inside begins to melt, releasing tremendous energy for overcoming old habits of lethargy and apathy.

It is a very different story with those in whom rajas predominates. They have left tamas behind them, often for the sake of achieving great success in the eyes of the world. Rajasic people are certainly more evolved than those governed by tamas, but unfortunately they are frequently the victims of tempestuous passions. They are the movie idols, the empire builders, and the marathon walkers who make newspaper headlines. They enjoy competing and breaking records; if there is a pie-eating competition, the rajasic man or woman will walk away with the prize. Such people may have great enterprise and remarkable digestion, but they often have little sense of direction. For them the greatest danger lies in getting caught in things that are enjoyable but meaningless.

It amazes me to see the extent to which rajas is running wild in the world today. It is rajas that drives individuals and nations to manipulate others for their own ends. It is rajas that drives us to pollute the earth for profit. And it is rajas that drives us to keep adding to our own convenience and comfort, even if it brings harm to our fellow creatures. One example is "junk food"—food that is produced essentially for profit rather than for nutrition. Years ago I read that we pay some thirty billion dollars on medical bills for ailments related to poor nutrition. Since that time the Surgeon General, the American Heart Association, the American Cancer Society, and other expert bodies have linked poor diet to a much larger percentage of health problems, many of which are the result of eating things because they look lavish, fill a craving for calories, or have a catchy theme song. More and more of the items I see on the so-called food shelves of today's supermarkets have only "empty calories": sugar and fat, but very little nutrition. We Americans consume on the average about *one-third pound* of sweetener per person per day: in terms of calories, nothing else every fourth day. Imagine giving your child a bowl of white sugar for breakfast, some lunch, and a glass of honey for dinner! And when I first heard about additives in food, I naturally thought they were to preserve our health. Then I learned that we eat dangerous quantities of chemical additives whose purpose is to prolong not our lives but the shelf-life of processed foods, so that a real banana can sit for weeks without changing much more than a plastic banana would.

Another sign of rajas is restlessness, which is endemic in our modem civilization. Whenever you see someone who is restless, who travels around the world once a year or takes up one job after another, this may be a sign that he or she has real potential for meditation. In this connection I remember a story about Paramahamsa Yogananda, the distinguished spiritual teacher from India who established the Self-Realization Fellowship in Los Angeles. One of Yogananda's students, James J. Lynn, was an oil magnate who had begun to see that money could not bring the security and lasting satisfaction he sought. When Yogananda asked Mr. Lynn in his simple, sweet manner if he would like to learn to meditate, Lynn replied, like many of us, that his desires made him too terribly restless; he had to keep on drilling for more and more oil. Beneath the restless surface of consciousness, however, Yogananda recognized a deep spiritual longing. He told Mr. Lynn to turn all his drilling desires inwards in meditation until he hit the deep strata of unitive awareness, where he would find an endless source of joy, security, and wisdom. Lynn responded with all the energy and enthusiasm that had gone into drilling for oil. First, through meditation and its allied disciplines, he learned to transform rajas into sattva, bringing every aspect of his life into balance. Then, through Yogananda's close guidance, he learned to go beyond the conditioning of the gunas altogether and attain the abiding joy of Self-realization. It is a perfect example of how the restless energy of rajas can be harnessed to reach the supreme goal of life.

Through meditation and its allied disciplines, all of us can learn like this to transform the self-directed energy of rajas into the selfless power that is characteristic of the third stage of consciousness, called sattva. Then instead of becoming angry, we will find it natural to forgive; instead of becoming irritated, we will find it easy to be patient; instead of grabbing all we can, we will work to fulfill the needs of others. People in whom sattva predominates appear serene, but we should never make the mistake of thinking they lack energy. Instead of scattering their energy over a lot of restless activity, they make effective use of it when it will do some good and conserve it when it will not. This sense of discrimination gives them an evenness of mind and constancy of action that make them a blessing wherever they go.

देवी ह्येषा गुणमयी मम माया दुरत्यया ।
मामेव ये प्रपद्यन्ते मायामेतां तरन्ति ते ॥१४॥
न मां दुष्कृतिनो मूढाः प्रपद्यन्ते नराधमाः ।
माययापहृतज्ञाना आसुरं भावमाश्रिताः ॥१५॥

14. These three gunas make up my divine Māyā, difficult to overcome. But they cross over this Māyā who are devoted to Me.
15. Others are deluded by Māyā; performing evil deeds, they have no devotion for Me. Having lost all discrimination, they follow the way of their lower nature.

Years ago I spent a week as a guest in an hospitable retreat not far from San Diego, where I had a magnificent view of the Pacific Ocean. I used to take long walks along the beach there and watch the surf, which makes me think of the restless sea of the mind and the "sea of birth and death" that we call everyday life. But what fascinated me was the surfers. I had never seen surfing in India, and I really enjoyed the ease with which these young people had learned to ride the waves.

One day I was surprised to see among the surfers a deeply tanned girl with Indian features. Sure enough, she had a good Sanskrit name, Māyā, and when she found out I was from India she invited me to her home for dinner just as my students used to do in India. Her parents were from the Punjab, a part of India noted for its hospitality, and in keeping with their tradition, I was given a real Indian feast. Then, after dinner, the daughter asked me if I could tell her the meaning of her name. I can still remember telling her that if I could explain this Sanskrit word *Māyā,* I would have given her the secret of life.

Māyā cannot be explained because it permeates everything; it conditions all our thinking and perceiving. Māyā is the hypnotic spell of separateness that is the source of all our confusion. It is very much like a kind of hypnotic trance, or a vivid but frustrating dream in which everything appears to be just the opposite of what it is. We see people as separate when we are all one; that is Māyā. We think that pleasure, or power, or material possessions will make us happy, that it is absurd to say "it is in giving that we receive." Yet the more we go after the things that please us, the less they seem to satisfy; the more we look for excitement, the more everything in life seems stale; the more we try to manipulate people, the more insecure we become. This is Māyā, which hides the source of joy from us and then drives us to look for joy everywhere but where it is.

In the Sanskrit scriptures, these two aspects of Māyā, the powers of concealing and diverting, are ascribed to the gunas of tamas and rajas. The gunas are the very substance of Māyā. Tamas, inertia, keeps us wrapped up in ourselves, always thinking we are the body and separate from everyone else. Then rajas comes along, restless energy, and whips up an endless series of desires for selfish satisfaction that sends us racing after mirage after mirage, always thinking that what we are after is just around the corner. We may have been down a particular blind alley a thousand times before, but with rajas at the wheel it doesn't matter; we're always surprised when we see the same old brick wall at the end. Sometimes there is a little twinge of memory: "Oh, yes, haven't I seen this wall before? . . . Why do I ever listen to you?" But rajas just says, "I say, old fellow, look over there; why don't we back up and try that alley across the way?" And before we have time to think, we've forgotten our suspicions and are off towards another dead end.

It is this bewildering razzle-dazzle of what we desire for ourselves that keeps us from seeing life whole. As long as we go after happiness just for us, as long as we see everything in terms of what we want for ourselves only, there will always be this wall of separateness between ourselves and others. And one of Māyā's cruelest tricks is that as we begin to get more frustrated, more lonely, more alienated behind our wall, we try to grab more fiercely at what we want and end up building the wall even higher.

Even before I took to meditation, I had a great love for natural beauty and a deep interest in people. I had a rather keen eye for human nature and could sympathize easily, and nothing could have convinced me that I was not seeing the world clearly. But all this was nothing like the way I see life today. Earlier, when I saw a mountain or a river or looked at the stars in the autumn sky, the response to beauty was deep and immediate, but it was still just an aesthetic response. Now, if I may try to put it into words, it's like seeing the beauty of the hills and the stream and the starry night and the faces of those around me and knowing that all this is one. That is what happens when the veil of Māyā falls. Afterwards, though you are back in the world of separateness and know how real it is for everyone still caught in it, you will never forget that all the bewildering array of differences in the world around you—different faces, different habits, different races, different beliefs—is just window dressing; beneath all this there is no one but the Lord.

When I came to this country on the Fulbright exchange program, all the talk was about how different everything was going to be; you'd have thought I was going to Mars. Some of the orientation programs I went to must have been intended to *dis*orient us, because the emphasis was never on what Indians and Americans had in common but always on how we differed. To me it was absurd, because all these little differences are only on the surface; they are no more significant than differences in food or dress. The mystic doesn't deny these differences; all he or she says is, "So what?" When our ship pulled into New York harbor we all stood at the rail and watched the skyline. I don't think I had ever seen a building more than three or four stories high, and here were buildings a hundred stories high. A British lady by my side looked at me and said, "Aren't you *overwhelmed*?" I just asked, "By what?" People don't get overwhelmed by more bricks piled on top of each other or more

wire strung together; they get overwhelmed when they see someone whose patience is inexhaustible. So that night, when my colleagues wanted to take in Times Square, they all stood around looking up at the tall buildings and the neon lights, but I was looking at
the people. That gave me more delight than anything else: seeing
how different they all looked and how alike they all were inside. It
really makes you appreciate the magic of Māyā to see Times Square
and realize that there is no one there except the Lord.

The explanation for all this is that it is not our eyes with which
we see; it is our mind. And the mind can operate only in a world of
differences. It has to have separate people and different things to
like and dislike; otherwise there isn't any mind. Where there is no
anger, no fear, no greed, no separateness, the mind just goes to
sleep; it cannot operate at all. There is nothing to get excited about,
nothing to take notice of; there is only pure joy, which is something
the mind simply can't experience. This is what the Buddhists call
the state of no-mind, and it gives us the clue to going beyond Māyā.
The more you can still the mind, which is the whole purpose of
meditation, the more you will be able to see beneath the surface
level of life and remember its unity. Everything that quietens the
mind helps to weaken the spell of Māyā, just as everything that agi-
tates the mind works to strengthen the spell of Māyā. That's why I
say over and over again not to think about yourself but to think always of others; give yourself freely, be patient always, slow down,
and don't ever dwell on your problems or your resentments, because these are the things that inflame self-will and fan the fires of
separateness. The agitation of the mind *is* Māyā, and if you can remember that you are seeing everything and everyone through the
medium of the mind, that will provide motivation for keeping it
calm and clear always.

चतुर्विधा भजन्ते मां जनाः सुकृतिनोऽर्जुन ।
आर्तो जिज्ञासुरर्थार्थी ज्ञानी च भरतर्षभ ॥१६॥

*16. Good people come to worship Me for different
reasons. Some come to the spiritual life because of
suffering, some in order to understand life; some come
through a desire to serve humanity, and some come
seeking self-knowledge.*

People come to the spiritual life for all sorts of different reasons.
First, and by far the most numerous, are those who come because of
suffering, either physical, emotional, or spiritual. Like most people,
before I began meditating I did not understand the lesson suffering
has to teach us. Only when I had some deeper awareness of life did
I realize the truth of my Grandmother's words, that the grace of
God often comes in the form of sorrow. If we are not prepared to
realize the unity of life, the Lord in his infinite love will let us suffer
until we are forced to change our ways.

Probably the most acute kind of suffering is the spiritual anguish
that comes from an intense sense of deprivation, of being alienated
from ourselves. When, suffering from this anguish, we turn inwards
in meditation, we find that the Lord has been waiting for years to
console us, support us, and inspire us. We may wonder how he who
is the embodiment of love can let us suffer so, until we realize that
his sole purpose is to bring us closer to him. The purpose of suffering is to take us beyond all suffering. It is the driving force to be
separate that is the cause of all our estrangement, and the person
who extinguishes his or her self-will has no more need of sorrow.

The second category Krishna mentions is *jijñāsu*, 'those who desire to know.' It is quite an interesting group. These are people with
a restless curiosity. They have tried all sorts of things in their search
for fulfillment: different restaurants, different nightclubs, different
countries, different drugs. But finally, after trying these things for a
while, they will conclude: "Going to restaurants only makes you
fat; taking drugs only leaves you addicted. There has to be more to
life than this."

This kind of restlessness is what drives people to seek out anything they haven't yet seen. If there is a veil over an empty box, they *must* peek under the veil to see what's hidden inside. Mention a big hole you saw by the roadside and they won't be satisfied until they go there and see this hole for themselves. Curiosity like this is the beginning of inquiry, which is the basis of knowledge in any field. The person who is curious about the nature of the universe, for example, asks all kinds of questions that don't usually trouble the rest of us: "Where does matter go when it passes into a black hole in space? Does it fall over the edge of the universe?" This same capacity for asking questions can be transformed into asking about the meaning of life.

There is another group of people in this category, too, who have shown up often in our classes in Berkeley: those who are artistic. With a half-humorous, half-serious tone, they will confide to me, "We know we have something inside, but we just can't get it out. There's a stoppage somewhere; the flow just doesn't come." I tell them, "Why not try meditation?" Meditation can unlock the reservoir of creativity inside every one of us. Near my village in Kerala there used to live a simple, uneducated man who had received deep inspiration from one of the greatest of Indian sages, Sri Ramana Maharshi. A friend of mine told me, "This man has written some poetry. You're a professor of literature; why don't you look at his work and evaluate it?" This is a job that every professor of English has to do at times, and having been steeped in the university tradition, I took it for granted that this man's efforts couldn't amount to much. After all, what could he know about meter, or scansion, or rhetorical devices? I wasn't prepared to take him seriously, but I accepted a manuscript in what looked like a child's handwriting and read a little. I was amazed. Here was living poetry from the depths of the heart. I hadn't seen anything like it, from my colleagues or my graduate students or in any literary magazines. Since then I have tried to warn people taking to meditation, "Watch out; you may become a poet."

This leads to the fourth group, those who take to meditation because they want to know what the purpose of life is and how to ful-

fill it. They have discovered that making money is not living, own-
ing an elegant home is not living, indulging the senses is not living,
acquiring a position of power is not living. Now they ask, "How can
we find lasting joy?" Eventually, everyone who is meditating sincerely and systematically will come to ask this question, even if they
had some other purpose in mind when they began. In time, many of
those who came with a particular emotional or physical problem
will become interested in tapping their deeper resources, and finally
they will join the ranks of those who want to know how to live in
permanent peace and abiding joy.

तेषां ज्ञानी नित्ययुक्त एकभक्तिर्विशिष्यते ।
प्रियो हि ज्ञानिनोऽत्यर्थमहं स च मम प्रियः ॥१७॥
उदाराः सर्व एवैते ज्ञानी त्वात्मैव मे मतम् ।
आस्थितः स हि युक्तात्मा मामेवानुत्तमां गतिम् ॥१८॥

*17. Unwavering in devotion, always united with Me,
the man or woman of wisdom surpasses all the others.
For such a person I am the highest goal, and he
or she is very dear to Me.
18. All those who follow the spiritual life are blessed.
But they who are always established in union with Me,
for whom there is no higher goal than Me, they may
be regarded as my very Self.*

The key word here is *nityayukta*, 'always united with Me.' Such a
person fills Sri Krishna's heart with joy, for with such people he can
lift the hearts and relieve the suffering of many, many others.

To inspire us, Sri Krishna goes on to say in the next verse:
"Whenever you see a person like that, you are seeing Me." Jesus
uses almost identical words when he tells his disciple Philip, "He
that hath seen Me hath seen the Father." It is a magnificent tribute
to the many men and women over the centuries from both East and
West who have devoted their lives to the Lord. Moses, Meister Eckhart, St. Teresa of Ávila, St. Francis of Assisi, John Woolman,
Jalalu'l-Din Rumi, Sri Ramakrishna, Mahatma Gandhi—all these

and many others of all religions were born as we were born, suffered more than we have suffered, and yet realized the divine unity underlying life by meditating and practicing selfless living until they were united with the Lord of Love. So when we see someone seated in a corner with closed eyes, completely absorbed in meditation, it is wise to remember that he or she is not just a friend or relative, but someone through whom the Lord is beginning to do his work.

बहूनां जन्मनामन्ते ज्ञानवान्मां प्रपद्यते ।
वासुदेवः सर्वमिति स महात्मा सुदुर्लभः ॥१९॥

*19. After many births the wise learn to meditate
on Me, seeing Me everywhere and in everything.
Such great souls are very rare.*

One of the names for Sri Krishna in Sanskrit is Hari, 'the thief.' The Lord is a divine pickpocket who has stolen our heart and then sent us out into the world to search for him. People who ski on precipitous slopes or go skindiving in exotic waters are really looking for the Lord. Others are looking for him in a safe-deposit vault or on the floor of the stock exchange. Scholars think they hear him calling from the library; the expression on their faces as they enter the stacks would make you think the Lord was curled up in a rare book. But no matter what we think we are looking for, all of us suffer ultimately from a gnawing sense of deprivation at being separated from our real Self.

In this verse, the Gita is using the traditional language of reincarnation to explain why some of us take a long, long time to understand that exploits like these can never fill the vacuum within us. In this view, selfless men and women are said to be highly evolved; they have learned to see through the games we all play. It is those who have had little experience of life who are fascinated with these games. Often, for example, it is the person born into a wealthy family who is detached from money and knows how to use it wisely. He or she has enough experience with it to know its true value. For those who have only recently acquired wealth—whom my Grand-

mother used to call "today's mushrooms after last night's rain" —
everything about money is still new; everything money can buy is
still exciting. Most of us have to play with material possessions a bit
in order to discover that they are just toys. That is the advantage of
living in an abundant economy. In a poor country, where the products of technology are expensive and hard to come by, people set a
high value on material things. Take the craze for television. Our
friend Sultana, who was born in Greece, tells me that when television first became available there everyone wanted to watch it,
even though all the programs were in other languages which most
people couldn't understand. In the United States, where there is
television all around us, it shouldn't take much imagination to see
that no amount of watching television can ever make us happy. The
same is true for everything else in the material world. Happiness has
nothing to do with having two cars in the garage, or a terraced
swimming pool, or the latest dress from Paris. Happiness lies within
us, and the more desires we have for this and that, the less happy we
are going to be. Nothing we can buy, nothing we can own can ever
fill the aching void within us, and the restlessness of modern living
is really a signal from the Lord that it is time to turn inwards and
find the source of all joy, wisdom, and security in our own hearts.

When we finally attain this source of joy, we shall see that there
is no one in the universe but the Lord. It is not an intellectual concept; everything we see will be whole, and everything will be full of
God. The beautiful expression in this verse might easily be the refrain of this volume: *Vāsudevah sarvam,* 'The Lord is everything';
there is no place where he is not found. St. Angela of Foligno uses
much the same language to describe her own experience of God:

> The eyes of my soul were opened and I beheld the fullness
> and perfection of God, in which were comprehended the whole
> world, both here and beyond the sea, and the abyss and ocean
> of all things. In all this I saw nothing but the power of God, in a
> way that is beyond the power of words to explain; so that the
> soul, through excess of marveling, cried out with a loud voice,
> saying, *This whole world is full of God.*

कामैस्तैस्तैर्हृतज्ञानाः प्रपद्यन्तेऽन्यदेवताः ।
तं तं नियममास्थाय प्रकृत्या नियताः स्वया ॥२०॥

*20. There are others whose discrimination is misled
by many desires. Following their lower nature, they
worship the gods of the sense-world in their actions.*

In the Hindu tradition, many of the forces which motivate our behavior are represented as gods and goddesses. There is a great deal
of practical wisdom to this, because these personifications give us a
vivid picture of these forces which all of us can understand. For example, people who build their lives on the pursuit of money are
called devotees of Kubera, the god of wealth, who lives in a temple
of twenty-four karat gold studded with sapphires, diamonds, and
rubies. Each time we play the stock market or switch jobs for better
pay, we are paying homage to Kubera in hopes that he will grant
our desire for wealth. Kubera's devotees see opportunities for making money everywhere, and people can become so driven by this desire that they will find ways of increasing their bank account even if
it means that someone else has to suffer.

The pleasure-seeker too has his god in the Hindu pantheon:
Kāma, the god of selfish desire, who is portrayed as an archer with
five arrows tipped with flowers—one for every sense organ—which
he shoots at the hearts of his devotees. It is a comment on our times
that a man's (or woman's) fancy for Kāma is no longer limited to
spring; worship is continuous throughout the year.

These two desires, for money and for pleasure, are the source of
most of our confusion in the modern world. This constant clamor of
I want this, I want that makes buddhi's job impossible. He is supposed to be listening to the Ātman and making intelligent choices,
but all he can hear is Kubera and Kāma trying to get him to go in a
hundred different directions at once. After some time of this, we
can't even imagine that there is a guiding principle in our lives at all,
and we wonder why there is so little purpose in what we do.

In the West it is often the mass media that create and perform
daily worship of these gods of money and sex. Now a third god is be-

ing added to the altar—the god of violence. Violence on television and in films is more than just a temporary form of excitement; these scenes of murder and assault get deep into our consciousness. Pleasure is glamorized, but instead of bringing joy, the drive for pleasure is leading to assault and molestation. Money is made the goal of life, but instead of bringing fulfillment, the craving for money and material possessions is spreading disregard for people, property, and resources. Gradually, we have become accustomed to living in a climate of fear. "Stop-thief" fashions such as handbags that sound an alarm and coats with purses sewn into their seams are featured in the stores. Homeowners and apartment dwellers are investing in elaborate, expensive alarms, closed circuit television, ultrasonic sensors, and computer-operated locks. These are advertised as security systems, but they should really be called *in*security systems because they only increase the fear of those who use them.

Those of us who have grown up under the influence of the mass media deserve sympathy and help, for it is very rare to have someone around to give us a higher alternative in life. This cannot be done by books or workshops or lectures. It has to be communicated through personal example, which is what *vijnāna* means. We cannot just settle for the intellectual approach, which is to analyze the problem and then go home; we have to show in our own lives that these spiritual ideals work. That is what Gandhi did. His whole life was a showcase for his experiments with nonviolence, not just in politics but in education and economics and many other areas too, and it had such an impact that in the long run I think historians will refer to our times not as the nuclear age but as the age of Gandhi. After all, the discovery of nuclear power only marks another revolution in technology. Gandhi's life marks a revolution of an entirely different order, for it showed that the problems we have been trying to deal with by manipulating atoms and manipulating nations can be solved for good by transforming ourselves.

Once, when a foreign correspondent asked Gandhi for a message he could take back to his paper, Gandhi wrote on a scrap of paper: "My life is my message." In this sense all of us are teachers in the example we give others, though often not in a particularly positive way. The man who lives for profit is a full-scale advertisement for making money the goal of life. He talks constantly about diversified investments, he vacations in Monte Carlo and Las Vegas, he dreams about the Dow Jones index; everything he does advertises his way of life. His life is an open book for anyone who cares to observe it, and those who observe carefully will see how the lust for money robs him of his capacity to love. On the other hand, the man or woman who lives for others is a constant reminder of the love and wisdom that come from selfless living. People like this do not need to preach or attract attention to themselves; we cannot help being drawn to them and drawing inspiration from their life.

यो यो यां यां तनुं भक्तः श्रद्धयार्चितुमिच्छति ।
तस्य तस्याचलां श्रद्धां तामेव विदधाम्यहम् ॥२१॥
स तया श्रद्धया युक्तस्तस्याराधनमीहते ।
लभते च ततः कामान्मयैव विहितान्हि तान् ॥२२॥

21. When a man is devoted to something
with complete faith, I unify his faith in that form.
22. Then, when his faith is completely unified,
he gains the object of his devotion. In this way,
every desire is fulfilled by Me.

There is a haunting verse in the Bhrihadāranyaka Upanishad which says:

You are what your deep, driving desire is.
As your deep, driving desire is, so is your will;
As your will is, so is your deed;
As your deed is, so is your destiny.

The key word here is one of the most important terms in the Gita: *shraddhā. Shraddhā* has a wealth of meanings; it may be a deep desire, or strong conditioning, or the underlying assumptions which shape our thoughts and actions. The basic meaning is faith—not just intellectual adherence to something, but what we believe in, what we trust in, in our heart of hearts. Shraddhā is the key to life.

It is our shraddhā, our conditioned assumptions, that shapes our thoughts and actions, and it is our shraddhā, our faith, that shapes our will and our destiny. We become what our shraddhā is, because all of us live out what we believe and desire in the deepest recesses of our consciousness.

The ancient Greek story about Midas is a story of shraddhā. Midas was obsessed with gold. He may have thought he was a man of many interests—music, horticulture, Olympian wines—but in the depths of his consciousness, his deepest belief was that wealth is the source of all joy. He found himself thinking about gold, dreaming about gold, wanting gold more and more as time went on. Gradually, without realizing it, he was thinking about nothing else. He wanted everything he touched to be turned to gold, just as there are people who want everything they do to make them a profit or bring them a little power or pleasure. And—so the story goes—the gods granted his desire. Midas got up one morning, picked up his toothbrush, and in an instant it turned to gold. Midas was ecstatic. In delight he hopped around touching everything in his palace and watching it turn to gold.

After a while, however, the novelty wore off, and Midas sat down to have some breakfast. He tried some grapes, but they turned to gold. So did his toast, and his egg, and even his Greek coffee. Midas was a little irritated; he was hungry, and he had enough imagination to suspect that there might not be much future in eating now that he had this golden touch. It raised some questions which he didn't feel like thinking about before breakfast. A little subdued, he went out to his garden to take his mind off his stomach. It was a beautiful Mediterranean morning. The roses he had been cultivating so carefully were still filled with the first liquid rays of the sun. Their beauty took him by surprise, and he bent over to pick one for his table. But in an instant the lovely petals turned into harsh, cold metal.

Midas was beginning to get the picture. He threw the gold rose into the bushes and muttered some bad Greek. Then, suddenly, he looked up and saw his little daughter running to greet him. Her smile was so bright that he forgot all about his golden toast and his golden rose, and he reached down joyfully to take her into his arms. The instant he touched her, she too turned into gold, leaving only a lifeless statue for him to love. At last Midas understood. Weeping, he fell to the ground and begged the gods to take away his curse.

Most of us, fortunately, are not as obsessed as Midas was. But his fate is not as fanciful as it might seem. Midas's shraddhā was in gold; for others it might be property, or power, or personal pleasure, but the result is very much the same. When we get caught in these things, we begin to mold our lives around them. All our capacity to love is trapped in getting what we desire, and without really wanting to, we begin to treat those around us as only figures in a game. Seen through our shraddha, they are scarcely real at all, and there are people who spend their whole lives together without ever really seeing each other, just because of their preoccupation with themselves.

There is no point in blaming people like this; to some extent, this is the conditioning of our times, and all of us have been affected by it. But all of us have the capacity to change our shraddhā. Through the practice of meditation, we can learn to withdraw our trust from the things that separate us from others—wealth and pleasure, power and prestige—and place it more and more in what contributes to the welfare of us all.

अन्तवत्तु फलं तेषां तद्भवत्यल्पमेधसाम् ।
देवान्देवयजो यान्ति मद्भक्ता यान्ति मामपि ॥२३॥

23. Those whose understanding is small attain only transient satisfaction. Those who worship the gods of the sense-world go to the gods of the sense-world, but my devotees come to Me.

Every deep desire is a prayer. In the deepest levels of our consciousness all of us are praying constantly, and when the prayer is intense enough and consistent enough, we will live out our lives in such a way that that prayer is answered. The difference is in what we pray for. If we worship the gods of the sense-world—wealth, power, pleasure, status—we will get more and more caught up in the world of change. Every day we will play that old game with the mirror: "Mirror, mirror on the wall, how am I doing?" And more and more often the mirror will reply, "Not so hot." But if we try to give all our love to the Lord of Love, Sri Krishna reminds us, we will gradually become unaffected by any change, even the great change called death.

Here again, the key to understanding this is *shraddhā*. Shraddhā supports our whole outlook on life. Everyone has faith in something; we cannot live without faith. When I get into our Volvo I have faith in the people who make Volvos. I take it for granted that there is still an engine there, that the wheels won't fall off, that the steering wheel is connected to something; that is shraddhā. When I take my friends out for ice cream in Berkeley and pay for it with little green pieces of paper, that is shraddhā which the storekeeper and I and everyone else in the country all share. If we didn't have this common shraddhā, the entire economy would collapse. Without shraddhā, we would be questioning everything; there would be time for nothing but worry.

It's very much like this at a deeper level, too. Just as we all share this belief in money, without which this whole game of buying and selling would collapse, so we all share the deep conviction that we are separate, that we are the body, that our nature and behavior are conditioned by our genes. In this verse, Sri Krishna is reminding us that the more we identify with the world of prakriti, the physical world of change, the more we will be subject to the ravages of time and eventually death. But by placing our shraddhā in the Lord, who is our real Self, we gradually come to remember our real nature, and the passage of time affects us less and less. Finally, when our faith in God is unshakable, we are united with him completely. Then, when the time comes to shed this body, there is no rupture in consciousness, any more than there is when we pass from one room to another.

This is the promise Sri Krishna is giving us in this verse. Faith in this promise is the highest kind of shraddhā. It is not blind faith; it is the trust in spiritual values, the confidence in their applicability, that comes as our experience deepens. We don't just go to bed one night and wake up with perfect faith; as the lives of all the great mystics show us, shraddhā grows over a long period of time, as we try these timeless values out in our own lives. All that the mystics ask at the beginning is that we trust them enough to give what they say a try.

This is much the way a scientist works. A scientist like Sir Isaac Newton doesn't build theories out of faith; his faith is in the method. He says, "Well, there is some reason to think that the fall of this apple and the motion of the moon are related; let's see if that proves true." He doesn't say they *are* related; he says, "Let's see." He has enough shraddhā in the idea to try it out; and gradually, after many experiments, his faith in a uniform force of gravity is unshakable.

Most of us, after this, never repeat these experiments, but we *do* trust the conclusion. At the most, I might go to the top of the campanile tower at our campus and drop a marble and a bowling ball at the same time, and when they landed at the same time, I would just say "Good, it *does* act equally on unequal masses" and be done with it. A great mystic like St. Francis of Assisi or Sri Ramakrishna would ask us gently, "Don't you at least trust us as much as Galileo or Sir Isaac Newton? We're not telling you about things we've read about or things we've heard from others; we're telling you what we know, from a lifetime of personal experience."

There is a story much like this in the Buddhist tradition. The Compassionate Buddha was once speaking to a large number of villagers about nirvāna and the way it can be attained. After he had finished, one of them asked: "Blessed One, everything you have told us about nirvāna is wonderful. All of us would like to go beyond sorrow and death. But this Eightfold Path of yours isn't easy, and if it doesn't work we would have thrown our lives away in looking for the impossible. How do we know there *is* a nirvāna that people like us can attain?"

The Buddha smiled. "Are there any mountains to the north of here?" he asked.

"Of course," the villager answered; "the Himālayas."

"How do you know? Have you been to see these 'Himālayas'?"

"No," the man admitted, "but everybody says they're there. My father has told me all about them; they're the source of the Ganges and it has to come from somewhere."

"Has your father seen these mountains?"

"No, but he heard all about them from *his* father, whose uncle went there on pilgrimage many years ago."

"Perhaps this uncle had a vivid imagination."

"Oh, no, he wouldn't have misled us like that! Everyone remembers him as a very honest man."

"My friend," said the Compassionate Buddha gently, "if you have such faith in the words of someone whom you know of only by hearsay, don't you think you can have faith in someone who has seen nirvāna and who stands in the flesh before you?"

अव्यक्तं व्यक्तिमापन्नं मन्यन्ते मामबुद्धयः ।
परं भावमजानन्तो ममाव्ययमनुत्तमम् ॥२४॥

24. Through lack of understanding, people believe that I, the Unmanifest, have been born as a person. They fail to realize my true nature, which transcends birth and death.

Shankara, the great saint from Kerala state in India, has a profoundly inspiring invocation which begins, "O Thou from whom all words recoil." This is the supreme, unmanifested Reality, called Brahman in the Sanskrit scriptures. Brahman cannot be described, for It has no attributes. As a youth, Shankara wanted to have the famous seer Gaudapāda teach him how to realize Brahman. After an extensive search, he finally found Gaudapāda on the banks of the river Narmadā. But when Shankara asked him to be his teacher, the sage refused. He had resolved to remain absorbed in union with the total Godhead, in which state there is no teacher and no one to teach. So he directed Shankara to his foremost disciple, the sage Govindapāda, who had realized the personal form of God.

In the ancient Hindu scriptures, union with the impersonal Godhead is called *nirvikalpa samādhi*. This is a state of pure, undifferentiated consciousness, and it is attained by very few. The more devotional form of union with God is called *savikalpa samādhi,* or union with the personal God. The devotee is absorbed in meditation on the Lord, but he still has one foot in the world of dualism. There is still a difference between subject and object for him, and he remains a devotee who is in communion with the Lord.

For the vast majority of us, limited as we are by our human condition, it is not possible to love the impersonal Godhead. We may feel intellectually attracted to the concept, but intellectual attraction is not enough. In order to undergo the tremendous transformation of personality that the spiritual life demands, we need a personal form of God that we can love, an embodied ideal that can draw us with all our heart. So Sri Ramakrishna says that God is with form and without form: the formless Godhead seems to take on form through the powerful lens of the devotee's love.

In an earlier verse in the Gita, Sri Krishna explains that whenever the human condition becomes heartbreaking, the Lord of Love is born on earth in the form of a human being, to rekindle our love for God. In Sanskrit this is called an *avatāra* or divine incarnation: someone like Jesus the Christ, or Sri Krishna, or the Compassionate Buddha. Laughing like us, talking like us, weeping like us, the incarnation of God seems to pass like us through all the changes of birth and death. But though the Lord allows himself to appear limited in this way, he is really beyond all limitation. Later, in chapter eleven, Sri Krishna will lift the veil of his Māyā for an instant to remove his disguise and reveal to Arjuna His cosmic form as Lord of the universe, who transcends all space and time.

I sometimes amuse my friends by imagining how our dogs and cats must think of God. It is a very helpful shift in perspective. Our dog Muka would tell his friend Hebbles, "What's all this talk about God as a human incarnation? God has four legs and a tail, and his barking resounds throughout the universe." And the cats would be saying, "Those dogs have no sense; *bow-wow* is all they know. God must be a cosmic Cat, filling the universe with an endless *meow*." It's easy to laugh at this sort of talk from dogs and cats, but we need to keep the same sense of humor with regard to our own quarrels about God. We too are trying to limit what cannot be limited, to confine in words that which cannot be confined.

नाहं प्रकाशः सर्वस्य योगमायासमावृतः ।
मूढोऽयं नाभिजानाति लोको मामजमव्ययम् ॥२५॥

25. Few see through my veil of Māyā; not knowing that I am without birth and changeless, the world is deluded.

The ice show we took our nieces to see recently is a good example of how Māyā works. Just before the show started, the stadium was plunged into darkness. After a fanfare of trumpets, lights of blue, gold, and rose began to play on the ice rink, and one by one, graceful figures in beautiful costumes came gliding onto the ice. Usually our finances give us the privilege of watching shows like this from afar, and distance makes the view even more enchanting. From our position the skaters were incredibly graceful, showing skill which must have taken years to develop. The costumes, the tinted lights, the makeup which must have taken an hour to apply, all made everyone appear breathtakingly beautiful. It was only after Māyā's show was over and the skaters had removed their makeup and shed their costumes for street clothes that I could see their real beauty, which came not from these external trappings but from the Lord of Love within us all.

Imagine watching an ice show for so long that you forget when you came in. It would never occur to you that there was a world outside, or that there was something much more real than greasepaint and tinted lights. The stadium would be your universe. Doesn't Hamlet say, "I could be bounded in a nutshell and count myself a king of infinite space"? You would spend your life studying the performances and analyzing the costumes, and if someone were to suggest that you turn in your ticket and get your money back you would object, "What are you talking about? This is the only show in town."

In a great leap of insight, the Hindu scriptures will tell us that all this world of separateness and change is Māyā, from the farthest galaxy to the body itself. Everything that is prakriti is Māyā, which means everything that is subject to change—not only matter, but mind and ego as well. Even the passage of time has no reality apart from the mind. Vast and varied as this universe is, it is only the surface of reality. It is real, just as a dream is real to the dreamer, but like a dream it is a lower level of reality out of which we can awaken.

We are so captivated by the promises of this dream that we do not want to wake up; in fact, we cannot even imagine what waking up would be like. All our attention is on the dream. But the mystics of all religions assure us that as our longing for fulfillment becomes more and more acute, and our dreams become more and more stale, we will begin to struggle to wake up into the state of joy. This is the touch of grace. As Sri Ramakrishna says, once the Divine Mother casts a glance at you out of the corner of her lovely eyes, the blandishments of Māyā will begin to fade. And when you finally awaken, you will rub your eyes in wonder that you ever could have been taken in by this dream of separate existence.

The wonder of this awakening can never be expressed in words, but it can be glimpsed in some of the marvelous stories we have in the Hindu tradition. One of these stories is about a famous sage named Nārada. Nārada was deeply devoted to Sri Krishna, and there are many stories told in the scriptures about their adventures together. One day, it is said, Nārada was taking a walk with Sri Krishna. The Lord was very pleased with his devotee and told him to ask for a boon, anything he might desire. Now, Nārada was already illumined. He had no personal desires worth speaking of, so he had to think some time before he could come up with an answer. Finally he remembered something even he had never understood, for all the breadth and depth of his spiritual experience. "Lord," he said, "explain to me how you have become the cosmos, from the smallest atom to the greatest star. Tell me how in every being you hide yourself in countless forms, so that people never see that beneath all life there is only One. Show me how you hide yourself as many; tell me the secret of your Māyā."

Sri Krishna smiled and did not answer immediately, for the secret of Māyā is the final riddle of existence. But he had to say something; after all, he had given his word. "All right, Nārada," he said. "But first, I am very thirsty; will you please bring me a glass of water?"

The sun was burning fiercely in the tropical sky, but Nārada ignored the heat and immediately set off for the nearest house to fetch some water. It took some time, for the village across the rice fields that had seemed so near proved to be a much longer walk than he had guessed. The sun beat down, and his feet grew tired; he began to think he might as well ask for *two* glasses of water, and drink the second one himself.

At last, very tired and thirsty, Nārada reached the village and knocked at the door of the very first house he saw. Who should open the door but a breathtakingly beautiful girl, who looked at him with such lovely dark eyes that he forgot all about his thirst. Nārada did not know what to say. He hemmed and hawed, and all the time he was hemming and hawing she just stood there with a gentle smile, looking at him with those eyes. Finally he blurted out, "Will you marry me?"

They got married and settled down, and Nārada was very happy. They had children, then some more children, and the children all graduated from school and got jobs in the village and settled down. Gradually, one by one, their children too got married and had children of their own. The years flew by. Nārada became the patriarch of a great dynasty; everything he turned his hand to prospered, and his family became a hundred strong, until their fields stretched for miles around.

Then, one day, a terrible flood overcame the village. It swept away cottages, it swept away cattle and human beings, and it devastated the land. Before his eyes, everyone in his family was drowned except Nārada, who was overwhelmed by grief. In a matter of hours, everything he had built up around him over the years—wife, family, home and lands—had been wiped out. With nowhere else to turn he cried out from the depths of his heart, "Help me, Lord!"

Immediately, as if a veil were lifted from his eyes, Nārada saw Sri Krishna standing before him with the peacock feather dancing in his hair and a playful smile on his lips, looking just as he had so many years before. "Nārada," Sri Krishna asked gently, "where is my glass of water?"

Then Nārada remembered, and he fell at the feet of the Lord. In one tremendous insight he had seen the nature of Sri Krishna's divine play.

वेदाहं समतीतानि वर्तमानानि चार्जुन ।
भविष्याणि च भूतानि मां तु वेद न कश्चन ।।२६।।

26. I know everything about the past, the present, and the future, Arjuna; but there is no one who knows Me completely.

Until the end of the last century, I think, astronomers took it for granted that the Milky Way galaxy was the whole of the universe. Any student who questioned that would have been failed on the spot. Now, less than three quarters of a century later, we know that there are a billion galaxies within the limits of the observable universe alone. Our own sun used to be the featured player in the drama of astronomy, everybody taking orders from him, everybody dependent on him; now he is just another extra. It's like taking Hamlet and giving him a job holding a spear in the wings; if he doesn't want to come, there are lots of others the Lord can call. When the first quasar was discovered, a lot of prestigious astronomers got together and agreed that it was just another star within our galaxy. It took only a few years for these same men and women to realize that this was actually something a million million times brighter than our sun, and so far removed from our galaxy that our imagination fails to grasp it. This is the nature of scientific knowledge: it grows through trial and error, and it is always capable of growing more; there is no end to it.

Scientific knowledge, in other words, is confined to the everchanging realm of prakriti. Its mode of knowing is the intellect, which can only proceed by dividing something further; that is why intellectual inquiry can never satisfy us with a last word. In Spinoza's language, this is all knowledge of the surface world. It can tell us a lot about the ripples, but it can never see below the surface to the vast ocean in which all these ripples are held together in one whole. That's why I'm so fond of that image of Sri Krishna wearing the galaxies in a garland about his neck. Until recently, astronomers have been studying one bead in this necklace. Now we have discovered there are two beads, and everyone is very excited: remember, each of these is a little cosmos much vaster than we can comprehend. Who knows? At the end of the century we may have even found a few beads more. But the mystics, though they may be deeply impressed by the beauty of all these worlds, understand that this is a necklace that simply has no end. They are not satisfied with two or three beads; they want to realize the Wearer.

The only way to understand creation is to know the Creator: after all, he wrote all the rules, which is just another way of saying he is the source, the underlying unity, from which all the laws of nature derive. As the Upanishads say, "What is that One by knowing which all other things are known?" This knowledge is jnāna, knowledge of the unity of life, whose laws never need to be revised. Astronomy textbooks have to be rewritten every few years; sometimes they are outdated while they are on the press. But a scripture like the Bhagavad Gita, or the Sermon on the Mount, or the Dhammapada of the Buddha can never become dated. The values these scriptures teach—patience, for example—are as valuable now as they were five thousand years ago. And five thousand years from now, when we may be transporting ourselves to other solar systems and eating algae in undersea restaurants with mermaids as waitresses and Neptune at the till, we will still need patience in order to be at peace.

इच्छाद्वेषसमुत्थेन द्वन्द्वमोहेन भारत ।
सर्वभूतानि संमोहं सर्गे यान्ति परंतप ॥२७॥

27. Delusion arises from the duality of attraction and aversion, O Bhārata; every creature is deluded by these from birth.

The Compassionate Buddha had a rather mischievous saying: "Not to have that which we want is sorrow; to have that which we do not want is sorrow." We have conditioned our nervous systems to one-way traffic only—away from what we dislike towards what we like. This is all right as long as everything is going our way, but unfortunately, all too often things are going someone else's way instead. Then it's as if everybody in town has decided to stage a motor parade down our one-way street the wrong way. The nervous system screams in protest, which it lets us hear about in all kinds of ways: tension, headaches, asthma, peptic ulcer, numbness in the toes. Most of us respond to this by putting up bigger and bigger one-way signs: "Stop! Do not enter! Go back! This means *you*." The Buddha would say, this isn't going to work; life *is* two-way traffic, and there isn't any way to change it. Instead of trying to make life fit us, it makes more sense to accommodate our roads to traffic in both directions. Then if things go our way, of course we will be pleased, but if things don't go our way we will be just as even-tempered and enthusiastic as before. For a long time in meditation this is what most of us are doing: reconditioning the nervous system to accept two-way traffic.

The Katha Upanishad gives us two words that shed light on this reconditioning: *preya* and *shreya*. Preya is what is pleasant now, though in the long run it leads to insecurity and distress. Shreya is what is permanently beneficial, though it sometimes seems unpleasant at first. We are so poorly educated in the art of living that we prefer temporary satisfaction, even though it may lead to permanent loss, to the adventure of bearing a temporary displeasure that leads to permanent fulfillment.

We have to make this choice between preya and shreya continually every day. When we see a chocolate éclair in the bakery window, for example, the immediate appeal of it is so great that before we know it we have gone into the bakery, eaten one or two, and bought a dozen to take home. It never occurs to us that we have a choice. There is a chocolate éclair in the window; we *like* chocolate éclairs; therefore we must go in and eat one. For two minutes of satisfaction we eat something that gives us cavities and puts on fat. But just as we have developed a taste for wrong food, so with a little effort we can develop a taste for food that is nutritious. I remember trying chocolate candy for the first time when I was a teenager in India; it took several tries before I could develop a taste for it. We may not be mad about whole-grain bread or green salads, but by cultivating a taste for food that is healthy and learning to prepare it with a creative flair, we can soon become as enthusiastic about fresh garden vegetables as we are about chocolate éclairs.

Like our habits of likes and dislikes in eating, tension too develops only with sustained practice. This is particularly true in personal relationships. The collision of likes and dislikes is greatest in situations where we have to work closely with other people. After all, they have likes and dislikes too, and theirs are not likely to be the same as ours. So one of the most effective ways of reducing tension is to learn to work harmoniously even with people who do not do things our way. In our āshram family all of us were raised in different homes, but we have all learned the skill of working together harmoniously. At first it was far from easy. In the kitchen, for example, one person liked to keep the salt near the stove, another used to put it in a cupboard; then the first would search through the cupboards to find the salt and put it back near the stove. In every little detail, agitation can creep in. Even the way food is served can be a source of irritation. The clever voice of the ego ventriloquist is constantly whispering inside, "I don't like this; that's not the right way." When this goes on inside us for many years, our nerves gradually get more and more tense until at last we cannot bear to live with others; we have to live alone.

It is by reversing this process of estrangement and doing what adds to the joy of others that we release ourselves little by little from the tyranny of likes and dislikes. For example, in taking a job we can look for something that benefits others instead of something that happens to pay very well or offers an office overlooking San Francisco Bay. At home we can learn to enjoy our partner's Waldorf salad even though we can't stand walnuts, or join in our children's four-square game now and then, or look for projects like a backyard vegetable garden which the whole family can enjoy together. When we begin looking upon everything as an opportunity to draw closer to others, the days of the ego are numbered.

येषां त्वन्तगतं पापं जनानां पुण्यकर्मणाम् ।
ते द्वन्द्वमोहनिर्मुक्ता भजन्ते मां दृढव्रताः ॥२८॥

*28. But those who have freed themselves from all
wrongdoing are firmly established in worship of Me.
Their actions are pure, and they are free from the
delusion caused by the pairs of opposites.*

Dvandva, the 'pairs of opposites'—happiness and sorrow, good and
bad, pleasure and pain, and all the rest—are the very texture of
Māyā. Self-will thrives on these dualities, especially likes and dislikes; they are the ego's way of self-expression. In every country and
every community, no matter whether rich or poor, there is a rare
type of person who from birth has very little self-will, who can forbear and forgive very easily. People like this are like freestone
peaches; you have only to open them up and the seed of self-will
falls out easily. The vast majority of us, however, are cling-peach
types. With cling peaches, the seed seems glued to the rest of the
peach. Not only does it not fall out easily; you have to put in a lot
of effort prying all around it with a sharp knife in order to pull the
seed out and throw it away. The knife the Lord gives each of us to
perform this operation of ego-extraction is double-edged; it has patience on one side and suffering on the other. Unfortunately, we
have no choice but to use this knife as long as we cling to our likes
and dislikes. But, Sri Ramakrishna would say, we don't have to go
on clinging forever. No one is making us cling but ourselves, and it
is up to us to let go.

The more you learn to change your likes and dislikes at will, the
more clearly you will be able to see the core of purity and selflessness that is the real Self in everyone. This is seldom easy. Some
people *are* a little more irritating and self-willed than others; there
is no doubt about it. But instead of criticizing such people, which
only makes their alienation worse, you can focus all your attention
on what is best in them. This is one of the most practical skills I have
learned from my Grandmother, and it can be tremendously effective in helping those around you. It is something like turning a flash-

light on a particular spot. I don't diffuse my attention to take in both positive and negative behavior; I keep concentrating on what is kind, what is generous, what is selfless, and the amazing response is that this kind of support draws out and strengthens these very qualities. Not only that, as they become more secure, such people begin to spread this consideration to their other relationships too.

My Grandmother had a very pungent phrase for difficult people: "A lash in the eye." We all know from experience how an eyelash in the eye can be so irritating that we just cannot think about anything else. That is exactly how difficult people affect those around them. But for the mystics, this lash in the eye is an opportunity for learning the skills in life that matter most: patience, forgiveness, and freedom from likes and dislikes. They will go and put their arm around someone who has been a thorn in their flesh and say with gratitude, "Without you, how could I ever have learned to be patient? How could I have learned to forgive?"

जरामरणमोक्षाय मामाश्रित्य यतन्ति ये ।
ते ब्रह्म तद्विदुः कृत्स्नमध्यात्मं कर्म चाखिलम् ॥२९॥

29. Those who take refuge in Me, striving for liberation from old age and death, come to know Brahman, the Self, and the nature of all action.

Growing up close to my Grandmother, I had the blessing of hearing early in life the tremendous truth that you and I are not this finite, mortal body but an eternal, immortal force. As a child I used to run home from school every afternoon to be with my Grandmother, and every afternoon I would find her standing by the front gate waiting for me. Eagerly I would tell her everything that had happened that day—what I had learned in school, what the teacher had said, what had happened on the playing field. One day, though, I came walking slowly up the road with a cloud of gloom over my face. "What's the matter?" my Grandmother asked. "Bad news, Granny," I said. "Today in geography our teacher told us that compared to the sun, we are just insignificant bits of dust." She laughed. "This sun will burn out," she replied, "but you and I will never come to an end."

This is true of every one of us. You and I were never born; therefore we will never die. We are not limited to this physical body; our real Self is divine. Compared with this Self, our sun is just a youngster. Astronomers tell us that it was born perhaps five billion years ago, long after countless millions of similar stars had come, blazed out their lives, and passed away; and, like them, in a few more billion years it will exhaust itself and die. Everything in the created world is part of this continuous process of birth and change and death. But this will in no way affect the Self, the eternal witness within your body and mine.

In the climax of meditation called samadhi we rise above physical consciousness completely, once and for all, to realize that this body is only an instrument which has been given us to use for the benefit of all. In these violent times, each one of us has a crucial role to play in reversing the destructive trends we see around us. Here Mahatma Gandhi gives a personal example we can all follow. So influential was his daily life that Nehru said of him, "Where he sat became a temple; where he trod was holy ground." We too can learn to make our contribution wherever we go by living not for our personal satisfaction but for the welfare of all—as the Buddha would say, *bahujanahitāya, bahujanasukhāya,* 'for the welfare of the many, for the happiness of the many.'

साधिभूताधिदैवं मां साधियज्ञं च ये विदुः ।
प्रयाणकालेऽपि च मां ते विदुर्युक्तचेतसः ॥३०॥

30. Those who see Me ruling the cosmos, who see Me in the adhibhūta, the adhidaiva, and the adhiyajna, are conscious of Me even at the time of death.

In this verse Sri Krishna uses three rather technical terms from the Upanishads. Arjuna is not familiar with these terms; he is a man of action, not a philosopher, and in the next chapter he will ask Sri Krishna to explain this verse. Here, however, he is completely absorbed in what the Lord is telling him about the time of death.

When we take to the spiritual life and begin to practice meditation, we come to see into the heart of life, and our awareness of unity in the world around us deepens immensely. Finally, we come to see the presence of the Lord everywhere: in the sky, in the sun and moon, in animals and birds, and of course in the "human face divine." For the God-conscious person, the wind sighing in the trees whispers of God; the waves sweeping across the beach sing the mantram. Everything is pervaded by the presence of the Lord.

When the mind is permeated like this with consciousness of God, there is no rupture in consciousness at the time of death. My Grandmother sowed the seed of this awareness in me while I was still a child. Every morning she would go to our ancestral temple to worship Lord Shiva. On returning home she always placed a flower from the temple behind my ear with this simple blessing: "May you be like Mārkandeya." In the Hindu scriptures, Mārkandeya is an illumined teenager whose parents had prayed for a son who would be completely devoted to Lord Shiva. Their prayer was granted, but with the sad condition that the boy would die on his sixteenth birthday. As a baby, Mārkandeya's first words were, "Shiva, Shiva," and his love for the Lord grew daily until it filled his consciousness.

Finally, however, the day of his sixteenth birthday dawned. His parents, overcome by grief, came to him and told him that Yama, the King of Death, would claim him that very day. When he heard this, Mārkandeya sat down in deep meditation and became united with Shiva, who is known as the Conqueror of Death. When Yama appeared to claim his victim, from the depths of Mārkandeya's meditation Lord Shiva arose to protect his young devotee. Placing one hand on Mārkandeya's head in infinite love, and with the other pointing his trident at the King of Death, Lord Shiva said, "Don't you know that anyone who takes refuge at my feet has gone beyond your power? Mārkandeya has now become immortal through my grace." This is the secret of going beyond death, on which Sri Krishna will elaborate in the following chapter.

इति ज्ञानविज्ञानयोगो नाम सप्तमोऽध्यायः ॥७॥

CHAPTER EIGHT

The Eternal Godhead

अर्जुन उवाच

किं तद्ब्रह्म किमध्यात्मं किं कर्म पुरुषोत्तम ।
अधिभूतं च किं प्रोक्तमधिदैवं किमुच्यते ॥१॥
अधियज्ञः कथं कोऽत्र देहेऽस्मिन्मधुसूदन ।
प्रयाणकाले च कथं ज्ञेयोऽसि नियतात्मभिः ॥२॥

श्री भगवानुवाच

अक्षरं ब्रह्म परमं स्वभावोऽध्यात्ममुच्यते ।
भूतभावोद्भवकरो विसर्गः कर्मसंज्ञितः ॥३॥
अधिभूतं क्षरो भावः पुरुषश्चाधिदैवतम् ।
अधियज्ञोऽहमेवात्र देहे देहभृतां वर ॥४॥

ARJUNA:

*1. O Krishna, what is Brahman, and what is
the nature of action? What is the adhyātma, the
adhibhūta, the adhidaiva?*

*2. What is the adhiyajna, the supreme sacrifice,
and how is it to be offered? How are the self-
controlled united with you at the time of death?*

SRI KRISHNA:

*3. My highest nature, the imperishable Brahman,
gives every creature its existence and lives in every
creature as the adhyātma. My action is creation
and the bringing forth of creatures.*

> *4. The adhibhūta is the perishable body; the adhidaiva is Purusha, eternal spirit. The adhiyajna, the supreme sacrifice, is made to Me as the Lord within you.*

This chapter begins like a seminar. Sri Krishna has just told Arjuna how to go beyond death, but he is teasing him by using words which Arjuna does not understand. So Arjuna keeps asking, "What does this mean? What about that?" Then he hesitates, his face full of doubt. There is still one more question. He has saved it until last because it bothers him most. Now his tone changes, and he asks in simple, direct words the searching question that has troubled thoughtful people in all religions. "At the time of the great change called death, how can I remember you in the depths of my consciousness? How can I become united with you and go beyond death?" The answer to this question is the theme of chapter eight.

The Chāndogya Upanishad, one of the oldest of the Sanskrit scriptures, tells us about a young man named Shvetaketu who has just returned home from the ancient Indian equivalent of our University of California. Having completed his formal education, Shvetaketu now wants to learn how to live, and he asks his father to teach him the secret of Brahman. In reply, his father gives him one of the greatest spiritual formulas anywhere in mystical literature: *Tat tvam asi,* 'That thou art': Brahman, the supreme Reality, and Ātman, our real Self, are one and the same.

This is a very difficult concept to understand, but the Upanishads bring it out with a vivid image. They say that this very Brahman, who is beyond all change and limitation, has brought all things into existence as a spider spins her web out of herself. It is not so much a process of creation as of emanation. A spider doesn't need to go out to a yarn shop and buy fine silk thread for her web; she has everything she needs right within her. Similarly, the creative power of the Godhead, Māyā, spins out the cosmos so that a little bit of the Godhead is present everywhere. Sri Ramakrishna will say that these two—Brahman and Māyā, the Godhead and the power that creates and dissolves Its creation—are inseparable, like fire and its power to burn. We cannot imagine fire without the power to burn, or the burning power of fire without the fire itself. Similarly, Sri Krishna is reminding us, it is just as absurd to talk about the cosmos as separate from the Lord, who is present everywhere and in every being.

In living creatures, this divine presence is called *adhyātma,* the Ātman or Self. *Adhibhūta* refers to the countless seemingly separate houses in which this Self dwells, of which our own body is one. This house is constantly changing. Only a while ago we were toddlers, as sweet and angelic as any baby we see today. Just look at your old baby pictures and you cannot help wondering what happened to that wide-eyed child of not too many years ago. With the passage of time the body inevitably undergoes certain natural changes, the last of which is death. The dweller within the body, however, is unaffected by these changes.

The implication is that the body is only a powerful tool which the Lord lends us for this life. He trusts us to look after this tool, and to recycle it when our time is up; but we are not it, and it is not ours to do with as we like. Just as there are specific steps to follow in caring for more conventional power tools like ripsaws or hedge clippers, there are specific steps we should take to keep our body healthy, too. We should eat nourishing food, get plenty of vigorous exercise every day and our full quota of sleep every night, and find time for wholesome recreation with our family. We don't have to fall for the belief that good food can be had only in gourmet restaurants; we can prepare good-tasting, nutritious meals at home and share them with family and friends. We don't have to go to an expensive health club for exercise; a good, brisk walk is excellent exercise at any age. All these things help to keep the body strong and the nervous system resilient, which are particularly important in the practice of meditation.

Adhidaiva refers to the Lord as the Inner Controller in all. It doesn't apply only to human beings; it means that the Lord is present as the Operator in all the natural forces around us. In the sun he generates heat and light; in the tree he makes new branches grow and blossom. The force of gravitation, the energy transformations in a cell, the beating of our hearts all take place under his direction, not from without but from within.

The next term, *adhiyajna,* refers to Him to whom any real sacrifice in life is made. It is a rather subtle concept. Whenever we give up something for the sake of others—a movie we want to see, a vacation we want to take, the money we'd like to spend on ourselves—it is really an offering, not so much to others as to our real Self. It is not that others do not benefit from these things; they do. But it is we who benefit most, because it is we who grow.

All spiritual progress requires the sacrifice of self-will, not so much in one grand gesture as in a thousand and one little acts of thoughtfulness during the day. The responsibility for making this sacrifice rests squarely on each one of us; no one can do it for us. Spiritual teachers are like signposts pointing the way to immortality, but it is we who must make the journey. This is quite reasonable. After all, when we pass a signpost on the freeway, we don't expect it to get into the driver's seat and do the driving while we lie down in the back to take a nap. Similarly, we cannot expect other people to pick us up and carry us along the spiritual path. It is up to us to meditate regularly and with sustained enthusiasm, and to reduce our separateness from others in every way we can.

Since most of us have rather large amounts of self-will, we cannot expect to get rid of it overnight. Those who are terribly eager may expect to put all their self-will and selfishness in one big truck and cart it all to the dump. Unfortunately, there is no truck big enough, and even if there were we would not have the strength to get all our self-will into it. The safest and simplest method for people like us is to cart off a little bit of selfishness every day, day after day, year after year, until one day we find to our great surprise that all our separateness has been removed. Then the compulsive identification with body and mind will be completely broken, and death will be no more a change than taking off a jacket, hanging it up, and going home. The Sufi mystic al-Ghazzali puts this beautifully in a poem composed while he was dying:

When my friends weep over my dead body,
Ask them, "Do you mistake him to be this?"
Tell them I swear in the name of the Lord
That this dead body is not I. It was
My dress when I lived on earth; I wore it
During my stay there.

अन्तकाले च मामेव स्मरन्मुक्त्वा कलेवरम् ।
यः प्रयाति स मद्भावं याति नास्त्यत्र संशयः ॥५॥
यं यं वापि स्मरन्भावं त्यजत्यन्ते कलेवरम् ।
तं तमेवैति कौन्तेय सदा तद्भावभावितः ॥६॥

5. If a man remembers Me at the time of death,
he will come to Me. Do not doubt this.
6. The goal a man pursues in life will occupy his mind
at the time of death; to that goal only will he go.

These verses are a quiet statement of a powerful spiritual law. Whatever we think about most, whatever we labor for most, whatever we desire most, that will be the content of our consciousness at the time of death. When we think about something constantly, it sinks deep into our consciousness, and when the time for death comes we will be able to think of nothing else. The Hindu and Buddhist mystics say that at that time the powerful desires in our deeper consciousness will explode like a depth charge, sending us into the next life.

There is a great deal of interest in reincarnation in the West today. Almost every week it seems I get mail announcing some workshop in rebirth, in which people talk about who they were in previous lives. I usually ask, "Don't they want to know who they are in *this* life?" It's a much more pressing question. But I must admit that reincarnation, as it is presented in the Sanskrit scriptures, offers a powerful explanation of how we shape our lives by our deep desires.

The Upanishads throw light on reincarnation in a very scientific way. Psychologists will tell us that in sleep we pass in and out of the state of dreaming and the deep, restful state of dreamless sleep. In the Upanishads, these levels of awareness—waking, dreaming, and dreamless sleep—are said to be only different orders of reality. In dreaming sleep, they tell us, consciousness is withdrawn from the body and the senses, and we live completely in the world of the mind. It's not a particularly restful state, as all of us can testify, and these sleep researchers can show us all kinds of diagrams to show that the mind factory is really working overtime during these hours of dreaming. But in dreamless sleep, consciousness is withdrawn from the mind as well, and we rest in the lap of the Self. In this state, we are completely unconscious; the ego is completely asleep. Here the Upanishads ask a very penetrating question: where is your personality when this takes place? You are not aware of any desires, any fears, so at that time you *have* no desires or fears. Yet they are all there latent in the room of the mind, waiting for you to come back in and pick them up again when you wake up into the dreaming or waking state.

In a flash of insight, the Upanishads tell us that this is just what happens between death and life. When we die, consciousness is withdrawn from the body just as it is in dreamless sleep, and just as all our desires and fears wait for us to reclaim them and live them out again in a dream-body, they wait until they can take form again in another physical body and another life. In both cases, it is the restless desire for personal satisfaction that draws us back into separate existence.

This is difficult to grasp at first, but all of us can understand that when we think about something constantly, when we desire something deeply, we are training our minds to be focused on this even at the hour of death. Our deepest desires at the moment of death sum up this life and determine the context for the next. The consequences of this are tremendous: what we do each day shapes our destiny. We do not suddenly wake up one morning free from the lurid dream of separateness; unitary consciousness is the result of long years of trying to act, speak, and think for the welfare of all. The choices we make throughout life have a powerful, cumulative effect. The other day I saw a sign in a restaurant which read, "You are what you eat."

How simple life would be if this were true! We could all be living in health and security simply by eating three good meals a day. Unfortunately, however, we are *not* what we eat; our body is. When the Compassionate Buddha gave us the Dhammapada, he did not begin by saying, "All that we are is the result of what we have eaten"; he said, "All that we are is the result of what we have thought."

In other words, it is the little choices we make every day that determine what we become. Life is the sum of all these small thoughts and actions. One of the many reasons I admire Mahatma Gandhi is that he could give his complete attention to the smallest problems of daily living as well as the immense problems presented by India's struggle for independence. Day in and day out, in even the smallest details, he did everything possible to realize the unity of life. This kind of determination was characteristic of Gandhi. From his early days as a student in London he refused to be overwhelmed by anything. When he was in London and could not find any vegetarian restaurants, he started cooking in his room. His specialty was carrot soup, but it is said that those who dropped in at his place at dinnertime never did so again. Then, when he was a lawyer in South Africa and the white barber refused to cut his hair, he did not become angry or try to get back at the man; he went out and bought a pair of scissors and cut his hair himself. The day after this historic haircut, when he went to court as usual, his fellow barristers teasingly asked him if the mice had been nibbling at his hair. Gandhi didn't mind; he just didn't like to depend on anyone, or to throw up his hands and say, "There is nothing I can do."

Meister Eckhart tells us, "Whoever has God in mind, simply and solely God, in all things, such a person carries God with him into all his works and into all places, and God alone does all his works." Those who use every minute of their lives to serve the Lord in those around them, as Gandhi did, carry God with them wherever they go. When the assassin's bullet took his life, the only word that escaped Gandhi's lips was his mantram, *Rāma*. He had made his life a continuous effort to remember the Lord, so he felt no hatred at the moment of death; his mind had no thought of anything but the Lord. Similarly, Sri Krishna promises each of us, "If at the time of death your heart is filled with love for Me, if your consciousness is permeated with love for Me, then you will come to Me. Of this there can be no doubt." Men and women of God all over the world have corroborated this countless times. They have imbued their consciousness with such depth of love that at the time of death they are able to maintain continuing awareness of God. Their bodies do suffer, because the body is subject to the stress of pain, but inside there is continuing awareness which neither physical pain nor emotional suffering can disturb.

तस्मात्सर्वेषु कालेषु मामनुस्मर युध्य च ।
मय्यर्पितमनोबुद्धिर्मामेवैष्यस्यसंशयम् ॥७॥

7. Therefore, remember Me at all times and
fight on. With your heart and mind intent on Me,
you will surely come to Me.

If shraddhā is the key to destiny, meditation is the key to shraddhā. Here it helps greatly to remember that the Gita is no pastoral discourse; it is set in the middle of a battlefield, with elephants trumpeting and swords flashing and conchs calling the regiments to battle all around. If the Gita were written today there would be bombers overhead and tanks rolling over the ground while Sri Krishna tells Arjuna how to go beyond death. The point is that if we really want to live—not just driven by negative conditioning, but in complete mastery of ourselves—then we have to be prepared to fight. This is the grimmest battle any human being can face, and it has to be faced every day, day in and day out, until victory is won.

It isn't possible even to dream how terrible this fight is until we get below the surface level of consciousness and begin to see the forces ranged against us. Even then, for a long time we do not guess their real strength; all we see is the front lines. First there is the infantry, which is fear—all kinds of fears, most of which we are not even acquainted with. We may not think we have much fear to reckon with, but it is as deep as our separateness, which cuts deep into the consciousness of every one of us. Then there is the cavalry, which is anger. If you can imagine the effect that cavalry and chariots had when they suddenly made their appearance in some of the great civilizations of the ancient world, you will see how apt a comparison this is; a cavalry attack is much more ferocious than infantry and much more difficult to conquer. But the real backbone of the army in ancient India was the elephantry. Throughout India's long history there have been many occasions when another country would try to plunder our rich material resources. But when these invading armies would look up and see huge armored elephants coming down on them by the hundreds, sometimes by the thousands, they would be panic-stricken. The elephantry is self-will, and it is a thousand times more fierce than anger and fear. All this is what we have to overcome in order to be masters of ourselves, and those who have won this battle, even giants like the Compassionate Buddha, will tell us that nothing on earth is more difficult, more precious, or more exhilarating than this victory.

This fight goes on twenty-four hours a day; even at night there are going to be skirmishes. The alarm goes off in the morning and the fight is on: to get up or not to get up? Years of conditioning are whispering to you to doze on a few minutes more; it's the distant thunder of the cannon on the battlefield. No mystic has ever denied that at a time like this, especially when it's cold outside, it's very pleasant to turn up your electric blanket and go back to sleep. All they will say is, "You're going to lose the fight." Here I can offer a simple and very effective tactic: don't stay there to weigh the pros and cons; throw off the blankets and jump out of bed. It will be a little difficult, but after a few days you will realize that the first skirmish of the war is over and you have won. It's a very good feeling, because this isn't a war in the grand old Clausewitz style. It's all guerilla warfare, and every skirmish counts.

So you jump out of bed, and the same instant you've won one encounter, you're in the middle of another one. Even once you're out of bed, the prospect of sitting down to meditate isn't exactly inviting. After all, the newspaper is waiting at your door; you can always sit in a beanbag chair with a cup of coffee and read the news instead. Nobody will say this isn't more pleasant than meditation. A beanbag chair may not do much for your spine, but at least it doesn't take much effort to sit in it; journalism may not be particularly non-violent these days, but it *is* stirring. Here it is that you don't even give the beanbag chair a glance, let alone the paper; you go straight to your meditation room, sit down quietly, and start trying to meditate.

But the fight has only begun. It's not as if you left the battlefield with the beanbag chair; the battlefield is right inside you. You're sitting quietly in meditation, trying to keep your mind on the Prayer of St. Francis, and after a few minutes you find you're a little drowsier than you suspected. It's very difficult to fight when you're getting sleepy in meditation. For one thing, if your meditation is going well, it may not be normal sleep that's coming on. It may be what the Sanskrit scriptures call *yoganidrā,* the wave of oblivion that comes over the mind when you try to stay conscious beneath the conscious level. In *yoganidrā* there's not much motivation to fight; there's not much will. But there is no choice; you have to fight. Otherwise you cannot go forward. And when someone asks me, "What do I do when I don't have much motivation?" I just say, "You *make* it much—by trying." There is no other way. This is a problem that will keep coming up in meditation for many, many years, and if you don't begin to fight it now you will find it almost impossible to take on the fight later on. The point is not ever to yield, to say, "There is nothing I can do." As my Grandmother used to say, there is always something you can do. If you yield, you have lost the fight; but if you do not yield, you are beginning to win.

Then you finish meditation, and after all these conflicts, all you want to do is take it out on the refrigerator. It's an opportunity again; it's another skirmish. Instead of tucking into things to which you have been conditioned—say, a few pieces of nice, light bread that weakens the body in twelve ways, loaded with butter and jam—you get out the whole wheat bread and the margarine. After two pieces of toast there's a foray by a third, but you fight it off. As you get to be a seasoned fighter, even your hand will get accustomed to fighting. Instead of reaching automatically for the coffee it will say, "Coffee, you're no friend of mine; all you give me is caffeine." Do you see why I say that there's no boredom in life once you take to meditation? You can't get bored in the middle of a battle; you've got to be alert all the time just to save your skin.

It's like this all day long. You go to work and immediately the ego says, "What's the least I can give here and the most I can get?" It's bad for work; it's bad for you; it's bad for everybody. So there is fighting again—you have to try to give as much as you can. At lunchtime you can sit around and join in some gossip, or you can take a fast walk repeating the mantram. And when you go home, you bring the battlefield with you even in the car; if you can keep calm, everybody in the cars around you will be a little safer.

By the end of a day like this, if you've really been giving your best, there is every reason to want a chance to come home, put your feet up, and hang up your sādhana until the next morning. It's a very reasonable request. The problem is, your opponent wouldn't even dream of fighting by the rules. In his book, any minute is right for a sneak attack. Things haven't been going so smoothly at home either. The children have had a bad day, the cat is missing, the dryer is broken; there are all kinds of problems. The natural reaction is to say, "I've had my share of problems already," and to take it out on the first person who comes to greet you. Of course, you have had your share of problems; no one is denying that. But the cat and the dryer have sprung this sneak attack, and the only choice is whether you're going to win or lose.

There is a thrilling kind of satisfaction in this. You step out of the car into no-man's-land and little Susie comes up to tell you that George has broken your new hi-fi. That's all; no "Hello, daddy," just this news about George. It takes real stamina to say at a time like this, "Oh, sure, let's see if we can fix it. After all, hi-fi's aren't eternal." It may be a hi-fi or a tennis racket or a sewing machine or anything else that is your favorite; the point is, you can come back even to an upset home and immediately set to work at bringing peace into it again. Nothing in the world can give more satisfaction than this, and nothing can make you more precious to those around you. Everyone in the family will be looking forward to your return.

Even your neighbors will be watching over the fence and saying, "There goes someone who really deserves a peace prize." They don't know that you're still fighting.

There's no end to this fight, and there is no end to the satisfaction it can bring, because there is always more you can give. Instead of rushing through dinner to go bowling, you can stay and listen with genuine interest to Susie's rambling account of what happened to her at school. That's what really makes a meal satisfying, not just the food. And after dinner, when you just want to go off to your room to watch the late show or plow on through *The Decline and Fall of the Roman Empire,* you can drop in at your neighbor's, where things have been getting a little strained, and say, "I've got the evening free; why don't your children come out with ours for ice cream so that you two can have a little time to yourselves?" You're not only fighting your own battles then; your example is making it a little easier for others to fight too, and helping to build up a neighborhood where there is solidarity and trust.

If you have been fighting like this all day and really giving it your best, it will be a great solace to go to bed at night. No waterbed in the world can ever give the kind of rest that comes when you have been trying your hardest all day to lead the spiritual life. Then, after your evening meditation, when you lie down, close your eyes, and give all your mind to the mantram, it is very much like dropping off to sleep in the arms of the Lord. When you fall asleep in the mantram it will go on in your consciousness throughout the night, nursing the wounds of the day and strengthening your spirit for the fight that will come the next day. You know now that you are fighting for the Lord, and He will give you all the health and strength and endurance you need until finally the battle is won, and you come—as this verse promises—to be united with Him forever.

अभ्यासयोगयुक्तेन चेतसा नान्यगामिना ।
परमं पुरुषं दिव्यं याति पार्थानुचिन्तयन् ॥८॥

8. When you make your mind one-pointed on the Lord through the regular practice of meditation, you will find the supreme glory of the Self.

A clever verse from ancient India describes the mind as a restless monkey that is stung by a scorpion, drunk, and possessed by a demon, all at the same time. We are all proud owners of this monkey, which gives us a clue as to why it is so incredibly difficult to bring our mind under control. Yet control it we must if we are to go beyond the conditioning of the mind.

The symbol of the monkey is easily understood in a country like India, where monkeys run about as freely as cats and dogs in the United States. Often in India you will see little monkeys trained to perform and entertain. My wife and I once saw a little one that had been taught to act just like a reluctant child on the way to school. He dragged his feet, kicked at pebbles, and kept looking back over his shoulder and watching the birds in the trees just as any schoolboy would. Then, on the way home, he jumped and ran cheerfully. Now, this restless creature did not learn schoolboy gestures overnight; his master trained him over a period of time. Similarly, we do not still our minds in a week or even a year; it takes a long, long period of steady, enthusiastic effort. We should never be impressed by anyone who claims to give us complete control over the conscious, preconscious, and unconscious levels of the mind in a four-week seminar. But even if it takes a lifetime to attain this state, it is worth all our time and attention.

It always amazes me to see the kind of skills people spend their time perfecting. We know of one boy who delivers his newspapers from a precarious perch atop his unicycle. On college campuses you will find a lot of students who have managed to embroider a whole garden of exquisite flowers on their blue jeans. These are all skills which demand a great deal of concentration to master, and whenever I see anyone with the capacity to excel in his or her chosen field, whether it is sculpture or gymnastics or jumping motorcycles over the Grand Canyon, I know that if that person would only take to meditation, he or she could really go far.

One of the signs that a person has this capacity for concentration is that he will not get distracted when he is talking with someone; all his concentration will be on the conversation. This is an art which all of us can cultivate; it will help our meditation and our personal relationships too. There is a story about Samuel Taylor Coleridge, the English poet, that illustrates this point. Coleridge was an enthusiastic talker, full of ideas and theories. One day, it is said, he saw his friend Charles Lamb on his way to his London office and went up to him, saying, "Lamb, stop a minute; I've a new theory of literary criticism. Wouldn't you like to hear it?"

Lamb said, "Sorry, old chap, but I've an appointment at the office."

"Let me give you just a few minutes' summary, then," said Coleridge. And he started on the theory that underlies the *Biographia Literaria*.

Now, just as Coleridge had developed a talent for talking, Lamb had developed a talent for escaping from long-winded conversations. So Coleridge, knowing Lamb's ways, grabbed hold of his friend's coat button to keep him from getting away. Minutes passed, an hour passed, and Coleridge went on and on; he had closed his eyes in concentration and was well into his exposition, secure in his hold on Charles Lamb's coat button. But he had underestimated his friend's resourcefulness. Lamb had pulled out a pair of pocket scissors, quietly clipped the button from his coat, and slipped away to get to his appointment.

Hours passed, and Lamb, who was a very busy man, went about his business in the City and forgot about his long-winded friend completely. But on his way home late in the afternoon, to his amazement, there was Coleridge, still hanging on to his button and holding forth on literary theory. It may be an exaggerated story, but it illustrates the concentration of genius. If only Coleridge had taken to meditation instead of drugs for inspiration, he could have gone very far on the spiritual path.

कविं पुराणमनुशासितार-
मणोरणीयांसमनुस्मरेद्यः ।
सर्वस्य धातारमचिन्त्यरूप-
मादित्यवर्णं तमसः परस्तात् ॥९॥
प्रयाणकाले मनसाञ्चलेन
भक्त्या युक्तो योगबलेन चैव ।
भ्रुवोर्मध्ये प्राणमावेश्य सम्यक्
स तं परं पुरुषमुपैति दिव्यम् ॥१०॥

9–10. The Lord is the Supreme Poet, the First Cause, the Sovereign Ruler, subtler than the tiniest particle, the support of all, inconceivable, bright as the sun, beyond the darkness of Māyā. Remembering him in this way at the time of death, through devotion and the power of meditation, with your mind completely stilled and your concentration fixed in the center of spiritual awareness, you will realize the Lord of Love.

The Supreme Poet is at work wherever we look; we can see his touch in the beauty of the sky, in the vast oceans and the rivers, in the mountains and forests, in all the creatures who live on the earth. Even our careless habits, which have covered the earth with a blight of pollution, cannot obscure the infinite beauty of the Lord reflected in every blade of grass, every drop of water. Look at even that humblest of flowers, the dandelion, the plague of gardeners and a nightmare to anyone who wants a perfect carpet of green for his front lawn. How beautiful even this little yellow flower is! Look at any leaf and you can see the miracle of life, the perfect pattern created by the Supreme Poet. The German mystic Nicholas of Cusa looks at a simple nut and sees in it the creative force of the Lord; in one little nut lies the potentiality of thousands of trees to come.

In the Upanishads the source of all this creativity is called "the uncaused Cause." If some scientist were to decide that the ultimate constituents of the universe are protons, I would ask, "Who put those protons there?" If an astronomer tries to tell me that the cosmos was born from a black hole, I would still want to know, "Who bored that black hole?" This line of questioning has no end within the world of cause and effect; we can always ask where that primordial particle or black hole came from. But this infinite regression of questions comes to a halt where the Lord is concerned. If you ask Sri Krishna who created him, he will say, "Me. I put myself here." In mysticism everywhere the Lord is called the Self-created, the First Cause, which means that everything else, including you and me, is an effect.

All this is not just beautiful poetry; it has a terribly practical point to it. In this verse and those which follow, Sri Krishna is telling Arjuna in very precise terms how to maintain unbroken awareness through the cataclysmic changes we call death. It is important to realize that whether we prepare for it or not, death will come to us all. As the Katha Upanishad tells us, the body is like a city with eleven gates, and just as historical cities change, grow old, and eventually become archeological relics, the body too is bound to come to an end. Yet, as all the world's great scriptures assure us, we do not have to die when the body dies. If we have trained our consciousness over the years to be united with the Lord, we shall be able to guard ourselves against the rupture in consciousness that takes place for almost all human beings when the body is shed.

The key to this almost unimaginable achievement is devotion. It is all very well to talk about the Ultimate Reality, the Great Void, but we cannot love a Void, and I doubt very much if ordinary people like us would find much about the Void to remember as we entered the moment of death. Here it is that we need the Lord in the aspect we can love and understand—the Supreme Poet, the sustainer and protector of all, from whom we came into existence and to whom we shall return. For this, we need a divine ideal like Sri Krishna, Jesus the Christ, the Compassionate Buddha, or the Divine Mother, a divine incarnation in which the supreme Godhead assumes a human form. We have only to look at the picture of Jesus holding a lamb or reassuring the children of Galilee for our hearts to go out to him. We have only to see one of those South Asian statues of the Buddha seated in meditation, full of compassion and tenderness, for us to want to become like him. The great incarnations come to live among us, to talk and laugh and weep like us, so that we can learn to love them more than we love ourselves. When we can love like this, it will be impossible for all our love not to flow to the Lord at the hour of our death. Absorbed in him completely, secure in the realization that we are neither body nor mind, we can shed the body as naturally as a dead leaf falls from a tree.

When we are setting out on this final journey, there should be nothing in our knapsack. We cannot afford to have a lot of things on our backs, like the hitchhikers we see on University Avenue all loaded down with transistor radios and guitars and camping gear. Similarly, on the last journey there should not be a movement in the mind. Every attachment, every desire, every resentment must be left behind, which means that the mind must be completely stilled. When there are no lingering desires and thoughts to tie us to the body, we can keep our minds absorbed in the Lord without any trace of reservation. This is the theme of the verses which are to come.

यदक्षरं वेदविदो वदन्ति
विशन्ति यद्यतयो वीतरागाः ।
यदिच्छन्तो ब्रह्मचर्यं चरन्ति
तत्ते पदं संग्रहेण प्रवक्ष्ये ॥११॥

11. I will briefly tell you of the eternal state all
scriptures affirm, which can be entered only by those
who are self-controlled. Those who are selfless in
their daily lives and free from selfish attachments
attain this supreme goal.

In a village in India it is impossible to be ignorant of death. Everyone knows everyone else, everyone's life is connected with the lives of everyone else, and it is not uncommon to hear that someone you saw only the other day, or with whom you played, or whose mango trees you used to climb, has passed from this life completely. It is a continual reminder of the transiency of all life. This kind of thing happened many times while I was growing up, and often people on their deathbed would send for my Grandmother to come sit with them and hold their hand and ease their hearts a little in going through the agony with which most people face death. I don't think any of them had much idea of my Granny's real stature, but everyone was aware that she was a great source of strength, and in moments like those all you had to do was look into her eyes to glimpse the great truth all scriptures tell us—that we are not the body, we are imperishable spirit, and death is no more than a change of rooms.

Even when I was a little boy, my Grandmother would insist that I come with her on these deathbed vigils. It used to horrify everyone in my family, for no one, certainly not I, ever had any idea of why she should want to take an impressionable child to scene after scene of agony. But no one would argue with my Granny. She was a very loving but a very determined spiritual teacher, and many years later I came to see that all those scenes of death and dying planted deep in my consciousness the fervent desire to go beyond death once and for all. The suffering I witnessed at those scenes still haunts me. There is no isolation from the dramas of birth and death as there often is in this country; life ebbed out in the presence of family and friends, and their grief used to add to the agony of the dying, which often went on for hours and sometimes even days.

Once, I remember, I took courage and asked my Grandmother why there had to be such suffering. Granny didn't have much of a way with words; she taught me by how she lived. So she didn't quote the Gita at me; she just asked me to sit down in a chair and hold on to the arms with all my strength. Then she tried to pull me out of the chair. I was a rather strong fellow, and I held on for all I was worth; but she was stronger, and with one painful wrench she had me up on my feet. "That hurt, Granny," I said. "Now sit down again, Little Lamp," she told me, "but this time don't hold on." I sat down again, and she reached down and lifted me gently into her arms.

This is the secret of facing death. As long as there is something we want to get out of life before we go—a little more money, a little more pleasure, a chance to get in a parting dig at someone we think has hurt us—there will be a terrible struggle with death when it comes. As long as we think we are the body, we will fight tooth and nail to hold on to the body when death comes to wrench it away. The tragedy, of course, is that death *is* going to take it anyway; it was never ours to begin with. So the great mystics all tell us, "Give it away now and be free." Give up all these selfish attachments; then, when death does come, we can give him what is his without a shadow of regret, and keep for ourselves what is ours, which is love of the Lord. There is great artistry in this; that is why it appeals to me so deeply. Death comes and growls something about how our time has come and we just say, "Don't growl; I'm ready to come on my own." Then we stand up gracefully, take off the jacket that is the body, place it carefully in Death's arms and go on home.

सर्वद्वाराणि संयम्य मनो हृदि निरुध्य च ।
मूर्ध्न्याधायात्मनः प्राणमास्थितो योगधारणाम् ॥१२॥

ओमित्येकाक्षरं ब्रह्म व्याहरन्मामनुस्मरन् ।
यः प्रयाति त्यजन्देहं स याति परमां गतिम् ॥१३॥

12–13. Remembering Me at the time of death, close down the doors of the senses and place the mind in the heart. Then, while absorbed in meditation, focus all energy upwards to the head. Repeating in this state the divine Name, the syllable Om that represents the changeless Brahman, you will attain the supreme goal.

A decade or so ago there seemed to be a veiled conspiracy to pretend that death did not exist. Now it is just the opposite. Courses on death are given on university campuses; books on death are prominent in every bookstore. Yet, though most people will now admit "Oh, yes, we know we have to die; everyone has to die sometime,"

I have met very, very few people—even including those with terminal illnesses—who really believed it. The proof is that if you
really believe you're going to die, you will do something about it.
That is where the Gita comes in.

Some of the books on death we see in stores go so far as to recommend shedding the body in a state of mind where the senses are sati-
ated. This seems to be the modern way—to hope to die with the senses all aroused. The Gita suggests a far different approach. It is not
much help to die in a state of sense-pleasure—say, after having eaten
a gourmet meal. The ultimate goal is to be able to shed the body
without any rupture in consciousness at all, and for this we must be
prepared to train ourselves for decades.

These two Gita verses follow closely the very precise description
of the death process given in the Upanishads. First, the Upanishads
say, the vitality of the senses is withdrawn into the mind. Then the
mind, along with the life-force, descends into the heart, into the
realms of deeper consciousness. Finally the Self, accompanied by
mental impressions, departs from the body, following one of the
tracks leading from the heart. In the case of the man or woman of
God, the Self is said to depart upward through the crown of the
head.

At the hour of death, the doors of the senses are completely
closed. If we are to maintain awareness of the Self at that time,
nothing can be allowed to take away from the complete concentration within. There is no hearing, no seeing, and there should be no
desire to see or hear. Everything must be centered on the Self. For
most of us, however, the onset of death precipitates a terrible longing for sensory experience and a feeling of agonized deprivation in
the mind. That is when the real agony of death begins. All the attachments we have formed, all the virulent self-will we have cultivated, tie us down in the mind completely so that we cannot break
loose. Yama, the King of Death, must tear us away. If I may use a
grim image, this tearing away is like being thrown through the
windshield in an automobile accident. It is horrible to be thrown
through the windshield, but it is much worse to be thrown through

the rigid barrier of self-will and selfish attachments when our body is wrenched away in death. This is the agonizing horror of death, even beyond the physical level.

I am not at all against alleviating the physical pain of death through the wise use of drugs, but these cannot relieve this kind of pain in the mind. The only way to be able to still the mind at the time of death is to train it from now on to be filled with love of the Lord, whom we must see in every creature around us. Then at death there is nothing in the heart but love of the Lord. There is no personal attachment or self-will; there is no conflict, no anger, no fear. The body may suffer, but there is no suffering in consciousness, for the mind is full only of the mantram or Holy Name.

One of the secrets of the Gita is how to use the mantram at the time of death. When vitality has been withdrawn into the mind and the mind into the heart, you have gone beyond the mind; therefore, you have gone beyond memory. This is a terribly practical point. You will not be able to remember the inspirational passage at that time. But when the mantram has become *ajapajapam,* when it repeats itself without any conscious effort, you do not need memory; you do not need coherence or connections between words. You do not have to remember to repeat the mantram; it will go on of itself.

There is a beautiful verse from the Mundaka Upanishad that describes ajapajapam:

> Take the great bow of the sacred scriptures,
> Place on it the arrow of devotion;
> Then draw the bowstring of meditation
> And aim at the target, the Lord of Love.
> The mantram is the bow, the aspirant
> Is the arrow, and the Lord the target.
> Now draw the bowstring of meditation,
> And hitting the target be one with him.

For the great mystics, the mantram has taken root and become established in their consciousness; the Holy Name echoes continuously in the depths of the heart. In sickness and in health, in favorable circumstances and in times of turmoil, the mantram continues to fill the heart and mind. When this happens, we are so established in God-consciousness that death loses its terror. At the time we shed the body there will be no break in consciousness, for we have become continuously aware of the Lord who dwells within.

The mantram mentioned in these verses is *Om,* which is not really an external sound. It is an internal sound, which may occasionally be heard in very deep meditation. The Sanskrit scriptures call it "the unstruck sound"; in Zen it is alluded to as the "sound of one hand clapping." The most ancient of all the mantrams in the Hindu tradition, *Om* is considered to be the fundamental vibration which pervades the cosmos. So *Om* is not just an idle sound, but a powerful spiritual formula. For the mystics, this sound may come and go in their consciousness. But at the time of death, when they have trained their consciousness to be completely filled with the love of the Lord, *Om* is the sound that will reverberate in their hearts, drowning all mortal noises.

अनन्यचेताः सततं यो मां स्मरति नित्यशः ।
तस्याहं सुलभः पार्थ नित्ययुक्तस्य योगिनः ॥१४॥

14. I am easily attained by the person who always remembers Me and is attached to nothing else. Such a person is a true yogī, Arjuna.

Our home on the Blue Mountain in South India was near the road to town, and every Saturday during the summer holidays the local tribal people used to go by our house on their way to the race track. They were a lively group when they passed our place in the morning. Somehow fifty of them could squeeze into a bus intended for thirty; they didn't mind having to stand the whole way with someone's elbow in their ribs, because they were having such a good time speculating on how much money they were going to win at the races. But in the evening it was a different story. The same bus would return shrouded in silence. My mother used to stand at the gate and watch them go by, and being a tender-hearted woman, she felt sorry to see them going home so depressed after all that cheering and singing in the morning.

This is the story of us all. We are conditioned to believe that we only have to pursue our pleasure, to pick up whatever profit we can and put it in our wallet; but the pleasure is never quite what we had hoped, and our wallet is sometimes snatched away in the bargain. In his mercy the Lord allows us a margin for experimentation, but after a while he expects us to get the point—that we cannot find fulfillment in making money or in stimulating the senses. Life on the sensory level is fraught with such frustration and anger that once we begin to make some progress on the spiritual path we can only ask, "How can people enjoy this kind of life?" We have only to look around us to see how much suffering there is in living for oneself— thinking about money and material possessions, comparing oneself with others, competing against even one's nearest and dearest. To the mystic, this is not living at all, and in an earlier verse in the Gita Sri Krishna says, "What most people call day is the night of ignorance to the sage."

In the deepest stages of meditation, when concentration has become complete, we go beyond the attraction of the sense-world once and for all. In this state, consciousness is withdrawn completely from fleeting pleasures and personal possessions, and all sense of separateness goes. All our vitality is consolidated within us, and the doors of the senses, which are usually in one position only— open to all incoming traffic—now swing completely shut. Consciousness has been withdrawn into the mind and the mind into the Self, just as at the moment of death. The all-important difference is that in meditation this is something we learn to do intentionally, over a period of many years of spiritual practice, so that instead of blacking out, our consciousness is intensely awake and filled with peace. In death all our selfish attachments are torn from us, but in the climax of meditation they have been thrown away of our own free will. Afterwards, when we return to the world of the senses, we are free to enjoy whatever is in harmony with the welfare of all, but we can never again be misled by anything life has to offer. We have already

died to our little self to come to life in the Ātman, our real Self. So
a great mystic like St. Paul will say, "I have already died to my little
'I'; how can I die again? *Not I, not I, but Christ liveth in me.*"

In every tradition there is a rare man or woman who embodies
this ideal, so perfectly symbolized by the Compassionate Buddha,
Jesus the Christ, and Sri Krishna, or by the Virgin Mary in the Catholic tradition and the Divine Mother in Hinduism. If you want to
see beauty in its most radiant form, look at men and women who are
trying to be like these, whose daily life reflects the divine presence.
The other day, seeing a particularly striking statue of the Compassionate Buddha seated in meditation, I could not help thinking with
humility but with great love: "I will do anything to be like him! I do
not care about what others think of me, about what image I project;
I just want to be like the Buddha."

मामुपेत्य पुनर्जन्म दुःखालयमशाश्वतम् ।
नाप्नुवन्ति महात्मानः संसिद्धिं परमां गताः ॥१५॥
आब्रह्मभुवनाल्लोकाः पुनरावर्तिनोऽर्जुन ।
मामुपेत्य तु कौन्तेय पुनर्जन्म न विद्यते ॥१६॥

*15. Great souls make their lives perfect and discover
Me; they are freed from mortality and the suffering
of this separate existence.*
*16. Every creature in the universe is subject to rebirth,
Arjuna, except the one who is united with Me.*

In the early days of the Blue Mountain Center I once gave a series
of talks on meditation to a group of hard-headed Kaiser businessmen, who followed most of what I had to say with attentiveness and
appreciation. Once, however, I happened to refer casually to the
Hindu and Buddhist concept of reincarnation. After the talk one of
these men came up, took me aside, and said very persuasively:
"You've been so rational all this time; you haven't said anything
that we can't accept, even with all our scientific training. Why do
you have to start dragging in these esoteric theories?"

Though reincarnation is emphasized in these verses, Sri Krishna is not going to require us to pass an exam on the theory of rebirth in order to attain the goal of life. There is no necessary connection between the practice of meditation and belief in reincarnation. We can believe in many births and still lead an unspiritual life, just as we can believe in only one birth and still lead a selfless life. But there is no contradiction at all between the theory of reincarnation and the theory of evolution. Both mystic and scientist agree on the stages through which life evolved; the mystic is only adding that there is another level than that on which the physical drama of existence is played out. In a crude form, each of us recapitulates these stages of evolution in the mother's womb, from the simplest organism—the single cell—up to the human being. To make this concept a little more personal, I like to imagine the dog-lover as once having been a little pup playing with a shoe, and when I come across someone who is especially partial to cats, I tell them they were once curled up by the fireside themselves, purring contentedly. The Sufi mystic Jalalu'l-Din Rumi expresses this universal evolution eloquently:

> I came forth from the Unmanifested
> And pitched my tent in the forest of life.
> I was a mineral, then vegetable,
> Then became an animal. I evolved
> Into a man, and in the company
> Of good people I wandered round and round
> The house of prayer. At last I chose the road
> That leads to Him, and became a servant
> At His gate. No longer were He and I
> Separate, for I was lost in Him.

Twelve years ago I had the pleasure of meeting Dr. Evans-Wentz, one of the world's foremost authorities on Tibetan mysticism. According to Evans-Wentz, the Tibetan contribution to the theory of reincarnation is vividly picturesque. Like the ancient Hindu sages, the Tibetan mystics say that we really have two bodies: the physical body, *sthūlasharīra,* and the subtle body, *sūkshmasharīra.* The subtle body, which consists of our thoughts and emotional tendencies, is immaterial, nonphysical. This is why we find it difficult to believe it exists, and go through life thinking of ourselves as being so many inches tall and weighing so many pounds. But within this physical sheath there is a subtle body too, which has an ego so many units broad, a lot of samskāras—what you call "hangups"—a subtle mass of tamas or inertia, some rajas or energy, and a little sattva or serenity.

At the time of death, this subtle body and the physical body part company. The physical body is shed and resolved back into its constituents of calcium, phosphorus, and other elements, while we go in our subtle body to a kind of prenatal waiting room which the Tibetan mystics call Bardo, the 'in-between state.' These mystics say that we often have to wait in Bardo for a long while before the proper situation for our next birth becomes available. The Upanishads tell us penetratingly that there is some similarity between this state and the state of dreamless sleep between two periods of waking. It can be a source of great consolation to those who are facing death. In deep dreamless sleep, the Upanishads add, our problems all disappear for the time being; we are not conscious of either the body or the mind. But when it comes time to wake up, don't we still wake up the same person, into a world that is changed only by a short passage of time? It is the same in Bardo. At the moment of death, consciousness is withdrawn from the physical body, and we get a long period of rest and recuperation. Then, when we are ready, we wake up again into the physical context to give it one more try.

The other day I went with my wife to a large drop-in clinic in Oakland for our annual physical examinations. One of the first tests they always give you is to see how long you can wait. Finally I presented my card, and they decided that I was who it said I was. It can take some time, because the only proof I have of my identity is not the kind that clerks are prepared to accept. Then they took me into another room, took away my clothes, and gave me a white paper gown to wear while I went from room to room to wait for test after test.

Bardo is very much like that. You have to stand in a queue to register; then you show your identification card to the receptionist and she tells you to sit in the waiting room until she calls your name. There's always a certain amount of waiting, because it's not easy for the administration to find the right constellation of circumstances for you. If you haven't been very kind to your parents in this life, you have to be born into a home where you will have rebellious children—which actually is not too difficult to find. If you haven't been very considerate to your wife, you have to be born into a context where you will have an irate husband, which also is not too difficult to find. And if you have been a very poor neighbor, walling yourself off and ignoring those around you, you have to be placed in a neighborhood where people will look right through you and not even remember your name. It's like that even down to your dog or cat; you have to have the right dog or cat in your home, too. Everything must be perfect for your future growth. When these circumstances are put together, among the millions of possible homes there is only one into which you can be born that is just right.

In this verse, Sri Krishna says that until we become united with the Lord, all of us have to keep coming back into our old context, exactly where we left off at the time of death. It is a brilliant theory, because it places the responsibility for our life in our own hands. If we can lead a selfless life, contributing to our family and community, then we will have made a better life for ourselves in our next birth. On the other hand, if we lead a selfish life marked by lack of love and respect for others, we are setting the stage for unfavorable circumstances the next time around. You and I are responsible for the situation in which we find ourselves, and there is no point in blaming our parents or our partner or our children for it. Instead we can take our life in our own hands, practice meditation, learn to reduce our selfishness, and create a better life now as well as for the next time around.

In other words, whatever context we find ourselves in is a suitable one in which to overcome our problems and grow to our full height. We tend to look upon the *other* home as peaceful, the other couple as perfect, the other parent–child relationship as ideal, but this is not very likely. Whenever she heard someone talking like this, my Grandmother used to remark pungently, "The jasmine in your neighbor's garden always smells sweeter." Most of us, if I may say so, have nice parents, and most of us have good friends and children. Naturally they all have certain liabilities as well as assets; this is part of the human condition. If our parents were completely perfect, they would not be here; according to the theory of reincarnation, they would have passed the parent test in the school of life *summa cum laude*. The very fact that we have come into this life shows we have some imperfections to correct. The mystics are loving realists. They don't say, "Let me see your angel's wings"; they remind us that we all make mistakes in life, and that without making a reasonable amount of mistakes, most of us cannot learn to improve. So none of us need be depressed about our past or present; on the path of meditation, even past mistakes can be made into powerful assets if we have learned something by making them.

To put it in simple terms, life is a kind of school where we keep coming back until we realize the unity of life. Only then can we graduate. Suicide, according to this theory, is the worst crime we can commit against ourselves. Both the Hindu and Buddhist scriptures agree that if a person commits suicide when he finds himself in an extremely difficult situation, he will be born again and again into a similar web of circumstances until he tries his best to improve that situation. Even in this life, the purpose of difficult situations is to get us to master something in ourselves, and until we do this by facing such situations squarely, they will come to confront us again and again, more complicated and more distressing each time around. No matter what circumstances we find ourselves in, however distressing they may be, the Lord expects us to try to reduce our selfishness and forget ourselves in contributing to the welfare of those around us. He does not promise any easy way out of our problems, but he does tell us that by eliminating our separateness we can be united with him and see him dwelling in the hearts of everyone, even our enemies. Then we shall have attained the goal of life and need not enter the cycle of birth and death again.

There is a powerful story about Arjuna's oldest brother Yudhishthira, who is a remarkable character in Hindu spiritual lore. One of his many names is Ajātashatru, 'he who has no enemies.' When he is banned from his kingdom with his brothers, Yudhishthira goes to live as an exile in the forest for thirteen years. During this time he is visited by sages who come to cheer him up and bring news of his kingdom and countrymen. One such sage, curious about his epithet, asked him, "Sir, how can you claim to have no enemies when you have been driven from your kingdom and subjected to more difficulties than ten men put together?" Yudhishthira replied, "It's true that I have been exiled for many years from those I love, but I don't think of my usurpers as enemies. I'm still prepared to serve them in any way that contributes to the welfare of all. They may call me their enemy, but as far as I am concerned, they are my friends." He had learned to see the Lord in every living creature, even in those who attacked and cheated him. This is the lesson which we are all born to learn, and the scriptures go on to say that Yudhishthira was not born again, but was reunited at the time of his death with the Divine Ground of all existence.

सहस्रयुगपर्यन्तमहर्यद्ब्रह्मणो विदु: ।
रात्रिं युगसहस्रान्तां तेऽहोरात्रविदो जना: ॥१७॥
अव्यक्ताद्व्यक्तय: सर्वा: प्रभवन्त्यहरागमे ।
रात्र्यागमे प्रलीयन्ते तत्रैवाव्यक्तसंज्ञके ॥१८॥
भूतग्राम: स एवायं भूत्वा भूत्वा प्रलीयते ।
रात्र्यागमेऽवश: पार्थ प्रभवत्यहरागमे ॥१९॥

*17. Those who understand the cosmic laws know
that the day of Brahmā ends after a thousand yugas
and the night of Brahmā ends after a thousand yugas.
18. When the day of Brahmā dawns, forms are
brought forth from the Unmanifest; when the night
of Brahmā comes, these forms merge in the Formless
again.
19. This multitude of beings is created and destroyed
again and again in the succeeding days and nights
of Brahmā.*

Hindu cosmology divides the history of the earth into four periods or ages called *yugas*. In *satya yuga,* the Age of Truth, right after creation, everybody put the welfare of the whole first, and there was a real kingdom of heaven on earth. This period is traditionally represented by a bull standing firmly on all four legs—steady, balanced, and secure. Gradually, however, selfishness crept into our desires. Pleasure and profit became more important, robbing mankind of support. In this period, *tretā yuga,* the bull loses one of its legs and begins to wobble. He is still able to balance, but not quite so steadily. Then, as self-will increases, the poor bull loses another leg, leaving him with one in front and one in back—a very precarious position, as you'll see if you can get a bull to demonstrate it for you. This third age, called *dvāpara yuga,* is characterized by a half-for-me, half-for-others attitude. You never know when someone is going to pursue his personal pleasure and when he is going to contribute to the happiness of the whole. Finally, the bull loses its third leg, which marks the beginning of our age, *kali yuga.* It is a very factual name for our era, because *kali* here means anger and violence, qualities which have come almost to dominate our times.

These four yugas taken together constitute one great yuga, or a yuga of the gods. One thousand such great yugas make up what is called a *kalpa,* which Sri Krishna here tells us is a day of Brahmā, the Creator. It's a very personal conception. The Lord wakes up and the world of name and form comes into play, very much as it does when we wake up out of deep sleep. Creation starts; matter and energy, time and space, all come into existence; the great chain of evolution begins. There are even some calculations made by the sages of ancient India as to how long all this should take; according to them, one day of Brahmā is 4320 million years.

But, the Hindu scriptures tell us, after a while the Lord becomes tired of all this cosmic play and wants to take a nap. When you or I take a nap there is no awareness of the world outside us; it drops out of our consciousness completely. So here the Lord curls up on his endless serpent Ananta, and the whole of creation, which the Sanskrit scriptures tell us is just a thought in the consciousness of the Lord, is withdrawn into a state of latency, with no more reality than the tree which will sprout from a seed. This state of primordial equilibrium is the night of Brahmā, in which everything is dissolved and all creation returns to the Unmanifest.

Recently I have been dipping into a few books on astronomy, because it fascinates me to see how easily the two major theories of cosmology are accommodated in the Gita. One of these is called the evolutionary or "Big Bang" theory; the other is the steady-state theory. Supposedly they represent opposite camps, but in the light of the Gita they become different aspects of one and the same truth. It's like picking up a cosmic kaleidoscope: turn it to the left, look inside, and the universe was created and will someday be dissolved; turn it to the right and look again, and the universe has neither beginning nor end. In meditation we gain a higher mode of knowing which enables us to look behind this kaleidoscope and see the Lord at his divine play, making beautiful patterns with galaxies and quasars, gathering the pieces back into his hands, and then spreading them out again into another magnificent pattern, another universe.

The Big Bang theory is similar in many ways to the insights we find in the Sanskrit scriptures. The first modern statement of this theory came from a Belgian priest, Abbé Georges Henri Lemaître, who conjectured that the universe began at a specific point in time, at least ten billion years ago. At that time it was an incomprehensibly dense mass which was equal to the mass of the universe today. All matter that ever existed was stuffed into what Lemaître called a "primeval atom" or "cosmic egg"—a term, by the way, which closely translates the Sanskrit term *brahmānda*. In one of his most pregnant statements, Lemaître suggests that in this primordial state there was not even time or space. Then the cosmic egg exploded, sending matter and energy outward in every direction. I can imagine the Lord jiggling the kaleidoscope ten or twelve thousand million years ago to make the universe start expanding, as it still is today.

When Lemaître formulated his theory he thought that the universe would come to an end someday, since no new matter was being created. But astronomers after him decided that there were some other alternatives. "After the universe explodes," they asked themselves, "mightn't the gravitational attraction of all this matter gradually slow its expansion to a halt? Eventually all the galaxies would start drifting in towards the center again until finally all matter would rush into a single point, forming a new cosmic atom. Then it would explode again, starting the universe once more." This theory of the oscillating universe, as it is called, is so close to the presentation of the Gita that I can almost see Sri Krishna smiling to himself and saying, "These fellows are beginning to catch on to my game." Just as we have day followed by night, then day again, month after month, year after year, so too the day of Brahmā follows the night of Brahmā over and over again without end. In India you often find the Lord represented as a mischievous little boy, and I can imagine little Krishna here chewing bubble gum, blowing the bubble of the cosmos out of his mouth, and then sucking it back in again, over and over.

The other camp of astronomers, the steady-state adherents, has had a good look through the cosmic kaleidoscope too. According to them, there was no specific beginning to the universe. It did not decide to start itself up at 12:30 on a Friday afternoon billions and billions of years ago; it has always existed and it always will exist, without beginning, without end. Not only that, it is continuously coming into being, because new matter is always being created as the universe expands. It sounds surprising, but as one astronomer points out—from the other camp—whether we talk about Big Bang or steady state, matter has to come into existence somehow, and it is no more unlikely for it to come little by little than in one big explosion.

One gifted proponent of the steady-state theory, Sir Fred Hoyle, is a particular favorite of mine, because he is capable of great insight and yet uses language that any of us can understand. I had an opportunity to attend one of his lectures on the Berkeley campus; before the talk I was sitting right behind him and was delighted to see the friendly way he greeted everyone, from the professor emeritus to the young graduate student. He was completely at home with his subject and made a number of very penetrating remarks, some of which had a creative touch that reminded me of the Gita. Of course Sir Fred was not able to refer to the supreme goal of life, which is usually considered out of bounds for astronomers, so his lecture ended on a note of pessimism. But a few of his more positive remarks can help us understand the cosmology of the Gita.

Hoyle's position is that all matter has a beginning, but the universe itself has neither beginning nor end. It is far greater than all these separate bits of matter of which it is composed. He also pointed out that the universe is everywhere. Substitute the word *Lord* for *universe* and you have the Gita; as Sri Krishna says earlier, the universe exists in him, so he is everywhere. Then, in a flash of insight, Hoyle suggests that there is a creative principle at work throughout the universe. Just as there is a nuclear field binding together atomic nuclei and a gravitational field binding together the stars and galaxies, so we can speak of a field of creation from which all matter comes. This creative source is similar to what the mystics call the Divine Ground underlying all that exists. An imaginative scientist tells us that matter comes forth from and returns to a creative field of forces; the mystic tells us that all creation comes forth from and returns to the Divine Ground of existence. It is a superb instance of how the principles of science converge on spiritual truths.

Recent evidence has led Hoyle to modify his position somewhat in an even more suggestive theory. In this new view, the mass of an object is not something independent of its environment; it is a function of the "mass field" of the universe as a whole. It's not just Hoyle's idea; other great scientists, including Einstein, have believed that the properties of the universe at any place are affected by the rest of the whole. Among other things, this means that mass can vary from place to place and from time to time. With rigorous mathematics, Hoyle points out that instead of talking about squeezing the whole mass of the universe into an infinitesimal point, we can talk just as precisely about a universe that has always been the same size, in which the total mass "cancels out" from time to time. The Big Bang still occurs, but it's not really a creation out of nothing; the universe as a whole was never created and will never be destroyed.

Examples like this are helpful in bridging the chasm of misunderstanding that has developed between science and the spiritual tradition. The reason for this misunderstanding is not in scientific or spiritual principles, but in not knowing how to use the contributions of science to interpret the insights of the mystics. In samādhi we develop the higher mode of knowing called *turīya,* which is a kind of intuitive leap beyond the intellect to a unified state of consciousness in which knower and known become one. In this state there is no Sir Fred Hoyle searching the universe with his powerful instruments; Hoyle and the universe are one. Then we get a glimpse of the Lord of the immense, starry heavens at work, boring black holes, twirling Milky Ways, and setting the universe in motion as effortlessly as a college student sends a Frisbee spinning through the air.

परस्तस्मात्तु भावोऽन्योऽव्यक्तोऽव्यक्तात्सनातनः ।
यः स सर्वेषु भूतेषु नश्यत्सु न विनश्यति ॥२०॥

*20. Beyond this formless state there is another,
unmanifested Reality, which is eternal and is not
dissolved when the cosmos is destroyed.*

When the universe is withdrawn into the Lord at the end of a kalpa, there is no more earth, no more sea, no more galaxies, no more life; everything is dissolved back into the formless state. But Sri Krishna says, "I will still be there, for I am eternal." It is a quiet way of telling us that we are immortal too. When the sun has burnt itself out, when the galaxy has disappeared into a black hole, Sri Krishna says, "I will still be here, and so will you, for I am your deepest Self." In the Katha Upanishad we have the same declaration in beautifully exalted words:

> The supreme Self is beyond name and form,
> Beyond the senses, inexhaustible,
> Without beginning, without end, beyond
> Time, space, and causality, eternal,

Immutable. They who realize the Self
Are forever free from the jaws of death.

Do you see the prize that is being offered us by the Lord? It is inconceivable, beyond the grasp of the most brilliant intellect or the most fertile imagination. It is so great that no price would be too high to pay for it; compared to this supreme goal, any material comforts or honors the world can offer seem utterly insignificant.

In other words, the mystics all say, if you want illumination, do not ask about the price. Do not complain, do not begrudge what the Lord takes from you; when you begin to see this wisdom and love within you, nothing else will seem worthwhile. Illumination is only for those who are prepared to pay the highest price, who will never haggle. When we have difficulties with the palate, when we cannot get up early for meditation, we are haggling. When we act self-willed, we are trying to bargain with the Lord, which means we can only lose.

अव्यक्तोऽक्षर इत्युक्तमाहुः परमां गतिम् ।
यं प्राप्य न निवर्तन्ते तद्धाम परमं मम ॥२१॥

21. Those who have realized the supreme goal of life know that I am unmanifested and unchanging. Having come home to Me, they are never separate again.

Whether we were born and raised in America or Europe, in Africa or Asia, none of these places is our real home. We are all transients on earth, and to most sensitive people there comes now and then a strange feeling of homesickness for our permanent home, which Sri Krishna calls here *mama dhāma,* the land of abiding joy and security within us. The main reason for restlessness, for the recurring impulse to travel, is this desire to find our real home. If we go to Iceland to find peace of mind, or try to escape to the "land of the kangaroo," as the travel advertisements put it, what we are looking for will only slip through our fingers. We will come back tired and frustrated, and those of us who are sensitive will confess that what we really want is something that the world of change and limitation can never give us.

In meditation we travel inwards, beyond the frontiers of time and space, to discover our true home. This is a journey to the land of light. To visit this land we do not have to reserve tickets or get a passport or a visa; all we need to do is throw away our biggest piece of luggage, the ego. If we can extinguish our selfishness, if we can put an end to our self-will and separateness, then wherever we go, whether it is Iceland or Australia, we will find ourselves in the kingdom of heaven.

In describing our true nature, Sri Krishna uses the word *akshara,* 'that which does not age, decay, or die.' Our real Self can never die, but it is the nature of the body to change continuously until it comes to the last great change that is death. My mother, who lives with us as an important member of our spiritual family, has a special way of remembering this fact. When she came to stay with us in this country, she brought with her from India a supply of ashes. The customs official must have been a little puzzled; probably he could not have guessed their grim purpose. Every morning she puts a mark on her forehead with these ashes to remind everyone, including herself, that someday this is what our bodies will become. There is a very practical purpose behind many of these Hindu customs, and often it is to help us remember that the purpose of life is to learn to go beyond death. Every mystic worth his or her mantram will tell us not to waste a single day, not to postpone the practice of meditation even a single morning, but to start living today in such a way that we will be able to transcend the body when death takes place.

I remember once reading a story about a man who kept putting off taking to the spiritual life in order to have just a little more pleasure, or one more windfall of profit. Again and again he vowed that next week, or next month, or next year, he would change his life. Then one night he had a terrible dream: he dreamed he was about to die. There was no chance now to change his direction; time had passed him by, and all the plans he had had for making a new start in life could never be. It was a terrifying experience, and as he struggled to wake up and shake it off he vowed passionately not to put off the practice of meditation a single morning more. But when he tried to sit up, he could not make his body obey him. Then, wide awake at last, he realized that the dream was true.

We cannot afford to put off changing our habits, even for what appear to be very good reasons. If we are not in the best physical condition, meditation will improve our health. If we have emotional problems, either with others or with ourselves, in meditation we will be able to get beneath these problems at their source. Any difficulty, any problem can be an incentive for practicing meditation. No matter how many drawbacks we may have, no matter how many mistakes we may have made, the Lord will accept us joyfully. This is why in Hinduism he is called Mitra, our truest friend.

पुरुषः स परः पार्थ भक्त्या लभ्यस्त्वनन्यया ।
यस्यान्तःस्थानि भूतानि येन सर्वमिदं ततम् ॥२२॥

*22. This supreme Reality which pervades all
existence, the true Self of all creatures, may be
realized through undivided love.*

This one short sentence gives away the secret of the spiritual life. The medieval *Cloud of Unknowing* says in very similar words: "By love may He be gotten and holden, by thought never." The supreme Reality cannot be attained by any amount of reasoning, for He is one and indivisible, beyond all duality. But by loving Him "with all our heart, and all our soul, and all our strength," we can come to live in Him completely and go beyond death here and now. And St. John of the Cross gives us the reason: we do not live in what we think; we live in what we love.

There is nothing abstract about this kind of love, nothing philosophical. Loving the Lord means loving those around us, in each of whom he is present as the innermost Self. The chief thing is somehow to increase our capacity to love. Here, at the beginning, everyone has the same question: how? I imagine people have been asking this question for as long as there have been spiritual teachers on earth. And the answer has been the same all along, in every spiritual tradition. There is a charming story about St. Francis of Sales, a very practical spiritual teacher in sixteenth-century France, that puts it beautifully. One of his disciples, a young bishop of the church, asked Francis how to attain perfection. Francis's answer was straight from his Master: "Love the Lord with all your heart, and your neighbor more than yourself."

These were scarcely new words to the bishop, and he was a little frustrated by them. "I don't want to know what perfection is," he objected; "I want to know how to attain it."

"Oh," said Francis. "Then you must love the Lord with all your heart, and your neighbor as yourself."

And that was all the bishop could get out of his friend, though he kept on asking several times more. Finally, seeing his frustration, Francis explained with words we can all remember: "Many people have asked me for a secret way to perfection, but there is no secret except undivided love of God, and the only way to gain that love is by loving. You learn to speak by speaking, to study by studying, to run by running, to work by working; in just the same way, you learn to love by loving."

Love grows by practice; there is no other way. Whenever you forgo something you want to do in order to give your time and help to those around you, you are increasing your capacity to love. Naturally, at the beginning, there will be reservations in your heart: "All right, we'll go to the opera—but I still want to go to *Gone With the Wind!*" That is the time to ignore your reservations, put on a smile, and repeat the mantram instead. As you begin to forget yourself and see how much your partner is enjoying the opera, or how much your little girl is enjoying her fourth performance of *Alice in Wonderland,* your reservations will fade away. St. Teresa of Ávila says beautifully, *"Amor saca amor"*: love draws out love. By putting the people around you first, you *are* loving more, not only them but the Lord himself, in whom they and you are one.

यत्र काले त्वनावृत्तिमावृत्तिं चैव योगिनः ।
प्रयाता यान्ति तं कालं वक्ष्यामि भरतर्षभ ॥२३॥
अग्निज्योतिरहः शुक्लः षण्मासा उत्तरायणम् ।
तत्र प्रयाता गच्छन्ति ब्रह्म ब्रह्मविदो जनाः ॥२४॥
धूमो रात्रिस्तथा कृष्णः षण्मासा दक्षिणायनम् ।
तत्र चान्द्रमसं ज्योतिर्योगी प्राप्य निवर्तते ॥२५॥

23. *There are two paths, Arjuna, which the soul
may follow at the time of death. One leads to rebirth
and the other to liberation.*
24. *The northern path, the path of light, of fire,
of day, of the bright fortnight, leads selfless souls
to the supreme goal.*
25. *The southern path, the path of smoke, of night,
of the dark fortnight, leads the others to the light of
the moon and to rebirth.*

These three verses borrow symbolic language from the Upanishads
to describe two paths which the soul travels after death. The meaning of these verses is rather obscure, and scholars have had some
difficulty in interpreting these two paths. One is called *uttarāyana,*
'the northern path,' and the other is *dakshināyana,* 'the southern
path.' The usual interpretation is that the northern path is a reference to the six months during which the sun appears to move across
the northern hemisphere of the sky, and the southern path is a reference to the six months of the sun's southern passage. This is the lit-
eral explanation, but for me it is much more practical to interpret
these paths in terms of the destiny we choose for ourselves.

Every one of us—rich or poor, educated or not so well educated—
has to choose continually between what leads to personal, private
satisfaction and what leads to the welfare of the whole. But while
most of us can appreciate the ideal of living for others, we still do
not know how to translate this ideal into our own lives. As long as
we are self-centered, we are not even likely to see what is in another's best interest, and often we make the wrong choices unwit-

tingly. Our problem has a very simple diagnosis: clouded vision. We have cataracts of self-will that keep us from seeing life as it really is. Even with the best of intentions we may do things that disrupt personal relationships, and then we give up and retire into our own seemingly safe pursuits. But clouded vision is not an incurable disease. It is possible for us to clear our eyes, and as we do so, we will be able to distinguish more and more surely these paths of light and darkness.

When I was growing up in my village, I heard from my Grandmother many stories that help to explain difficult verses like these in the Bhagavad Gita. One story, from the *Mahābhārata,* was of a patriarch called Bhīshma. Bhīshma was a splendid spiritual teacher, but unfortunately he was a teacher to the Kauravas, the forces of darkness, and though he tried to win them away from violence, they would not listen to him. Unable to understand his teaching, they ignored his warnings and went to war against Arjuna and his brothers at Kurukshetra, the very battle in which the dialogue of the Gita unfolds. Bhīshma was mortally wounded in this battle. Pierced by many arrows, he lay in agony for fifty-eight days—"on a bed of arrows," as the epic poet says. Despite this terrible suffering, however, he kept his body alive through a great effort of will until the sun had crossed the equinox from the southern hemisphere to the northern, so that he could shed his body during the northern path of the sun, the time considered auspicious for death according to ancient Hindu tradition. He was prepared to suffer any amount of pain in order to attain the path of the sun, the path of light and unity.

My Grandmother never read a book on the Gita, but all these things were a natural part of her daily life. She was a simple Hindu woman with complete, unshakable faith in Sri Krishna's message, and for her, to believe something was to live in accord with it. When she was stricken with a fatal illness at the age of seventy-seven, which is a ripe old age in India, it was the dark period of the sun's path, the six months of dakshināyana. In spite of our doctor's prediction that her death was imminent, my Grandmother, who had utter faith in Sri Krishna, bravely kept her body functioning until the period of uttarāyana came. Her deep faith in the Lord enabled her to wait until the remaining months of the southern path were finished. Then, as soon as uttarāyana began and the sun entered its northern path, she gave up her body. It showed us all that anyone with great love for the Lord, who lives not for herself but for the welfare of those around her, has a deeper will to sustain her and support her.

We, too, should count no cost too high for attaining the realization of God. When we start training our senses, most of us who have not had any experience of this discipline suffer acutely. But we should cheerfully put up with any feelings of deprivation, for the time will come when training the senses is a source not of suffering but of joy.

In this verse, uttarāyana is called the path of light; dakshināyana is the path of darkness. Those who let their senses run amuck, who follow the call of self-will, are traveling on the dark path. Often such people quickly lose their vitality and fall victim to sickness; and in the latter part of life they find themselves left in the worst state any human being can endure—having all the strong desires they had when young but no capacity to indulge them; having fierce self-will and no one left near them on whom it can be imposed. Feeling life to be desolate, they wait for death to come and relieve them of their burden. That is the path of darkness. There are millions of people treading this path because they cannot bear to pay the price of suffering that comes in changing habits; they cannot face the suffering that comes in reducing self-will. This is the price that is asked. If we remember this interpretation of the path of light and the path of darkness, these three verses can provide deep motivation for the practice of meditation.

शुक्लकृष्णे गती ह्येते जगतः शाश्वते मते ।
एकया यात्यनावृत्तिमन्ययावर्तते पुनः ॥२६॥

*26. These two paths, the light and the dark,
are said to be eternal, leading some to liberation
and others to rebirth.*

In the Hindu scriptures, there are said to be seven realms of consciousness, each of which is associated with a particular center along the spinal column. In most human beings, who have not made a disciplined effort to arouse spiritual awareness, the evolutionary energy called *kundalinī* circulates among the three lowest centers. These are the centers of physical consciousness, connected with the functions of the body. It is when kundalinī rises to the higher levels of consciousness, the fourth center and beyond, that you begin to see the light spoken of in this verse.

Along with this vision of light comes a greater capacity to see life clearly, because every experience in the depths of meditation has its effect on daily life. This is the test of any so-called spiritual experience: does it have a beneficial effect on your conduct and character? If at any time, especially during meditation or at night, you experience a vision of light or have some similar experience, the following day there must be an immediate benefit. Old inhibitions will have fallen away; a long-standing conflict in personal relationships may be resolved; you will have a much clearer perception of the unity of life. This is the test. If such changes do not take place, I would say your experience has not been a valid one. But if these changes do occur, then there is no mistaking your progress.

When you have been leading an ordinary life for many years, for a long time you will have no perception of the light within. If you manage to rouse kundalinī to the fourth center, there will seem to be only a few dim rays of light. Actually, the mystics say, the room is full of light; it is only that you haven't yet learned to see inside. As Cardinal Newman puts it, you are still "blinded by the garish day." You cannot yet see clearly, but you are beginning to make out the outline of things. You now have a consuming enthusiasm for meditation, and you are beginning to perceive the unity underlying life. It is not enough now to be concerned for your family's welfare alone; you must expand your love to a much wider circle. You cannot help grieving when a child in Africa is hungry, and you feel a sense of loss even at the death of the smallest creature—not out of sentimental attachment, but out of a deep awareness of unity.

Slowly, as kundalinī begins to travel upwards towards the fifth center, at the level of the throat, you begin to see more and more clearly. At last, after many long years of intense spiritual struggle, kundalinī reaches the center between the eyebrows, the center of Krishna-consciousness or Christ-consciousness. Then you see quite clearly. As St. Paul tells us in those wonderful lines from Corinthians, "Now we see as through a glass darkly; but then we shall see face to face." The Hindu scriptures call this state *savikalpa samādhi,* a state of deep concentration in which we have the vision of our chosen spiritual ideal. After that we will see the Lord present everywhere, which means we can never bring ourselves to harm any living creature.

When, in a few very rare men and women, kundalinī finally rises to the seventh center, there is nothing but light, a light that can never be seen by physical eyes. This is the complete unitive state, called *nirvikalpa samādhi.* The light is so bright it is like the direct light of the sun, which we cannot bear to look at lest our eyes be burned or our vision lost forever. This is why it is so important on the spiritual path for us to strengthen our will, train our senses, and master our passions; otherwise we cannot bear to look at even a small ray of this light, let alone the dazzling radiance of samādhi. Only the rare person who has prepared himself or herself over many decades or many lives can withstand this stupendous experience, which is the goal of spiritual evolution.

This ascent through the seven centers of consciousness is the bright path, the path of the sun, which is also called *devayāna,* 'the path of the gods,' 'the divine path.' It is this path we set out on when we make the choice to practice meditation and turn our backs on petty, personal pursuits. The Mundaka Upanishad describes very precisely those who travel by this path to reach the supreme state:

> But those who are pure in heart, who practice
> Meditation and conquer their senses
> And passions, shall attain the eternal Self,
> The source of all light and source of all life.

On the other side is the dark path, the path of the moon. The moon has no light of its own; it has only borrowed light. When they stood on the moon, our astronauts said, the earth looked beautiful but the moon was cold and bleak, completely devoid of life, altogether unlike the shimmering image we have of it in earthly skies. In the Gita, the path of the moon symbolizes the path of greater and greater darkness. To me this refers not to astrological phenomena but to successive stages in life. When we dwell on ourselves, indulge ourselves more and more—eating what is not nourishing, eating too much, growing addicted to alcohol or to drugs—in the long run, as Jesus says, the whole body becomes filled with darkness. Health goes, and health is the light of the body, the very basis of beauty. Those who do not have the will to control their senses soon lose not only their health but their physical beauty, too.

Look at those who pursue the life of pleasure—people who are often envied for their wealth or youth, as in the song my friend Jeff sings, "If I had his money, I would do things my way." The Gita would say, "If you had his money and did things your way, you would probably just fall sick." In our twenties, we can get away temporarily with quite a lot—if we want evidence of the mercy of the Lord, all we have to do is look at our past and see what we have got away with. But we are not going to be in our twenties for the rest of our lives. Finally, as the Buddhist scriptures are so fond of telling us, we must all grow old. Then, after the ebullience and vitality of youth have passed, we may well be left feeling rootless, without any direction in life at all. We can still be vitally alive even in our last years, but not when we use our body for pleasure or cling to it for security. Then the body will lose its strength far more quickly than is necessary.

The more self-willed we are, the more darkness there will be inside. Always in the dark, we will always be insecure, not knowing how to relate to people or how to be at home with others. Not knowing how to love or how to be loved: that is the path of darkness. Just as in meditation we go from light to more light and finally to light that is infinite, so in living a selfish life we go from darkness to increasing darkness—not only on the physical level, but on the emotional level also.

As self-will increases, rigidity increases too. Rigid people cannot change habits; they have to have their way always. Most tragically, they cannot even understand how other people can have different ways and different conditioning. Without this understanding, how can they be patient? After thirty, it becomes increasingly difficult for the impatient person to learn patience, increasingly difficult for almost all of us to change our ways. There is no statement more poignant to me than an older person saying, "I can't change." I hear this often, and not only from older people, either. I always reply that everybody can change. It is going to be more and more difficult as we grow set in our ways, but no matter how long we may have spent on the path of darkness, we can always cross over to the path of light.

नैते सृती पार्थ जानन्योगी मुह्यति कश्चन ।
तस्मात्सर्वेषु कालेषु योगयुक्तो भवार्जुन ॥२७॥

27. Once you have known these two paths, Arjuna, you can never be deluded again. But to attain this knowledge, your perseverance must be unfailing.

In Sanskrit the delusion of separateness, symbolized by the path of darkness, is called *līlā,* the play of the Lord. It's not a play that takes place somewhere off Broadway; the entire universe is līlā, and it is the Lord, simultaneously wearing countless billions of masks, who plays all the parts.

The tragic part of this play is that all of us have forgotten that we are in costume. We have been playing our little drama for so many billions of years that we have forgotten who we really are. Little by little we have become completely entangled in the part we are playing. This is the delusion of Māyā. It is only when our ego is dissolved and our self-will extinguished that we make the remarkable discovery that we, along with everybody else, have been participating in a cosmic theatrical production, sometimes playing our role well and sometimes botching our lines completely.

Some time ago, for example, we saw Richard Burton and Elizabeth Taylor in a film version of *The Taming of the Shrew*. Both of them played their parts with enthusiasm, and I greatly enjoyed the crucial scene when Petruchio finally bends a bedraggled Kate to his self-will:

> "Kate, I say it is the moon that shines."
> "I *know* it is the moon."
> "Nay, then, you lie; it is the blessed sun."
> "Then, God be blessed, it *is* the blessed sun."

It was all very convincingly done. But I couldn't help wondering what would happen if Richard Burton kept on thinking he was Petruchio after the scene was shot and they both went home; I don't think he would have got so far. Yet that is just what we do in life; we forget all about our costumes and makeup and keep on acting the same old part twenty-four hours a day.

Tragically, the drama we are acting out isn't always a comedy; all too often it's more like *Othello* or *King Lear*. Try watching *Othello* with real detachment; then, when Othello is raving in jealousy, you'll want to climb up on the stage, tap him on the shoulder, and say, "That's just a *handkerchief* you're getting so excited about; you can get four of them for a dollar at Penney's. It's your imagination that is driving you into a frenzy." Even in life, that is all that is behind most of our misunderstandings. At breakfast our husband or wife makes some innocent remark that we don't appreciate and in a few minutes, because of what we imagine he or she was saying, both of us are so agitated that we cannot even finish our toast. Do you see the absurdity of it? We are getting indigestion not over what was said or even what was meant, but over our *idea* of what the other person really meant. That is why the Buddha says so penetratingly, "The problem is not with the other person; the problem is with your mind." When our mind is calm we can see clearly, and we can act all our parts in life with consummate artistry. This is a very refreshing change of perspective. I think it was Noel Coward who was asked for the secret of good acting. He replied, "Speak your lines clearly and don't bump into people." When all is said and done, when you can get through life without bumping into people, you have managed a great deal.

Once I began to see through this game of līlā, I used to go into my classroom very much as if I were going onto the stage. I would put on my professorial robes, put on a suitably intellectual look, and say, "Now you're Eknath Easwaran the professor of English," and I would go into my classes and give them all a really good show. Not only that, I used to do all the paperwork in just the same spirit. But when the last class was over and it was time to go home, I would hang up my professorial role right there with the robes, and step into my next role like one of those quick-change artists you see in the circus. There is a lot of satisfaction in this, and once you master it you have gone a long way towards mastering the art of living.

वेदेषु यज्ञेषु तपःसु चैव
    दानेषु यत् पुण्यफलं प्रदिष्टम् ।
अत्येति तत्सर्वमिदं विदित्वा
    योगी परं स्थानमुपैति चाद्यम् ॥२८॥

28. There is merit in studying the scriptures,
in selfless service, in giving of oneself, and in going
against self-will, but the practice of meditation
carries you beyond all these to the supreme abode
of the Lord of Love.

Meditation is the very basis of the spiritual life. It is meditation that enables us to understand the teachings of the mystics and apply them in our daily life; it is meditation that gives us the immense power to stay patient and forgiving when all our conditioning is crying out for an eye or a tooth. There is nothing exciting about meditation, nothing glamorous, and I have never presented it as anything but a lot of hard, hard work. But when the alarm goes off in the morning, even in the dead of winter when the bed is warm and the blankets don't want to let them go, my friends get up for their meditation with eagerness and enthusiasm every day, rain or shine,

well or not so well, because they know now from their own experience that meditation is the key to the art of living. This is the theme
of the next chapter.

इति अक्षरब्रह्मयोगो नाम अष्टमोऽध्यायः ॥८॥

CHAPTER NINE

The Royal Path

श्री भगवानुवाच
इदं तु ते गुह्यतमं प्रवक्ष्याम्यनसूयवे ।
ज्ञानं विज्ञानसहितं यज्ज्ञात्वा मोक्ष्यसेऽशुभात् ॥१॥

SRI KRISHNA:

1. Because of your faith, I shall tell you the most profound of secrets: obtaining both jnāna and vijnāna, you will be free from all evil.

A few years ago, at a Halloween party we gave for the children at our āshram, my two nieces Meera and Geetha made me up to look like a maharaja. It didn't take much in the way of props; most of the disguise was a silk sari tied into a turban, with a fancy crest which my wife had picked up for ten cents in some bargain basement. When I went to show my mother—who still hasn't figured out what Halloween is all about—I asked her playfully, "Well, do I look like a maharaja?" With great love in her eyes she answered simply, "You *are* a maharaja." It wasn't just figurative language. *Rāja* means king, and rāja yoga is meditation, the 'royal path,' because by mastering meditation we become masters of our lives.

This chapter opens with the same theme with which we opened this volume: jnāna and vijnāna. These are the fruits of meditation. Jnāna is knowledge—not of the natural world, but of the unity of life. Vijnāna is the artful capacity to apply this knowledge to the problems of daily living. Sri Ramakrishna says that intellectual knowledge is like knowing that you can get a fire from two sticks;

jnāna is actually making the fire. But vijnāna is cooking rice on the fire, eating it, and being strengthened by its nourishment.

In other words, jnāna and vijnāna together make up the art of living. This art is not a luxury; it is a dire necessity. Not long before he died, Arnold Toynbee, one of the most perceptive historians of any age, observed with deceptive simplicity that the main reason our civilization has made so much progress in science and technology is that a lot of people have applied themselves to science and technology. That's all; there is no inherent reason. We have applied ourselves to the "arts" of war, so now we can kill everyone on earth several times over. We can manipulate genes; we can transplant vital organs from one body to another; we can send coded messages into outer space so that anyone out there receiving these messages will be intrigued about who we are. We can do all these things because a lot of people have tried to do such things, over a period of time. And Toynbee adds, if we remain ignorant of the meaning of our lives, if we can't even live in peace together as individuals or as nations, it is only because we have been writing all our entries on the other side of the ledger.

There is no need to get despondent over this; it is only a matter of lack of balance. There is nothing wrong with science or technology. The problem is simply that they cannot give themselves a sense of direction. No amount of studying the physical world can ever give us knowledge of spiritual values. It is we human beings who must give direction to what we investigate, what we invent, what we apply; otherwise we are racing along at an impressive rate with no one at the wheel. If we want to change the situation in which we find ourselves today, Toynbee is telling us, we have to get behind the wheel. If we gave even a little of the attention we now give science to what Sri Krishna calls here *brahmavidyā,* the 'supreme science' of Self-knowledge, most of the problems that threaten our world could be banished once and for all.

Here it is interesting to look at a current area of investigation in the neurosciences, the divided brain. The two sides of the brain seem to have very different functions. The left half, which is highly analytical, tends to dominate personality; it specializes in intellectual skills like speaking, writing, reasoning, and mathematics. This is the half with which researchers feel most comfortable: they at least understand what it is good for, even if they don't know how it does what it does or why. But the right half of the brain is much more of a mystery, because its contribution is not to intellectual capacities but to ill-defined realms like creativity, intuition, and the appreciation of beauty. However, though we do not know much about how the brain functions in these areas, or what else the right half of the brain does which we haven't yet discovered, virtually everyone agrees that you can't get along well in life with half a brain. If you have spent all your life putting muscles on the left side of the brain, you may be able to eat and sleep and work crossword puzzles and carry on an intelligent conversation, but to be a whole person you need to develop the right side of the brain as well.

This is what happens in the practice of meditation. Meditation *is* the integration of consciousness, and one of the many physiological developments that take place naturally as our meditation deepens is that all the activities of the brain begin to come into balance. In some of the Sanskrit scriptures these developments are said to take place with the rise of kundalinī, or evolutionary energy, through the spinal column towards the brain. When, after many years of sincere effort in meditation, kundalinī finally reaches the crown of the head, the billions of cells in the brain all burst into integrated activity. This is samādhi, the stupendous climax of meditation, and it brings about a complete transformation of personality. Afterwards there is a never-ending flow of creative power for solving the problems around us, and the immense endurance not to rest until a lasting solution can be found.

To take just one example of this approach, look at the problem of violence. From international organizations down to local communities, everyone is concerned about the spread of violence, but it never seems to occur to anyone that this is a problem that can actually be solved. Everywhere the assumption seems to be, "We just have to learn to live with it." In my language, that means we will only learn to die with it. To prevent robbery and assault, we are told to put more locks on our doors, to train our dogs to bite even worse than they bark, to install burglar alarms that will upset the whole neighborhood, and to carry harmful chemicals in our pockets or purses for spraying would-be attackers. All these are just palliatives; they do not touch the causes of violence at all. I am not denying that there are some first-aid measures, such as gun control legislation, that should be put into effect as soon as possible. But the root cause of violence is separateness, and until we do something about separateness, violence is going to increase unchecked no matter what else we do.

Here the solution of the mystics is daring in its simplicity: we can show, through our own example, how to build rich, steadfast personal relationships everywhere we go. After all, this is what gives life meaning: not money, or prestige, or power, or even pleasure, but plenty of deep relationships that cannot be shaken by any change in fortune. If you think it is farfetched, just try it. Start with your home and begin to rebuild your neighborhood. Get to know your neighbors; make your home the center of your life. Don't go to some other neighborhood every night for entertainment or sit alone with the television; go out for walks with your friends, share your porch with your neighbors on summer evenings, do things with your children and the children of those around you. It is when all the houses on your block are separate Bastilles of loneliness—or worse, just empty shells—that a neighborhood begins to be plagued by violence. When you live in a community of trust, full of friendly relationships and human activity, problems like violence will not arise at all. Not only that, they will be replaced by a way of life that is so much more satisfying that people will look back on these days of separateness and fear as a nightmare from which they have awakened into day.

राजविद्या राजगुह्यं पवित्रमिदमुत्तमम् ।
प्रत्यक्षावगमं धर्म्यं सुसुखं कर्तुमव्ययम् ॥२॥

*2. This royal knowledge, this royal secret, is the
greatest purifier. Supreme and imperishable, it is
a joy to seek and can be directly experienced.*

Many years ago I was taken to the library of someone who had col-
lected almost all the books ever published on meditation in any language. I had never seen so many books on meditation in my life,
and I told my host, "You must meditate regularly."

He coughed apologetically. "Actually," he explained, "what
with all these books to study, I don't have time for meditation."
Then he asked politely, "You must be familiar with most of these
titles?"

I, too, coughed apologetically. "No," I said, "I don't have time
to read many books on meditation. I use the time to meditate."

It is not enough to read about meditation, or talk about meditation, or do research on meditation; if you want Self-realization, you
have to learn to meditate. And there is only one way to learn to
meditate—through trying to meditate. Wasn't there someone who
said he would never get into water unless he had learned to swim?

Meditation is often presented as a pleasant experience in which
you hear birds singing and see flowers blooming while you float
along in a wonderland. Actually, floating in a wonderland is just
the opposite of meditation. In order to learn to meditate, you have
to put in a great deal of work. For a month or two the person who
has just taken to meditation will tell you all about how grand it is.
But it is only fair to point out that, once you really get started, this
initial surge of enthusiasm is going to wane. To guard against such
ups and downs, I would make several suggestions.

First, it is very helpful to meditate with others. A group of friends
meditating along the same lines can meditate together and draw
support from one another. As Jesus says, "Where two or three are
gathered together in my name, I am present in the midst of them."
It is especially helpful if husband and wife can meditate together,

even if it takes some rearranging of schedules. Any family in which
both partners meditate is blessed, and children growing up in such
a household will have a legacy of security on which they can draw
throughout their lives.

Second, be very regular about your meditation. There is a saying
in India that if you miss meditation just one morning, it takes seven
mornings to make it up. You can see that if you miss seven mornings, you have a big job on your hands. So please do not ever skip
your meditation, no matter what the temptation. If you are ill, or if
you are feeling exceptionally well and think you don't need any
meditation that day, that is just the time you should meditate. The
ego is such a clever customer that it waits for the slightest opportunity to regain any territory it may have lost.

You can make time for meditation anywhere. I have sometimes
had to meditate on the train or even in the faculty lounge, and on
board ship on my way to this country I used to have my meditation
on the sports deck, which is a remarkably quiet place early in the
morning when the games enthusiasts are still asleep. If you can always meditate at the same time of day, too, you will find that helps
a great deal. The mind becomes used to behaving itself when the
time for meditation comes around. If you are still asleep, it will start
to nag at you and say, "It's six o'clock; if you don't get up now
you're not going to have time for breakfast," and when you sit
down to meditate, the mind will gradually resign itself to a little discipline for half an hour.

Third, it is very important to practice the disciplines related to
meditation, such as repeating the mantram and putting the welfare
of those around us first. These are elaborated on in the Introduction
in my eightfold program for spiritual living. Meditation taps a
source of tremendous power, and the other seven steps in this program play a vital role in harnessing this power so that it can be
used wisely for the benefit of all.

Fourth, check all your living habits very carefully—your food,
your sleep, your exercise, everything. To make steady progress in
meditation, you need to be as careful as an athlete during training—
eating only good, nourishing food in appropriate quantities, getting

the amount of sleep you need rather than more or less, and getting plenty of physical exercise. Meditation is turning inwards, and it needs to be balanced by plenty of physical activity. This body of ours is meant for motion, and one of the best ways to see that it gets it is by walking whenever you get the chance: to work, to the post office, before breakfast, after dinner. A long, fast walk is not only excellent exercise; it is relaxing and invigorating, especially when it is combined with the mantram. For those who are young, hard physical work is good too, especially when it is at something that benefits those around you.

Finally, I would emphasize the need to be with people and to contribute to life around you. When you are meditating regularly, you need the counterpoise of being with family and friends. As you begin to taste the security and joy within, you may develop the tendency to bask in this inward state. From my own experience, I would say that this is just the time to turn your attention outwards. Unless we maintain close relationships with those around us, there is the danger of getting caught inside, locked within the lonely prison of the ego. To learn to live in harmony with others, to feel at home with everyone, we need the close ties of a wide circle of family and friends. None of us can afford to retire into ourselves and "do our own thing" if we want to become aware of the unity of life.

After singing the praises of meditation, I would like to give a few precautions now concerning its practice. For one, make sure that you are concentrating fully on the words of the inspirational passage and not letting them slip away from your grasp as meditation deepens. Following the passage is rather like flying a kite, carefully letting the string pass through your fingers as you watch the kite become just a speck in the sky. If you do not pay enough attention to the string, which is the passage, it will slip from your grasp and you will lose the kite, which is concentration. So if you find stray words, or odd sounds, or lights and colors trying to coax your attention away, please ignore them and give your attention more and more to the words of the inspirational piece. It is important, right from the first days of meditation, to develop the habit of not letting distractions get the better of you.

Of course, the mind is going to wander somewhat in spite of your best efforts. The one thing necessary is to keep bringing the mind back whenever distractions disturb you. As St. Francis of Sales points out, "And even if you did nothing during the whole of your hour but bring your heart back and place it again in our Lord's presence, though it went away every time you brought it back, your hour would be very well employed." After many years, your concentration is going to take you into the depths of the unconscious mind. What you will be attempting to do then is to enter the unconscious while remaining completely conscious. At that time, even if you can remain awake in this uncharted area, you will not know how to walk. That is where the inspirational passage serves as a lifeline, helping you travel the vast realms of the unconscious in security. There are certain areas in the mind which resemble an Alice's Wonderland of fears and fancies, but as long as you keep the words of the passage as your lifeline, you will be able to discriminate between the facts and fictions of the unconscious.

Another common problem to guard against is sleep in meditation. Sleepiness is bound to come as your meditation progresses, so it is good to prepare for it now. As concentration deepens, the neuromuscular system relaxes. One sign of relaxation is a very happy look on the face; then, the next thing you know, your head may be on your chest. Often people are not aware that they have gone to sleep in meditation, and sometimes they continue in this state for as much as fifteen minutes. To avoid this, draw yourself away from your back support into a firm, erect posture the moment you feel sleepy. If that isn't enough, open your eyes and repeat your mantram—*Jesus, Jesus, Jesus* or *Rāma, Rāma, Rāma*. But when you do this, do not let your eyes wander; your mind will wander as well. Choose some spot in front of you that helps to focus your attention—it might be a picture of Sri Krishna, or Jesus, or the Compassionate Buddha—and let your eyes rest on that while you repeat your mantram. After a while the wave of sleep will pass, and you can close your eyes again and continue with the words of the passage.

It is important to keep on memorizing new passages for use in meditation; then the words will always be fresh with meaning. The Prayer of St. Francis of Assisi is a beautiful one, but if you try using nothing else for several months, it will become so familiar that the mind will not be sufficiently challenged and may move through the words mechanically. There is a wide range of inspirational passages from the world's great spiritual traditions, some of which I have mentioned in the Introduction to this volume.

In India we have a peculiar yellow fruit called the amla which is a great favorite with children. When I first bit into an amla, I thought there must be some mistake; it was so sour that I wanted to spit it out. But my Grandmother told me to keep chewing. I made a wry face but kept on chewing, and slowly it began to get sweeter. Finally it became so sweet that I asked if she had any more. Meditation is like this amla fruit. At first it is not exactly pleasant, but if you stick with it and never let anything come in the way, the time for meditation will become the most precious part of the day.

अश्रद्दधानाः पुरुषा धर्मस्यास्य परंतप ।
अप्राप्य मां निवर्तन्ते मृत्युसंसारवर्त्मनि ॥३॥

3. But those who have no faith in the supreme law of life do not find Me, O scorcher of the foe; they return to the world, passing from death to death.

The word used for faith here is *shraddhā*—literally, 'that which is placed in the heart.' Shraddhā is what we believe will bring us the fulfillment that all of us are seeking—not what we think will bring us fulfillment, but what we really believe in our heart of hearts. In this sense, everyone has faith in something. Just look at people who are devoted to skiing, who love the challenge of hurtling down precipitous slopes at top speed on two little pieces of fiberglass. These are people with a tremendous amount of energy and enthusiasm and nothing to do with it. They need an outlet for all this energy, so they jump at the most difficult challenge they can find. But no less tremendous than their energy is their faith—that skiing has the power to make them happy. All of us have our own equivalent of skiing, whatever we think will bring us lasting joy. The tragedy is that wherever this faith is in something outside us—money, or drugs, or personal pleasure, or the thrill of the dangerous and the unknown— it is inescapable that someday we are going to be let down. So the Buddha warns pointedly, "Don't ever put your faith in what is changing; it *has* to fail you in time."

One of the most tragic examples of misplaced shraddhā is substance abuse. A CBS documentary in 1986 reported that 60 percent of the world's illegal drugs are used in the United States, reflecting the frightening rise in cocaine addiction. But alcoholism may still be the country's biggest drug problem. Over twelve million Americans have symptoms of alcoholism, and more than 57 percent of adult Americans report that they are "current users." The human being has to put faith in something, and these are cases where shraddhā has got locked in a bottle or a packet of powder. It is especially tragic with young people, most of whom, I feel, turn to drugs when they look around them and find no channels where the natural idealism of youth can flow. We should never look down on such people. All of us are searching restlessly for fulfillment, usually in the wrong places, and the thirst for spirits, as William James said, is really a spiritual thirst for the living waters of life.

The Gita takes an extremely positive approach towards this problem. It says that even though our faith may not be in something that is particularly relevant to living, the very fact that we are capable of such faith means that there is hope. Once our faith is changed, we can become as enthusiastic a spiritual aspirant as we were a skier or world traveler. For the skiers, all I have to tell them is, "Your kind of skiing isn't worthy of such faith. How would you like the challenge of skiing *up* the slope?" This is meditation: no chair lift, no towline, no source of momentum at all. You must ski uphill, against all that is easy, against every impulse that says, "Go your own way; do your own thing." Anyone who can respond to a challenge like this has the capacity to transform shraddhā, and when shraddhā is transformed, the alcoholic may emerge a stronger person than the teetotaler, because he or she has access to tremendous drives which now can be brought under control.

मया ततमिदं सर्वं जगदव्यक्तमूर्तिना ।
मत्स्थानि सर्वभूतानि न चाहं तेष्ववस्थितः ॥४॥
न च मत्स्थानि भूतानि पश्य मे योगमैश्वरम् ।
भूतभृन्न च भूतस्थो ममात्मा भूतभावनः ॥५॥
यथाकाशस्थितो नित्यं वायुः सर्वत्रगो महान् ।
तथा सर्वाणि भूतानि मत्स्थानीत्युपधारय ॥६॥

*4. I pervade the entire universe in my unmanifested
form. All creatures find their existence in Me, but I
am not limited by them.
5–6. Behold my divine mystery! These creatures
do not really dwell in Me, and though I bring them
forth and support them, I am not confined within
them; they move in Me as the winds move in every
direction in space.*

This is a paradox which lies at the very heart of the mystical experience. The Lord is present in every living creature, in every atom,
yet he is in no way limited by any of these forms. In the climax of
meditation, when we have the tremendous experience of union with
the Lord, we too will be lost in wonder that he whom the galaxies
cannot contain, whom the entire cosmos cannot contain, is contained in your heart and mine.

This is the mystery of Māyā. How is it that this hand of mine appears solid and brown? Physicists would tell me it is not solid and
brown at all, but a pattern of countless tiny nodes of energy, like the
swirl of winds in the air. If I see it as having a fixed shape and color
and call it my hand, that is just because of the inherent limitations
in my perception. In other words, its shape and other characteristics
are not in the world outside me; they are in the very fabric of thinking and perceiving. In the great leap of insight that comes in samādhi, the mystics tell us that all this world of names and forms is
nothing but the Lord. As Shankara says so beautifully, "Names and
forms are like gold bangles and bracelets; the Lord is like the gold."

Towards the end of *The Tempest,* Shakespeare uses the language of great poetry to convey a similar idea:

> Our revels now are ended. These our actors,
> As I foretold you, were but spirits, and
> Are melted into air, into thin air.
> And, like the baseless fabric of this vision,
> The cloud-capped towers, the gorgeous palaces,
> The solemn temples, the great globe itself—
> Yea, all which it inherit—shall dissolve
> And, like this insubstantial pageant faded,
> Leave not a rack behind. We are such stuff
> As dreams are made on, and our little life
> Is rounded with a sleep.

Aldous Huxley, who was associated for many years with Swami Prabhavananda in this country, commented: "Prospero is here enunciating the doctrine of Māyā. The world is an illusion, but it is an illusion which we must take seriously, because it is real as far as it goes, and in those aspects of the reality which we are capable of apprehending. Our business is to wake up, , , , We must continually be on our watch for ways in which to enlarge our consciousness. We must not attempt to live outside the world, which is given us, but we must somehow learn how to transform it and transfigure it. . . . One must find a way of being in this world while not being of it. One must find a way of living in time without being completely swallowed up in time."

Sometimes, to remind him that he is not the body, I tease my friend Jim by telling him there is no Jim there at all; it is only an energy process walking down the road. The truth is that until I have the direct experience that he is really the Ātman and the body I see is just Māyā, there is a Jim there. As long as we live in Māyā, we have to treat these names and forms as real. But we should never forget, even for an instant, that under all these disguises there is no one but the Lord.

सर्वभूतानि कौन्तेय प्रकृतिं यान्ति मामिकाम् ।
कल्पक्षये पुनस्तानि कल्पादौ विसृजाम्यहम् ॥ ७ ॥
प्रकृतिं स्वामवष्टभ्य विसृजामि पुनः पुनः ।
भूतग्राममिमं कृत्स्नमवशं प्रकृतेर्वशात् ॥ ८ ॥
न च मां तानि कर्माणि निबध्नन्ति धनंजय ।
उदासीनवदासीनमसक्तं तेषु कर्मसु ॥ ९ ॥

*7. At the end of the age these creatures return to
unmanifested matter; at the beginning of the next
cycle I send them forth again.
8. Again and again I bring forth these myriad forms
and subject them to the laws of prakriti.
9. None of these actions bind me, Arjuna; I am
unattached to them, so they do not disturb my nature.*

According to the Hindu scriptures, the universe is created and
dissolved over and over again. In the interregnum, everything in
the universe rests in a primordial state without any differentiation,
without time or space. But in the instant of creation this equilibrium
is disturbed, setting loose the long chain of action and reaction in
which all the elements and forces of the universe become manifested.

The personal aspect of this is that in each of these cycles, the
whole of creation is said to be evolving towards the unity of life.
When, after billions of years, we come into the human context, the
Hindu scriptures say we must come back over and over again until
we learn to go beyond the biological conditioning of animal life and
realize that beneath all these forms of creation, we are all one in the
Lord.

In other words, according to this view, all of us are going to be
saved. Sooner or later, even if we do everything possible to put it off
for billions of years, every one of us must reach the highest state of
consciousness. If we drag our heels, the very painfulness of our mistakes and our separateness will slowly force us to change our ways.
That is what evolution means on the human level. Just as a species

blindly evolves certain characteristics by exposure to the world around it, we are constantly shaping ourselves by the consequences of everything we do. This is the law of karma, which states unequivocally that any suffering we cause to other people *must* come back to us. It is an inescapable consequence of the fact that all of us are one. That is why it grieves me so deeply to see anybody treating another person harshly; it's like hitting yourself with your own hand.

In the traditional classification, there are three types of karma. The first may be called "cash" karma, because it is all over with immediately. John hits Joe, and Jim hits John; there is no suspense, and John's karma comes to a fast end. The second kind is more painful; it is the consequences we reap from past actions. "Others fear what will happen tomorrow," says the Sufi mystic Ansari of Herat; "I fear what happened yesterday." The Compassionate Buddha describes this kind of karma as an arrow we have already shot: it is on its way, and the best we can do is accept the suffering that comes from it and learn from that suffering not to shoot that arrow again.

The third type of karma is that which we are about to create right now, in the immediate present. This is karma over which we have some control. If we can't do anything about the arrows we have shot in the past, we can at least refrain from shooting more arrows in the future. Often we find ourselves in a situation where our passions have been roused, our anger is ready to burst, and all we can think of is retaliation. The arrow rests on the bowstring and the bow is drawn, ready to shoot. But, says the Buddha, we do not need to let the arrow go; the choice is up to us. That is the time to repeat the mantram, relax our hold, and put the arrow safely away.

Here it is that the Hindu mystics make a really daring proposal. We do not need to let ourselves be buffeted towards the Lord by our own karma over millions and millions of years; we can take our evolution into our own hands. That is precisely what meditation is for, and great mystics like Sri Ramakrishna or St. Catherine of Siena are really pioneers in consciousness who have gone millions of years beyond us in human evolution. Patanjali, the great teacher of rāja yoga in ancient India, tells us that any of us can make this great leap; the capacity is within us all. We are all born with enough vital energy for the journey, and a little extra to play around with while we get used to the car. The choice is ours what we do with this energy. Some of my friends tell me that in their earlier days, they used to leave their house in Berkeley early Monday morning fully intending to drive straight to New York City. They would stop at the grocery store for some orange juice, then go to a friend's house and listen to a record or two, then remember to get some incense on Telegraph Avenue, and by the time it was nightfall they would still not have got out of town. But there are some people—St. Francis of Assisi, Mahatma Gandhi—who want so badly to get where they are going that they don't spend any time on side trips. They put all their energy into the practice of the spiritual life and do everything they can to learn not to repeat the mistakes that all of us make. Every one of us can choose to do this, and the harder we try, the farther we will go.

In the Sanskrit scriptures there is a vivid dramatization of this immense leap across evolution into the unitive state. The story is about Mārkandeya, the boy whose devotion to Lord Shiva rescued him from death in his sixteenth year. In this story, with all the daring of a teenager, he asks Sri Krishna to explain to him the secret of Māyā. It's a question which allows for some rather imaginative answers. As soon as the words are out of the boy's mouth the Lord disappears, and in one great roar all the seven seas rush in around Mārkandeya and rise up to the clouds in flood, the way they did in Genesis before the world was made. Everything is engulfed in the waters, not only the earth but the sun and all the starry firmament. And Mārkandeya, the boy who had gone beyond death, floats on these cosmic waters for billions of years, evolving from lifeless matter up the long ladder of animate existence.

Suddenly he bursts into the human context. Life after life of selfish existence passes; he begins to shed all his selfishness and develops great devotion to the Lord. Then he sees in the distance a wonderful little baby, dark like the monsoon cloud, lying on a banyan leaf on that endless expanse of water. In a flash of recognition, Mārkandeya recognizes the baby Krishna, playing on the waters just as any other baby does, with one of his toes tucked into his little rose-bud of a mouth.

A thrill of unutterable joy runs through Mārkandeya at the thought of lifting and cradling in his arms this divine infant, whose playfield is the universe. But all these eons have been just one gentle breathing out of the baby Krishna, one day of Brahmā; now he begins to breathe in again, and Mārkandeya is sucked inside through that tiny mouth into the body of the Lord, where he sees in wonderment all the galaxies of the universe suspended in the cosmic night. Outside there is again nothing but the primeval waters; matter and energy, time and space, everything is inside while creation rests.

The experience must have lasted for billions of years. Then baby Krishna breathes out again. Mārkandeya is thrown out, and he is so overcome that he embraces little baby Krishna in adoration and tries to find words to express his gratitude for this vision of the Lord's Māyā. But the baby disappears in his arms, and Mārkandeya finds himself back in his own āshram seated in meditation. It's a magnificent rendering of what can happen in samādhi, when we see that all the vast sweep of evolution is only the play of the Lord.

मयाध्यक्षेण प्रकृतिः सूयते सचराचरम् ।
हेतुनानेन कौन्तेय जगद्विपरिवर्तते ॥१०॥

10. Under my watchful eye the laws of nature take their course. Thus is the world set in motion; thus the animate and the inanimate are created.

I remember an article in *Scientific American* entitled "Why Doesn't the Stomach Digest Itself?" It is a rather practical question. How is it that the stomach, which secretes hydrochloric acid able to dissolve metal, does not harm itself? What protects it from the corrosiveness of its own chemistry?

Scientific research gives us extensive information on the physiology of the body, but it cannot help us know who is closer to us than this body of ours. Although we spend millions of dollars on coronary care units, we do not know who is in our heart of hearts.

Textbooks now have precise illustrations of the lens of the eye and the cochlea buried in the inner ear, but no book can show us who it is that sees, who it is that hears.

Everywhere we look we see evidence of the miracle of life. On the beach where we took our walk this morning, I was watching a little creature of which I'm very fond, the sandpiper. It waited for a wave to break, and when the water was about to reach its toes it ran off so fast that I could hardly see its legs. Where does it get the power to run? Science can describe its legs—the angle at which they move, their velocity, the condition of the sand, the wind's resistance—but the power that enables the tiny sandpiper to outrun the tide is the power of God.

In the operations of the body, in the movements of the stars, every expression of energy in the universe is the power of the Lord. When the sun converts hydrogen into helium, the energy released is the power of the Lord, just as is the energy released in your body in the process of digestion. It is all the same energy; that is what the unity of life means. The Lord *is* the power of the universe, and the Law governing all laws. This doesn't mean that the laws of motion or thermodynamics are incorrect; these laws are only aspects of the law of unity which supports all existence.

One of the key phrases in this verse is *jagad viparivartate,* 'the universe turning around.' When the universe began to evolve, the Sanskrit scriptures say, the power behind that evolution was the creative aspect of the Lord. From that dynamic imbalance, the interplay of all the forces of nature began, never to cease until they are withdrawn again into the Lord at the end of the age. It's as if the cosmos is an immense globe like those globes of the world that children are so fond of spinning. The Lord gives this globe one big slap from inside and it goes on spinning for billions on billions of years.

In the Hindu tradition, this idea that the Lord is the source of all law is conveyed in all sorts of stories, many of which I heard often from my Grandmother. One of these stories is from the *Mahābhārata,* in which this dialogue of the Bhagavad Gita takes place. Arjuna's enemy, Karna, had taken a vow to kill him in battle. Karna was an exceedingly skillful warrior and was armed with supernatu-

ral weapons, but as the battle raged, even though Arjuna was losing
ground, his charioteer, Sri Krishna, seemed in no hurry to come to
his aid. Then, just as Karna aimed the fatal arrow at Arjuna's head,
Sri Krishna caused the earth to sink beneath their chariot. The arrow passed overhead, leaving Arjuna unharmed. My Granny told
me stories like this in a very matter-of-fact manner, because to her
it seemed obvious that he who made the whole cosmos could tell the
earth to sink for his devotee's protection. To her there was no conflict here with the laws of nature; the lower laws of physical phenomena had simply been superseded by a higher law for the time
being.

There is another story about the great mystic Shankara, whose
mother was an ardent devotee of the Lord. Every morning she used
to walk several miles to the river for her bath and then to the temple
for her daily worship. One day she fell during this journey, and her
friends had to carry her home. Shankara, who was a teenager at the
time, was grief-stricken. He took the Lord severely to task for not
taking better care of his mother. After all, his mother was going to
the temple to worship the Lord; shouldn't He protect her? It is said
that the Lord murmured something about being distracted by the
problems of the world and promised to make amends for this lapse.
Then he told the river to flow closer to Shankara's home. To this
day geologists speculate about the peculiar changes in the course of
this river. There may be numerous other explanations, which I do
not deny in the least, but they do not conflict with the capacity of
the Lord to effect any number of wonders from within the forces of
his creation.

Nothing can take place without the power of the Lord. Sri Ramakrishna used to say that the Divine Mother even hears the footfall of
the ant. Ever since I read this I cannot look at an ant without imagining the Lord listening to the *thud, thud, thud* of its tiny feet. Jesus
gives us the same truth when he says, "Not a sparrow falls without
the will of the Father." Just imagine the supreme master of the cosmos keeping track of all the sparrows in his huge map room. His
eyes are everywhere; he sees everything and hears everything because he is everything. If his secretary reports a comet is creating a

bit of trouble, he says, "Straighten it out." Astronomers on earth, watching this comet, may gather from all over the world for a conference on its idiosyncrasies, but no conference can ever reveal who set the comet in motion. We can study the physics, the chemistry, the biology of our small corner of the universe, but only through the practice of meditation will we be able to meet the Supervisor.

अवजानन्ति मां मूढा मानुषीं तनुमाश्रितम् ।
परं भावमजानन्तो मम भूतमहेश्वरम् ॥११॥
मोघाशा मोघकर्माणो मोघज्ञाना विचेतसः ।
राक्षसीमासुरीं चैव प्रकृतिं मोहिनीं श्रिताः ॥१२॥

11. The immature do not look beyond physical appearances to see my true nature as the Lord of all creation.
12. The knowledge of such deluded people is fraught with disaster, and their work and hopes are all in vain.

To help us change our direction in life, Sri Krishna occasionally uses some rather strong language. The word he uses in these two verses is *mūdha*, 'slow-witted.' Anyone who cannot see below the surface of life, who believes only in what can be touched and measured, Sri Krishna says, simply is not thinking intelligently. When we think there is no more to life than physical objects and sensations, when we identify ourselves completely with the body and deny that there is any unifying principle in life, everything we do will be futile; there will be no fulfillment in life at all. That is the nature of the physical world: everything in it is limited; everything is fleeting. Not only that, Sri Krishna warns us, this is not something that affects us alone. There can be great danger in living on the surface of life, because there will always be this blindness about the welfare of the whole. Even with the best of intentions, people with this kind of shallow vision can be led into activities that really endanger life around them.

To take just one example, look at the people who think that by producing more and more and consuming more and more, we will eventually reach the land where all troubles end. The phrase Sri Krishna uses for this self-centered way of life is quite contemporary: *moghāshā moghakarmāno,* 'with vain hopes, and with work in vain.' Those who go on producing for the sake of profit, who continue to consume for the sake of pleasure, will end in futility and frustration. Many of our business empires and technological exploits, built on the idea of unlimited material progress, are now facing the fact that the earth's resources are very limited indeed. To the mystic, the real problem is not with our resources; it is what we are trying to do with those resources that is futile.

As we are forced to give up some of these activities, we make a marvelous discovery that the mystics have been trying to tell us about all along: a simple life can be a joyful life. By "simple life" I do not mean a romantic return to a rustic state. Nor is simplicity something we must just put up with because we are running out of energy. The simple life is much more creative and practical than most of us imagine. It is a life that values human qualities, one that is rich in lasting relationships with family and friends and community.

Most people do not have time to get to know their neighbors, or listen to what their children have to say, or be sensitive to the needs of their friends. They are too busy traveling between their city condominium and their country cabin. They have to work additional hours to buy two cars; then they need separate kitchens, separate bank accounts, separate televisions, separate sets of silverware, separate everything, all because they cannot live in harmony. Finally, they lose the capacity to exercise choice over their lives; the living room must be redecorated again and last year's car has to be traded in for a new model. Before they know it, life has become incredibly complicated—and far from satisfying.

Simple living can be beautiful, right down to the smallest details. Some of the Japanese homes I have been in are remarkably beautiful with just a few well thought-out touches. On the other hand, I have also been in elaborate homes where I had to watch every move for fear of knocking an antique off its pedestal. Unfortunately, the more possessions we accumulate, the more we are possessed by them. It is only after we begin to taste the joy of simple living that we realize that these accessories can actually stand between us and our fulfillment.

Our modern way of life seems to be making us busier and busier about less and less. This is the vain superficiality Sri Krishna is warning us against. The more we divide our interests, our allegiances, our activities, the less time we have for living. The simple life doesn't mean a drab routine; it means giving our time and attention to what is most important. For parents, it means having time and energy to devote to their children—and no matter what the latest psychological theory may tell us, our children can never grow to their fullest without continual support from the parents, particularly the mother. For friends, simplicity means taking the time to deepen a relationship, and remaining loyal in times of trouble. To remain loyal even when someone is causing us a great deal of trouble, we must know that person very well, well enough to warn him when he is about to make a mistake. Such relationships take time. We cannot get to know someone intimately in a day or establish a lasting relationship during a weekend conference. If we spend eight hours a day at our job, an hour or so at a bar after work, and the evening watching television, where is the time for cultivating close friendships? But if we simplify our lives, we shall find plenty of time and energy to be together with our circle of family and friends. These are discoveries all of us can make.

महात्मानस्तु मां पार्थं दैवीं प्रकृतिमाश्रिताः ।
भजन्त्यनन्यमनसो ज्ञात्वा भूतादिमव्ययम् ॥१३॥

13. But truly great souls seek my divine nature.
They worship Me with a one-pointed mind, having
realized that I am the eternal source of all.

The vast majority of people have many-pointed minds. Just go to a large department store on the day after Christmas; everyone's attention is divided between the sale tables, an old acquaintance, a crying child, and the exchange of unwanted gifts. When a person's eyes are darting in every direction like this, it's not only a sign of restless eyes; it's a sign of a restless mind as well. Once this kind of distraction becomes a habit, nothing in life can hold our interest. We take up bowling, but after a week or two we become bored; we decide to master classical guitar, or pick up a little French, or learn to skin dive, but very soon we will want to do something new. But as Ecclesiastes says, "There is nothing new under the sun." There is a limit to the new things we can do in this world, and the more restlessly we search for novelty, the less likely we are to be successful at anything we take up.

The key to this problem is not more new things but better concentration. Boredom and fulfillment have nothing to do with the world outside us. When we can give our attention to it, the classical guitar seems fascinating; when we cannot give our attention to it, it seems dull. The guitar itself is neither fascinating nor dull; all the interest is in the attention we can bring to bear on it. If we can learn to make the mind one-pointed, we will be interested and effective in everything we do.

When I was a little boy, I saw an experiment by one of our science teachers which illustrates the power of concentration. Without giving us a clue as to what he was going to do, he picked up a lens, put a lot of paper underneath, and let the rays of the tropical sun pour through the lens. We watched quizzically for a minute, totally unprepared for the climax. For a while nothing happened at all. Then there was a thin little curl of smoke, and all of a sudden the paper burst into flames. We thought it was some kind of magic. But our teacher explained that there was no magic at all; the heat that had been diffused had been brought together to bear on one point through the lens.

This is more or less what we do in the practice of meditation. Most of the time, the capacities of our mind are wasted in innumerable little cravings for things which do our bodies no good, our minds no good, and no one else any good either. Ordinarily we have no way of harnessing these little cravings; that is why most of us are not as effective as we could be, do not have particularly secure relationships, and are not able to make the contribution to life that we would like. So the question is, how do we make the mind converge? And the answer is, through the practice of meditation.

In meditation, when you go as slowly as you can through a passage like the Prayer of St. Francis without letting distractions creep in between the words, you are learning to focus your attention completely on one train of thought. Gradually your whole thinking process will become slowed down, which releases a great deal of tension and removes a great deal of conflict. It takes many years to achieve this kind of mastery of the mind, but finally, when your consciousness is unified completely, you will be able to keep your mind calm, clear, and concentrated even in the most agitating circumstances.

Slowing down thoughts is one of the most effective methods for changing negative habits of thinking. As long as the mind is working furiously, it's not possible to stop it; it's not even possible to make a turn. But when you are able to see thoughts going by in single file, you can recognize them and say, "Hey, you're no friend!" You can choose not even to say hello to a negative thought, and its power to agitate you will be completely lost. This is how we learn not to identify ourselves with our thoughts, which means we have the power to pick and choose which thoughts to think.

To do this requires more than just the practice of meditation; we also need to cultivate a one-pointed mind throughout the day. There is a great deal of energy dissipated when we do or think several things at once. To be insecure, for example, consumes a lot of energy. You can't simply sit back and say, "Now I'll be insecure"; you have to put in a lot of time comparing people, thinking about what others did to you to foil your plans, and dwelling on how much you are to be pitied. All this requires a lot of energy. Last evening we had a fire in our fireplace, and to keep the fire going for about one hour we had to pile on a big stack of firewood and keep on piling on more. If it had been really cold and we had had to keep that fire for many more hours, we wouldn't have had any firewood left at all. That is how insecurity works; you have to go on feeding it constantly, and there is no energy left for anything else.

Later, my friend Rick—who probably learned about fires when

he was living in the jungles of Paraguay—explained to me that we had built the fire wrong and used the wrong kind of wood. So to-night he got us a good, heavy log, one that burns slowly and puts out a lot of heat, and if we hadn't finally put it out it would still be burning now. Instead of piles and piles of wood, all we needed was that one log. There is a good deal of potential energy in a log like that, but it's all very carefully conserved. Only a little of the wood needs to be consumed to give light and heat to all. It is the same with vital energy. When you scatter your attention everywhere, you really get drained—if you want proof of it, just spend a day window-shopping and see how you feel when you get home. But when you can work slowly, with complete concentration, at one thing at a time, very little energy is consumed. At the end of the day there will still be a lot of firewood left, which is what unshakable security means.

सततं कीर्तयन्तो मां यतन्तश्च दृढव्रताः ।
नमस्यन्तश्च मां भक्त्या नित्ययुक्ता उपासते ॥१४॥

*14. Constantly striving, they make firm their
resolve. They worship Me without wavering and, full
of devotion, sing of my divine glory.*

Pelagius has a strong but very practical aphorism on the spiritual life: "If you don't want to fall back, you have to keep running forward." If that is what is required just to keep standing still, you can imagine what is called for to make real progress. To go as far as you can in meditation, you need to be striving every minute. Every morning you renew your commitment to the spiritual life.

From my own experience, I would say that the problems get tougher the farther one proceeds along this path. Palate problems—which seem to be omnipresent in the beginning—are, after all, not so serious, because you can always refrain from eating. If you don't pick up your fork and put food in your mouth, no one is likely to do it for you. If you are tempted to overeat, you can always run out of the house and go for a fast walk. Similarly, if you feel yourself drawn to a rock concert, you can give your money away instead; if you don't have money with you, there's not much danger of getting past the box office. In other words, these are not serious temptations because they are external. That is the positive, practical side of Jesus' words when he prays, "Lead us not into temptation": do not put yourself in situations where your will may break down; do not go in and ask for trouble.

So physical indulgence is not a very grave problem. The real problems come in the deeper stages of meditation. Then you are no longer on the surface level of consciousness, and you begin to see the roots of your problems, which go deep. On the surface you see only innumerable little weeds, which you think can simply be pulled up and thrown out. But as your meditation deepens you will see that what you thought were twenty weeds have actually only ten roots. Then, deeper still, you see that these seemingly ten roots are actually ten shoots off five stout stems, each of which is so strong that you scarcely know how to get at it. At last you get to the taproot, which is self-will. Then the going really gets rough. After this long journey you realize that you have only been trekking across the prison of the ego. There are no doors, no windows, no exits of any kind. Imagine finding yourself in a room where there is no door, where you cannot even move or turn around. What effort do you make against a blank, seamless wall? That is the problem.

These problems in the deeper stages of meditation are gigantic simply because they are not outside you any more; they are inside. When they come, you cannot help fighting; there is nowhere to go. You cannot say, "Don't look at me; I'm a lover, not a fighter. Let me know when it's all over." When you come face to face with the ego in the basement of consciousness, you have to do something about it. Every morning in your meditation for a long, long time you will have to fight this battle with the ego, which will call for every ounce of endurance you can muster and a little more. But every defeat only strengthens your resolve.

I saw this kind of fierce resolution the other day in a film of two fellows climbing a sheer rock wall in Yosemite. They had all sorts of climbing gear, but what is more important, they had commitment. As the commentator said, what is essential is to decide to leave the ground; after that, it is just a matter of going on. The beginner may look at the steep face of Washington's Column and say, "I'd better think twice about this; a fall from there is going to be *bad*." But these young men were dedicated climbers; they made the initial decision and then never even once thought of turning back.

These climbers were following a system of cracks up the cliff, pounding pitons into the cracks and then hanging their ropes from these pitons and slowly pulling themselves up a little higher. Everything went well until they got halfway up the face of the peak. Then the crack system stopped, and above them stretched a sheer, unclimbable rock wall with not even the tiniest crack into which to pound a piton to go higher. At that point most people would shrug, give up, and go back down to Glacier Restaurant to console themselves with a big dinner. But these two fellows had set their hearts on the top, and nothing could make them quit. The sheer impossibility of their situation only deepened their resourcefulness. One of them started swinging like a pendulum from one ledge to another, looking for a new crack system. Finally he found one, and while I watched amazed they picked up their climb from this new point and made it to the top of the peak.

In meditation too we need this kind of tenacity, the capacity to keep on climbing when the going gets rough. More than once, as we continue to climb, we will reach a point when the crack system ends. This is an inescapable part of the spiritual ascent, and it will test our dedication to the fullest. Then it is that instead of getting anxious or depressed, we renew our resolve and give everything we can to find some way to go farther. Our responsibility is only to give our very best; the outcome we leave to the Lord. When he sees that our sense of dedication is strong enough to withstand the rigors of the climb ahead, a little door will open in our consciousness and give us access to the deeper resources we need to continue climbing.

There is a beautiful story in this connection about St. Teresa of Ávila, the great Christian mystic of sixteenth-century Spain. Teresa spent decades founding convents throughout Spain, traveling long distances over terrible roads in every kind of weather. In most places she had to work with people who were adamantly opposed to her order. Often she was ill and physically exhausted, but her determination and enthusiasm never wavered. Then, towards the end of her life, she was struck in an epidemic of influenza. After that she never recovered her physical strength. But in the dead of winter the call came from her superior to inaugurate a new convent at Burgos. Teresa hesitated; after all, she was very ill. But the Lord, she said, reproved her: "I am the true warmth. What is there to be afraid of?"

As Teresa and her companions set out in their mule-drawn carts, sky and earth seemed fused in one torrential stream of water. The carts became so mired that the nuns had to wade much of the distance in their sandals. Teresa was shaking from head to foot from the exposure and her illness, but she was determined to obey the Lord and him alone.

Next day, the river Arlanzón had to be crossed. When they reached what had been the bank, all they saw was an enormous sheet of water. All the bridges had been carried away by the flood and there was only a makeshift footbridge, which was so narrow that at the slightest movement of the current, carts, mules, and nuns would roll right into the raging flood. Teresa's carriage moved forward first. Those who were still on the bank saw it swerve and stop, then begin to tip as if to fall into the torrent below. Teresa jumped out and hurt herself. While the river raged just below her feet, she stood clinging to the cart. "Lord," she exclaimed, "amid so many ills why do you add this to all the rest?"

In the depths of her consciousness she heard a voice reply: "Don't be upset, Teresita; that is how I treat my friends."

"O my Lord!" Teresa replied, as only his beloved handmaiden could. "No wonder you have so few of them!"

The Lord must not have been displeased with this answer, for the whole caravan reached the far bank unharmed.

Of course, Teresa was a great saint, so the Lord made great demands on her. But he tempers the wind to the shorn lamb, and all he asks of little people like you and me is that we remember him constantly in all the small daily encounters in our family and our community. For most of us, that is quite challenge enough.

ज्ञानयज्ञेन चाप्यन्ये यजन्तो मामुपासते ।
एकत्वेन पृथक्त्वेन बहुधा विश्वतोमुखम् ॥१५॥

15. Others follow the path of jnāna, spiritual wisdom: they see that where there is One, that One is Me; where there are two, they both are Me; they see my face everywhere.

This verse has puzzled those who look for a hidden meaning. Actually it is a simple account of what happens in the climax of meditation, when we realize that all creation is one in the Lord. Then, though we still see beauty in all the abounding variety of life, we will always be aware that underlying this variety there is only the Lord, who the Sufis say beautifully is the "face behind all faces." This is the hallmark of the mystical experience everywhere. In Jewish mysticism there is a charming anecdote about a Hasidic master who had to put on his glasses in order to remember that people around him saw things as separate, for otherwise he saw everyone and everything as One. And the Shvetāshvatara Upanishad says:

> The Lord dwells in the womb of the cosmos,
> The creator who is in all creatures.
> He is that which is born and to be born;
> His face is everywhere.

In the Krishna tradition, there is a little story I like very much which illustrates this vision of unity. Once again, it is a story about Nārada, a sage who was deeply devoted to Sri Krishna. On this occasion, Nārada asked the Lord to tell him the deepest truth of the spiritual life. Sri Krishna has a rather playful way of answering these questions, and this time he just smiled mischievously and disappeared, leaving Nārada standing bewildered in the bustling street of a village he had never seen before. Nārada was not one to be at a loss, but even he didn't know what to do. Was he still in heaven, or was he back on earth? He waited and waited for Sri Krishna to re-appear, but there was no sign of him anywhere.

Finally, Nārada began to get hungry. In India it has been a tradi-tion for thousands of years for householders to give food to wander-ing spiritual aspirants; it is a great blessing for the householder and the whole family. So Nārada took out his wooden bowl and went up to the nearest house to ask for a little food. But when the door opened Nārada gave a start, for the woman who answered had Sri Krishna's eyes. Not only that, as she handed back the bowl, he was sure she gave him just the hint of a wink before she disappeared into the shadows of the house again and closed the door.

A little bewildered, Nārada went on to the next house, where a whole family was just sitting down to dinner. This time there was no wink from the lady of the house, but a little boy with those same eyes ran over to greet him and said a little too mischievously, "Sir, have you ever seen Sri Krishna? Can you sing us some of his praises?" It was like that in every house. In one place it was an in-fant, in another a teenager, in a third the grandmother, but in every family Nārada visited, one of the family was the Lord. At last he realized that for all the differences in age and appearance, there was no one in that village except the Lord, and in that instant of realization the village disappeared and Nārada was back with Sri Krishna again in the heavenly realm of Vaikuntha.

अहं क्रतुरहं यज्ञः स्वधाहमहमौषधम् ।
मन्त्रोऽहमहमेवाज्यमहमग्निरहं हुतम् ॥१६॥

*16. I am the ritual and the sacrifice; I am true
medicine and the mantram; I am the offering and the
fire which consumes it, and he to whom it is offered.*

This verse and those that follow serve as a prelude to chapter ten, in which the Lord will describe the endless glory of his attributes. Here the Lord is drawing his illustrations from parts of ancient Ve-dic ritual, but when he talks about sacrifice, he means the sacrifice of our self-will. When I want to see how well someone is doing in meditation, I don't ask if he or she is seeing visions or hearing voices; I look to see how easily that person can go against his or her self-will. This is the way to make progress on the spiritual path, and in this verse the Lord is reminding us that whenever we turn our backs on ourselves in order to move closer to him, it is he within us who is prompting us to make the offering.

The dynamics of this process are quite interesting. Breaking through to a deeper level of consciousness in meditation is very much like trying to open a door which keeps banging shut. You just cannot keep it open; every time you open it a crack, the handle slips out of your hands and the door slams shut. At the beginning this is only frustrating, but eventually it becomes quite tantalizing. The more you are able to peek through the door, the more your concentration is drawn to what is on the other side. It is as if the Lord is standing on the other side of the door, opening it a little until you can almost see in and then quickly closing it again. Finally you decide you are going to keep that door open, come what may. You will get up from meditation with the door haunting your memory; you will go through the day without being able to get it out of your mind. This is a very hopeful sign, because it means that even in your unconscious you are working on ways to get your foot in the door.

In general, there are two ways you can strengthen yourself to solve problems like this, which are bound to come as your meditation deepens. The first is to look for an opportunity to defy your self-will. When you begin to get the motivation, you will find hundreds of opportunities for this every day. Wherever there are likes and dislikes, wherever there is friction in personal relationships, that is an opportunity for going against self-will.

The second very powerful ploy for getting through that door into deeper consciousness is to defy a strong desire. It may be for cigarettes, or for alcohol, or for some selfish activity that benefits no one—whatever it is, large or small, power is locked up in that desire. When you come to an obstacle in meditation and find that you cannot break through, you will discover the important connection between desire and will. Desire *is* will. Every strong desire has a great deal of will locked up in it; the problem is that usually we do not have any control over it. This is what happens in compulsive desires, the biggest and most powerful of which is sex. Every time you turn against a strong desire, it immediately strengthens the will. Often you can see the results the very next time you sit down for meditation. Whenever you can do this you will find your physical and emotional health improving, your relationships deepening, and your energy increasing. These are signs that you are going forward.

If the desire is particularly strong—something to which you have been conditioned over a period of several years—you can think of it as a continual source of power. Every time that desire comes up and you defy it, there is power generated. Once you get a taste of this and you really want to make progress in your meditation, you won't just wait for a strong selfish desire to start to pick you up; you will go around ferreting out all sorts of little cravings everywhere.

This desire to go against desires is the surest sign of grace. To give you an idea of how far it can go, the moment a desire rises in my mind and starts to tell me what to do, my immediate response is to defy it. Then I have to step in, tap myself on the shoulder, and remind myself that after all, it *is* time for dinner, and there is nothing wrong with a moderate helping of spinach crepes. It is a wonderful state to be in, because it means I am always master in my own little house of the mind.

When you keep on digging away at a powerful desire over a period of years, the great day will come when you can get underneath it and pluck it out at the root. Then it is like opening a perpetual spring of power; where that desire used to be, there is now continuous access to the vitality it used to consume. You will see the effects of a breakthrough like this in every aspect of daily living. Your patience will be greater; your relationships and security will deepen; even your body will be bathed in the restorative waters of this spring. One of the surest signs that you have changed to a deeper level in meditation is that some emotional or physical problem that had been bothering you for years—a digestive problem, or asthma, or chronic headache, or high blood pressure—will begin to disappear. So Sri Krishna says, "I am *aushadham,* your best medicine";

the more you draw on him, the more he will heal, not from without but from within.

In making this sacrifice of self-will, the mantram can be a tremendously effective ally. Unlike meditation, the mantram does not call for strenuous discipline; anyone can repeat a mantram and benefit from it. We are all familiar with the power of words, if only through the effect advertisements have on what we do and even what we think. Millions of people, for example, know that smoking causes cancer; we have irrefutable evidence of this today. Yet the number of people who smoke is on the increase. To see why, we have only to look at the billboards and magazine advertisements all around us; the advertiser's words go right into our consciousness. But just as Madison Avenue's words work to condition our desires, the Holy Name from any of the world's great religious traditions can free us from this conditioning. All we have to do is keep on repeating the mantram in our minds whenever a desire threatens to make us do what it says.

It sounds too simple, but just try it and see how powerful the mantram can be. The next time you are angry or afraid, go out for a long, fast walk repeating the mantram. Do not take your anger out on others, but use this strong emotion to drive the mantram deep into your consciousness. You don't need to wait for a chance to exit gracefully, either; just take to the nearest door. When you return, the transformation in your consciousness will more than make up for any toes you might have stepped on on your way out.

Similarly, when you have a compulsive urge to eat something or do something—especially if it is not good for you—go for a long walk repeating the mantram. In an hour's time, the urge will pass away. When the urge is upon you, you feel like you must yield or explode. All your concentration is on the cigarette you must smoke or the hot fudge sundae you must eat. But if you can switch your concentration over to the Holy Name, you will forget the cigarette or the sundae completely. Sometimes, of course, the mantram is like a car that hasn't been driven for a long, long time; when you try to start it up, at first it only groans and growls. But all you need do is just keep trying—once it gets going, the mantram will run smoothly.

पिताहमस्य जगतो माता धाता पितामहः ।
वेद्यं पवित्रमोंकार ऋक्साम यजुरेव च ॥१७॥

*17. I am the father and mother of this universe, and
its grandfather too; I am its entire support. I am the
sum of all knowledge, the purifier, and the syllable
Om; I am the sacred scriptures, the Rik, Yajur,
and Sāma Vedas.*

When parents in an Indian village want their sons or daughters to
go to college, which is beyond the means even of most middle-class
people, they look for a college in a place where they have relatives.
Then their children can stay right in the relatives' home. This is not
looked upon as an imposition; it is something that everybody does,
and if your sister leaves her son with you for four years while he
studies engineering, you can always console yourself that when the
fellow grows up and gets a job, others will billet their sons or daughters on him. But an even more important reason than saving money
is that with this arrangement there is the same family atmosphere,
and if your son comes back a little late one night, he will be taken to
task just as if he were at home.

In this verse, the Lord is assuring us in his own very personal way
that he is responsible for us completely. No matter how old we are,
no matter where we stray, we can count on his support. The other
side of this, which he is too tactful to mention outright, is that he is
not going to let us get away with a single, solitary thing. He will
keep on taking us to task, severely if the situation demands, until
we are prepared to be selfless always.

This verse personifies the nature of reality with the Hindu flair
for the dramatic, but we find the same basic insight in modern science. The language is quite different—instead of the Lord we have a
unifying force of nature—but the truth is the same; the Lord *is* the
unity of life, the Divine Ground in which all forces in the cosmos co-
here. The same laws govern the universe everywhere. The elements
here are the same as those in the farthest reaches of the universe,
and so are the forms of energy. So Sri Krishna says, "I am the sum

of knowledge: knowing Me, you know that which supports all things." It is the language of Spinoza also. And the Chāndogya Upanishad explains beautifully: "As by knowing one lump of clay we come to know all things made of clay—that they differ only in name and form, while the stuff of which all are made is clay—so through that spiritual wisdom, dear one, we come to know that all life is one."

गतिर्भर्ता प्रभुः साक्षी निवासः शरणं सुहृत् ।
प्रभवः प्रलयः स्थानं निधानं बीजमव्ययम् ॥१८॥

18. I am the goal of life, the Lord and support of all,
the inner witness, the abode of all. I am the only
refuge, the one true friend; I am the beginning and end
of creation, and the receptacle for the eternal seed.

The Lord is everything for us. When we become God-conscious, all our needs are met; all our deepest desires are fulfilled. Sri Krishna says, "I am the supreme goal of life, your sole support; you have no other master than me. I am the eternal witness within you, your true home, your only refuge; when everyone else deserts you, I am still your friend." Jesus puts it in very simple words: "Follow me; I am the way, the truth, and the life."

In a beautiful little poem, St. Teresa of Ávila tells of the deep security that comes when we find our refuge in the Lord:

> Let nothing upset you;
> Let nothing frighten you.
> Everything is changing;
> God alone is changeless.
> Patience attains the goal.
> Who has God lacks nothing;
> God alone fills all her needs.

Let nothing upset you. That is the first result of this realization: you become unupsettable. It means that none of your energy will be wasted, and you will have a long life with abounding energy to carry on the work of the Lord. *Let nothing frighten you.* There is going to be tragedy in life for everyone—loss of money, loss of face, loss of loved ones, and finally loss of everything on earth. You may grieve, but you never get oppressed by any loss, because through the deprivation you can see the Lord present always.

Everything is changing. The more experience I have of life, the more I appreciate the stark grandeur of this line. The other day I received a letter from India telling me that somebody I knew, somebody I loved, somebody I used to work with is now no more. When we move into the second half of life, this is the news that will come to us more and more often. The Katha Upanishad exclaims hauntingly, "Like corn, a man ripens and falls": everything is changing, and everything that changes is going to pass away. *God alone is changeless:* turn to him, love him with all your heart, and you will be secure always; you will find fulfillment everywhere you go.

Patience attains the goal. The logic is as ruthless as the words are beautiful. No matter how difficult a situation is, no matter how difficult another person is, everything and everyone must yield to patience, which outlasts all obstacles. In the heart of every storm in life there is always this unchanging center which is the Lord, and when you can bear with those who rage against you and keep your trust in them, you are helping them to trust and respond to their real Self. If you can only be patient and remember these lines of Teresa's—"everything is changing; God alone is changeless"—those who oppose you, those who differ from you, those who make life impossible for you will *have* to respond; it is only a matter of time.

Who has God lacks nothing. That's why everybody throws away their defenses before a person who has realized God. Such people do not lack anything at all, so they have nothing to try to get from anyone. They live for our benefit, not for their own. You can take what you like from them; they will still be full. They can give anything away; they will still be full. You can give them any kind of trouble; they will still be full. As Teresa concludes beautifully, *God alone fills all their needs.*

तपाम्यहमहं वर्षं निगृह्णाम्युत्सृजामि च ।
अमृतं चैव मृत्युश्च सदसच्चाहमर्जुन ॥१९॥

*19. I am heat and light; I give and withhold the rain.
I am immortality and I am death; I am what is and
what is not.*

Working through the forces of nature, the Lord gives life with one
hand and takes it away with the other. Not only is he the force sus-
taining life; he is the force behind change and death as well, and the
power which we harness to go beyond death to immortality. Therefore, as Swami Vivekananda is said to have remarked, if we can understand the meaning of death, we will understand the meaning of
life. In Somerset Maugham's powerful novel *The Razor's Edge,* a
young American, Larry, who is the hero of the story, sees one of
his friends lying dead on the battlefield. With consummate skill,
Maugham conveys in one short sentence the profound shock in
Larry's consciousness: "The dead look so dead when they are
dead." All of us can benefit from this rather grim reminder and put
all our effort into going beyond death here and now.

In the Upanishads there is a profound statement that whatever is
in the outside world is within our consciousness also. Many of the
forces Sri Krishna talks about in verses like these apply not only to
the natural world but to events we experience as our meditation
deepens. When the Lord says he is heat and light, for example, he is
not just referring to the sun. The mystics of all traditions describe
the blazing effulgence that can take place in the final stages of meditation. If you are meditating sincerely and systematically, the time
may come when you experience a sudden, dazzling flash of light in
the head. It will be so intense that you might even open your eyes
thinking that the sun is rising, only to discover that it is still the
small hours of the night. Such flashes give a glimpse of the radiance
that is within us. When at last our self-will has been removed, the
Lord can show us his divine glory, which the Gita will tell us is like
the splendor of a thousand suns rising at the same time. It is no won-

der the man or woman who has become united with the Lord is radiant with lasting joy.

For the great majority of us, this experience would be quite overwhelming if it came on all at once, so the Lord in his mercy spreads out our spiritual development over many years. The Indian mystics are fond of drawing a comparison with the Hindu wedding processions that are a common sight in the villages. When a wedding is about to take place in a Punjabi village, the villagers can hear the band playing long before they see anything. Then the first part of the wedding party, the men bearing banners and presents, comes into view. When the villager hears the music and sees the banners and gift-bearers approaching, he calls to his friends, "There's a wedding coming!" They stop their work to watch the procession, but for a long time they still do not see the bride or the bridegroom. Instead, the father-in-law comes by with great majesty, dominating the scene with his measured stride. Then comes the horse on which the bridegroom rides, covered with garlands. You can see the horse but not the bridegroom; all that is visible is a giant bouquet, behind which, if you look closely, you may see an arm or a bit of an ear. Finally, the wedding party reaches the bride's home. The bridegroom gets down from the horse, the flowers are taken away, and the bridegroom and bride stand before us together at last.

It is very much like this on the spiritual path too. You do not see the Lord right away, but in the later stages of meditation there will be a number of signs that he is on the way. My suggestion is not to look for these signs. When you keep waiting for something to happen in meditation, you are actually keeping yourself from going deeper, and anything you experience is not likely to be valid. If you are waiting for a deep-hued monsoon cloud, the symbol of Sri Krishna, to float across your mind's eye, you may find yourself thinking in meditation: "'Lord, make me an instrument of thy peace' . . . *Where is that cloud?*" When this happens, you are no longer meditating. So do not pay undue attention to anything you experience in meditation. If the experience is genuine, it will bear fruit in your life the very same day, whether you dwell on it or not.

But if you allow yourself to get excited over it, a depression will come in its wake and your progress will be impeded.

Then the Lord says, "I give and withhold the rain." St. Teresa of Ávila describes the soul as a garden which must be watered by meditation, which she calls interior prayer, until the Lord gives it the rain of grace.

> It seems to me that our garden can be watered in four ways: by taking the water from a well, which is hard work; or by a water wheel and buckets, when the water is drawn by a windlass (I have sometimes drawn water in this way; it is less work and yields more); or by a stream, which waters the ground much better, for it saturates it more thoroughly and there is no need to water so often, so that the gardener's work is much less; or by heavy rain, when the Lord waters it with no labor of ours, a way infinitely better than any of the others.

For a long time, meditation is like drawing water from a very deep well. The well in my ancestral home in Kerala is about a hundred feet deep, and during the summer, when the sun is scorching the plains of India, people who draw water from the well have to use almost the full hundred feet of rope to lower the bucket down into the water. Often in a very poor village the bucket will have leaks, so that by the time it reaches the top, even after all their struggle, the women have only half a bucketful to take home. This is how it is when we start meditation; our bucket will have quite a few leaks. We will meditate with great concentration and finally succeed in filling the bucket with the soothing waters of forgiveness, but then the leaks—impatience, irritation, resentment, indolence— begin to sap our will until we wonder sometimes if our bucket is anything more than a lot of holes put together. We may even have struggled a great deal to bring the bucket up, only to find that there is no water in it at all. On days like that we are tempted to say, "There just isn't any water in the well." "Oh, no," Teresa would answer, "there is a lot of water in the well; you just need to plug up the holes." There is no beginner's luck in meditation. In the beginning it is only hard work and more hard work, because we can rely only on ourselves.

After some years of leading the spiritual life and practicing meditation, our awareness becomes deeper. Now, Teresa says, meditation is more like drawing water with the help of a Persian wheel—a large wheel with many buckets hung around the rim, each of which scoops up water as the wheel goes around. It is a marvelous image, which St. Teresa draws not from books but from the things she observed around Ávila. In this second stage of spiritual living, you still have to do a lot of hard work, but instead of having one old, leaky bucket you now have many good buckets. Now you are able to water the garden more abundantly with less effort, and the peace obtained in meditation is not drained away by the little anxieties and resentments of the day.

In the third stage, Teresa tells us, we see a little brook making a channel into our field, as if to say, "Just keep your bucket in a corner and let me do the watering." The effort needed to keep the mind still in meditation is becoming less and less, and the waters of selflessness now flow continuously. St. Teresa says of this state: "The Lord is now pleased to help the gardener, so that he may almost be said to be the gardener himself, for it is he who does everything." When we are able to forget our own needs in trying to solve the problems that threaten us all, the Lord is beginning to act through us. He is the Operator, and we become the instruments of his peace. Finally, Teresa says, the grace of the Lord descends in a shower, bathing the garden constantly in a gentle rain.

त्रैविद्या मां सोमपाः पूतपापा
यज्ञैरिष्ट्वा स्वर्गतिं प्रार्थयन्ते ।
ते पुण्यमासाद्य सुरेन्द्रलोक-
मश्नन्ति दिव्यान्दिवि देवभोगान् ॥२०॥
ते तं भुक्त्वा स्वर्गलोकं विशालं
क्षीणे पुण्ये मर्त्यलोकं विशन्ति ।
एवं त्रयीधर्ममनुप्रपन्ना
गतागतं कामकामा लभन्ते ॥२१॥

*20–21. Those who follow the rituals given in the
Vedas, who offer sacrifices and take soma, free themselves from evil and attain the vast heaven of the gods.
There they enjoy celestial pleasures. When they have
enjoyed these fully, their merit is exhausted and they
return to this land of death. Thus observing Vedic
rituals but caught in an endless chain of desires,
they come and go.*

According to the traditional interpretation, people who take to the
spiritual path to gain worldly ends, for the sake of their own private
happiness, go after death to a heavenly realm where the satisfactions they have been searching for will be multiplied many times.
Eventually, however, these pleasures will be exhausted. The grand
time will come to an end, and they will return to good old terra
firma to learn to make wiser choices the next time around.

There is another, more practical way these verses can be interpreted to apply to daily living. When you practice meditation for
the sake of some private, personal goal, without training the senses
and putting other people first, it can be a tremendously dangerous
combination. The deeper resources in your consciousness are beginning to flow into your hands, giving you the capacity to fulfill
some of your deepest desires, but you have no control over what
these desires are. You may be able to amass an immense amount of
money, acquire great prestige, even live a very long life, but there

will be no more direction to your life than before. It's all quite possible; in fact, I have known some people whose lives illustrate these verses perfectly. Instead of going to the orthodox Hindu heaven of the gods to have a grand time, they go to Acapulco or the south of France to live their life in just the way they like. It's not necessarily unaesthetic; after all, these are people with highly refined desires and all the means with which to satisfy them. They have their meditation every morning by the Mediterranean, go for a brisk swim in some secluded cove, and then have a good, nourishing breakfast in the finest restaurant around. For entertainment they don't sit and watch *The Godfather;* they fly to London for the new opening of *King Lear* or spend a week or two in Salzburg for a Mozart festival. And wherever they go, people get interested in them. Photographers like to take pictures of them for the weeklies; journalists gather to ask them all kinds of questions because the answers are always interesting. And they derive great pleasure from all of this; it is the fulfillment of their dreams.

But then, the next verse says, look at where all this leads. *Kshīne punye martyalokam vishanti:* after a while, all these things begin to tire you. *Kshīne* means 'worn out,' exhausted; the Sanskrit word for tuberculosis comes from the same root. All this adulation becomes a nuisance; the questions and the questioners become a bore. You get tired of the Mediterranean and try the Caribbean for a season, but it's the same old crystal blue water, the same questions from the press, the same kind of company as you left behind. What has happened is that you have become tired of pleasure, but you don't understand that; you think you have become tired of Nice and Cannes. So you start growing a beard, wearing dark glasses, registering in hotels under a false name; and instead of luxurious restaurants, you begin to frequent little out-of-the-way places where the furniture is deliberately mismatched and the food is served in handmade bowls. Everything that used to please you now begins to irritate you—the radical becomes a reactionary, the reactionary becomes radical, the profligate becomes more puritanical than a Puritan. Such people have simply grown tired of living for themselves, and all this time has been misspent as far as the spiritual life is concerned. As this

verse reminds us, they will have to return to the "land of mortals"—
the everyday world—and try again to live in harmony with others
and contribute to the welfare and happiness of those around them.

Meditation is a tremendously powerful discipline, and there can
be real danger if it is misused for selfish ends. I get frightened sometimes at the literature I receive by mail: learn to meditate and you
will be able to influence people; learn to meditate and you will be
able to get whatever you want. There will always come a time when
these powers will turn against you. That is the theme of Marlowe's
Faustus, and at the end of the play, when Faustus is faced with destruction of his own making, he cries out in haunting lines:

> Mountains and hills, come, come and fall on me . . .
> O soul, be changed to little water drops
> And fall into the ocean, never to be found!

There is no place to hide when the powers you have developed
and misused turn against you. To take an extreme example, even the
story of Hitler may be interpreted in this way. Not too long ago I
saw a powerful film in which Sir Alec Guinness, a very accomplished actor, brought Hitler to life as a maniac with tremendous
power to influence the will and lives of other people. In the end the
same destructive forces he had created turned against him and his
party and tore them to pieces. It is for our own protection that most
of us will not be able to make real progress in meditation unless we
are trying sincerely to train our senses and to put the happiness of
all those around us first. But if we are giving our very best to all the
disciplines of the spiritual path, our progress will be swift and safe.

अनन्याश्चिन्तयन्तो मां ये जनाः पर्युपासते ।
तेषां नित्याभियुक्तानां योगक्षेमं वहाम्यहम् ॥२२॥

*22. Those who worship Me and meditate on Me
constantly, without any thought for their own welfare,
I will provide for all their needs.*

Many years ago, when we started the work of the Blue Mountain
Center of Meditation in Berkeley, we had hardly any money and

not many dedicated friends to help us. I used to do part of the grocery shopping and the gardening; Christine was receptionist, accountant, secretary, editor of our newsletter, cook, chauffeur, you name it. Most people looked upon the whole thing as a foolhardy venture. My friends asked me, "How much money do you have in the bank?" They always looked a little depressed when I would tell them I didn't have a bank account. "Without substantial financial support," they warned me sincerely, "by yourselves, you cannot build any organization in this country."

"Exactly," I replied. "We are not building it by ourselves."

"Then you must have a sponsor?"

"Yes, the very best."

"Who? The Ford Foundation? Rockefeller?"

"Better than that: Sri Krishna."

Usually there would be a stunned silence; they seemed unwilling to credit the Lord with solvency. But I wasn't joking at all; I had the promissory note right in this verse. When we devote ourselves wholeheartedly to the spiritual life, without any reservation for ourselves, Sri Krishna says, *Yogakshemam vahāmyaham:* "Not only am I entirely responsible for your spiritual progress; I am also responsible for paying your bills."

No mystic from any spiritual tradition East or West has ever found this guarantee to fail. In the early years of the Center, I remember, at a time when things were looking particularly thin, we looked in our donation bowl after the evening's class and found a bill so large that I don't think I had ever seen a picture of that particular president before. It kept the wolf from our door for several weeks. Even Christine was a little surprised, but I have to say that I was not; I had already learned that I could trust the Lord to keep his word. On another occasion that same year we opened the bowl and found nothing but a big sheaf of Blue Chip stamps. We went out and bought seven folding chairs to use in our meditation classes, and now when I see those same chairs being used in our āshram and look around to see how much the Center has grown, it always makes me remember the promise of this verse.

येऽप्यन्यदेवता भक्ता यजन्ते श्रद्धयाऽन्विताः ।
तेऽपि मामेव कौन्तेय यजन्त्यविधिपूर्वकम् ॥२३॥
अहं हि सर्वयज्ञानां भोक्ता च प्रभुरेव च ।
न तु मामभिजानन्ति तत्त्वेनातश्च्यवन्ति ते ॥२४॥

*23. Those who worship other gods with faith
and devotion will also come to Me, Arjuna, but
by other paths.*
*24. I am the object of all worship, and every act of
selfless service is done for Me. But those who fail to
realize my true nature must be reborn.*

When we were living on the Blue Mountain, my wife and I met an
American spiritual aspirant who had come to India after World
War II. He had grown up in a Christian family and graduated from
Harvard, but when he began to feel a great need for a deeper purpose in life he went to an āshram in India, presided over by an orthodox Hindu teacher from Bengal. He lived with his teacher and
practiced meditation for twelve years, which is the traditional period of sādhana. I remember him telling us in amazement, "Here I
travel all the way from Boston to Bengal, where they worship
Mother Kālī and Lord Shiva; I practice meditation with a Hindu
teacher and use a Hindu mantram, and who should reveal himself
in the depths of my consciousness? Not Sri Krishna, not Lord Shiva,
but Jesus the Christ."

In our case, too, there is no need to debate the pros and cons of
various incarnations. We can leave the choice in the capable hands
of the Lord. One person may be meditating on the Christ, another
on the Buddha, a third on Sri Krishna, but the names do not make
the slightest difference. If we are meditating sincerely and regularly
and trying our best to eliminate self-will, all of us are going to be
united with the Lord one day. When we call upon Jesus or the Buddha, we are calling on Sri Krishna too; when we call upon Sri Krishna, we are calling equally upon the Christ, or Allah. When I was
teaching at the university, I had a student whose name was Shiva-

rāmakrishna—his father hadn't wanted to take any chances when he named him, so he just covered all the bases with one name. I used to tell him, "Wherever heaven is, you'll find your way to it; at least one of those names is sure to open the right door."

Though you may not be greatly drawn towards any particular incarnation when you start meditating, gradually the time will come when you will have such longing for the Lord that you will feel the need for a divine ideal of your own—an *ishtadevatā,* as it is called in Sanskrit. Often, however, you may not know which incarnation is most suitable for you. You feel drawn to "gentle Jesus, meek and mild"; then you have a look at the Buddha, full of compassion for everything that lives, and you feel torn between the Buddha and the Christ. In such cases, it is good to leave the decision to the Lord. He—or she—will come to you in whatever form fulfills your deepest needs. At the appropriate point on the spiritual path, it is not unlikely that in a dream you will see a great incarnation or hear his or her name. You may see Jesus carrying a lamb, or you may hear resonating in your consciousness the mantram associated with the Compassionate Buddha, *Om mani padme hum.* Then there will be a tremendous response in the depths of your heart that will leave no doubt in your mind.

यान्ति देवव्रता देवान्पितॄन्यान्ति पितृव्रताः ।
भूतानि यान्ति भूतेज्या यान्ति मद्याजिनोऽपि माम् ॥२५॥

*25. Those who worship the devas will go to the realm
of the devas; those who worship their ancestors will be
united with them after death. Those who worship
phantoms will become like phantoms; but my
devotees will come to Me.*

The key to this verse is that we become what we meditate upon. If we meditate for the sake of solving a particular physical problem, often that problem will be solved. If we meditate for the sake of solving some emotional problem, that too can be solved, if we are sincere and systematic in our practice. "But," Sri Krishna says, "if you meditate on Me, you will go beyond all your problems." As

Jesus reassures us, "Seek ye first the kingdom of heaven and every-thing else will be added unto you."

This is practical advice. We cannot find joy by solving a physical problem if we still have a lot of emotional difficulties. If we go to heaven's gate, St. Peter will say, "Your cholesterol level is less than 220; your blood pressure is 120 over 70; you don't have any cavi-ties. But what a lot of fear, anger, and greed you have! Sorry, old chap, can't admit you this time. Come back again when you've learned a little patience." Similarly, after we have made our for-tune, St. Peter will still say, "You've shown a lot of enterprise and enthusiasm, but we don't need money up here. Why don't you use it to work for a worthy cause, and then come and see me?" But if we seek first the kingdom of heaven, all our other needs will be pro-vided for as well.

The Hindu tradition has a genius for dramatizing the desires which shape our lives. In the *Rāmāyana,* for example, the demon king Rāvana is the perfect symbol of selfish power. Rāvana has a brother named Kumbhakarna, the personification of indolence and apathy, who sleeps for six months of every year. When we sit back and fail to contribute to life, this verse reminds us, we are worship-ing Kumbhakarna. When we live for ourselves, we are praying to Rāvana to take us to his kingdom and make us his servants forever. In other words, it is we who choose the kingdom to which we go, even in this life, by our choice of what to desire. If we want to go to the kingdom of heaven, it is only appropriate that we not walk in the other direction.

Similarly, Sri Krishna warns, there are those who let their desires entangle them in the past. Ancestor worship is not an exotic custom, confined to communities which have yet to enter the modern age. Visit the home of an established family and look at the gallery of paintings and photographs on the walls. Your host or hostess will gladly give you a guided tour. "Here is my great-great-grandfather, who founded our town; here is my great-aunt Agatha, who dined at Buckingham Palace." It is true that our great-great-grandparents may have had many qualities worth emulating—for one, they had a simpler way of life, from which we can learn a great deal. But we have to use our discrimination and select from the past only what is most helpful for today's world. I understand there is a special society of people in this country who want to live as they did prior to Independence, in the days of the British Empire. The tragedy of such people is that often their wishes come true. They can come to live completely in the past, which means that in the present they are no more than ghosts. It is very much the same with people who pretend to be others. Whenever my wife and I take a walk in Berkeley or San Francisco, we see people who are pretending to be their favorite movie star or tennis champion or rock musician. Once we went to a restaurant where the waitress was trying to be like Shirley Mac-Laine. I was tempted to tell her I was Walter Matthau. By trying to be someone else, these people have no life of their own. They, too, become ghosts.

In another sense, this "world of spirits" Sri Krishna mentions here refers to the vast continents of fear, anger, and greed within our consciousness. The more we dwell on any negative emotion, the deeper we wander into its uncharted domain. For example, most of us are prone to all manner of fears, from loss of life to loss of hair. When we look in the classified pages to see how we can have hair grafted, or spend hours training our hair to cover a little bald spot, the motivation is really fear. As more and more hairs continue to fall out, our sense of security goes with them, for the more we dwell on a fear, even a little fear, the bigger it becomes. So in my case, when it began to look as if my head was going to become quite bald, I remember saying in the spirit of true renunciation, "All right, let it all go." Time may have diminished my hair since then, but it has not diminished me. My niece Meera, who likes everything about me, even goes so far as to say admiringly, "Uncle, what beautiful hair you have!"

When we are meditating, instead of welcoming fear by giving him attention, we can politely tell him to leave. If our meditation is going well, he will slink out muttering, "Sorry; I must have the wrong address." Fear wants us to worry about him. He will tempt us to study his genealogy from the time of William the Conqueror, and by the time we have finished discussing his life history he will have drawn us into his realm and shut the door behind us. Many people live in this world of fear, in which they are upset by continual anxieties. They are prone to a number of psychosomatic ailments which can lead to serious diseases, and they suffer from estrangement in their personal relationships because they are suspicious even of those they want to love. Such people can benefit greatly from meditation. Fear is concentration of which we are not the masters; it is a way of dwelling compulsively on ourselves. In meditation we gain the capacity to withdraw our attention from our problems and concentrate on the needs of those around us. When we do this, we find ourselves really coming to life in the present while our fears simply fade away.

पत्रं पुष्पं फलं तोयं यो मे भक्त्या प्रयच्छति ।
तदहं भक्त्युपहृतमश्नामि प्रयतात्मनः ॥२६॥

26. Whatever I am offered in devotion with a pure heart—a leaf, a flower, fruit, or water—I accept with joy.

Now we are entering the climax of this chapter. In some of the most beautiful language in the Gita, the Lord is inspiring us to make everything an offering to him. Leaves, flowers, fruit, and water are often used for ritual worship in India. In one widely used ritual, the worshiper stands before the divine image and repeats the names of the Lord, offering a flower petal at the deity's feet with each name. Sri Ramakrishna used to worship the Divine Mother in this fashion, but with a divinely peculiar twist of his own. He would close his eyes and begin repeating the beautiful names of the Divine Mother, but soon, completely absorbed in her, he would lose all outer consciousness and begin throwing the lotus petals on his own head rather than towards the image. Such was his devotion to the Divine Mother that he had become united with her.

The practical approach to this verse is to look upon everything that we do, no matter how seemingly insignificant, as a gift to the Lord. If we hoe the garden carefully so that our family can have fresh vegetables for dinner, that is an offering to the Lord. If we work a little more than is expected of us at something that benefits others, that too is an offering to the Lord. Everywhere, in every detail of daily living, it is not a question of quantity or expense that makes our offering acceptable; it is cheerfulness, enthusiasm, and the capacity to forget ourselves completely in helping those around us. The verse that follows will go into some of the ways in which this offering can be made.

यत्करोषि यदश्नासि यज्जुहोषि ददासि यत् ।
यत्तपस्यसि कौन्तेय तत्कुरुष्व मदर्पणम् ॥२७॥

*27. Whatever you do, make it an offering to Me—
the food you eat, the sacrifices you make, the help
you give, even your suffering.*

Every term in this verse has a practical application in our daily living. The first is *yat karoshi:* "Whatever you do, make it an offering to the Lord." Instead of doing what pleases you, what you are accustomed to, what feels right to you, try to do something that benefits someone else instead. It may be distressing at first, but if you are making your best effort, the Lord will accept your offering. The proof of it comes in your daily living. The Lord isn't sitting at an altar somewhere and accepting what we offer him; he is right inside, and when we do something that pleases him it means that there is tension released at a very deep level throughout the body and mind.

Then the Lord says, *Yad ashnāsi:* "Whatever you eat, make it an offering to Me." Considering the wealth of this country, it has always surprised me how poorly many Americans eat. Some of my friends were telling me the other day that it is not uncommon for people to have only a cup of coffee and a roll for breakfast, often topped off with a cigarette. Over the years such inadequate food habits contribute to very poor health—and in the case of mothers-to-be, the damage is not only to them but to their unborn children, too. Some advertisers no longer even bother to call what they are marketing "food"; they just say "products." When we sit down to dinner, most of us don't want to eat products; we want food—and tasty, nourishing food at that. It is so easy to cultivate a little back-

yard garden and have fresh fruits and vegetables for lunch or dinner. Even if there is no more than a window box or a small plot by
the back door, we can still grow a few vegetables. We don't need to
resign ourselves to food that has become stale or polluted with
chemicals, or to products that have no food value at all.

In Sanskrit, however, "eating" refers to more than food. The Gita
means whatever we consume, not only through our mouths but
through our eyes, ears, and skin. Just watch children with their eyes
glued to the television: they are having a big meal, often full of sex
and violence. Since the average American household watches television an astonishing seven hours a day—one hour more than in
1977—these "TV dinners" are rather large. At best, like junk food,
they displace real nutrition: the human interactions by which a child
learns to love, understand, feel, and give. At worst they spoon in the
lowest possible image of the human being. "You are what you think,"
the Buddha warns. We all have a responsibility not to support any
media production that fills our minds with junk thoughts and images.

Next Sri Krishna tells us, *Yaj juhoshi:* "Whatever you offer in renunciation, make that an offering to Me." This is hard-hitting advice. He is not asking us to renounce our antique almirah or our
tickets to the World Series; the sacrifice the Lord wants us to make
is our self-will. It is not ideological differences that cause family
conflicts or lead to clashes between man and woman; it is self-will.
Reducing self-will is a terribly painful renunciation to make, because the ego will try every trick in the book to undermine our efforts. Fortunately, every one of us has a defiant streak that can
enable us to turn against our self-will and overcome it. Eventually
there is a tremendous sense of exhilaration in this, because it frees
us from the conflicts which make life so miserable for us today.

The practical question is how to make this offering of self-will. I
would suggest starting on a very small scale. Just as the mountain
climber does not begin with Mount Everest, you cannot get rid of
all your self-will immediately. You start with little things. When
you go out to dinner with a friend, instead of choosing carefully just
what you like, have what the other person is having instead. It
might be your favorite, but more likely it will be something you

would just as soon pass over. That is the time to smile and eat. It is especially good if husband and wife can do this, for then there is the motivation to learn to like what the person you love likes. In such cases you cannot help moving closer to each other, for you will have got a little of your self-will out of the way. If you can even ask for seconds, you can mark that day on your calendar; the ego has started to pack his bags.

Then Sri Krishna says, *Dadāsi yat:* "Whatever you give, make it an offering to Me." The finest gifts we can give are forgiveness and patience. We can't give anyone joy or security by increasing her bank account or adding to his collection of vintage wines. The only thing these gifts will increase is the gross national product, and after some experience of life we should be able to see that there is no connection between the gross national product and real security. In the spiritual lore of India there is a story that the Lord whispered only one word in our ears when he sent us into the world: "Give." Give freely of your time, your talent, your resources; give without asking for anything in return. This is the secret of living in joy and security. The moment you expect reward or recognition, you are making a contract.

Even parents and children suffer from this contract relationship. While I was teaching at the university in India I met some parents with good intentions who wanted to make their boy or girl into the scientist or musician they had never been. I used to be very close to most of my students, and they didn't mind confiding in me that their real talent lay in some other field. Parents can help their children tremendously by avoiding this "I gave this to you, therefore you do that for me" approach, encouraging them instead to follow their own star.

My Grandmother, who did not know how to read or write, showed great wisdom in what she expected of me. I remember how she responded to my downfall in mathematics. I was in high school and had just been introduced to the world of Shakespeare, which was so glorious to me that my mind was full of Capulets and Montagues, of Falstaff and Prince Hal. I forgot all about my mathematics class, and when my mathematics test came, I didn't do very well. As

I came home from school, my friends teased me with, "How could this possibly have happened to you?" My family was even less understanding. Only my Grandmother remained unperturbed; she did not say a word about it.

That night I made up my mind to go to the top of the class in mathematics, just to please my Grandmother. Her attitude of not losing faith in me gave me such motivation that I took to Euclid like a blood brother and did extremely well. Immediately, most of my family wanted me to become an engineer. I tried to tell them that I had no deep commitment to Pythagoras or Euclid, that my heart was given to literature, but the elder members of my family simply told me, "Nonsense. You've done very well in mathematics. India needs engineers and pays them well, too, so you should become an engineer." They had picked out the engineering college and even the courses I should take. My Grandmother did not get drawn into this debate, but when I was leaving for college she gave me her support in a way I shall always be grateful for: "Follow your own star." It was the soundest educational advice she could have given. After all, if I had become an engineer I don't think I would have been too eager to cross a bridge of my own design.

Finally Sri Krishna says, *Yat tapasyasi:* "Whatever you suffer, make it an offering to Me." This is the crux of sādhana. It is not easy to forgive someone who is bristling with hostility. It is not a simple thing to help someone who irritates you and frustrates your attempts to mend an estranged relationship. Until we learn these skills, there can be a lot of anguish in going against our self-will when everything within us is crying out to let it have its way. But if we are to make progress on the spiritual path, we have no choice but to face this suffering and grow.

To use the language of the Compassionate Buddha, we all suffer from ourselves. Most of us are inclined to lay the blame for our problems at our parents' or our partner's doorstep, but the culprit is not 'he' or 'she'; it is 'me.' The day we can tell ourselves honestly, "You created this mess all by yourself; now you can get yourself out all by yourself," we have become strong enough to pull ourselves out.

शुभाशुभफलैरेवं मोक्ष्यसे कर्मबन्धनैः ।
संन्यासयोगयुक्तात्मा विमुक्तो मामुपैष्यसि ॥२८॥

*28. In this way you will be freed from the bondage
of karma, and from its results both pleasant and painful. Then, with your heart free, you will come to Me.*

All of us have had moments of regret when we look back upon the
past—particularly upon our early days, when we were ignorant of
the pitfalls of life and simply did not know which was the way to fulfillment. But on the spiritual path it is essential not to look back either in sorrow or in anger. Here the Gita can console and strengthen
us, because it takes into account how easy it is for us to make mistakes. Instead of condemning us or criticizing us, the Gita shows us
how we can correct those mistakes through the practice of meditation.

When we suffer from guilt about the past, it is very much like a
record player when the needle gets stuck. We are playing our favorite song, "I should have known better," and it keeps on repeating,
"I should have known better, I should have known better . . ." The
same thought goes round and round, and every time it goes round
the groove becomes deeper. At times like these we forget that there
is any other song in our repertoire. But there is a breathtakingly
simple solution to this problem: all we need to do is reach out, lift
up the needle, and move it to a new song.

This is what we do in meditation, when we recall our mental energy from dwelling on our thoughts. It is not the mistakes we have
made that torment us; it is our dwelling on those mistakes. All this
obsessive repetition charges them with power, and just as a demoli-
tion unit can go into a building and defuse a bomb, in practicing
meditation we can defuse a memory of its power to hold our attention and agitate us. When thoughts of the past are coming up—as
they will for almost all of us—what I would suggest is, don't pay any
attention to them, and don't let anyone else talk to you about them
either. It is very much like dealing with a distraction in meditation:
you don't fight it directly; you simply withdraw your attention from

the distraction by giving more concentration to the words of the passage. Here, instead of dwelling on your mistake and talking it over with all your friends, go for a long, fast walk repeating your mantram. You will find that this is all it takes to change the needle to a new, positive line of thinking.

But it's not enough if we simply repeat the mantram; we need to keep from putting the needle on that same old groove again. When we ask the Lord to forgive us, most people look upon it as a passive prayer: "Lord, forgive us, please." If we are going to keep on committing mistakes and saying, "Lord, forgive us, please," our whole life will be spent between erring and repenting, erring and repenting. From the little I know of Sri Krishna, he will say, "What about tomorrow?" He *will* forgive us; there is no end to his mercy. But as one physician used to say, "The Lord may forgive us our mistakes, but our nervous system will not." Every time we repeat a mistake, every time we dig the groove a little deeper, we are making it more difficult for our nervous system to change.

In my interpretation, therefore, forgiveness means learning to draw upon the deeper powers in our consciousness and change the wrong ways of thinking that have conditioned us to make these mistakes. No matter what we may have done in the past, it is always possible for us to change. That is why the mystics say that the Lord's forgiveness is always held out for us to take. But the choice to reach out and take it is left to us.

Most people in the modern world object strongly to the concept of divine punishment, because they think it means there is somebody in outer space meting out sentences with a firm hand. So instead of talking about sin and punishment, I prefer to talk about mistakes and consequences. It is the same thing; the only difference is in the language. Here the Compassionate Buddha's approach is very easy to understand. He would say when we are angry, we are punishing ourselves; anger is its own punishment. On the physical level, for example, when we are angry our respiration changes, and in the long run this may lead to asthma. Our digestion is affected, and after many years of this we can develop serious digestive problems. Even dandruff is like that. Dandruff is not inflicted by God; it is a light sentence which we impose on ourselves. When we have been eating wrong food, or smoking, or not getting enough exercise, we are working hard at giving ourselves a really stiff punishment, and the way to ask the Lord for forgiveness is to draw on the power released in meditation to give up smoking and change our wrong habits of eating and behaving so as to have a peaceful heart.

If you want to see the miracle of the Lord's forgiveness, you have only to look at how complete this change can be. To give you just one example, I have had friends who have given up alcohol after many years of heavy use, and I have been overwhelmed at the mercy of the Lord when I see how swiftly they can learn to relate to people well and overcome many of their physical disabilities after all those years of abuse. Even though we may have serious problems, none of us need throw up our hands in despair and say we can never stand straight again. Whatever the mistakes of our past are, however much they may have affected our body and mind, there is such resilience in our consciousness that by changing our ways, all of us can release ourselves in a large measure from the consequences of our past.

समोऽहं सर्वभूतेषु न मे द्वेष्योऽस्ति न प्रियः ।
ये भजन्ति तु मां भक्त्या मयि ते तेषु चाप्यहम्॥२९॥

29. I look upon all creatures equally; none are less dear to Me and none more dear. But those who worship Me with all their heart live in Me, and I come to life in them.

This verse is simple but very deep in its significance. In sweet words, the Lord tells Arjuna: "I have no favorites; race or sex, place of birth or social status make no difference to Me. All that is important is that your life be devoted to Me."

Arjuna looks at Sri Krishna quizzically. "Then why is it," he asks, "that you often say of a particular devotee *sa ca me priyah,* 'I am wildly in love with him, head over heels in love with her'?" So the Lord explains gently the relationship he has with those who are completely devoted to him. "Those who meditate on Me with all their heart, who try to see Me in every creature, live in my love and security completely." Then he adds, "I who am infinite, whom all the galaxies cannot contain, I live in such people too."

When we begin to realize the magnitude of this statement, we shall have profound veneration for our real Self, the divine spark within us. The Compassionate Buddha calls this body of ours a frail clay pot. Who can fathom the wonder of the Lord of the cosmos taking up residence in this brittle little vessel? The Hindu greeting *namas te* expresses this reverence for the Lord of Love, who dwells within each one of us. It means "I bow unto you"—not unto Jonathan Swift or Tom Jones, but to Him who is seated within Jonathan Swift, Tom Jones, and you and me.

अपि चेत्सुदुराचारो भजते मामनन्यभाक् ।
साधुरेव स मन्तव्यः सम्यग्व्यवसितो हि सः ॥३०॥
क्षिप्रं भवति धर्मात्मा शश्वच्छान्तिं निगच्छति ।
कौन्तेय प्रतिजानीहि न मे भक्तः प्रणश्यति ॥३१॥

30–31. Even a sinner becomes holy when he or she takes refuge in Me alone. In a short time that person is completely dedicated to the spiritual life and attains to boundless peace. Never forget this, Kaunteya: no one who is devoted to Me will ever come to harm.

These beautiful verses have been a source of consolation to millions of men and women down the ages, for they remind us that no matter what our past is like, even what our present is like, none of us is ever lost in the eyes of the Lord. All of us are only frail human beings—"born to trouble," as the Bible puts it, "as the sparks fly upward"—and all of us have committed mistakes in the past, mostly in our ignorance of the unity of life. That is human conditioning, which every one of us shares. But just as it is our nature to be liable to these mistakes, all of us have the inborn capacity—which is never lost—of erasing this futile writing on the wall which we ourselves have done through many years of wrong living.

When we really understand the implications of this approach, so loving and yet so practical, we will never again be oppressed by the burden of the past. During the many years in which I have been teaching meditation in this country, I have come into intimate contact with hundreds of thoughtful people, young and old, some of whom have led lives of no earthly benefit to anyone, not even themselves. It always touches me deeply to hear such people confide how lonely they have made themselves, how estranged from the loving support of those around them, how despairing of any chance to change. I do not pretend that their past has been flawless; I do not ask about their past at all. Instead, I remind them that no amount of mistakes can ever banish the Lord of Love from our hearts. He is always there, and because he is always there, we always have the choice to turn our backs on the past completely and learn to live in peace with ourselves and in harmony with those around us.

In other words, as Jesus puts it so tenderly, all of us are children of God, and however misguided our conduct may be, a loving father—or, as we would say in India, a loving mother—does not disavow his or her children. That is the deep appeal of Jesus' parable of the prodigal son. Here is a young man who has received his full legacy from his father and gone away to squander it all in riotous living, painting the towns red from one end of Judea to the other. Naturally, as the wheel of his deeds begins to turn against him, he eventually finds himself alone and friendless, utterly without resources, without even the means to feed himself. Then he understands the enormity of what he has done, and stricken with grief, he decides to return to his father's house—not for a second legacy, but merely to work for his father as a servant rather than starve in a foreign land. And it is a very moving scene when Jesus tells us that the father, in the joy of seeing his son again, runs out to meet him on the road, and embraces him, and returns the young man to his full legacy with great love and ceremony, saying in words that we can remember always: "This my son was dead, and is alive again; he was lost, and now he is found."

There is no question here of the nature of our mistakes. In every country, in every tradition, the annals of mysticism are filled with stories of men and women whose errors in life may have been much worse than ours, but who have managed to reverse their lives completely once they glimpse this birthright of forgiveness within us all. Sometimes it is those with the greatest capacity for doing harm to themselves and others who become tremendous channels for good, for when it is harnessed, all their aggression, all their militancy, all their destructiveness can enable them to go very far on the spiritual path. I think it is St. Teresa who says beautifully that the sun of God's love is always shining, and though we may have kept the curtains drawn for a whole lifetime, filling our hearts with darkness, once we reach out and open the curtains there is no darkness so deep that it will not be dispelled by the brightness of that light.

But it is not enough to say that we are all children of the Lord; we have to learn to act as children of the Lord. In my ancestral home in India, when the younger girls were just learning to cook on our wood stoves, they would sometimes spill a little curry or burn a little rice, and their mothers or aunts would sometimes criticize them for being all thumbs. On such occasions, my Grandmother would always say for the benefit of both generations, "In order to learn to cook, you have to burn a little and spill a little." But then she used to add to the girls, "But if you never do anything but burn and spill, you will never learn to cook." It is very much the same in our lives too. I have great sympathy for people when they come and tell me of the mistakes they have committed, because I know how easy it is for all of us to make such mistakes ourselves. But where I get bewildered is when they go on committing those same mistakes without doing their best not ever to commit them again.

All of us, as human beings, have the marvelous capacity to relearn all our patterns of living, to change every liability into a strength. I am always amazed at how quickly this transformation can take place. Here is someone who has been eating unhealthy food for years, and in a few months he is able to change his habits completely. There is someone who has been suffering from terrible bouts of anger, and after a few years of meditation she has already begun to change anger into compassion and hatred into love. Even if we have been in the slough of despond for fifty years, we need not work fifty years to get out of it. This is divine mercy. Even though we may have been very selfish, even if we have developed all kinds of unpleasant habits over the years, such as smoking, or drinking, or always brooding on ourselves, Sri Krishna says, *Kshipram bhavati dharmātmā:* we swiftly become the soul of goodness, often even stronger in body and mind than we were before these negative habits began to drain us of our strength.

As our spiritual awareness deepens and we begin to see ourselves more clearly, there will be times when past mistakes will swim into our vision and do their best to consume us in guilt or regret. At such times, it is essential to repeat the mantram and turn all our attention outwards, away from ourselves. Analyzing our mistakes and dwelling on how to repay them is of no earthly benefit at all. But here I can offer one consoling application of the law of karma. If, when you were in Milwaukee, you happened to say something insulting about your girlfriend's dog, it is not necessary to go to Milwaukee and find your old girlfriend or her dog to make amends. Every dog you treat with kindness will be a proxy for that dog. If you have treated a particular person badly, even if you can no longer win that person's forgiveness, you can still win the forgiveness of yourself, of the Lord of Love within, by bearing with everyone who treats you badly and doing your best never to treat anyone else badly again. This is the tremendous practical implication of St. Francis's words, "It is in pardoning that we are pardoned." Whatever we have done, we can always make amends for it without ever looking backwards in guilt or sorrow.

Here the question I like to hear is, How do we do this? We are convinced of the folly of looking backwards, of analyzing our weaknesses or our guilt; now how do we go about changing ourselves so that all of these habits can be unlearned? This is the purpose of meditation and its allied disciplines, which gradually give us the wisdom to see what changes to make in ourselves and the will and skillfulness to translate these changes into our daily lives.

First there is the physical level, which is very much the level of the body and the senses. As the Buddha would say, we are not punished for our sins, we are punished *by* our sins, and I think that many of the serious diseases which have become so widespread today—heart disease, hypertension, digestive and breathing disorders, even many kinds of cancer—are influenced by things like poor diet and smoking and environmental pollution, which are entirely within our means to avoid. Even if our problems are not of this kind, a healthy body and a relaxed, resilient nervous system are essential if we are to overcome the emotional problems to which all of us are subject in some measure.

So the first step we must take once we take to meditation is to change our way of living. To begin with, our attitude towards food begins to change. Instead of eating what benefits only the palate, what appeals to our taste, we begin to eat what benefits the body. Then our whole attitude towards exercise begins to change. Where we used to drive to the corner to post a letter, we now begin to walk everywhere—after breakfast, during our morning break, every time we get a chance. Walking briskly while repeating the mantram is excellent exercise; it can go a long way towards releasing tension, and as one doctor I was reading says, virtually every muscle in the body is utilized except the jaws. And whenever we get some free time—a day off, or a weekend, or a summer vacation—instead of doing something that pleases no one but ourselves, we can give our time and our energy to people or worthwhile organizations who are in need. All these are changes we can make in our external lives which strengthen us immensely to turn our backs upon the past.

But external changes like these are only the beginning. On the emotional side, even those with strong, healthy bodies, who lead very temperate lives, are not immune to the restlessness, the loneliness, the insecurity that we see all around us today. Here, meditation and the allied disciplines can give us such peace of mind that negative states such as insecurity and depression can be banished from our lives forever. This takes more time than physical changes, but it is within the reach of every one of us. Then, when we can make these changes, the Lord says, *Shashvacchāntim nigacchati:* in a very short time our hearts will be at peace, and we will live at peace not only with others but with ourselves.

Arjuna is overwhelmed by these statements, because he sees in this promise of Self-realization how infinite is the mercy of the Lord.

Arjuna's mother is Kuntī, and this mighty warrior has become so like a little child in his gratitude and his love that Sri Krishna calls him by a very tender name: *Kaunteya,* 'Kuntī's child.' He says, *Kaunteya, pratijānīhi:* "Always remember"—when the senses get turbulent, when the ego becomes rebellious, when the world threatens to overpower you—*na me bhaktah pranashyati:* "those who are devoted to Me, who meditate on Me, will never come to harm." It is a promise which has been verified by so many mystics that we can trust it as an eternal spiritual law.

मां हि पार्थ व्यपाश्रित्य येऽपि स्युः पापयोनयः ।
स्त्रियो वैश्यास्तथा शूद्रास्तेऽपि यान्ति परां गतिम् ॥३२॥
किं पुनर्ब्राह्मणाः पुण्या भक्ता राजर्षयस्तथा ।
अनित्यमसुखं लोकमिमं प्राप्य भजस्व माम् ॥३३॥

32. All those who take refuge in Me, whatever their birth, race, or sex, will attain the supreme goal; this realization can be attained even by those whom society scorns.
33. Kings and sages too seek this goal with devotion. Therefore, having been born in this transient and forlorn world, give all your love to Me.

No matter who we are or what our past, every one of us can become aware of our real Self, the Ātman, which is beyond any barrier life can erect—nationality, race, sex, social status, anything.

In India, there is a story about a poor peasant boy who came from one of the so-called lower castes. This boy was a great lover of Lord Shiva, always repeating Shiva's name and meditating on him. So when it came time for the annual festival to celebrate the glory of Shiva, this boy desperately wanted to go. But all his days were committed to working in the rice fields of his landlord, whose permission he had to obtain before he could go. The landlord was a very wealthy man but not a very spiritual one, and he just laughed at the boy's request: "Imagine you wanting to go to the Shiva festival, which is usually attended by brahmins! What do you know about the scriptures?"

The boy replied, "I don't know anything about the scriptures. I can't even read or write. But I have such love in my heart for Shiva that even the sound of his name thrills me."

"That's all very well," said the landlord, "but the rice fields are ready for harvesting and I need you here." Then he added in an unkind joke, "Have the harvest completely finished by tomorrow morning, and I will give you permission to go."

Now, normally a rice harvest takes many days of backbreaking labor, and there was no way in which even a small part of this work could be done overnight. But the boy was undaunted, for his landlord had given him an opportunity that a boy of his caste would ordinarily never get. He went home, sat in his hut in deep meditation, and asked Lord Shiva from the very depths of his heart: "I have such a good landlord; he has promised to let me go to your temple and celebrate your glory if I can harvest all the rice from the fields by tomorrow morning. Help me, O Shiva, so that I may go to your festival." Then, after he had laid his prayer at the feet of the Lord, the boy was so full of faith that without any doubts troubling him further, he lay down and fell asleep.

Early the next morning an excited crowd of villagers gathered outside his hut. Not only had the fields been completely harvested; the rice bundles were neatly tied and arranged on the bullock carts, ready to go. Everybody was crying, "Miracle! Miracle!" Even the landlord was profoundly moved. He asked the boy to forgive him and to explain how this miracle had been performed. The boy replied in utter guilelessness: "What is there so miraculous about it? I love Shiva, and he is the Lord of the universe. I just told him I had a little job to do before I could go to his celebration." This is the faith that harvests rice fields and moves mountains, and it may be attained by any of us, no matter what our birth or background or social status.

Today, however, most of us find it so easy to support the underdog that I would like to say a good word in favor of the upper dog, too. Just because someone is cultured, or wealthy, or has led a good life, he or she is not barred from going far on the spiritual path. In my experience, those who have undergone all the discipline it takes to become scholars, doctors, engineers, lawyers, artists, and scientists can take to meditation very easily. All they have to do is take the energy, concentration, and effort they used to achieve excellence in their field and turn it towards the supreme goal of life. Wherever you find people who can concentrate with absorption, you have found promising potential spiritual aspirants. Once they understand how to harness their capacities through the practice of meditation, such people can grow to great spiritual heights.

मन्मना भव मद्भक्तो मद्याजी मां नमस्कुरु ।
मामेवैष्यसि युक्त्वैवमात्मानं मत्परायणः ॥३४॥

34. Fill your mind with Me; serve Me; worship Me always. Seeking Me in your heart, you will at last be united with Me.

This is the refrain of the entire Bhagavad Gita. The Lord sums up the supreme secret of the spiritual life in one word, *manmanā:* "Let your mind be filled with Me." Let your heart dwell only on the Lord and let nothing else distract you. In your dreams, see the Lord; in your sleep, hear his voice. Under no circumstances must you ever forget him. In the deeper stages of meditation, the Lord will put you to some simple tests to see if you have unified your consciousness in him. He may strike a great blow at you, and when your whole being is agitated he will say, "Now let me see you meditate." It is a stiff, honest test. The mind may rise in tides of turmoil and object, "How can I meditate when you have struck at me like this? I'm completely stunned." If that is so, you haven't passed the test. But if you have been meditating steadily and enthusiastically over a long period of time, your mind will remain centered on the Lord no matter what blows life deals you. Whatever reverses come your way, your heart will always be filled with love. Then the Lord will say, "You pass." When he says that, all your problems pass, too.

Under no circumstances should we forget that the Lord alone is worthy of our deepest love. We should never sacrifice our meditation for the sake of any other interest. When we base our life on meditation, our health, our security, our intellectual and creative capacities *have* to improve; there is no other alternative. If we try in this way to fill our hearts with love for him, we will be united with him without any doubt at all.

इति राजविद्याराजगुह्ययोगो नाम नवमोऽध्यायः ॥९॥

CHAPTER TEN

Divine Splendor

श्री भगवानुवाच
भूय एव महाबाहो श्रृणु मे परमं वचः ।
यत्तेऽहं प्रीयमाणाय वक्ष्यामि हितकाम्यया ॥१॥
न मे विदुः सुरगणाः प्रभवं न महर्षयः ।
अहमादिर्हि देवानां महर्षीणां च सर्वशः ॥२॥
यो मामजमनादिं च वेत्ति लोकमहेश्वरम् ।
असंमूढः स मर्त्येषु सर्वपापैः प्रमुच्यते ॥३॥

SRI KRISHNA:

*1. Listen further, Arjuna, to my supreme teaching,
which gives you such joy. Desiring your welfare, O
great-armed warrior, I will tell you more.
2. Neither gods nor sages know my origin, for I am
the source from which the gods and sages come.
3. Whoever knows Me as the Lord of all creation,
without birth or beginning, knows the truth and
frees himself from all evil.*

When I was a boy, growing up in village India, I used to belong to
the Boy Scouts. We were very much like Boy Scouts everywhere:
we had the same khaki shorts and shirts, and a little patrol ribbon—
ours was an elephant—and even a tenderfoot badge. The only difference was that the official uniform included a green turban.

Not far from our village there was a dense forest, and one of the
things we used to do as Boy Scouts was tracking. We would divide
into two groups and then one group would go hide in the forest,

leaving all sorts of clues about where they had gone—tearing off one leaf and placing it next to another, breaking a twig in a particular way, things like that. Then the rest of us, after a decent wait, had to go through the forest very observantly and try to find and interpret all these little signs. We would roam around in our khaki shorts and our green turbans, peering closely at everything, and now and then someone would spot something out of the ordinary and exclaim, "Aha! That's not nature; that's some Boy Scout!" I wasn't very good at this game, but fortunately there were others who were quite skillful and we always worked as a team. At last, after we had found several of these signs, one of these more skillful chaps would look up into a tree, squint his eyes, and say, "Hey, that's not a monkey; that's our Scout leader!"

This is what the Lord has done; he has strewn little signs of his presence throughout the universe, and the person who is very observant, who is very spiritual, will always see these signs and recognize where the Lord is to be found. Most of us see these signs but pass over them; we do not recognize them for what they are. But as our eyes begin to clear through the practice of meditation, when we see someone being extremely patient, someone who can listen quietly to criticism without retaliating or losing his temper, we will think, "Aha! That's not my friend Richard; that is the Lord in Richard."

Richard may leave broken twigs of patience, torn leaves of kindness, but the men and women who have realized God leave big signposts of His presence everywhere they go. There is a marvelous story about a man looking for the Buddha the way one follows the tracks of an animal in the jungle. He went around asking people everywhere, and whenever he found a person whose life had been transformed he would exclaim to himself, "Those are the tracks of a really big elephant!"

This chapter is rather like a divine tracking manual, in which Sri Krishna tells Arjuna a few of his favorite signs. Though the Lord is present everywhere, the expression of his presence varies throughout the infinite variety of his creation. Wherever perfection is approached, his glory is revealed a little more—among people, among trees, among stars, in all the qualities of life. As the Persian mystic Jamī writes:

> To display His eternal attributes
> In their inexhaustible variety,
> The Lord made the green fields of time and space
> And the living garden of the cosmos,
> So that each branch, leaf, and fruit reveal
> His innumerable glories.

बुद्धिर्ज्ञानमसंमोहः क्षमा सत्यं दमः शमः ।
सुखं दुःखं भवोऽभावो भयं चाभयमेव च ॥४॥
अहिंसा समता तुष्टिस्तपो दानं यशोऽयशः ।
भवन्ति भावा भूतानां मत्त एव पृथग्विधाः ॥५॥

4–5. The different qualities found in living creatures have their source in Me: discrimination, wisdom, understanding, forgiveness, truth, self-control, and peace of mind; the dualities of pleasure and pain, birth and death, honor and dishonor; nonviolence, charity, equanimity, contentment, and perseverance in spiritual disciplines.

All the faculties of life have their origin in the Lord: not only pleasure but pain too, not only honor but dishonor too. It is not that the Lord is capricious or unloving; these are distinctions that we make ourselves. Once we make ourselves whole, we see everything as whole, which is what it means to see the Lord everywhere. But until then, as long as there is division in our minds, everything is split into two: good and bad, right and wrong, pleasant and unpleasant, friend and foe.

There is a story by Edgar Allan Poe called "The Purloined Letter" in which a certain cabinet minister steals a letter and then threatens to blackmail its owner. The Paris police almost take the man's apartment apart looking for the letter—inside the vases, up the chimneys, behind the walls, everywhere they can think of—but none of them is able to find even a clue. Only the amateur detective

Dupin is able to guess where it is: in the most obvious place possible, lying on the man's desk in front of everyone's eyes.

This is what the mind has done to us. The Lord is all around us,
but we cannot see him as long as we have to depend on the mind,
which has an unfortunate obsession with cutting everything up into
two. It is pointless to blame the mind for this; it cannot help itself.
Do you remember Charlie Chaplin in *Modern Times*? He plays a
worker on an assembly line, whose sole job all day long is to take
his wrench and tighten one particular bolt a quarter turn. After a
day of this, doing the same thing over and over again, even on his
way home he walks along tightening everything a quarter turn. This
is how the mind is. It has its tool chest of saws for every possible
purpose, and every time it runs into something—objects, ideas, perceptions, people—it pulls out a hacksaw or a pocket chain saw and
saws that thing into two. That is all that is required; we cannot see
the unity of life anywhere.

In practice, all that this collection of saws amounts to is likes and
dislikes. As your meditation deepens and you begin to see the ways
of your mind more clearly, you will notice that there is a constant
chorus of likes and dislikes going on inside. Usually we are not
aware of this chorus because it goes on beneath the surface of consciousness. But if we could listen in on a little of what literary critics
call the "stream of consciousness"—really it is more a stream of
unconsciousness—we would be embarrassed to see how petty this
chorus can be. Just watch your mind when you respond to a person;
what is it you are really responding to? "I don't like his walk; it
looks too pompous. I don't like her voice; it grates on my nerves."
What about your walk? What about your voice? Once, when I was
responsible for recording something for All India Radio, I played
back one of the programs for a student to hear. She listened to it all
with a rather pained expression, and afterwards she commented,
"That's a really unpleasant voice. I don't like it." The voice was her
own; she hadn't recognized it at all.

As long as the mind feels compelled to keep us posted on its opinions like this, consciousness has to be divided, which means that we
are going to be tormented by vacillation and lapses in everything:

in our loyalty, in our patience, in our security, in our capacity to see clearly and make wise decisions anywhere in daily living. All the qualities in this verse have a role to play in helping us see through this fog of separateness, called *moha* in Sanskrit. *Moha* literally means 'delusion.' *Sammoha* is 'super-delusion,' and the word used here is *asammoha,* 'without any trace of delusion,' which means complete awareness of the unity of life. I have translated *asammoha* as "wisdom" because in its practical application, it means that you will never be deluded by anything the world has to offer—money, pleasure, power, prestige, anything.

Sammoha is the distorting medium of self-will through which all of us perceive life. Self-willed people go around in this kind of ego-fog always; that is why they are constantly bumping into people and running down blind alleys. Everything is distorted: friends appear menacing, harmful activities promise fulfillment, and the road to happiness that looks so shimmering in the fog turns out to be the road to the dump. As your vision begins to clear through the practice of meditation, you really have to rub your eyes. It will scarcely seem like the same world, and yet nothing will have changed except your way of seeing.

One of the most practical ways I know for clearing our eyes of this fog of suspicion and self-will is *kshamā*. Kshamā is not only forgiveness, it is patience, forbearance, and understanding too, all wrapped into one. No matter how much we feel we have been wronged, no matter how much we feel others may not appreciate us, we should learn to be patient and to forgive—not only because it helps those around us, but because it helps us to free ourselves from the pall of suspicion and resentment. Gradually, as our eyes become clearer, this can save us a good deal of embarrassment. Because of the distorting mirror of self-will, most of us are liable to complain at some time or other: "Why is so-and-so always rude to me? I said hello to her this morning and she didn't even answer." It is only when we learn that the lady in question had received bad news that morning, or was up all night with her baby, that we realize we had not been wronged at all. It was only because we were so wrapped up in ourselves that we took her silence personally.

Bearing with people, especially those who really do cause us problems, is the essence of forgiveness. It is not particularly helpful to do this with a feeling of martyrdom, either; we need to bear with people cheerfully. But this does not mean making ourselves into a doormat. Letting people take undue advantage of us is not helpful for them any more than it is for us. Instead, we can learn to bear with them and at the same time improve the situation with their help.

When it is necessary to show our love by expressing disapproval, we should learn to disagree constructively. Sri Ramakrishna advises us to hiss gently when necessary, but not to bite. This is particularly applicable in relationships with children, who can be ingenious at needling us to see how far they can go. What they are trying to say is, "Hiss at us so we'll know when to stop." I saw the value of a well-timed hiss when I was out for a walk with our dog Muka, who tries to play with every creature he sees. He found a snake in the garden and offered to play with it. The snake was doing whatever snakes do early in the morning, and when Muka tried to get it to play there was a sharp *hsss!* and Muka came hopping out of the grass like a jackrabbit.

The secret of seeing through *sammoha* is in not dwelling on ourselves. The more we think about what *we* enjoy and don't enjoy, what *we* want and don't want, the more we are going to be caught in this net of separateness, cut off from others and from ourselves. So Sri Krishna says, *Tushti:* "Be content with what life sends you." Don't be a beggar, sitting with your little tin cup and begging of life, "Please give me a few cents of pleasure, or at least don't give me any pain." Don't ask always what you can get from life, but *dānam:* ask what you can give. Stand up to your full height and give freely to those around you—your time, your resources, your talents, your extra clothes or vegetables from your garden, whatever you have. It doesn't matter whether the gift is simple or modest; what matters is that it be given freely, wholeheartedly, without any reservations, without even the left hand knowing what the right hand is doing. You are not wealthy simply because you have a lot, you are wealthy when you have given a lot away; and the more you give, the more you will have to give—not in money, but in the richness of your life.

It is not enough in life to do no harm; we should be able to contribute to life wherever we go. In the Hindu tradition we have a story about a man who was the perfect model of respectability, who always did what the letter of the law demanded of him. He never offended anybody or injured anybody; he always kept up with the Ramaswamis, and when he was called on to give a speech he always had a grand audience, because he used to tell them just what they wanted to hear. When the time came for this man to pay his final bill, he was taken before Chitragupta, a kind of cosmic auditor in the Hindu scriptures. Chitragupta looked up the man's record and there it was, not a single entry on the debit page. Chitragupta was really impressed, because even in the case of the great mystics there are debit entries, sometimes rather a lot of them. "Wow!" he said. "I've never seen anyone like you." Then he turned to the credit page and stared in astonishment, because that page was completely blank too. Chitragupta just stood there and scratched his head; he didn't know what to do. The man had never let anybody down, never helped anybody; never offended anybody, never loved anybody—he couldn't be sent to heaven, but on the other hand he couldn't be sent anywhere else either.

Finally Chitragupta took the chap to Brahmā, the god of creation in the Hindu Trinity. "You made this guy," he said; "what shall I do with him?" Brahmā looked at the statute books and couldn't find anything to cover the case, so he said, "Send him over to Krishna." And Sri Krishna said, "The buck stops here." He examined the record very carefully and there, almost illegible, was an ancient credit entry: "Gave two cents to a beggar at the age of six." "There," Sri Krishna said; "return his two cents and send him back to try again."

महर्षयः सप्त पूर्वे चत्वारो मनवस्तथा ।
मद्भावा मानसा जाता येषां लोक इमाः प्रजाः ॥ ६ ॥

6. The seven great sages and the four ancient ancestors were born from my mind and received my power. From them came all the creatures of this world.

The Hindu tradition has a gift for personalizing the forces of nature and of the mind, and to me these seven great sages and the four ancient ancestors of all living creatures represent the laws by which the universe and life evolved. As ruler of the cosmos, the Lord delegates his duties to specific powers. These are not just the laws of the physical world. In Hindu and Buddhist thought, there is no real distinction between the world outside us and the world of thoughts and feelings within, and the same unity that keeps the outer world running smoothly governs the world within us too.

Whenever we try to harm each other we are violating this law of unity. Today it should be clear to any sensitive man or woman that when we inflict suffering on others, we only destroy ourselves. Our world today is like a jet airliner without a pilot, in which most people are so busy trying to save their own seats that they can't be bothered to think about the plane. We are prepared to fight all the other passengers and even to rip our seat out of the floor if that is what it takes to have it all to ourselves.

All of us can play an important part in the conquest of violence by throwing our full weight behind peaceful, effective programs for eliminating the situations from which violence arises. But most important, we need to do everything we can to remove every trace of hostility and resentment in ourselves. The violence that is flaring up all around us on our streets and on our campuses is not so much the result of social conditions as the inevitable expression of the hostility in our hearts. Hostility is one of the most infectious diseases I know of, and whenever we indulge in a violent act or even in hostile words or expressions, we are passing this disease on to those around us.

To take just one example, look at what can happen in even a little family quarrel. When we quarrel at home, it is not just a domestic problem; we are contributing to turmoil everywhere. Suppose Tom Jones gets up on the wrong side of the bed, sits down at the breakfast table, and dares Amelia to tell him where she ever learned to make coffee. Amelia, being upsettable, gets upset. Tom goes off to work in a black cloud, and just to make sure that his day will be irritating, he keeps on rehearsing what he's going to tell Amelia when he gets home. And Amelia, who is doing the same thing, is still so upset two hours later that she makes an unkind remark to the clerk in the store, who takes it out on the next ten customers.

These are small things, but over the day, day after day, they all add up. In the language of Hindu psychology, all these little moments of irritation and resentment build up into a samskāra, which means that they become a habitual response to everything around us. When a samskāra like this becomes deeply ingrained, almost anything can trigger a hostile reaction, often without any rhyme or reason. You have only to pick up the morning paper to see how commonplace this kind of reaction has become. That is why it is so important for all of us to learn to respond to hostility with patience and good will, and never to say or do anything that adds to this chain reaction of anger.

This applies not only to our words and actions; it applies even to the look on our face. It is said that the English satirist Jonathan Swift enjoyed his pessimism so much that he used to wear mourning on his birthday and go around with a scowl. Probably he thought it was no one's business but his own. But depression is everybody's business. In my teaching days in India, when I would remind a student that he was looking a little gloomy, he would object, "But sir, it's *my* face." I would reply, "Yes, but it's we who have to look at it." Not even the look on our face is our own business; all these things affect the people around us.

एतां विभूतिं योगं च मम यो वेत्ति तत्त्वतः ।
सोऽविकम्पेन योगेन युज्यते नात्र संशयः ॥७॥
अहं सर्वस्य प्रभवो मत्तः सर्वं प्रवर्तते ।
इति मत्वा भजन्ते मां बुधा भावसमन्विताः ॥८॥
मच्चित्ता मद्गतप्राणा बोधयन्तः परस्परम् ।
कथयन्तश्च मां नित्यं तुष्यन्ति च रमन्ति च ॥९॥

7. Whoever understands my power and the mystery of my manifestations comes without doubt to be united with Me.

*8. I am the source from which all creatures evolve.
The wise remember this and worship Me with loving
devotion.
9. Their thoughts are all absorbed in Me, and all
their vitality flows to Me. Seeing Me in one another,
talking about Me always, they are happy and fulfilled.*

In Sanskrit there is a vivid name for the Lord, *Prānadā*, 'he who
gives us *prāna*.' Prāna is energy, power, in the most basic sense of
the word. All forms of energy in the universe are only different
manifestations of prāna, which is one and indivisible. It is by prāna
that the sun burns, the clouds rain, and the wind blows; it is by
prāna that cells reproduce, the eyes see, the mind thinks, and the
heart loves. Physicists throw light on this when they say that behind
all matter is a field of energy, a unified field of forces. The language
is different, but the idea they are expressing is the same: it is all the
same prāna, whether we class its action as physical, mental, emotional, or spiritual.

The practical application of this is that it is the Lord, Prānadā,
who gives us this prāna. As the Prashna Upanishad tells us, "Prāna
is born of the Self. As a man casts a shadow, the Self casts prāna
into the body at the time of birth." Therefore, the mystics ask,
where do we get the idea that anything can be ours? We hang on
dearly to our car, our savings, our stereo tape deck, yet not even the
life in our bodies is ours; everything belongs to the Lord. So a great
mystic like Shankara will tell the Lord, "What is there to renounce
in this world? There is nothing here that I can call my own; everything is already yours."

Do you see the humor of this? It is as if I were to go up to my
friend Jeff and say, "Jeff, I renounce your guitar once and for all."
He would say, "What do you mean? It doesn't belong to you, it belongs to me." So where is the difficulty in renouncing it? Whatever
we give up on the spiritual path, this is all it amounts to: we are
simply letting the Lord know we understand that everything has always been his.

As we come to realize this on a deeper and deeper level—not intellectually, but in our hearts, so that it is reflected in our daily living—a great deal of the tension in our lives will begin to dissolve. When we want to have something that cannot be ours, we are putting ourselves on the horns of an impossible dilemma, and naturally there is tension below the surface level of our consciousness. This kind of constant tension wastes a good deal of prāna. It is very much like leaving the lights of your car on all night: when you get up in the morning, you find your battery is dead. That is what is happening when we go through life always feeling a little under par, a little unequal to what the day may bring; prāna is continuously draining out in the basement of our consciousness.

In deep meditation, however, we learn to get hold of the switches of our prāna, which means getting control of our desires. Only then do we have the choice to turn the switch off and conserve the energy it would drain. Whenever we can do this, the results are immediate; the entire nervous system relaxes a little, and the very next day the battery will have more power. Eventually we get our hands on the master switch of the whole circuit, which is sex. It is a very satisfying state of affairs. If we choose to, we can close the switch and all our vital capacity will be at our disposal. But we can also choose to leave the switch off, which is like pulling the plugs of all the appliances in the house. There is no outflow of prāna anywhere, which means that every part of the body is at rest.

Then, as this verse puts it, all our prāna is flowing to the Lord, who is within. The immense security of this state cannot be described; it has to be experienced to be understood. You know from your own experience that there is no limit to the power of the Lord within you, so there is no limit to your love or your capacity for service. The Hindu scriptures describe this state as *pūrnatā*—complete fullness, in which nothing can ever be lacking. There is no better example of the Lord's sense of humor: in giving up what was never ours to begin with, we are filled with everything; all our deep desires are fulfilled.

तेषां सततयुक्तानां भजतां प्रीतिपूर्वकम् ।
ददामि बुद्धियोगं तं येन मामुपयान्ति ते ॥१०॥
तेषामेवानुकम्पार्थमहमज्ञानजं तमः ।
नाशयाम्यात्मभावस्थो ज्ञानदीपेन भास्वता ॥११॥

*10. To those steadfast in love and service I give
spiritual wisdom, so that they may come to Me.
11. Out of compassion I destroy the darkness of
their ignorance. From within them I light the lamp
of wisdom and dispel all darkness from their lives.*

With infinite tenderness, the Lord lets it dawn on us only gradually
that we are not separate, that we belong entirely to him. If this realization were to come overnight, ordinary people like you and me
would not be able to withstand it; it would be more than our nervous systems could bear. That is why the Lord is so gentle with us;
he spreads the transformation from separateness to unity out over
many years so that all these changes in the mind and body can take
place gradually, often at such a deep level that we are not even
aware they are taking place until we look back and remember how
we were some years before.

I like to illustrate this gradual ascent to unity with the trip up to
my home high on the Blue Mountain in South India. The scorching
heat of the Indian summer begins early in March, and in the old
days, when I was a professor in Central India, I used to count the
days until summer vacation when I could leave the crowded cities
and the hot, dusty air of the plains behind me. On the very same
evening of the last working day I would be on the train for Madras,
and we used to pull into Madras Central Station twenty-four hours
later just in time to catch the Blue Mountain Express. It was a long,
hot, tiring journey, and it was a very satisfying moment when I
could open my eyes after the morning's meditation and see the Blue
Mountain beckoning on the horizon as we reached Coimbatore.

But even though there would be just fifty miles more to go, the
journey would be far from over. At Coimbatore I had to leave the

train and get onto a bus, and for a long, long time the bus would
make its way slowly along the twenty-five mile road to Mettupa-
layam at the foot of the Blue Mountain. If you don't know the road
and close your eyes, it's easy to imagine that you're climbing. But
all you have to do is open your eyes and look out the window at the
cars and roadside merchants and bullock carts to see that you are
still very much on the plains. It is a dull, dreary journey, with nothing to recommend it except that it has to be put behind you. The
real climb is yet to begin.

Then, as the bus begins to climb, the scenery changes, and the
road becomes beautiful. First you see areca nut palms, swaying
gracefully in the wind, and then the dense forests of the foothills,
full of wild animals like tigers and elephants. Then, as the bus
climbs above three thousand feet, there are rich coffee plantations
and terraced tea gardens, dotted with silver firs whose leaves sparkle
in the sun. And there was a particular point where I used to feel the
cool, invigorating air of the mountains. It was almost as if I could
draw a line where that change would occur. The hot, dry, dusty air
of the plains would suddenly leave us, and my whole body and mind
would drink in the cool, bracing air of the hills.

It is very much like that on the path of meditation. For a long,
long time you are on level ground. You *are* traveling forward, but
it's still on level ground; the air is still dry and dusty, and you get
gas fumes occasionally. But all this time, though you may think that
you are getting nowhere, you are building up momentum for the
climb ahead. It is only after you have been very diligent about your
meditation, after you have been very loyal in keeping your eyes always on the goal and very resolute in observing the disciplines of
the spiritual life, that the scenery will begin to change. But change
it surely will, and these changes will be reflected in every aspect of
your daily living. It is a sure sign that you are entering the foothills
and beginning to leave the plains behind. At work, you may find
that you can get along with someone who always seemed to special-
ize in rubbing you the wrong way. When you go into a bookstore,
instead of looking for books on literary criticism or getting glued to
a sensational novel, you will begin to ask if there is a new edition of

the Bhagavad Gita or an anthology of mystical poetry. And instead of going to restaurants where food lacking in nutritional value is served at outrageous prices, you will find yourself looking for vegetarian restaurants where the food is nutritious and the prices are within range.

At first your family may look askance at the way your life is changing, and your friends may raise their eyebrows at your flagging interest in old pursuits. If you don't have a certain amount of detachment from your opinions, this criticism may be difficult to take. At home in Berkeley you may be calm and true to your convictions, but as you walk slowly up the driveway to your parents' home, your security begins to waver. Then the door opens and the head of the household greets you with, "What's this I hear about meditation?" All security vanishes. You become either apologetic or defensive, state your case too vehemently, and find yourself in a very difficult position. But as you begin to gain security, you will be able to answer gently but firmly, "Yes, I'm trying to live a spiritual life, and I think it will benefit all of you, too." They may never have heard of the Bhagavad Gita; they may give an embarrassed cough and say, "That's not the life for us"; but they will begin to respect your efforts. After a while, when they see that you can be secure in the face of opposition and ridicule, that you can be true to your convictions and still keep your sense of humor, their critical remarks will change. Your father will tell your mother, "I never thought he had this in him"; your mother may even begin to tell her friends, "We might be able to take a leaf from her book."

During this first half of the ascent we have to travel under our own power. We have to make all the decisions ourselves; we have to strengthen our will and turn our backs on all sorts of temptations. It is only after this first part of the climb has been accomplished, after we have prepared ourselves, that we find the air becoming fresh and exhilarating. Then, slowly, during the second half of the ascent, we begin to realize that there is an inner power not our own which is drawing us forward. It is almost like reaching five thousand feet and then looking down from a narrow path to see how awesome the precipice is; one slip could plunge us to disaster. It makes us realize how miraculously we have been protected by the Lord all along the path. And though we can see the sheer, rocky peaks rising above us, we come to have a quiet faith that the same grace that has brought us this far will give us the support and inspiration we need for making the most difficult, most dangerous part of the climb which lies ahead.

Finally, at the very end of the spiritual ascent, we will reach a point beyond which we cannot go by our own effort. Though we must do everything we can to purify ourselves completely, the great mystics all testify, it is not possible for a human being to be finally united with the Lord by any amount of willing; it is up to the Lord to draw us to him if and when he chooses. This is a period of joyful agony, of watching and waiting as a bride waits for her bridegroom, for as Jesus says, the Lord will come as unexpectedly as a thief in the night. But finally, when we least expect it, the auspicious moment of union comes. Then, the Hindu mystics say, it is as if a lamp is lit in a temple which has been dark for many years: one minute the room is full of darkness; the next minute every corner is ablaze with light.

अर्जुन उवाच
परं ब्रह्म परं धाम पवित्रं परमं भवान् ।
पुरुषं शाश्वतं दिव्यमादिदेवमजं विभुम् ॥१२॥
आहुस्त्वामृषयः सर्वे देवर्षिर्नारदस्तथा ।
असितो देवलो व्यासः स्वयं चैव ब्रवीषि मे ॥१३॥

ARJUNA:

12–13. All the great sages and seers—Nārada, Asita, Devala, and Vyāsa, too—have called you the supreme Brahman, the highest abode, the supreme purifier, the self-luminous, eternal spirit, first among the gods, unborn and infinite. Now you have declared these things to me yourself.

Arjuna's words here emphasize the unity of all religions. All the great spiritual teachers speak of the same Reality and inspire us to strive for the same supreme goal. All have come to tell us of the divine spark within us. But for some curious reason, it is very difficult for us to accept our divine nature. This has always puzzled me. We pay money for books about how destructive we are; we stand in queues to buy magazines that emphasize our capacity for making trouble; we go to encounter groups where we agitate each other over our weaknesses. Then, when Jesus comes to tell us that the kingdom of heaven is within us, we say, "There must be some mistake." It is to convince us that our real Self is always pure and eternal that men and women of God keep arising among us and repeating the good news, that the source of all joy and security is right within.

सर्वमेतद्द्तं मन्ये यन्मां वदसि केशव ।
न हि ते भगवन्व्यक्तिं विदुर्देवा न दानवाः ॥१४॥
स्वयमेवात्मनात्मानं वेत्थ त्वं पुरुषोत्तम ।
भूतभावन भूतेश देवदेव जगत्पते ॥१५॥

14. Now, O Keshava, I believe that everything you have told me is divine truth. O Lord, neither gods nor demons know your real nature.
15. Indeed, you alone know yourself, O supreme spirit. You are the source of creation and the master of every creature, God of gods, the Lord of the universe.

Arjuna confides in Sri Krishna, "Every word that you say goes right to my heart. How can I ever think of knowing you completely?" This is one of the deepest questions asked in the scriptures. How can we talk about knowing God, write about him, speak about him, become an authority on him, if he is without name and form? The Hindu sages tell us that all we can hope to become is the dust of his lotus feet; Christian mystics will say all we can hope to do is touch the hem of his garment.

The Lord is everywhere; there is nowhere that he is not. We can never know him through our physical senses, but for the man or woman of God, he is more real than any object of the senses can be. When St. Francis of Assisi says he sees Jesus, we should not think he is talking figuratively just because he saw what others did not. Similarly, when St. Teresa of Ávila says, "His Majesty told me so," she is not referring to something she heard from King Philip; she *did* hear her King, but not with the outer ear. Sri Ramakrishna, who worshiped God as the Divine Mother, would sometimes break off in the middle of a sentence and tell his disciples, "Shh! Mother is coming; I can hear her anklets jingling." This is not hearing in the way we hear the jingling of coins or the tinkling of glasses; the Divine Mother is so real to him that he hears her in the very depths of his consciousness.

In his trenchant way, Meister Eckhart says that people think they can see God the way they see a cow. Actually, Eckhart tells us, we see God with the same eye with which he sees us. It is an image which I enjoy very much. Imagine peeking through a keyhole and discovering you are looking right into the eye of the Lord! We cannot know God in the usual way of knowing, the way we know the phenomenal world. He is the Ātman, the divine Self within us, and it is by identifying ourselves with this Self that we realize the Lord.

वक्तुमर्हस्यशेषेण दिव्या ह्यात्मविभूतयः ।
याभिर्विभूतिभिर्लोकानिमांस्त्वं व्याप्य तिष्ठसि ॥१६॥
कथं विद्यामहं योगिंस्त्वां सदा परिचिन्तयन् ।
केषु केषु च भावेषु चिन्त्योऽसि भगवन्मया ॥१७॥

16. Tell me all your divine attributes, leaving
nothing unsaid. Tell me of the glories with which
you fill the cosmos.
17. O Krishna, you are the supreme master of yoga.
Tell me how I should meditate to gain constant
awareness of you. In what things and in what ways
may I meditate on you?

Arjuna is asking how he can become aware of the Lord always, in everything he does and in everyone around him. In meditation, when we are concentrating completely on a passage like the Prayer of St. Francis—"It is in giving that we receive; it is in pardoning that we are pardoned"—we *are* meditating on the Lord; forgiving and giving freely are among the ways in which the Lord manifests himself in human beings. But it is not enough to meditate on him like this for an hour or so a day. We must learn to meditate on him always, which means bringing these qualities to life in our thought and action and learning to see the divinity that is within those around us too. This is not something sentimental, something we can do by sending cards saying "The Lord lives in you." We learn to see the Lord in those around us by *trying* to see the Lord in those around us. It is essentially a matter of practice, of constantly reminding ourselves over and over again throughout the day.

This is exactly what we are doing when we repeat the mantram, which is the name of the Lord. For those who have difficulty in remembering to repeat the mantram, I sometimes suggest putting a discreet little sign—"Repeat the Mantram"—wherever they are likely to see it frequently. Or, if they have a flair for the artistic and don't want to raise unnecessary questions from friends and coworkers, they can always write their mantram out in some original and decorative way—say, in the shape of an elephant, because an elephant never forgets. The point is somehow to remember the mantram; how we remember it is a matter in which there is considerable room for imagination.

The mind has a tremendous natural capacity to dwell on things, and in repeating the mantram we are channeling this capacity to train the mind to dwell constantly on the Lord. It is the same capacity, only we are giving it a different focus. There is a little story in the Hasidic tradition of Judaism in which a man asks his *zaddik* or spiritual teacher, "Do you mean we should remember the Lord even in the give-and-take of business?" "Yes, of course," the rabbi replies. "If we can remember business matters in the hour of prayer, shouldn't we be able to remember God in the transactions of our business?"

Finally, when we become established in the Lord, we shall see his glory everywhere, wherever there is beauty or excellence in the world around us. If I may say so, due entirely to the grace of my spiritual teacher, my Grandmother, this is how I see life today. When I see the first green shoots pushing up through the ground after a rain, or our dog Muka running on the beach, or a mother being very patient with her child, it is the Lord I see as the essence, the inner Ruler in us all. Once we learn to see the world like this, there will be no need for external reminders; we will not forget even for a moment that everything in the world is sustained by the power of the Lord.

विस्तरेणात्मनो योगं विभूतिं च जनार्दन ।
भूयः कथय तृप्तिर्हि श्रृण्वतो नास्ति मेऽमृतम् ॥१८॥

18. O Krishna, who intoxicate people with love for you, tell me in detail your attributes and your powers; I can never tire of hearing your immortal words.

When you live in a royal palace, Sri Ramakrishna says, even if you are not exactly in the royal family, a little of the royalty rubs off on you as well. In India, even if a man is only the tenth footman in a royal palace, everybody thinks of him as a glamorous figure—his address is the royal palace. Even here it is like that; there is glamor in being a member of the White House staff, even if all you do all day is pluck out dandelions on the President's lawn. You still work at the White House, and sometimes you even get to go inside; you may have caught a glimpse of the President's little girl and perhaps even have picked up her pen and returned it to her when she was on her way to school. It's true that the Joint Chiefs of Staff won't even look at you, but when you go home everyone will listen with bated breath about how you picked up Amy's pen.

That is what is happening in this verse too. There is a little of the Lord's infinite glory present in all of us, and the deeper we go in our meditation, the more this glory will shine forth in our daily living. That is why, when we really begin to be serious about the practice of meditation, we never become tired of hearing about the glory of God from someone who is speaking from personal experience.

Like Arjuna, the more we hear, the more we want to hear, because every word inspires us to reveal more of this divinity that is within us all.

श्री भगवानुवाच
हन्त ते कथयिष्यामि दिव्या ह्यात्मविभूतयः ।
प्राधान्यतः कुरुश्रेष्ठ नास्त्यन्तो विस्तरस्य मे ॥१९॥

SRI KRISHNA:
19. All right, Arjuna, I will tell you of my divine powers. I will mention only the most glorious; there is no end to them.

In response to Arjuna's eager request, Sri Krishna begins to describe the glory that lies within all of us. It is a reminder that there is no limit to the power we can draw on for selfless work through the practice of meditation. Compared to the state we can reach, the condition we are living in today is really a dream. In the verses that follow, the Lord will be giving us a glimpse of what the world looks like to the person who is awake.

अहमात्मा गुडाकेश सर्वभूताशयस्थितः ।
अहमादिश्च मध्यं च भूतानामन्त एव च ॥२०॥

20. I am the true Self in the heart of every creature, Arjuna, and the beginning, middle, and end of their existence.

In no other language with which I am acquainted is there a term for our real nature so precise as this word *Ātman*. All it means is 'the Self'—not the little self, the changing, self-centered personality with which most of us identify ourselves, but the higher Self, our real, changeless personality, which we discover in the very depths of our consciousness.

One of the most consoling implications of this is that no matter what mistakes we may have committed in the past, no matter what liabilities we are oppressed by in the present, our real Self can never be tarnished; the core of our personality is always pure, always loving, always wise. In both East and West, the mystics illustrate this by drawing a comparison with the sun. Even when it is completely hidden by the clouds, even when we close our eyes to it, the sun is always blazing away with the same radiance. Similarly, even if we have done our best for many years to cover up the splendor of the Ātman, it is still there, as radiant as ever, in our heart of hearts. We don't have to make ourselves loving or patient or forgiving; we have only to remove from our superficial personality everything hostile, everything impatient, everything resentful. When all these coverings are removed, the beauty of the Ātman will shine forth unimpeded.

The Hindu scriptures describe this discovery in wonderfully simple stories. One of these is about a prince who is kidnapped by a band of robbers when he is very young. He forgets all about the lap of luxury, about palaces and culture, even about his mother and father; he just grows up as a bandit, learning to master the bow and arrow and ambush passers-by and disappear into the woods without being seen. And for twenty years, this is the only life he knows.

Then one day the king's spiritual teacher happens by. Many years have passed; the little child is a grown man now, rough and cocksure, looking for all the world like anything but a king's son. But the spiritual teacher looks at him closely: beneath his violent manners, this young bandit has the king's features, the queen's eyes, even a hint of regal bearing. The teacher recognizes him as the king's son, and with great love in his heart he goes up to him, embraces him, and calls him "your royal highness."

The bandit is outraged. "What do you mean? I'm not your royal highness or anybody else's; I'm a bandit, and everybody in this kingdom is afraid of me."

But the teacher's faith is unshaken. Instead of being repulsed by this young man's bad manners, he puts his arm about him and begins to tell him stories about his childhood—how his father used to carry him on his shoulders, how his mother used to sing him to sleep with the mantram, how life used to be in the palace. And gradually the prince begins to remember. "Go on, go on!" The spiritual

teacher continues his stories, and finally, in the depths of his consciousness, the young man's memory clears. He draws himself up
straight, his eyes are bright and steady; he has become a different
man. "Now I recall," he says slowly, as if awakening from a dream.
"I'm not really a bandit at all. I'm not bad, I'm not violent; I simply
forgot who I was." He throws his arms about his teacher. "You're
my greatest friend," he exclaims; "you helped me to remember who
I am!" And truly a prince now, he goes home to his father, the king.

आदित्यानामहं विष्णुर्ज्योतिषां रविरंशुमान् ।
मरीचिर्मरुतामस्मि नक्षत्राणामहं शशी ॥२१॥

*21. Among the shining gods I am Vishnu; of lumi-
naries I am the sun; among the storm gods I am
Marīci, and in the night sky I am the moon.*

From the earliest times, men and women must have wondered
about the sun, the moon, and the stars in the heavens, the forces
governing the storms and the cycles of light and darkness. Even
those of us who are not astronomically inclined must have had moments when we asked the sun, "What are you doing there?" or the
stars, "Are you friendly with one another?" Now, in this century,
astronomy has developed high-powered instruments for looking
beyond the galaxy we live in to probe a universe much vaster and
more wonderful than we had ever imagined—a universe in which
there are billions of other galaxies, each with millions of solar systems, all held together in the embrace of a unifying force.

To me, this unifying force is the infinite love of the Lord, oper-
ating on the physical level. Just as all of us are one, so all things in
the created universe are one in the Lord. That is why he is called
Vishnu, 'he who is everywhere.' When the Lord puts his arms
around creation so that it can work in harmony, this is love on a
cosmic scale. Just as people live together as a family fostering each
other's welfare and happiness, so the cosmos is a family in which
every member is related. If even a distant planet like Neptune or
Pluto were removed from the solar system, life here on earth would

be a little different for us all. There is no possibility of anything in the universe—a sun, a star, or you and me—existing separately. Each part derives its significance from the whole, which is what the mystics call the indivisible unity underlying all life.

When Sri Krishna says he is the sun, this can be interpreted with both scientific precision and spiritual wisdom. The sun is the source of heat and light, both of which are necessary for life on earth. We can ask ourselves, "How has it been possible for the sun to give out this heat and light continuously for more than six thousand million years?" The astronomer and the physicist account for this heat in terms of hydrogen being converted into helium. With a dramatic touch they compare the sun to a hydrogen bomb exploding continuously for millions of years, and they add that it takes twenty million years for this energy to reach the sun's surface from its center, where the temperature is thirteen million degrees. But they cannot tell us why this process goes on or who is responsible for it. For this we have to draw upon the wisdom of spiritual insight.

I like to imagine Sri Krishna standing quietly in the center of the sun in an incomprehensible whirlwind of heat and light, playing on his magic flute. On a hot summer afternoon, when the temperature in our city goes up to ninety-five, my friends come home exhausted and consume gallons of iced lemonade. Now imagine the Lord, whom we are calling Sri Krishna, standing comfortably in the midst of thirteen million degrees and playing on his flute. If he were to play a little louder the temperature of the sun would go up, affecting life on earth; even a small rise in the earth's temperature and we could not survive. And if the Lord should allow his hidden melody to become a little softer, the temperature of the sun would fall, again making life on earth impossible. The question that any scientist would ask is, "How is it that this thirteen million degrees at the center of the sun gives the perfect temperature for life on earth?" It cannot be dismissed as an accident. According to the Gita, the sun has an inner law—or, to be more personal, an inner ruler—which maintains a perfect balance of energy, pressure, and temperature. This balance is an expression of the divine unity of existence, which keeps all the local forces working together so that the unity of the solar system may be maintained.

वेदानां सामवेदोऽस्मि देवानामस्मि वासवः ।
इन्द्रियाणां मनश्चास्मि भूतानामस्मि चेतना ॥२२॥

22. Among the scriptures I am the Sāma Veda, and among the lesser gods I am Indra. Among the senses I am the mind, and in living beings I am consciousness.

The Vedas are the sacred scriptures of Hinduism. They are four in number—Rig, Sāma, Yajur, and Atharva—and together they form the source of India's perennial philosophy, which extends in an unbroken tradition over more than five thousand years. *Veda* comes from the Sanskrit root *vid,* 'to know,' and the Vedas teach the only essential knowledge, which is to know who we are. Socrates gives us the same injunction: *Gnōthi seauton,* 'Know thyself'; that is the beginning and end of wisdom. For this kind of knowledge we need to practice meditation, which gradually awakens a transcendental mode of knowing latent in all of us.

When I talk about a "transcendental mode of knowing," people sometimes raise their eyebrows. It is beyond the range of their experience, so they have no way of judging it. In answer, I sometimes tell them about a cat we had staying with us when we returned to the United States from India. Woosh was a very sophisticated cat. Not only was she widely traveled, she had a special diet, an elaborately decorated scratching post, and all sorts of toys for recreation. But I am sure that if we could have asked her what she thought the highest faculty of knowing was, she would have answered, "Instinct." In her next incarnation, if she were to become a human being, she would probably tell us it was reason; but as long as she is a cat, instinct is the highest mode of knowing open to her. Similarly, just as human beings develop reason, which is an evolutionary step beyond instinct, so the mystics develop a higher mode of knowing with which they see life whole.

The second line of this verse deals with the mind and consciousness. The mind—*manas* in Sanskrit—not only records the perceptions of the other senses, it can re-experience a perception even though nothing is immediately perceived by the senses. There is an important connection here with desire, for sense desires, especially obsessive desires, thrive on this faculty of recollection. Even if we are miles away from a pizza, when we remember one and want it we can easily recall just how it looks and tastes. If we are a little compulsive about eating, we may even dwell on all the pizza perceptions of our past experience. In doing this, of course, we are only deepening our pizza samskāra, our pizza obsession, making it harder to resist eating *two* pizzas the next time we get a chance. The Gita would ask, where is the freedom in this? In terms of the damage we do our will, the difference between the pizza we dwell on and the pizza we eat is mainly a matter of calories—and even that difference disappears when, after dwelling on pizza for so long, we overeat the next time we get a chance. So the mind is by far the most important and powerful of the senses, and we can master the senses only through the mind.

Most of us have let the mind go unattended for such a long time that cultivating it requires full-time effort. I was admiring our vegetable garden this weekend and was pleased to see that the tomatoes and corn were doing very well. Then I noticed another crop which was really flourishing. I didn't recognize that particular variety of greens, so I asked my friend Sarah about it. She explained, "Those are the weeds." This is very much the usual state of the mind. If there were an exhibit of mind-weeds, most of us could enter some rather fascinating crops.

Anger is one of the worst of these weeds; it spreads over every inch of ground and keeps other plants from growing. But all negative states of mind—fear, hostility, jealousy, depression—make it difficult for useful plants like kindness and consideration to grow. It is not a question of our soil being infertile; it is that very few try to get rid of the weeds. There are even people who admire these weeds, who talk about weeds of anger and fear as though they were lilies and lotuses. Unfortunately, when we talk about our problems, write about them, think about them as we fall asleep, we are driving them deeper into consciousness. After a while the roots may go so deep that we cannot pull them out. So instead of dwelling on the negative aspects of the mind, let us turn our attention to the positive side and make the mind a beautiful garden. By practicing meditation regularly and repeating the mantram whenever a weed tries to send out a new shoot, we can trim back our negative tendencies and eventually weed them out of the mind forever.

In Hindu psychology, it is important to remember that the mind is not thought of as being conscious any more than a television set is, or the engine of a car. Just as the body is the external instrument we use, the mind is the internal instrument; it reflects consciousness, but it is not conscious itself. So Sri Krishna adds that he is not only the mind; he is consciousness itself in every living creature. If you go to a potter's stall in an Indian bazaar, you will see all types of pots, tall and short, stout and slender. But the tall pot does not contain a different kind of air than the short pot; all of them are filled with the same air. Similarly, though each of us is quite different in appearance, underneath all these variations we are all one. Inside each of us is the same pure, undifferentiated consciousness, the Ātman, the same in you as it is in me.

रुद्राणां शंकरश्चास्मि वित्तेशो यक्षरक्षसाम् ।
वसूनां पावकश्चास्मि मेरुः शिखरिणामहम् ॥२३॥

23. I am Rudra and I am Shankara. Among the spirits of the natural world I am Kubera, god of wealth, and Pāvaka, the purifying fire; among mountains I am Meru.

Shankara means 'he who brings about our lasting welfare'; *Rudra* means 'he who makes us grieve.' Both are traditional names of the Lord of Love, and in the one short phrase with which this verse opens, Sri Krishna is giving us one of the deepest secrets of life: often the grace of the Lord comes to us in the form of sorrow.

One of the most distressing facts of life is that most of us do not learn without a certain measure of suffering. The question we must ask is whether we prefer to be stunted or to suffer some distress and grow up. Suffering in life comes as an enemy only when we do not know how to receive it as a friend. We can either benefit from suffering to improve our health and security, or we can become frustrated and embittered because we cannot change our ways of living under the impact of pain.

Several days ago I went with a friend to a restaurant just to see what people are eating. It was one of the better restaurants in the area, yet these educated, cultured people were eating the worst possible kind of food. It always amazes me on such occasions to realize how strong the human system is. It is a wonder that our bodies continue to function; it is only the mercy of the Lord that prevents us from causing ourselves more physical problems than we do. If you want to see how perfect the nervous system can be, look at a sleeping infant, as relaxed as a cat curled up in the sun. Yet thirty-five years or so later, many of us have managed to throw a big spanner into the machinery of the body. Tension, high blood pressure, chronic headaches, and peptic ulcers don't arise overnight; these are problems we slowly develop by making ill-considered decisions day after day, year after year.

Suffering is like the red signboard on the freeway: "Go Back; You're Going the Wrong Way." The first time I saw this sign I thought the freeway designers had borrowed a slogan from the Gita; it has the practical touch of Sri Krishna. First the Lord puts up a little sign saying "Pain Ahead," but we continue on our way. Then he puts up another, bigger sign, "Turmoil Coming," but still we don't pay attention. Finally he sets an enormous blockade. Most of us do not know how to respond, and instead of putting on the brakes we step on the gas. Then we wonder why we crash.

The mature person responds to Sri Krishna's first signboard. As soon as there is even a little suffering, physical or mental, he starts looking around to see how to improve his ways of thinking and behaving. Often, of course, this presents a practical difficulty. When we have become addicted to wrong habits over a period of time, it is terribly difficult to change them. I have known people who want to give up smoking, drinking, or drugging, but who do not have the will to carry out their desire. Here it is that meditation comes into play. Almost all my friends who meditate regularly have been enabled to give up such addictions, for meditation gives us the will and wisdom to go against our previous conditioning.

This same capacity to change habits can be applied to the way we use our natural resources. The serious problem of pollution in our air, lakes, rivers, and oceans is just as much a source of suffering as physiological disorders, and it too is a warning: we have mercilessly exploited the environment and will have to change in order to survive. The ocean, for example, is not just something that stands between us and Paris or Tahiti; it is an underwater world where four fifths of the creatures of earth live. In these vast depths there are gorges deeper than the Grand Canyon, peaks higher than Mount Everest, and great plains which stretch for hundreds of miles. All life depends ultimately on our oceans, yet the amount of oil, sewage, and industrial effluent that we are pouring into them threatens to turn this vast, teeming world into a wasteland. This is a flashing red warning signal telling us to reassess our way of living and simplify our needs so as to reduce the demands we make on the precious resources of the earth.

In spite of what the popular media may tell us, we should not pretend that there is no pain at the core of life. Whether in Africa or America, whether poor or prosperous, people are suffering everywhere; that is the nature of life. Even if we live in the midst of plenty, we do not say goodbye to pain. As our spiritual awareness deepens, we will find it impossible to go after our personal pleasure or profit when there is so much suffering to alleviate in the world around us. I often describe the mystics as hard-nosed. It is they who really know the facts of life; most of us live in a private fantasy land where we think that if we keep up an appearance of prosperity, everything is all right. We have only to open our eyes to see that behind this facade, there is sorrow all around us—not just on the grand scale of war and poverty, but in millions on millions of anonymous, private lives. The more we close our eyes to this suffering, the more we shall have to suffer ourselves, for the simple reason that this is what it takes to rouse us out of our complacency and make us go to the help of those around us.

So the Lord adds that he is Pāvaka, the fire that purifies. A few years ago on a trip to Yosemite we stopped to visit an abandoned mining town, where we saw an exhibit about how gold is purified. It is a good analogy for what happens on the spiritual path, where the Lord comes with his fire, hammer, and anvil to burn away our selfishness and forge us into shape. The immature person takes one look and says, "Thank you very much, but I'd rather stay covered with this crusty ego." But the person who can go far will ask the Lord, "Put me on the anvil and use your heaviest hammer; I want to be freed from this ego-crust once and for all." When a person is able to say this, he or she has outgrown the need for suffering. The Lord may lift his hammer, but it does not fall. Instead he throws it aside and embraces that person in loving arms.

पुरोधसां च मुख्यं मां विद्धि पार्थ बृहस्पतिम् ।
सेनानीनामहं स्कन्दः सरसामस्मि सागरः ॥२४॥

24. Among spiritual teachers I am Brihaspati, and among military leaders I am Skanda. Among bodies of water I am the ocean.

Brihaspati is often mentioned in the Hindu scriptures as a tremendous spiritual teacher. It is not possible for the vast majority of us to approach the stature of such a teacher, but it is important to recognize that all of us, whether we like it or not, are in the role of teacher to those around us every waking hour of the day. This is especially clear in our relationships with children. Anyone who spends much time with children knows that they do not do what we ask them to do but what they see us doing. Education is based on a breathtakingly simple proposition: we teach by what we are. It is easy to buy a book on patience and security and give it to our children, but if we are impatient ourselves, no amount of reading will teach them to be otherwise. If we want our children to be patient, secure, and selfless, we have to give them an example of these qualities in our personal life.

This is a continuous struggle, so Sri Krishna adds that he is not only the ideal teacher, he is the ideal warrior too. Skanda is an invincible general in the scriptures who destroyed the forces of evil. It is a reminder to all of us that even the most aggressive temperament can be harnessed in this struggle to become commanders of ourselves.

Kālidāsa, one of India's greatest poets, has written a long epic poem relating the story of Skanda's birth, youth, and victory over the demon Tāraka, who symbolizes tyranny and evil. Tāraka was so powerful that all the gods had been defeated by him in battle over and over again. They had even had to vacate their homes because heaven itself was not safe against his rage. Only a son born of the great god Shiva could have the power to destroy this demon, so the gods went to this eternal bachelor and begged him to bring forth a son. Kālidāsa's poem tells how Pārvatī, Himālaya's daughter, after failing to attract Shiva by her unequalled beauty, finally wins his love by taking to the spiritual life. They are married, and Skanda is born to destroy Tāraka and his demon armies. It is a beautiful story, because Skanda is born not of physical passion but of Shiva's self-control. That is why he has the power to defeat Tāraka and rescue the cosmos from its misery.

Next Sri Krishna says he is the ocean. When the Lord is represented as sleeping on the cosmic ocean, it is not just the sea outside; he is also reclining on the sea inside. In one sense this is consciousness, but even on the physical level it can be illustrated as well. The same type of salt solution that was in the sea eons ago, bathing and nourishing the first cells when life began, is in our body fluids today. The oceans cover seventy percent of the earth's surface, and this same kind of fluid makes up almost seventy percent of the human body. It is not too far-fetched to say that we have a little of the sea flowing in all of us, giving sustenance to the millions of cells which compose our bodies.

The noted marine biologist and explorer Jacques Cousteau remarked that the ocean has become a universal sewer where all pollution ends up, so much so that a swimmer can contract an infection from just one swim in some of our more contaminated seas. Just as the sea outside is becoming polluted, the environment inside us suffers from pollution, too—the constant pollution of anger, fear, and greed, all of which we can clean up through the practice of meditation.

महर्षीणां भृगुरहं गिरामस्म्येकमक्षरम् ।
यज्ञानां जपयज्ञोऽस्मि स्थावराणां हिमालयः ॥२५॥

25. Among the great seers I am Bhrigu, and among words, the syllable Om; I am the repetition of the Holy Name, and among mountains I am the Himālayas.

Bhrigu is associated with one of the most beautiful stories I know of about the infinite mercy of the Lord. According to this story, there was once a thriving āshram in ancient India where men and women worshiping the Lord in different forms—Shiva, Rāma, Krishna, the Divine Mother—all lived and meditated together in harmony, each respecting the other's chosen way. Then one day Nārada happened to stop by. This Nārada appears in many of our stories. He was a great devotee of Sri Krishna, and spent much of his time traveling around from one holy place to another, where he showed a certain gift for stirring up spiritual controversy. So at this āshram Nārada asked mischievously, "Do you all worship the Lord in different forms?"

"Yes," one of the members of the āshram said, "the Lord takes on different forms to meet the needs of his devotees. Knowing that, we find it easy to meditate together and respect each other's spiritual ideal."

"That's very good," Nārada agreed. "But one of those ideals must be best, don't you think? Which do you think it is?" Then, while the members of the āshram began to talk over this idea, Nārada quietly slipped out and went on his way.

A month or so later, when Nārada returned, the āshram was in a hubbub. Cliques had formed, and some people wouldn't even talk to each other. Everyone was convinced that his or her approach to God was best. Some said that Shiva was the perfect embodiment of the Lord; others said Krishna; others said it was Rāma or the Divine Mother. "This is silly," Nārada said. "Why don't you go find out?"

"I'll go," volunteered Bhrigu, who loved the Lord with all his heart. "I'll test Sri Krishna's love myself; then you'll see why I say that there is no limit to his forgiveness." Bhrigu went up to Sri Krishna, who was sleeping with his head on the lap of his consort, Lakshmī, and while the rest of the āshram looked on in horror he kicked the Lord on the chest. Everyone was terrified; they expected Bhrigu to be burned up on the spot. But Sri Krishna simply opened his eyes and immediately saw into Bhrigu's heart. "It takes great faith to subject Me to a test like that," he said tenderly, "but now everyone has seen that there is no limit to my forgiveness. This mark your foot has left on my chest will be my adornment, *srīvatsa;* I will wear it always." It is a beautiful illustration of why Sri Krishna is called Kshamāsāgara, the ocean of *kshamā*—forgiveness, patience, and compassion all in one.

"Among words," this verse continues, "I am *Om,* and the repetition of the Holy Name." It is so easy to repeat the mantram or Holy Name that at first most of us cannot believe that it is charged with the power of the Lord. Only after we use it for a while do we begin to see that repeating the mantram is not just a mechanical exercise; it is a direct line to the Lord within—as I like to put it, "calling the Lord collect." We don't make any promises; all we do is repeat the mantram when we are agitated—angry, or afraid, or speeded up, or caught in worries or regrets—and the Lord opens a little door to the reserves of our deeper consciousness.

In college I used to be very interested in public speaking; it is an interest which still serves me well today. Whenever there was a talk being given I used to go to hear it, no matter what the subject, just to study the presentation and the delivery and all the little tricks of the trade. The principal of the school, whom I admired greatly, saw my enthusiasm and encouraged me in all this, and whenever there was an opportunity to speak or to debate I used to volunteer to go and represent our school. But no matter how often I spoke before an audience, the period of waiting to be called to the podium always turned my knees to rubber and my stomach upside down. It didn't matter how many times I had faced an audience before; I was always afraid that when my name was called I would trip on the stairs or open my mouth and find that no words would come out.

When I confessed this to my Granny, she had a very simple piece of advice: not to go over my notes, not to try to size up my audience, just to repeat the mantram. It was so simple that I didn't put much faith in it, but because of my love for her I promised to give it a try. The next time I had to face an audience I sat quietly awaiting my turn and repeating *Rāma, Rāma, Rāma*—and every now and then I would slip in, "I hope it works." After a while it became "*Rāma, Rāma, Rāma . . .* I think it works!" And now, on the basis of many years of experience, I can assure you with complete certitude, I *know* it works. At first it may just be a first-aid measure, but after many years, together with meditation, the mantram can enable us to transform our consciousness and rise to our full stature.

Most of us do not even suspect the height to which we can rise through the practice of meditation. On the walls of the Capitol in Sacramento is a line of poetry which I like very much: "Give me men to match my mountains." It makes me proud to remember that in India, where we have the highest and most majestic mountains in the world, there has been an unbroken tradition of spiritual giants, men and women of such tremendous stature that they tower as high above you and me as the Himālayas above the plains below. That is why the last line of this verse sounds so sweet to me. To my partial eyes, I don't think there is any symbol of spiritual awareness more beautiful than the Himālayas, the 'home of perpetual snow,' higher than which no human being can climb.

Here Sri Krishna is reminding us that there are Himālayan ranges inside us, too: the Himālayas of consciousness. When you begin meditating you enter the foothills, and as your meditation deepens, you climb higher and higher. Finally you reach the top of one of the lower peaks. But there is no time to sit down and congratulate yourself; another peak is already beckoning to you, saying, "Come and conquer *me.*" This is the challenge of meditation. Your legs are aching and your oxygen supply is exhausted. You have been waiting for the chance to sit down for a rest, but you just cannot be satisfied with anything less than the highest. So you start climbing again, hoping there will be a chance to build a little shack when you get to the top. But no sooner do you reach the summit than you see an even more magnificent mountain ahead of you. Then you realize that you have only been warming up; the real challenges are just beginning.

This is putting restlessness to work. Show me someone who is restless and I can help that person harness his or her restlessness in climbing the vast Himālayan ranges of consciousness, where the peaks never end. Even if, after years and years of climbing, you finally reach Mount Krishna, or Mount Christ, or Mount Buddha, you will see that there is no way to conquer these heights in the span of one human life; and even if it were possible to stand at the summit of these vast peaks, you would still be standing only at the foot of the highest of all mountains, Mount Brahman, lost completely beyond the universe.

अश्वत्थः सर्ववृक्षाणां देवर्षीणां च नारदः ।
गन्धर्वाणां चित्ररथः सिद्धानां कपिलो मुनिः ॥२६॥

26. Among trees I am the ashvattha, and among the gandharvas I am Chitraratha. Among divine seers I am Nārada, and among sages I am Kapila.

The ashvattha is the holy fig tree, important in both Hindu and Buddhist traditions. This tree, which lives for a very long time, is the basis for the image of the Tree of Eternity in the Upanishads— the cosmic tree with its root above, in God, and its branches here below on earth. You and I are its fruits; we are here on earth to satisfy the hunger of those around us.

This tree suffers if even the smallest leaves are injured. It is as if the leaves of a magnolia tree were to divide themselves into north and south and then wage war over the trunk; the whole lovely tree would soon die. This is the absurd situation we create between individuals, communities, races, and nations, when we forget that we are all part of one whole, the beautiful Tree of Life.

In the next epithet Sri Krishna tells Arjuna that he is Chitraratha, the leader of the gandharvas. The gandharvas are a little like angels in the Hindu scriptures. Just as in Judaism and Christianity you have cherubim and seraphim and other orders of the heavenly hosts, so in Hinduism we have gandharvas, devas, and other beings inhabiting the realms beyond earth. In particular, the gandharvas are cosmic musicians, and are responsible for what Shakespeare called the "music of the spheres." The scriptures tell us there is music everywhere if we have ears to hear it. In the language of mysticism, every star is singing; throughout the universe there is a symphony. There is music even in the subtlest of cosmic radiation, to which scientists listen with delicate instruments; there is music even in the sap running through the trunk and branches of a tree. Thomas Huxley tells us that "the wonderful noonday silence of a tropical forest is after all due only to the dullness of our own hearing, and could our ears catch the murmur of the tiny maelstroms as they whirl about in innumerable myriads of living cells which constitute each tree, we should be stunned as by the roar of a great city." This is not a mystic speaking; it is a great biologist, using the language of mysticism to describe a biological phenomenon. Everywhere the Lord is singing his divine melody, only we are unable to hear it with our small, sensuous ears.

In the Sanskrit scriptures, there is a unique figure among the gandharvas called Nārada. Nārada is not just a celestial figure; he is an illumined sage of divine stature, a fervent devotee of Sri Krishna who often acts as intermediary between the heavenly realms and the world of men. Usually he is portrayed as floating in space playing on his vīnā and singing the praise of the Lord, and in many Hindu religious plays he is given a part even when he is not essential to the action, just because he is such a familiar symbol of devotion. Something of a spiritual correspondent, he is always carrying news from one āshram to another, motivating aspirants to greater effort by remarks like, "Yes, you're doing well enough; you're not falling asleep in meditation. But do you know that in the āshram I just visited, two people attained illumination last week?"

Nārada had immense wisdom, but being a member of the monastic order he was under the impression that householders like you and me are not capable of much progress on the spiritual path. Sri Krishna has a soft spot in his heart for householders, and one day, it is said, he got the opportunity to correct Nārada's perspective. The two were walking together in heaven, and Nārada was taking advantage of his love for the Lord to ask him all kinds of questions. "Lord," he asked finally, "why do you like these householders so much? They're not very regular in their practice. One minute they're enthusiastic and resolve to be very spiritual, and the next minute they've forgotten all about it."

Sri Krishna had a way of not answering Nārada's questions directly. This time he said, "Look, Nārada, here's a little oil lamp. Why don't you carry it around this temple three times; then I'll answer your question. But don't let the flame go out."

The Lord gave Nārada the lamp, and Nārada lit it and went outside. As soon as he was out of the door, the Lord called Marut, the wind, and said, "Now blow for all you're worth!" Marut blew up a real typhoon, and then he called in his relatives to help him make it a hurricane. Nārada was hard put. The north wind was blowing and the south wind was blowing, and there he was with this little oil lamp which he couldn't let go out. But being a divine sage, he wasn't completely without resources. He held the lamp close and huddled over it to shield it from the wind, and somehow or other he managed to get around the temple three times with the flame still flickering. When he finally got back to Sri Krishna he was a little disheveled but still undaunted. "Well, Lord," he said breathlessly, "here is the lamp."

Sri Krishna smiled. "Tell me, Nārada," he said. "You're always singing my praises and repeating the mantram. While you were going around the temple just now, how many times did you remember to repeat my Name?"

Nārada hemmed and hawed. "With all this wind blowing, the

north wind and the south wind . . . actually, Lord, I'm afraid I didn't remember you even once."

"You see, Nārada," Sri Krishna said, "these householders have so many problems—television, and the generation gap, and Madison Avenue to contend with; the wind is blowing against them all the time. If they are able to remember me only a little part of the day, I am very pleased." It is a good story to remember whenever we find it difficult to remain calm and patient in all the storms of daily living.

Then, among sages, the Lord says he is Kapila, a spiritual teacher in ancient India whose stature was so tremendous that he was content to remain unknown. We know virtually nothing about his life. He was not interested in whether those who came after him would remember his vital statistics; he wanted only that we follow his teachings. If we could have interviewed Kapila he would have said, "Why do you want to know when I was born? How will knowing my height and weight help you realize the unity of life? None of this is relevant to going beyond suffering." All Kapila's greatness is inferred from the legacy he left behind him, which has influenced virtually every spiritual tradition in India since his time. Patanjali, who wrote the classic Indian text on meditation, follows Kapila's *sānkhya* philosophy and may have been one of his direct disciples, and the Bhagavad Gita, the Katha Upanishad, and the teachings of the Compassionate Buddha himself all show the strong stamp of the sānkhya outlook. An old Sanskrit saying testifies to the immense effectiveness of these teachings: "There is no knowledge like sānkhya, no power like yoga." Sānkhya, the philosophical aspect, gives us a systematic diagnosis of our human predicament; yoga—rāja yoga or meditation—gives us the cure.

In this verse Kapila is called *muni,* 'the silent one.' What is meant here is not silence of the tongue but silence of the ego. For the sages who have forever silenced their self-will, this is a perfect name. After many years of meditation, when you have risen above body-consciousness and your ego has been dissolved, you will have gone beyond the words of the inspirational passage. Then you will find yourself on the very seabed of consciousness, where everything is still. This stillness is the greatest source of joy, for the cacophony of self-will is the cause of all our suffering in life. The mind is completely still, so there can be no anger, no greed, and no fear.

उच्चैःश्रवसमश्वानां विद्धि माममृतोद्भवम् ।
ऐरावतं गजेन्द्राणां नराणां च नराधिपम् ॥२७॥

27. I was born from the nectar of immortality as the primordial horse and as Indra's noble elephant. Among men, I am the king.

This verse refers to the story in the Hindu tradition about the churning of the cosmic ocean to bring forth life as we know it. The story is a little reminiscent of the passage in Genesis which describes how the spirit of God moved upon the waters of life. According to the Hindu scriptures, before creation there was only a vast ocean of undifferentiated consciousness. Then the gods of light, representing the forces of selflessness and goodness, and the demons of darkness, representing the forces of selfishness and violence, took the head and the tail of the serpent king, Vāsuki, and began churning the cosmic ocean in order to obtain the nectar of immortality. Out of this churning, life as we know it began to evolve, and many creatures sprang forth.

In its practical application, the churning of the cosmic ocean is the churning of primordial, undifferentiated consciousness, and the creatures that come forth are the mighty forces released from the unconscious during meditation. The Lord brings out these forces within us so that we can work as his instruments, adding to human welfare and to world peace. Those who work for the welfare of the whole are leaders among men, which is the meaning of "king" in this verse. This is leadership based on love and service; it is leadership that is granted rather than taken for oneself. When we give up our private interests like this for the sake of serving others, two divine qualities are released which are essential to effective, selfless leadership. The elephant of Indra, king of the gods, is the perfect symbol of power; Indra's white horse, called the king of horses, symbolizes the gracefulness that comes when immense power is combined with complete self-control.

During the churning of the cosmic ocean, before these precious gifts emerged, all the poison of selfishness and separateness came to the surface. This poison threatened all life, and no one, neither gods nor demons, knew how to get rid of it. Then Lord Shiva said, "Let me drink it myself, to save the world from its own selfishness." He took the concentrated poison and drank it, but his queen, Pārvatī, was so anguished at the sight that she put her hands around his neck to keep the poison from going down his throat. So one of the most loving names for Shiva is Nīlakantha, from *nīla*, 'blue,' and *kantha*, 'throat': 'he whose neck turned blue' when he drank the poison of the world to save all creation. This is what true leadership means: even if there is sorrow and suffering, it is our privilege to take it on ourselves rather than let others become victims. When we choose to suffer for others rather than let our family, our country, or our world suffer, we become a little like Nīlakantha.

Finally, after the poison, out of the cosmic ocean came the nectar of immortality called *amrita*. *Mrita* is cognate with the word *mortal*, and amrita is that which makes us immortal. This was the ambrosia the gods and demons were hoping to find by churning the sea with the serpent Vāsukī. The nectar of immortality is what all of us are seeking, and we will find it eventually if we are vigilant in practicing meditation. In meditation we dive into the sea of the mind, where we learn how to transform all our poisonous, negative tendencies into selfless qualities. When at last we rid our hearts and minds of all fear, anger, and greed, the nectar of immortality will emerge. It is a symbolic way of saying that we rise above physical consciousness to realize that we are a permanent force for the welfare of all.

आयुधानामहं वज्रं धेनूनामस्मि कामधुक् ।
प्रजनश्चास्मि कन्दर्पः सर्पाणामस्मि वासुकिः ॥२८॥

28. Among weapons I am the thunderbolt. I am
Kāmadhuk, the cow which fulfills all desires; I am
Kandarpa, the power of sex, and Vāsuki, the king
of snakes.

Here Sri Krishna uses *vajra,* the thunderbolt, as a symbol of the
power of selflessness, which cannot be broken by any other power
on earth. In the Vedas, Indra, leader of the gods, carries the thunderbolt as his weapon; it is with the thunderbolt that he slays the
cosmic demon. The story of how this weapon was made is a marvelous one. The gods were terribly distressed at the strength of the
forces of violence in the world, so they went to Indra and asked him
to conquer this violence and separateness. His strange reply was,
"I must first have an invincible weapon, which can be made only
from the bones of a sage who is pure and perfect."

The devas searched far and wide for such a sage. They told many
spiritual aspirants of their plight. "Oh, yes," the aspirants would
say, "we would like to help you out. What can we do?" The unexpected answer was, "Give us your bones." As it turned out, the aspirants preferred having their bones inside them instead, and so the
search went on.

Finally the devas came to Dadhīci, a simple, sweet figure who
had come to identify himself so completely with all life that everyone's suffering was his own. The devas confessed, "We are at the
end of our tether. Violence is rising high on all sides, and we haven't
been able to get the weapon we need to stop it, for it can be fash-
ioned only from the bones of a sage who is pure and perfect."

"If you will accept it," Dadhīci reassured them, "my body is
yours. You don't have to look any further." He sat down in meditation, united himself with the Lord, and shed his body so it could
be used for the happiness of mankind.

This capacity to do anything to relieve the suffering of others is
a sign of invincible power. We usually misuse the word *power* to

mean the capacity to destroy another country, or race, or fellow creature. This is not power; this is a liability. Power rises from within us. The power that we have to forget ourselves, to subordinate ourselves to the welfare of the whole, is the only power that is real.

As long as we have the desire and the resoluteness to contribute to life, we need not be diffident about our efforts to solve the problems that face us. The Lord tells us in this verse that he is Kāmadhuk, the wish-fulfilling cow. This mythical cow satisfies desires that are for the general welfare, but if there is any personal taint in our wish, she will not grant it.

Because I come from India, people used to ask me if I consider cows sacred. I used to tell them, "Of course I do—and tigers, buffaloes, beavers, and Chihuahuas, too. All animals are sacred to me." We are learning more and more about the nutritional advantages of vegetarianism, but I would say the more important point about not eating meat is that it makes for sound spiritual living, because it affirms the unity of life. In India, where we have a tradition of vegetarianism stretching back thousands of years, we have a loving, protective feeling for most of our animals. In my ancestral home, for example, my Grandmother used to give our cows beautiful Sanskrit names. When visitors came to our home and my Grandmother gave them the news, she would always include the latest about the cows, who were just like members of the family to her. "Shanti is not doing very well today," she would say. "Shoba's calf is eating better now." My mother kept cows, too. One of them grew to a ripe old age and developed rheumatism, and my mother used to tell her friends with wry humor, "Both of us are rheumatic." Once someone suggested she sell the cow. Her answer was perfect: "That's like asking my son to sell me." The cow had served us well, giving us milk, yogurt, and butter for many years. Out of simple gratitude my mother wanted her to live her last years in comfort.

Kandarpa and *Vāsuki* are references to the power of sex. Vāsuki is the serpent who was used in churning the cosmic ocean, but it is also a symbol of kundalinī. And *Kandarpa* is one of the names for Kāma, who is the Cupid of Sanskrit literature. These are ways of saying that the Lord is the power of sex, because sex holds the key to life. One of Kāma's many names is *Pancashara,* 'he who has five arrows in his quiver,' each tipped with the flowers of spring. On college campuses it is easy to see Kāma busy at work. He pulls out his first arrow, which has ten flower-power, and quite a few students fall; one shot and they are down. But there are some who say, "I've got to work hard and get into medical school; I haven't got time for archery." For them, Kāma pulls out a second arrow with twenty flower-power and down they go; medical school is forgotten. Then there is the postdoctoral research fellow, who thinks he is flower-proof. For him Kāma pulls out the third arrow, and he falls victim to its thirty flower-power. So far, the man or woman who is self-controlled most of the time has managed to escape. But spiritual aspirants too can have moments when their vigilance nods, when Kāma can claim them with the fourth or forty flower-power arrow. Finally comes the person who is almost invincible, who has gone some distance on the spiritual path. Kāma waits patiently for a long time, until just the right moment comes. Then he quickly uses his fifth and last arrow, against which no one can be completely safe.

I would say, beware of the first arrow. The minute you see it coming, repeat your mantram and leave the scene. Here Jesus gives us simple, sound advice: "Lead us not into temptation, but deliver us from evil." Given the constant drone of the mass media, most of us have become so susceptible to Kāma's arrows that we need to be particularly careful about not putting ourselves in situations where we are likely to be swept away. Our most effective protection against turmoil is to not base our relationships on sex. Whenever a man and a woman put each other's welfare first, romance will never come to an end; they will fall more deeply in love every day.

अनन्तश्चास्मि नागानां वरुणो यादसामहम् ।
पितॄणामर्यमा चास्मि यमः संयमतामहम् ॥२९॥

29. I am Ananta, the cosmic serpent, and Varuna, the god of water; I am Aryaman, the noble ancestor of mankind. Among the forces which control the universe, I am Yama, the god of death.

Ananta is the endless serpent on which the Lord, in the form of Vishnu, is said to sleep. This cosmic serpent, as we saw in the previous verse, is also a symbol for the evolutionary energy called kundalinī. Just as we need gasoline to drive our car, so we need the power of sex to rouse kundalinī up the spinal column to the highest center of consciousness in the head. If we want to evolve to the highest level possible, this is the power we must use. Fortunately, there is no limit to this energy once we have begun to put it to spiritual use; that is why it is called *ananta,* 'without end.'

Aryaman, another figure from Hindu mythology, is the symbol of all that is noble in our ancestry. This is a reminder that we owe a great debt to those who have gone before us—our parents, our grandparents, our teachers, and everyone else who has helped make us what we are today. You can imagine your grandfather looking out of your eyes, because it is his tendencies that you have inherited. Sometimes I tease my young friends by saying that when we add twenty-five years to them, we get their mother or father. It works the other way, also: the next time you see a mother and daughter together, try subtracting twenty-five years from the mother and you will have the daughter. It is a very fine compliment to tell a daughter that she looks just like her mother, or a son that he is like his father. Whatever inadequacies our parents may have, they brought us into this world and therefore deserve our complete respect. Once, I remember, we took my Grandmother to a big store in a nearby town. She looked around carefully, and when we were leaving we asked her, "Well, Granny, what do you think of this store?" "You can get everything you need here," she replied, "except the love of your father and mother."

Finally, the Lord makes a strong remark: "Among the forces which control the universe, I am Yama," the King of Death. Yama is a rather frightening figure in the Sanskrit scriptures, but he can be a good teacher to those who want to receive his message. In the Katha Upanishad, the daring teenager Nachiketa goes straight to Yama to learn how to go beyond death. "You're the King of Death," he tells him; "who could have a better teacher than you?" When we face the implications of death squarely, it can give us all the motivation we need to take to meditation and learn to overcome our identification with the body once and for all.

Today, when life is so cheap and violence surrounds us, the theme of conquering death is particularly relevant. It is all too easy to resign ourselves to the constant threat to life and accept without question half-remedies which only feed the fires of violence. Take the problem of holdups, which are rapidly becoming commonplace. It is no answer to carry a gun; that only endangers our own life and the lives of innocent people around us. For a lasting solution we have to help our society change its values, and the best place to begin is for all of us to stop playing up money and material possessions. It is much more difficult to do this than to arm ourselves, but no other solution goes to the heart of the problem. When we are constantly being goaded to buy more, to own more, to measure everything in dollars, it is only a matter of time before we think we can't be happy without a new sports car or Tiffany diamonds or a trip to Acapulco. Our cupidity is inflated in even the smallest matters. When I first came to this country, I was amazed to see how gas stations compete with each other. I thought they would be offering better gasoline or better service; instead they offer you a drinking glass or a can of nuts. My first response was, "Are we supposed to put these in our tank?" Even the strongest person can be affected by this incessant appeal to get, get, get, even if it is things we do not need or really want.

To help our society free itself from this deadly conditioning, we need to show that what makes life worth living is not money but personal relationships. We don't do this by talking about it; we do it primarily by our own example. In their hearts, I think everybody knows that money and possessions can satisfy only for a short, short time. The problem is that most people do not have a clear, appealing alternative. But the person with a rich family life and deep, lasting relationships, who is always interested in other people and is not easily shaken by their ups and downs, is a reminder of the real meaning of life wherever he or she goes.

All of us can make of our lives this kind of shining example. Instead of spending our time making extra money, we can spend time with our family and friends, rediscovering the joy of being together. We can simplify our lives so we do not need that second sports car, and instead of taking to the road every weekend or sitting in front of the television, we can start some community project like a vegetable garden with our neighbors. Turning off the television to work with family and friends like this is not a sacrifice; the relationships it enriches will be a source of lasting satisfaction.

Another source of violence is the constant emphasis placed on sex. Now, for example, it is dangerous for college and university women to walk alone in the evening even on campus. You and I can counteract this source of violence in many different ways—by not buying magazines or books that play up sex, by writing to newspapers and television stations when their programs are objectionable, by not giving box-office support to movies which exploit sex. More than that, we need to show in our own lives that rich, lasting, fulfilling relationships between man and woman *are* possible when there is complete loyalty and mutual respect. Sex can have a beautiful place in such relationships, but if loyalty is absent, if sex is made the basis of the relationship and both parties are content to go their own ways, tragedy is going to follow for everyone concerned.

प्रह्लादश्चास्मि दैत्यानां कालः कलयतामहम् ।
मृगाणां च मृगेन्द्रोऽहं वैनतेयश्च पक्षिणाम् ॥३०॥

30. Among animals I am the lion; among birds, the eagle. I am Prahlāda, born among the demons, and of all that measures, I am time.

Some of the greatest characters in the Hindu scriptures are teenagers, and one of them is Prahlāda, who had boundless devotion to the Lord. The example of Prahlāda, Mahatma Gandhi tells us, was one of his earliest inspirations as a child. Born into a demonic society full of disharmony and violence, Prahlāda steadfastly kept his eyes on the divine unity of life. In spite of his family's objections, in the face of all sorts of obstacles and trials, he remained unswerving in his devotion to the Lord of Love. Throughout India he is deeply loved as a model of bhakti yoga, the path of love and devotion.

Then Sri Krishna quietly slips in one of the most powerful statements in this chapter: "I am time." It has far-reaching implications, for our inability to see below the surface of life is closely tied to our preoccupation with time. Almost everything we do is under pressure of time. The constant emphasis is on hurry, hurry, hurry, and our greatest praise goes not to those who can do something better but to those who can do it faster. Just see the absurdity of this speed mania. Yesterday somebody was telling me about a camera that can develop film in ten seconds instead of sixty seconds. My comment was, "What am I to do with the fifty seconds I have saved?"

Instead of trying to do things faster and faster, it is more effective to work at a steady pace with complete concentration. The person who does things very fast usually does a shoddy job. At my university in India, I often saw students go into the examination hall, dash off their answers, and leave, saying, "We finished the whole thing in an hour's time." To be accurate, they ruined the whole thing in an hour's time. An experienced observer can spot the good student easily: it is the person who studies the question first and tries to understand exactly what the examiner is asking. The student who is in a hurry, who begins writing immediately, often gives the examiner stone instead of bread.

When we work under the constant pressure of time, traveling as fast as we can and eating on the run, we are making our nervous system tenser and tenser. Eventually it simply goes out of control. When you see a person being rude or thoughtless to those around him, it can help to remember that he may not really be unkind; his nervous system may simply have been pushed beyond the limit. Instead of adding to their burden by giving tit for tat, we can help such people by being patient and courteous ourselves and by helping them to slow down.

Gradually, as we learn to slow down the mind through the practice of meditation, we begin to free ourselves from any compulsion of time. But we do not do this by throwing our watches away. Living in the midst of the world, I am always very particular about being on time, because being late affects not only us but everyone around us too. Being late makes for greater hurry and greater tension for everyone involved, and it tends to accumulate throughout the day. So even when I go out to a film or a play I like to arrive half an hour or so early, so that there is plenty of time to find a parking place, get the tickets, and find good seats without stepping on people's toes. This is the way to become master of time and gradually slow down the furious pace of living.

पवनः पवतामस्मि रामः शस्त्रभृतामहम् ।
झषाणां मकरश्चास्मि स्रोतसामस्मि जाह्नवी ॥३१॥

31. Among purifying forces I am the wind, and among warriors I am Rāma. Among water creatures I am the crocodile, and among rivers I am the Ganges.

The wind is a powerful purifier; without the wind to keep impurities from accumulating, our atmosphere could not continue to sustain life. On more than one occasion now, the Bay Area has been so stifled with smog that children have been asked not to run or play for fear that they might breathe too much of this deleterious air. Then a strong wind blows in from the ocean, and on the following morning the sky is blue and the hills stand out clearly, glad to be clothed in the clean air again. In tropical countries like India, when there is no wind, the air can become so still it is suffocating, and many people sleep outdoors under the stars to catch any gentle breeze that blows.

In most ancient cultures the wind is deified as a divine power, endowed with tremendous capacity for both evil and good. My friend Bron has been telling me about the chinook, which is a hot wind you have only in America, east of the Rocky Mountains. What is surprising is that it makes its appearance in winter. One March day in Montana, it raised the temperature thirty-one degrees in just three minutes. In the dead frost of winter, the chinook can come down from the mountains like a corps of angels to rescue herds of cattle from death by freezing and starvation. Another interesting wind

I've been reading about, the harmetan, has earned the title of "doctor." It blows from the hot, dry Sahara to the humid coast of Africa. Following the professional services of Dr. Harmetan, ague disappears, the pangs of arthritis are relieved, and everyone is invigorated. But it is not only extraordinary winds like these that purify; even a gentle breeze does its part to keep our air circulating so that impurities don't accumulate. The whole globe is enveloped in a mantle of giant wind systems, all kept in constant motion by the immense power of the sun. One scientist has calculated that the energy driving these systems is equal to that of seven million atomic bombs. All this is part of the continuous miracle which sustains life.

In this verse, Sri Krishna is reminding us that the same power for purification which is found in the wind is found in you and me. Any person whose life benefits others is a purifier. In contrast, any person who spreads anger and fear, who pursues his own interests at the expense of others, is like smog; he afflicts people wherever he goes. Look at his home and you will see how the eyes of his family smart, how their hearts burn with the selfishness that hangs in the air. Unfortunately, each one of us today is polluted with the smog of self-will to some degree. But through the practice of meditation we can learn the science of purification. This is simply another way of describing the skill for transforming hatred into love, resentment into compassion, and fear into fearlessness that comes with sustained practice of meditation. The person who has this inner fortitude, whose spirit cannot be broken by any adverse circumstances, is a purifier.

Then the Lord says, "I am Rāma." Rāma is the hero of the Indian epic the *Rāmāyana*. Like Sri Krishna, he is a divine incarnation of the spiritual power of Vishnu, the Preserver in the Hindu Trinity. Vishnu came down to earth many times to save humanity from danger, and he came as Sri Rāma before his incarnation as Sri Krishna.

Rāma is deeply loved in India because he represents the perfect son, the perfect husband, and the perfect king. His wife, Sītā, is equally cherished as the perfect wife and mother. Rāma and Sītā were always deeply devoted to each other, and were loyal through all sorts of trials. In the *Rāmāyana,* the story of these trials takes on deep spiritual significance. There, as Sri Ramakrishna used to say, Rāma represents the Lord, and Sītā the human soul. Rāma is so loyal to his father that to fulfill a rash promise his father made, he gives up his kingdom and goes into exile in the forest for fourteen years. Of her own accord, Sītā goes with him, giving up all the comforts of the court in order to be with the one she loves. During their exile, Sītā is abducted by a demon king called Rāvana, the embodiment of the ego. At the end of many trials, Rāma succeeds in slaying Rāvana and is reunited with Sītā. This mortal combat between Rāma and Rāvana, like the battle which is the backdrop for the Bhagavad Gita, is the struggle between the selfless and selfish urges within all of us, and the reunion of Sītā and Rāma represents the unitive experience which is the supreme goal of life.

This story of Rāma and Sītā is known all over India. In countless homes, especially in the villages, it is read and told over and over again, because it conveys spiritual values in a vivid way that even children can appreciate and absorb. Mahatma Gandhi was especially fond of the *Rāmāyana,* for his mantram was the name of Rāma, who is the perfect embodiment of one who never swerves from truth. After many years of conscious effort, Gandhi made *Rāma* an integral part of his consciousness. Then, when the assassin's bullets struck him at point-blank range, he was able to greet his attacker with *Rāma* on his lips and infinite compassion in his heart.

Among creatures that live in the water, Sri Krishna says he is the crocodile. We saw some crocodiles in the aquarium the other day, and what impressed me most about them was their almost impenetrable armor. This is the kind of armor we have to develop in order to withstand the onslaught of life. To meet every challenge as it comes, we cannot allow vacillations in fortune and fame to affect us. One well-known film star has confessed that he chose to go into films to gain as much attention as possible, thinking that he would find security. It was the one thing he did not find. Security is armor which we must learn to put on *inside* of us; we cannot get it anywhere outside. Every time we are patient in the face of agitation, every time we return forbearance for resentment, we strengthen this armor and deepen our security.

The final epithet has profound mystical significance, for the Ganges, the sacred river of India, is a symbol of the life-force contained in sex. In sex lies the secret of life itself. That is why I always repeat that sex can have a beautiful place in a relationship between man and woman where there is complete love and loyalty. In meditation we gradually gain control over this deep drive, so that instead of being its victim, subject to every whim of desire, we become its master. Then sex becomes a source of tremendous creative power which draws people together in the unity that underlies us all.

सर्गाणामादिरन्तश्च मध्यं चैवाहमर्जुन ।
अध्यात्मविद्या विद्यानां वाद: प्रवदतामहम् ॥३२॥

32. I am the beginning, middle, and end of creation.
Of all the sciences I am the science of Self-knowledge,
and I am reason in those who debate.

Patanjali, the great teacher of meditation in ancient India, tells us to take to the spiritual life so that we may realize who we are. To me, this is real education—not education for degrees but education for living, which is a perfect description of meditation. Meditation enables us to find, right in the context of our daily lives, the answer to that most important question, "Who am I?" We may know all about wines, or skiing, or even English literature, but until we learn who we really are, nothing else we learn or do can ever give us fulfillment, security, or peace of mind. The Lord is asking us here, "Before you try to learn everything else, why don't you give half an hour every morning to learning about yourself?"

In this verse Sri Krishna does not try to impress us with terms like "transcendental wisdom" or "the clear light within"; he uses simple, chaste language: "I am reason." Sometimes when I hear people discussing the possibility of intelligent life on other planets, I am inclined to ask, "Is there intelligent life on earth?" Far from expecting an age of mysticism, I hope only for an age of reason, which is noticeably absent in most of our activities today. For example, how can we live in harmony with our family and friends if we persist in returning anger for anger? How can we bring about lasting peace by adding to the probability of nuclear holocaust? To live in the midst of conflict with peace in our hearts, transforming those around us through patience and forgiveness, requires enormous internal strength, which is gradually developed through the practice of meditation.

अक्षराणामकारोऽस्मि द्वन्द्वः सामासिकस्य च ।
अहमेवाक्षयः कालो धाताहं विश्वतोमुखः ॥ ३३ ॥

33. Among letters I am A; among grammatical compounds I am the dvandva. I am infinite time, and the sustainer whose face is seen everywhere.

In many alphabets, including Sanskrit, *A* is the first letter; when the Lord says that among letters he is *A,* it is a grammatical reminder that he is the origin of all life. As Jesus says, "I am the alpha and the omega"; we come from him and we return to him. We may be born into the world through our parents, but our real origin is divine.

Dvandva is another reference to grammar. Sanskrit authors were fond of making big words by running smaller words together, sometimes so many of them that they wander off onto the next page like a snake. The most democratic of these compounds are called *dvandvas*; usually all their smaller words have equal value. But there may be another reason why Sri Krishna singles out the *dvandva* here. Sanskrit scriptures are full of *dvandvas* of opposites to describe life on the physical level: *sukhaduhkha,* 'pleasure and pain'; *labhālabha,* 'profit and loss'; *jayājaya,* 'victory and defeat.' Duality is the very nature of the world of change, and if we are to live in freedom we have to learn to dispel this fog called *dvandvamoha,* the delusion of separateness which keeps us from seeing that life is one.

In the last verse but two, the Lord told us he was time the mea-
surer; now he says that he is infinite time as well. This is the eternal
present, which we sometimes glimpse in the deeper stages of meditation when all awareness of the world of change has been withdrawn. Then we begin to understand just how relative time is. The
passage of time has no reality of its own; it is very much a part of
the functioning of the mind.

All of us are familiar with this. When we are absorbed in something we like very much, hours can pass before we know it, but
when we are doing something we dislike intensely, every little second seems to drag on endlessly. Patanjali would say that this has
nothing to do with the world outside us; it is a matter of the mind
being concentrated. When we are doing something we like, all our
attention is on the present; when we have to do something we dislike, the mind is always wriggling out into the past, or the future,
or its own little world of might-have-been.

In this connection, there is a good story about Dr. Albert Einstein—probably apocryphal, as a great many of these stories are—
which tells how this delightful man of genius had to sit through a
talk which seemed to have no direction and no end. Einstein was a
very patient man, but after some time of this he began to shift uneas-
ily from side to side and look down at his hands. Finally he leaned
over and whispered to a friend sitting next to him, "I have discovered only relativity; this fellow has discovered eternity."

The practical application here is that eternity is within the reach
of every one of us. By gradually learning to still the mind through
the practice of meditation, we can learn to live in the Eternal Now.
Then we can enjoy not only what we like, but what we dislike as
well. More than that, as we begin to live more and more in the
present, we make the exhilarating discovery that past and future
exist only in our minds. It is a tremendous realization, for it means
that we are released from any burden of guilt about the past and any
anxiety about the future. We think that past and future are real because we keep brooding over what we have done and what others
have done to us, what we will do and what others will do to us. But
it is not past and future that are real; it is our brooding on the past

and the future that is real. If we could withdraw our attention from these will-o'-the-wisps, many of our problems would simply dissolve.

Many years ago I stayed at the home of an hospitable woman in the Bay Area who happened to believe in ghosts. Her home had a beautiful view which took in a cemetery nearby, and though she was very fond of me, nothing I could say could convince her that ghosts from that cemetery did not pay her visits at unlikely times. So one day I announced casually that I was going for a walk in the cemetery to meet one of these ghosts myself. When I returned she was wringing her hands. "Did you see any ghosts?" she asked anxiously.

"Oh, yes," I said. "Three."

"What did you do?"

"I told them you were too nice a woman to be living in fear all the time, and that they should go away and leave you alone."

"And what did they say?"

"They said, 'We can't. As long as she believes in us, we *have* to stay.'"

She stared at me for a second and then laughed out loud. Because of her affection for me those simple words had gone in deeply, and after that she was never afraid of ghosts again.

Whenever we worry about something in the past or the future, what we are doing is setting up our own little haunted house and peopling it with our own special ghosts—Aunt Agatha, looking the way she did when she scolded us at the dinner table twenty-five years ago, or our little boy disguised as Marlon Brando in *On the Waterfront*. To banish these ghosts, all we need to do is stop thinking about them. They will never bother us again, because they were never there at all.

As we learn to disentangle ourselves from past and future and bring our consciousness to rest in the present, we enter into eternity. The Compassionate Buddha gives us the key to understanding how this happens in his doctrine of momentariness, called *kshanikavāda,* which tells us that there is no inherent connection between one moment and the next. Every moment is unique and discrete. When our concentration is complete, we rest like a king in the present, not concerned with what happened in the past, not anxious over what might happen in the future. Completely absorbed in the present, we are able to give our best concentration to everyone we deal with and everything we do.

The last epithet, *Vishvatomukha,* means 'he whose face is everywhere.' Nicholas of Cusa says that in every face there is the face of the Lord, hidden behind a veil. This divine face can be seen only when we enter into what Nicholas calls "mystic silence," which is what samādhi may be said to be.

मृत्युः सर्वहरश्चाहमुद्भवश्च भविष्यताम् ।
कीर्तिः श्रीर्वाक्च नारीणां स्मृतिर्मेधा धृतिः क्षमा ॥३४॥

34. I am death, which overcomes all, and the source of all beings still to be born. I am the feminine qualities: fame, beauty, perfect speech, memory, intelligence, loyalty, and forgiveness.

Over and over in these chapters the Lord is driving home to us that he is not only life and love, he is also death—*mrityuh sarvaharah,* by whom all of us one day are going to be struck down. No good spiritual teacher will fail to drive this into our consciousness, for once it penetrates our hearts we will give everything to the practice of the spiritual life; we will not let a day pass without doing our very best to surpass our efforts of the day before. The conquest of death is such an immense achievement that a lifetime is not too long for it, and when we let even a single day slip by, we are letting life itself slip through our fingers.

In the Hindu and Buddhist traditions we say that even a lifetime is not enough; all of us have been working towards this conquest for many lives. To me, the argument for reincarnation was summed up pithily by one of our children: "I don't want to be dead *always.*" The Lord of Love, by whatever name we call him, is not likely to keep us dead forever. Each time around we have the opportunity to conquer death, and each time most of us decide that we have other things to do instead. The Lord waits patiently while we experiment for a number of years, but finally, if we have still not learned that the purpose of life is to go beyond death, he comes to take us back for "R and R," rest and recuperation. Then, when the right circumstances develop for us to take up where we left off, he gives us a strong, new body and sends us forth to try again.

All this is very much like a loving father, but in many parts of India—particularly Bengal, where Sri Ramakrishna was born—we don't talk about God as our Father but as our Mother. I think it is a particularly appropriate perspective for this verse, for the selfless love of a mother for her child is the perfect symbol for the love the Lord has for every one of us. Just as we have been born on earth to our earthly mother, all of us are children of the Divine Mother. In the Krishna tradition, one of the names of the Lord is *Hiranya-garbha,* the 'womb of the cosmos.' She is the Source from which the universe was born, and the Upanishads, echoed by some theories in contemporary astronomy, tell us that when her creation becomes so vast that it threatens to disperse itself forever, she gathers the galaxies and all their creatures into herself to be born again. In the beautiful words of Christian mysticism, we all come from God, abide in God, and return to God, who is the Divine Mother of us all.

Sri Ramakrishna used to say frequently that we should look on all women as the embodiment of the Divine Mother. What he meant is that the qualities which make for a perfect woman are the qualities which make for a deeply spiritual person. This is the sense of Sri Krishna's reference to "feminine qualities" in this verse: it does not apply only to women; it applies equally to men. In the totally integrated person, man or woman, there is a part that is masculine and a part that is feminine. In the Hindu tradition this is represented by a glorious image called Ardhanārīshvara—one half thoroughly masculine, the other utterly feminine, united in one person. It is unrealistic to deny that there are masculine qualities, just as it is unrealistic to deny that there are feminine qualities. There are both, and each is meant to be completed by the other. Gandhi was like that; there was never more of a soldier than Gandhiji when he was fighting for truth, and no one more tender when he was nursing the sick or comforting a little child. Here all that is best in man and all that is best in woman have come together. There is no contradiction in this, no discrimination, no competition; there is only completion. It is not only women who love such a man, and not only men who love such a woman; everyone loves the person who has realized the unity in which man and woman are one.

As a boy, growing up under the guidance of my mother and my Grandmother, I absorbed this attitude naturally at an early age. The family tradition in which I grew up in the state of Kerala is like no other culture with which I am acquainted. It is a matrilineal tradition, highly civilized, in which women have had equal rights with men for centuries. One of the practical consequences of this is that while most boys and girls in India grow up almost in different worlds, I spent my first sixteen years under the roof of a large joint family in close daily contact with girls as well as boys, women as well as men. It still impresses me to remember how the ideals of that tradition were passed on to all of us by the quiet example of our women. Even when I was very young, I used to admire how girls no older than I was could put others first and win people over by their patient example with a grace that most of us boys never managed to achieve at any age, even when we tried. My Grandmother was the perfect flower of that tradition, and it was from her that I learned how perfectly the qualities mentioned here apply to either sex.

Some of these qualities deserve special attention, because they have no precise English equivalents. *Sri,* 'beauty,' has nothing to do with superficial attractiveness; it refers to the inner radiance that shines in the eyes of those who are selfless. I have never seen anyone so beautiful with *sri* as my Grandmother, even in the twilight of her life. My Granny was not given to praising people easily, and she always took a deep interest in the women who married into our ancestral family because of its ancient matriarchal heritage. There were not many brides who could meet her expectations of what a woman should be, but when she saw one who did, she would say with quiet approval, "That girl has *sri* in her face." No one could have asked for higher praise.

Dhriti, 'loyalty,' is a precious quality that we have almost lost sight of today. In relationships between man and woman, especially where sex is concerned, I think loyalty is considered old-fashioned, even unrealistic. Yet without loyalty, it simply is not possible to love.

When I first came to this country, everybody was talking about freedom. Between men and women, the idea was that if you came together freely, you were always free to walk out; this was supposed to be a complete safeguard against unhappy relationships. When my friends would talk this way I used to answer, "Oh, yes, you *are* free to walk out of such a relationship. There is no obligation; there are no bonds; there are not even any ties. But what happens if you go on doing this is that you never acquire the capacity to love."

Loyalty is the quintessence of love. When two people tell each other, "As long as you do what I like, I'll stay with you, but as soon as you start doing things I don't like, I'm packing my bags"—to me that is not love; that's indifference. Loving somebody means that even when they trouble you, you don't let yourself be shaken; even when they are harsh to you, you don't move away; even when they make a mistake that hurts you, you don't go off and make the same kind of mistake to hurt them. All of us are so liable to human error that unless we have some capacity to bear with the errors of others, we will not be able to maintain a lasting relationship with anybody, which is the tragic situation that many people find themselves in today.

I am not idealizing man–woman relationships when I talk like this. Despite what the media tell us, there is nothing easy about learning to love. It takes a lot of hard work, and if you want a relationship to get deeper and deeper with the passage of time, you will go on strengthening it all your life. Naturally there are going to be differences between you and your partner; that is the nature of life. Even identical twins have differences of opinion, and they come from the same combinations of genes and the very same background; why should two people from, say, New York City and Paris, Texas, expect life together to be smooth sailing? Even on the honeymoon there are going to be difficulties, and all too often one party is going to write home after the first week and say, "I never thought it would be like this!" You open Pandora's box expecting a lot of doves and out come a couple of bats instead. Here it is the mystics who are the real romantics, because they are the most practical. They won't get upset or despondent; they will say, "The doves are there; they're simply lying low. Why don't we get to work and clean out these bats?" This is the approach I learned from my Grandmother, which I try to apply in everything: never to dwell on the negative, but always to respect the potential in other people and help them to realize that potential through your support.

To do this we need *kshamā*—forgiveness, patience, the capacity to forbear. Kshamā is so important that I look upon it as another aspect of yoga. In the last chapter we discussed rāja yoga, the royal path of meditation; here we can introduce kshamā yoga, the path of patience and forgiveness, which will come into its real beauty in the climax of this volume in chapter twelve. It is a path that is suited to people in all walks of life, from all religious backgrounds.

Poets like to write about love, popular singers like to glorify love, but nobody ever bothers to sing the praise of patience. Yet in order to love others you must have tremendous patience, to bear with them come what may. None of us are born with this capacity, but all of us can develop it through practice. In a situation where there is a lot of friction, where others differ from you and everything seems to be going wrong, don't move away; move closer. It will be difficult, especially at the beginning. You may have to grit your teeth, you may have to bite your lip to keep from saying what is in your mind; and then of course you need to smile too, which doesn't add up to an especially pretty picture. It is a demanding art to do this gracefully, but I can give you an image from which you can draw consolation.

On the Blue Mountain in South India we had a little garden with a number of peach, pear, apple, and cherimoya trees. These trees had never been pruned; they had been allowed to grow in any direction they liked, and the garden was so small that they were all crowded close together. Their branches were tangled, fresh growth was choked by the snarl of dead limbs, and it was impossible for them to bear good fruit. It took a lot of work to prune that garden, and when we were done the trees looked denuded. All the dead branches had been cut away and nothing new had begun to grow. It was only when spring came that I was convinced that the pruning hadn't been a mistake, when I saw those trees all gracefully wearing their fresh leaves and decked with blossoms.

When we have free-roaming, unpruned self-will like this, when we've been letting our likes and dislikes run rampant for twenty or thirty years, the process of pruning can be quite painful. Not only that, we will not always be at our best. Sometimes we may be able to forbear gracefully, but there are going to be times when our smile looks like a grimace or we have to rush out the door repeating the mantram. This is the pruning period, when life can look pretty drab; the dead branches of our old habits will be lying all around us and the new leaves will not yet have begun to grow. But for all of us, if we keep at our pruning carefully, the spring is bound to come. There will still be gardening to do, but when we see our new ways blossoming and the good fruit we have begun to bear for others, this pruning of self-will will be a source of lasting satisfaction.

बृहत्साम तथा साम्नां गायत्री छन्दसामहम् ।
मासानां मार्गशीर्षोऽहमृतूनां कुसुमाकरः ॥३५॥

35. I am the Sāma Veda and the Gāyatrī. Among the months I am Mārgashīrsha, and among seasons I am spring, the season of flowers.

The Sāma Veda, one of the oldest of the Hindu scriptures, is so sonorous that it used to be sung. But no human recitation can compare with the beauty of such a passage in deep meditation, when concentration on the words is complete and each word reverberates through consciousness with unearthly beauty. The joy of this experience is so great that nothing the senses can offer is even worthy of comparison.

The Gāyatrī is a mantram from the Rig Veda, the earliest of the Hindu scriptures; it has been used throughout India for thousands of years. I interpret the word *gāyatrī* to mean 'that which protects the reciter against all harm.' The most enthusiastic Gāyatrī recitation I ever heard in India was not by any Indian, but by a Swiss friend with a good ear for music who used to recite it very much in a Wagnerian manner. But to reap the benefits of a mantram, you do not need to appreciate music or even be able to carry a tune. The Lord isn't going to listen to your recitation and say, "No, no, Roberta, let me hear that A again." All he is interested in is that we repeat the mantram whenever possible, with sincerity, concentration, and love.

Among months the Lord is Mārgashīrsha, the first month of the Hindu year. It is as if Sri Krishna is asking us to make a New Year's resolution to remember him in those around us throughout the year. Then he adds that among seasons he is the springtime, because all over the world spring is the season of birth, beauty, and joy. The birth that is meant here is the birth of the Lord in our hearts, which in the language of all the great religions is called our second birth, in which we wake up into eternal life.

द्यूतं छलयतामस्मि तेजस्तेजस्विनामहम् ।
जयोऽस्मि व्यवसायोऽस्मि सत्त्वं सत्त्ववतामहम् ॥३६॥

36. I am the gambling of the gambler and the radiance in all that shines. I am effort; I am victory; and I am the quality of sattva.

Some years ago I was in a bus depot and happened to hear the conversation of some people waiting for the bus to Reno. Everyone seemed to have his own foolproof system for blackjack, worked out through long research. Not only that, each person I listened to was absolutely convinced that his system could never fail. Even if the last time around they had lost their shirt and their T-shirt too, their faith was not affected. "Something was wrong with that dealer, or the angle of the table," they would say. "Or maybe the stars were all wrong. But this time my turn is going to come, and I'm going to double the stakes." As far as I could make out, they all had the same system: the more you lose, the more you double the stakes. Then, when you finally win, your losses are made up.

Now, according to the Gita, the gambler is not merely trying to win a game or break the bank; he is looking for the source of lasting satisfaction, which is the Lord. This is the compassionate view, which looks into the gambler's heart. People don't go to Las Vegas or Monte Carlo to make money or even to enjoy the thrill of winning; they go in search of the joy and security that can only be found within. It is very much like the man in one of my niece's favorite riddles. She takes delight in posing riddles for me, which I am seldom able to answer, and this time she asked: "Why was a man looking under the streetlight for the quarter he lost at the other end of the block?" The answer is really to the point: "Because there was more light there." This is very much our predicament. We are all looking for fulfillment in life, but most people are looking in places where they can never find what they are looking for, because the source of fulfillment is not outside us but within. We can render a real service to people like this by showing them that the thrill of winning can only be lasting when it comes from winning mastery of ourselves.

Next the Lord praises *vyavasāya,* 'effort.' Whenever you find the capacity to work enthusiastically for a selfless cause, the Lord is present, right in the effort itself. This does not include erratic effort, where we get up early and work nonstop until midnight, then go to sleep and do not wake up for two days. One of my schoolmates in high school actually did this; he went to sleep on Monday and woke up on Wednesday. We were all amazed. He couldn't understand why we were doing geography that day instead of history, because he didn't realize he had slept through an entire day. Such people do things on a heroic scale at the outset; then, when enthusiasm wanes and boredom sets in, they want something else to hold their fleeting interest. But there is a rare person who becomes more enterprising and resourceful with every difficulty that comes his or her way. Such people achieve success in any walk of life, and once they begin to harness their enthusiasm to achieve a selfless goal, they can really go far. So Sri Krishna adds here, *Jayo 'smi:* 'I am victory.' Mahatma Gandhi, one of the most inspiring examples of spiritual transformation I know of in this century, tells us out of his own experience: "Any man or woman can achieve what I have if he or she would make the same effort and cultivate the same hope and faith." And then he adds magnificently, "Full effort is full victory."

When you are really making your best effort on the spiritual path, there is a slow but tremendously potent rise of the spiritual energy called *kundalinī*. To an experienced eye, the marks of this rise are unmistakable. There is such drive, such resoluteness, such an indomitable will to achieve the goal of life no matter what stands in the way, that the mystics of both East and West use the image of fire to describe their personal experience of this power. To those around them, it is almost like seeing a human missile; every ounce of fuel is channeled into this tremendous attempt to reach an almost unreachable goal.

But finally, after samādhi is achieved, everything is transformed. Those who have become established in this state are so tranquil, so deceptively serene, that we might make the mistake of assuming that all their power has been consumed. It has not: it has become almost limitless, but now it is completely under control. It is like getting a second engine. You may have a Model T body, but now you get a Ferrari engine; just a touch of the accelerator and in seconds you can be at top speed. And then, the Hindu scriptures say, kundalinī is no longer fire; it is light. Going up, when all you can manage is to keep it under control, kundalinī is fire; but when it comes down again, to bathe all the centers of consciousness and release their deepest resources, it comes down as light. This divine radiance is called *tejas* in Sanskrit, and Sri Krishna is telling us here that this same light is within everyone, and it is the same radiance in the sun, in the stars, as in us all. Kabir says:

> The moon shines in my body,
> But my blind eyes cannot see it;
> The moon is within me,
> And so is the sun.

वृष्णीनां वासुदेवोऽस्मि पाण्डवानां धनंजयः ।
मुनीनामप्यहं व्यासः कवीनामुशना कविः ॥३७॥

*37. Among the Vrishnīs I am Krishna, and among
the Pāndavas I am Arjuna. Among sages I am Vyāsa,
and among poets, Ushanas.*

The references to Sri Krishna in this verse reveal a wealth of meanings. First and foremost, Sri Krishna is the eternal, immutable, infinite Reality whom we call God—the source of all joy, all security, all beauty, and all wisdom, present in the depths of our consciousness. But in another aspect, the historical aspect, Sri Krishna is a divine incarnation who was born on earth. He was a member of the Vrishnī clan; he played as a child, grew to be a handsome young man, and went through all the stages of human life.

These two—the eternal Godhead and the divine incarnation—are different aspects of the same supreme Reality. Similarly, the Compassionate Buddha was born a prince of Kapilavastu and grew to be a young man with a lovely wife and child; we know of his struggle to find the answer to the meaning of life. The life of Jesus the Christ is familiar to all of us too; we know of his birth in Bethlehem and his death on the cross. There is no contradiction between the historical aspect of the Lord and the supreme Reality, which was never born and will never die. All these incarnations are simply different manifestations of the same Reality. In the next chapter, Sri Krishna, the perfect divine incarnation, will give us a glimpse of his immortal, omnipresent nature. Then, after revealing his cosmic form, the Lord will once again assume his role in the human drama as Arjuna's guide and companion.

When my wife and I were in India we had to make a choice between going to the Taj Mahal and going to Vrindāvana, the historical birthplace of Sri Krishna. We still have not seen the Taj Mahal. Instead we took the evening train to Vrindāvana, and as it was a slow-moving train, we were able to watch leisurely all the timeless scenes of village India as we passed by. It was dusk, the "hour of cow dust," when the cows come home from the pasture raising dust with their hooves, and the scene around us immediately brought to mind the stories of Sri Krishna as an irresistible young cowherd. Vrindāvana is the perfect setting for these stories, with the river Yamunā winding round the village and Mount Govārdhana standing as a nearby sentinel.

Some of the most delightful episodes in Sri Krishna's life take place on this mountain. According to one legend, Indra wanted to test Sri Krishna to see if he was really a divine incarnation or just an imposter. So Indra, god of storms, told the rain, "Send down a deluge on Vrindāvana, and we'll see what this Krishna can do." Torrential rains poured down, and the whole village was in danger of being swept away. When Sri Krishna's friends begged him to protect them from the flood, he smiled, picked up Mount Govārdhana just as we would pick up a push-button umbrella, and held it up above the village to protect everyone from the rain. So one of the names for the Lord is Giridhara Gopāla, "he who holds the mountain as an umbrella to shelter all those who seek his refuge." It is a simple way of saying that we do not need to be afraid of any challenge when we seek the Lord's help.

In another story, Brahmā, god of creation, stole the calves and cowherds of Vrindāvana and hid them in a mountain cave. As the sun was setting, Sri Krishna went to look for his friends but could not find them. The families of these cowherds were eagerly waiting for their children to return home, and Sri Krishna couldn't bear to think how much they would worry if their children were late. So through the great power of his Māyā, he made himself appear as the missing cowherds, cows, and calves. Everyone apparently went home as usual, only this time there was unusually great joy in each home. The parents found their sons so perfect that they could not understand how they could ever have yelled at them, and their cows that night were such gentle creatures that no one wanted to part from them again. Nobody guessed that this was the perfection of the Lord appearing in the form of their sons and their cattle.

When Sri Krishna says, "Among Pāndavas I am Arjuna," Arjuna must be melting in ecstasy. He has given all his heart to Sri Krishna; he has eyes only for him; he has no thought other than of him. Because every corner of his consciousness is filled with love for the Lord, Sri Krishna says, "I am in him always, and he is united with Me."

Then the Lord says that of sages he is Vyāsa. Vyāsa was not only a great sage but a great poet as well—in fact, he is the author of the *Mahābhārata* itself, the epic in which the Gita is the crowning jewel. So the Lord says that he is also Ushanas, the poet of poets. It is to remind us that if we have artistic talent, whether for poetry, painting, speaking, dancing, or music, we should use it in the service of the Lord to bring deeper awareness of the unity of life. Kālidāsa, another of the giants of Indian literature, wrote in one of his early epics: "I am like a little pygmy trying to pluck a fruit from a tall tree; I have no gift for poetry. How I would love to be a poet so I could sing the praise of the Lord!" According to legend, his desire was so deep and so selfless that the Divine Mother, called Kālī, appeared to him and wrote on his tongue the mantram *Om*. He took the name Kālidāsa, 'the servant of Kālī,' and became a genius in Sanskrit poetry and drama, using all his creative capacity to sing the praise of the Lord.

दण्डो दमयतामस्मि नीतिरस्मि जिगीषताम् ।
मौनं चैवास्मि गुह्यानां ज्ञानं ज्ञानवतामहम् ॥३८॥

*38. I am the scepter which metes out punishment,
and the art of statesmanship in those who lead.
I am the silence of the unknown and the wisdom of
the wise.*

The Lord is not only the lawgiver; he is the law and that which enforces the law as well. *Danda*—'scepter' or 'stick'—is a strong term in Sanskrit, implying punishment, penalty, or consequences. Since many people have some resistance to words like sin and atonement, I usually substitute terms like mistakes and consequences. This leaves no room for misunderstanding. For example, if we overeat, it is not a law passed by Congress that gives us dyspepsia. "He or she who overeats will suffer stomachache for three days, or three nights, or both" is not a law on the statute books; it is a law written within every cell of our body. This is the principle of mistakes and consequences, which we can ignore only at our peril.

Once our eyes begin to open, we shall see this principle working behind the scenes in all sorts of situations. Take vacations, for example. I have been looking at the advertisements for cruises in *The New York Times*. Much of the emphasis is not on seeing new lands or learning new languages, but on eating. One ad boasts, "We never give you the same menu twice during our world tour." Another describes the ship's twenty-two kitchens and one hundred eighty one cooks, and tries to entice the reader by saying, "We serve four gourmet meals daily, and you can come to the dining room anytime for a snack." If we were to go on a tour like that we would probably need to be met by an ambulance, and our friends would not be able to recognize us at all. "That's not my friend Jimmy," they would say; "that's some fat fellow." For some, it would take a month in the hospital to repair the damage of this overeating and underexercising. Overeating has obvious consequences—overweight, gastrointestinal problems, probably high blood cholesterol, and an increased likelihood of heart attacks, to name just a few—which eventually force us to correct our unhealthy living habits. The beauty of the Gita's approach is that it makes health our birthright, no less than security and joy. But in order to claim this birthright, we have to learn to make wise choices.

Then Sri Krishna says that in leaders he is statesmanship. This is statesmanship of an unusually high order, the mark of which is the capacity to return good will for ill will and nonviolent resistance for violence. Unfortunately, many of us have been conditioned to look upon violence as a way of solving problems. But one of the laws of life is that hatred can never cease through hatred. As the Buddha tells us, hatred ceases only through love. We cannot break this law; we can only break ourselves against it by not observing it in all our relationships. When, against the background of evolution, we come into the human context, the law of the jungle is superseded by the law of unity, which Jesus phrased perfectly: "Bless them that curse you, and do good to them that hate you."

It is not difficult to understand what happens when we violate this law, which applies from the individual level to the international. No matter what the situation, violence will never cease when met with violence. World War I, for example, was supposedly fought to bring lasting peace. But the Treaty of Versailles which ended it, far from healing the wounds of conflict, broke the spirit of Germany and paved the way for World War II. In those days there were very few who could see the futility of seeking peace through war. Now most thoughtful people are beginning to agree that the world is one, that all life is one, and that a war anywhere on this planet threatens the welfare of us all.

यच्चापि सर्वभूतानां बीजं तदहमर्जुन ।
न तदस्ति विना यत्स्यान्मया भूतं चराचरम् ॥३९॥

39. My seed can be found in every creature, Arjuna, for without Me nothing can exist, neither animate nor inanimate.

Recently I have been reading a little of Spinoza, a mystic of the seventeenth century who was as unorthodox in the eyes of his Jewish community as Meister Eckhart was to the Christians of medieval Germany. Some of the things Spinoza says I like very much; they have the ring of personal experience, and they should appeal to any good scientist even if he or she professes not to believe in God. Spinoza calls God by a very surprising name: Substance. It is a very apt choice of words—*sub-stance,* "that on which everything in the universe stands." It is very much the same language that Eckhart uses when he talks about the Divine Ground of existence. The Lord *is* substance, the only reality; everything else is shadow. Here, because Arjuna is not very philosophically inclined, Sri Krishna puts it more personally: "Without Me," he says, "nothing else could exist, because I am present everywhere."

"As the idea of a circle is to all circles," Spinoza says, "so is God to the universe." If I want my friend Jeff, who is an architect, to build a complex of buildings where we can carry on our work, I don't let him start with a few bricks and some old recycled boards and just let everything grow like Topsy; I ask him to put every detail into one coherent plan. It may take longer, but at least that way I know that we won't end up with two false ceilings and a door opening onto the wall of the building next door. It is very much the same with the Lord. He has the blueprint for his creation worked out so that every detail follows from some previous detail, and when the time comes he just gives the word and the universe unfolds in all its endless diversity.

In some traditions this is the language that is used, where the Lord is the Architect, or the Designer, or the cosmic Watchmaker. In the Hindu tradition, however, we prefer to talk not about plans but about seeds. That is why Sri Krishna says here, "My seed can be found in every creature": just as in the unseen genetics of one tiny seed there is the potential for countless full-grown trees, the whole of creation is implicit in the Lord of Love.

नान्तोऽस्ति मम दिव्यानां विभूतीनां परंतप ।
एष तूद्देशतः प्रोक्तो विभूतेर्विस्तरो मया ॥४०॥
यद्यद्विभूतिमत्सत्त्वं श्रीमदूर्जितमेव वा ।
तत्तदेवावगच्छ त्वं मम तेजोंशसंभवम् ॥४१॥

40. But there is no end to my divine attributes,
Arjuna; these I have mentioned are only a few.
41. Wherever you find strength, or beauty, or spiritual
power, you may be sure that these have sprung from
a spark of my essence.

With these verses Sri Krishna gives the message of this whole chapter: wherever we see selflessness or forgiveness, wherever we see someone choosing to suffer rather than bring suffering to others, we can be sure that the Lord is present there. To see God, we do not need to look for some physical or psychical manifestation. Patience and forgiveness are not just moral qualities, but forces for unity that are latent within us all.

Like physical forces, these spiritual forces are universal. It is not only human beings that respond to patience, to forgiveness; animals respond too. Among the legends that surround St. Francis, there is a wonderful story about a fierce wolf who had been troubling the town of Gubbio until finally he was captured by the townsfolk. In their fear, the people of Gubbio wanted to put an end to the wolf's life. But St. Francis, aware of his unity with the wolf as only a child of God can be, went up to this fierce, frightened animal and scolded him just as he would an erring disciple. Francis was so full of love for all creation that not even a wild animal could see in him anything to fear, and the wolf lowered his head and listened humbly while the friar scolded him. After that he was a model of good behavior, and soon the entire town came to love him.

अथवा बहुनैतेन किं ज्ञातेन तवार्जुन ।
विष्टभ्याहमिदं कृत्स्नमेकांशेन स्थितो जगत् ॥४२॥

42. But of what use is it to you to know all this, Arjuna? Just remember that I am, and that I support the entire cosmos with only a fragment of my being.

Out of his love for Arjuna, Sri Krishna has patiently listed some of the ways his presence is manifested throughout creation. Using the example of ancient sages and modern householders, of mythological creatures and even grammatical compounds, the Lord has told us that he is in every creature and in every activity. In whatever reveals perfection, beauty, and awareness of unity, he is present. But now, having played the part of the professor and satisfied Arjuna's desire for knowledge, Sri Krishna warns him not to get lost in endless lists and categories. It is enough if we know that the Lord exists, and that his unifying force holds together the billions of galaxies throughout the cosmos with their countless forms of life. In the next chapter Arjuna will beg his friend to show him this infinite, universal form.

इति विभूतियोगो नाम दशमोऽध्यायः ॥१०॥

CHAPTER ELEVEN

The Cosmic Vision

अर्जुन उवाच
मदनुग्रहाय परमं गुह्यमध्यात्मसंज्ञितम् ।
यत्त्वयोक्तं वचस्तेन मोहोऽयं विगतो मम ॥१॥
भवाप्ययौ हि भूतानां श्रुतौ विस्तरशो मया ।
त्वत्तः कमलपत्राक्ष माहात्म्यमपि चाव्ययम् ॥२॥
एवमेतद्यथात्थ त्वमात्मानं परमेश्वर ।
द्रष्टुमिच्छामि ते रूपमैश्वरं पुरुषोत्तम ॥३॥
मन्यसे यदि तच्छक्यं मया द्रष्टुमिति प्रभो ।
योगेश्वर ततो मे त्वं दर्शयात्मानमव्ययम् ॥४॥

ARJUNA:
*1. Out of compassion you have taught me the
supreme mystery of life. Through your words my
delusion is gone.*
*2. You have explained the origin and end of every
creature, O lotus-eyed one, and told me of your
own supreme, limitless existence.*
*3. You have told me about your infinite glory,
O Lord. Now I long to see you as the supreme Ruler
of all creation.*
*4. O Krishna, if you think my love is strong enough
to absorb the glory of this vision, show me your
immortal Self.*

Swami Vivekananda, one of the foremost disciples of Sri Rama-krishna, used to say that religion *is* realization of God; nothing less can satisfy us. As a teenager, then called Narendra, he had struggled with all sorts of doubts. Like many young people today, he was tormented by questions about the meaning of life. He searched the worlds of literature and philosophy, but nowhere could he find an answer that satisfied him. Then he turned to highly regarded spiritual teachers, and to each he posed the same blunt question: "Have you seen God?" Always the reply was no.

Finally he heard of a saint who lived quietly at a little temple of the Divine Mother outside Calcutta. Narendra found his way there and went straight up to this little man to ask the same burning question he had asked all the others: "Have you seen God?"

Ramakrishna smiled. "Of course," he said. "I see God more clearly than I see you now. You I see only with my physical eyes, but God I see with every cell of my being."

This quiet authority, which can come only from experiential knowledge, is the unmistakable stamp of the vision of God. After becoming established in this vision, the God-conscious person may seem to be quite ordinary, but under this surface appearance he or she is no longer a separate, fragmented creature but part of the ir-resistible love force that we call God.

After years of enthusiastic effort, the Lord may reveal himself to us too in some small measure. Then we shall see into the very heart of life. This vision may last for only a moment or two, but it leaves behind an unforgettable awareness of the living presence of the Lord. Afterwards, no matter what their color or background or po-litical persuasion, we see everyone as this divine force. It is because we do not have this immense frame of reference that little pleasures get amplified out of all proportion. Once we have tasted the joy of this experience, the ordinary pleasures of life become insipid in comparison. All our desires will be unified around one great desire to recapture this experience, and we will cry, like David, "As the hart panteth after the water brooks, so panteth my soul after thee, O Lord."

When this great longing comes to us, the Divine Fisherman has got his hook into us forever. Isn't it Eckhart who says that the more we thrash about, the deeper the hook enters? We may try to run away, to do everything we can think of to get free; but finally, when we get a glimpse of who it is who has caught us, we realize what a blessing it is to be caught so firmly by the Lord.

श्री भगवानुवाच
पश्य मे पार्थ रूपाणि शतशोऽथ सहस्रशः ।
नानाविधानि दिव्यानि नानावर्णाकृतीनि च ॥५॥
पश्यादित्यान्वसून्रुद्रानश्विनौ मरुतस्तथा ।
बहून्यदृष्टपूर्वाणि पश्याश्चर्याणि भारत ॥६॥
इहैकस्थं जगत्कृत्स्नं पश्याद्य सचराचरम् ।
मम देहे गुडाकेश यच्चान्यद्द्रष्टुमिच्छसि ॥७॥

SRI KRISHNA:
5. Behold, Arjuna, a million divine forms,
with an infinite variety of color and shape.
6–7. Behold the gods of the natural world, O Bhārata,
and many more wonders never revealed before; be-
hold the entire cosmos turning within my body. These
are the things you desired to see.

Now Sri Krishna is beginning to reveal his universal, cosmic form, in one of the most magnificent portraits of the Lord I have seen anywhere in mystical literature.

In the Upanishads, the body is picturesquely called a little city, whose ruler is the Self. Recently I have been looking into quite a few books about the body, the immune system and the senses and all the mechanisms of health and disease, and the more I read, the more apt this image seems. If we could see life as a bacterium might, the body would be as busy as Bombay or New York City. It is a world of its own, so vast that learned societies of bacteria could study it and publish papers on its workings for generations and never suspect either the existence of the Ruler or of anything more vast outside.

In a breathtaking leap of spiritual insight, the Hindu scriptures go on to say that just as this body is only the city we live in during our life on earth, so the whole universe is no more than the body of the Lord. This is the cosmic vision that Arjuna is entering now. It is a beautiful image. When the Lord goes out into the world, he dresses as Sri Krishna, or the Buddha, or Jesus the Christ, and goes about looking just like one of us. But when he goes back home after a hard day's work, he takes off these forms and wears all the galaxies of the universe as casual garlands about his neck. That is why Sri Krishna is always represented as dark blue in color; it is to remind us that his body is really the infinite vastness of space and time.

To get some idea of the scale of this vision, look at the sheer vastness of the universe. Even at one hundred eighty-six thousand miles per second, it takes four years for light to reach us from the nearest star. Our own galaxy is more than one hundred thousand light-years across, and yet it is only an infinitesimal part of the universe. How long does it take for light to traverse the universe—assuming that it is possible at all? We can get some dim idea if we remember that some of the stars we see at night may have ceased to exist thousands of years before the light from them reaches our eyes. In looking outward into the depths of space, astronomers remind us, we are also looking backwards into the depths of time, and the light we see from faint stars on a clear night may have set out on its journey before there were human beings on earth to see.

On this cosmic scale, the stars that seem to us to be eternal are not much more long-lived than fireflies on a summer evening. Like all created things, they too have a beginning and an end. Born out of great clouds of dust and gas, they pour out energy over a few billion years and die, often in the fierce throes of a chain of explosions from whose remains new stars will someday be born. This drama has been going on throughout the vast universe for billions of years, and will go on for billions of years more; and the Sanskrit scriptures, echoed by many modern astronomers, remind us that even this is but a single act in the Lord's drama. Before and after the universe we live in, there stretch an infinitude of universes equally vast in space and time. As one Indian mystic wrote:

Let the Himālayas themselves become
The black pigment from which to make the ink,
And the ocean the bowl to contain it;
Let the whole universe serve as parchment,
And the celestial kalpa tree as pen;
Let this pen be held by Sarasvatī,
Goddess of wisdom, and let her write on
Through all eternity: she will not reach,
O Lord of Love, the end of your glory,
Nor find a limit to your dazzling splendor.

न तु मां शक्यसे द्रष्टुमनेनैव स्वचक्षुषा ।
दिव्यं ददामि ते चक्षुः पश्य मे योगमैश्वरम् ॥८॥

8. But these things cannot be seen with your physical eyes; therefore I give you spiritual vision to perceive my form as the Lord of creation.

Our eyes, like our other senses, are meant for registering changes in the world outside us. They are fine for letting us know when the traffic light turns red or when it is time to get up in the morning, but when it comes to going beyond change they are completely helpless. That is why in meditation we learn to withdraw all the senses gradually from the world of change. In deep meditation, when concentration on the inspirational passage is almost complete, we do not hear the cars on the road outside or the planes overhead; all our consciousness is withdrawn from the senses in a state of intense awareness within.

When we achieve this kind of concentration, we begin to discover that there is no real barrier between the world outside us and the world within the mind. As one British philosopher has put it, "outside" and "inside" are distinctions that we make mostly out of convenience; in both kinds of experience, outer and inner, what we are really perceiving is the contents and the impressions of our own mind. In other words, we see things not as they are but as we are. As long as our eye is multiple, as Jesus puts it, we see everyone around us as separate, and we cannot help trying to manipulate them when they do not behave the way we think they should. But when our consciousness becomes unified through the practice of meditation, we no longer see a world of separate fragments; we see all creation as one indivisible whole.

"Some people," Sri Ramakrishna said, "think that God cannot be seen. Who sees whom? Is God outside you, that you can see him with your eyes? One sees only one's Self." The vision Arjuna is about to have, in which all of space and time is comprehended in the body of the Lord, is not something he will see outside himself; it is something he will experience in the very depths of his consciousness.

संजय उवाच
एवमुक्त्वा ततो राजन्महायोगेश्वरो हरिः ।
दर्शयामास पार्थाय परमं रूपमैश्वरम् ॥९॥
अनेकवक्त्रनयनमनेकाद्भुतदर्शनम् ।
अनेकदिव्याभरणं दिव्यानेकोद्यतायुधम् ॥१०॥
दिव्यमाल्याम्बरधरं दिव्यगन्धानुलेपनम् ।
सर्वाश्चर्यमयं देवमनन्तं विश्वतोमुखम् ॥११॥

SANJAYA:

9. Having spoken these words, Hari, the master of yoga, revealed himself to Arjuna as the supreme Lord. 10. He appeared with an infinite number of faces, ornamented by heavenly jewels, displaying unending miracles and the countless weapons of his power. 11. Clothed in celestial garments and covered with garlands, sweet-smelling with heavenly fragrances, he showed himself as the infinite Lord, the source of all wonders, whose face is everywhere.

In this supreme vision the Lord reveals himself as having an infinite number of faces, and Arjuna sees the Lord in every face, in every creature. It can fill us with awe to realize that in our parents, our partner, our children, and our friends it is the Lord who is looking into our eyes, listening to us, responding to us. This is why we can learn to love the Lord while living in the midst of family and friends. Once the barrier of self-will falls in any of our close relationships, we will find the One—whether we call him the Christ, Sri Krishna, the Buddha, or Allah—in everyone around us.

Here the Lord appears to Arjuna as the source of miracles, not the least of which is the gift of life itself. Our every breath, our every heartbeat is a miracle; so are the wind blowing in the trees and the sun shining in the sky. We do not have to search the universe for miracles; they occur morning, noon, and night every day of our lives, only our eyes are not open to them. If we were in tune with this continuous miracle of life, we would put an immediate end to conflict—whether in our homes, between races, or among nations. We could not rest in peace until every creature was free from exploitation and violence and the threat of nuclear holocaust. As Mahatma Gandhi put it, "There can be no happiness for any of us until happiness has been had for all."

दिवि सूर्यसहस्रस्य भवेद्युगपदुत्थिता ।
यदि भाः सदृशी सा स्याद्भासस्तस्य महात्मनः ॥१२॥

12. If a thousand suns were to rise in the heavens at the same time, the blaze of their light would resemble a little the supreme splendor of the Lord.

You and I cannot look directly at the sun without damage to our eyes; its power is so immense that a minute fraction of the energy it radiates into space, diffused over ninety-three million miles and tempered by our atmosphere, is enough to sustain all life on this planet. Now we are asked to imagine a thousand of these suns rising at the same time in the depths of Arjuna's consciousness; his whole being is flooded with light. The intellect lies helpless, unable to grasp the immensity of this splendor; even the imagination swoons.

"When the soul looks upon this Divine Sun," St. Teresa says, "the brightness dazzles it . . . . And very often it remains completely blind, absorbed, amazed, and dazzled by all the wonders it sees."

Yet even this is still poetry, still understatement. The Lord is the source of all light; every sun, every luminous nebula in the cosmos is just a bead in his necklace. There are quasars, we are told, a million million times as bright as our own sun. The universe is filled with light; it pulsates with the power of the Lord.

The greatest wonder is that this tremendous radiance reflected throughout the cosmos shines within us too. As our spiritual awareness grows, as our separateness goes and our ego dissolves, we will experience a tremendous effulgence spreading throughout our consciousness, which no experience of the senses can ever help us comprehend. But Jesus gives the perfect description: "Thy whole body shall be full of light."

तत्रैकस्थं जगत्कृत्स्नं प्रविभक्तमनेकधा ।
अपश्यद्देवदेवस्य शरीरे पाण्डवस्तदा ॥१३॥

13. There, within the body of the Lord, Arjuna saw all the manifold forms in the universe united as one.

Here we have a glimpse of the mystery of the universe, which fills both mystic and scientist with awe. I get spellbound when I read about some of the discoveries in astronomy and atomic physics and realize that all this is just an infinitesimal part of the glory of the Lord. Even professional astronomers admit that the mind reels before some of these discoveries; the intellect cannot grasp their implications. We cannot even look at our own sun, and here are quasars that are millions of times brighter than our sun. We are told there are neutron stars in the universe where matter is so dense that a tablespoon of it is conjectured to weigh forty trillion tons. When matter gets this dense, the force of gravity is so immense at the core that the star is liable to collapse internally from its own weight, and millions and millions of tons of matter just disappear into a "black hole" in space—a bottomless hole with zero volume. You and I ask,

"What kind of a hole is that? Where did all that matter go?" And the astronomers can only shrug; they just don't know.

Now, in wonder, Arjuna sees that this whole vast universe of incessant change is all one in the Lord. The Gita will express this oneness in the language of poetry, drawing on all sorts of images from Hindu mythology. But the discoveries of science throw light on Arjuna's experience of unity too. Biologists tell us that every living thing, from a simple virus to a human being, has essentially the same DNA. It is a very personal tie that binds us to the beasts of the field and the birds of the air; even the plankton in the ocean are our kith and kin. But the unity extends deeper still, for the elements of life are the very same elements that are found throughout the universe, created in the depths of stars and strewn through space in the explosions of stellar death.

In the language of modern physics, the fabric of space and time, matter and energy, is continuous throughout the universe, from the nucleus of an atom to the farthest galaxy. To a great physicist like Albert Einstein, all forms of matter and energy are interrelated, and every point in the universe—say, an electron in one of the atoms of my hand—is affected by the rest of the universe as a whole. If we could see life at the subatomic level, the material objects we cling to for security would dissolve into patterns of energy, and the universe would be nothing but a sea of light. It is a precise description, but it is the language of Sri Ramakrishna too. On this level, we are at the very threshold of matter. The atomic particles of our everyday world are not fixed or solid; they come and go in and out of existence in the smallest fraction of a second. It is as if the Lord is teasing us in this subatomic world by playing a game of hide-and-seek. He comes and goes so quickly that we can never be sure where he is; no sooner do we think we have caught him than he slips away.

The deeper we probe into the nature of the universe, whether it is the vastness of space or the infinitesimal world within the atom, the more we shall see the glory of the Lord revealed. When I look at pictures taken through an electron microscope or the telescope at Mount Palomar, I don't see only beautiful, abstract patterns; I see illustrations for the Gita, showing the myriad forms of creation flowing from the Lord. Even the Andromeda galaxy and I have a common bond. In microcosm and macrocosm, the Lord holds all together in his embrace.

ततः स विस्मयाविष्टो हृष्टरोमा धनंजयः ।
प्रणम्य शिरसा देवं कृताञ्जलिरभाषत ॥१४॥
अर्जुन उवाच
पश्यामि देवांस्तव देव देहे
सर्वांस्तथा भूतविशेषसंघान् ।
ब्रह्माणमीशं कमलासनस्थ-
मृषींश्च सर्वानुरगांश्च दिव्यान् ॥१५॥

14. Filled with amazement, his hair standing on end with joy, Arjuna bowed before the Lord with folded palms and spoke these words.

ARJUNA:

15. O Lord, I see within your body all the gods and every kind of living creature. I see Brahmā, the Creator, seated on a lotus; I see the ancient sages and the celestial serpents.

Once, it is said, the women of baby Krishna's village came running to tell his foster mother, Yashoda, that her little boy had been eating sand. Baby Krishna denied everything, but his mother saw the look in his eyes and caught hold of his chin to try to see for herself. Krishna obligingly opened his little mouth wide. There, within that little rosebud of a mouth, Yashoda saw the vast starry sky with its innumerable worlds, and all the creatures that had ever lived and would ever be born. It must have lasted only for a moment, but Yashoda was overcome with fear and wonder, for this was the child she had been scolding and treating like her own.

This is the vision that Arjuna is entering now, which is beyond anything that words can express. Some of the greatest figures in the world's spiritual traditions have been left speechless by the vision of

God. Moses, it is said, returned silent from his encounter on Sinai, though his face was ablaze with the glory of the Lord. St. Paul lay paralyzed for three days and three nights after his vision of light on the road to Damascus. Pascal, a brilliant mathematician and writer, could only set down fragments: *"Certitude, certitude; sentiment, joie, paix"*—certitude, emotion, joy, peace. And St. Thomas Aquinas, the architect of Catholic theology, said simply after his experience, "All that I have written is no more than straw." Even the theories of modern physics become poetic when they try to describe the unity of life, and though their images may be more sophisticated than the sages and celestial serpents of this verse, I wonder if they have any more capacity to inform our deeper understanding.

But even if this vision of unity cannot be conveyed through words or pictures, it can be communicated in more subtle ways. It is said that of all the ways of giving spiritual instruction, the highest and most effective is through the living, personal example of an illumined teacher. Such people express the awareness of unity in everything they do, and through a kind of spiritual osmosis, those who love their teacher deeply can absorb this awareness and slowly learn to put it into practice in their own lives. That is why it is said that spiritual awareness is not so much taught as caught. I learned this from my Grandmother, who is one of the most accomplished spiritual teachers I have seen or even read about in the annals of mysticism. She scarcely ever spoke about these things, but she was so skillful in conveying her awareness that it was not until much later, when I finally turned to meditation, that I realized that she had been my spiritual teacher all along. Most people have to find a teacher. I was literally born into my teacher's arms, and even now it fills me with wonder to see how every day I become a little more like her, trying in a small way to live out the awareness of unity which she, in her infinite love for me, implanted in my heart when I was growing up.

अनेकबाहूदरवक्त्रनेत्रं
पश्यामि त्वां सर्वतोऽनन्तरूपम् ।
नान्तं न मध्यं न पुनस्तवादिं
पश्यामि विश्वेश्वर विश्वरूप ॥१६॥

*16. I see infinite mouths and arms, stomachs and
eyes, and you are embodied in them all. I see you
everywhere, without beginning, middle, or end.
You are the Lord of all creation.*

In Sanskrit, one of the names of the Lord is Vishnu, 'he who is everywhere.' Vishnu has a thousand names, which comprise all together one of the most sonorous of Sanskrit poems, and almost
every name is to remind us of the all-embracing, all-pervading
presence of the Lord.

It is said that when the suffering of Mother Earth became too
great for her to bear, she came to Vishnu, the Lord of Love, and
begged him to incarnate himself in a human body to lead humanity
back to the unity of life. That is the story behind baby Krishna's
birth, and just as with Jesus and the Compassionate Buddha, there
are a number of stories surrounding this event which every Hindu
knows from childhood, which help convey in simple language what
it means for the Lord to be born among us in human form.

According to the Hindu tradition in Kerala, a baby is not given a
name until it is a year old. Then there is a big feast to which all the
friends and relatives of the family come to celebrate his or her birth
when the name is given. Now, when baby Krishna was born, very
much as with the baby Jesus, there was a prophecy that caused the
king of the realm to want to take his life. But his parents managed
to spirit the baby away to foster parents in the country almost as
soon as he was born, and so it is in their home that the naming day
celebration takes place. As is traditional, his foster parents, Ya-
shodā and Nanda, invite a great sage named Garga to give their new
child his name. Neither Yashoda nor Nanda nor anyone else in the
village knows little Krishna's real nature, but Garga has only to see
the baby to realize that he has been asked to give a name to the Lord

Himself. He falls to his knees to worship the newborn child, and then he asks the foster mother and father, "What name can I give to a little boy who already has a thousand names?"

It is a beautiful way of reminding us that the Lord is in everyone, that all of our names are his names. It isn't just a thousand names; that is the poetic way of saying it. He has, at present, about four billion names, for he is within the heart of everyone on earth. The infinite numbers of arms and eyes in Arjuna's vision are not the product of an artist's imagination; in the depths of his consciousness, Arjuna is seeing the Lord of the universe simultaneously wearing the countless masks of all his creation. Ramdas, who is one of the most practical and inspiring mystics of this century, tells us:

> Whenever we see any form, we must see not only the external form, but also the indwelling Reality. This is the true vision which liberates us from the sense of diversity and makes us realize the oneness of all existence. This is the message of the rishis. It is not merely in particular holy places and solitudes that we should have this vision, but even in the marketplace and the bazaar we should be able to maintain the consciousness of unity in diversity. We must feel the divine presence always about us.

किरीटिनं गदिनं चक्रिणं च
तेजोराशिं सर्वतो दीप्तिमन्तम् ।
पश्यामि त्वां दुर्निरीक्ष्यं समन्ता-
द्दीप्तानलार्कद्युतिमप्रमेयम् ॥१७॥

17. You wear a crown and carry a mace and disk.
Your radiance is blinding and immeasurable; it fills
the universe with light like the fiery sun blazing
in every direction.

Even Emily Post would appreciate the way the orthodox Hindu worships the sun; it is a very personal way of saying thank you to him who makes it possible for us to live, to work and play, to go to school, or even to make money. For us he is not just the sun; he is

Divākara, "Mr. Daymaker." We draw our light from him, we draw our heat from him, we get our food from him; all life depends on the continuous miracle of the sun.

Here again, the astrophysicists can help us understand the dimensions of this miracle. Every second of every day for fifteen billion years, they say, 657 million metric tons of solar hydrogen are converted into 652.5 million metric tons of helium through a process of nuclear fusion—the same basic transformation as in the hydrogen bomb. The heckler will say, "Wait a minute; what happened to that other four and a half million tons of hydrogen?" And Mr. Daymaker replies, "That is what gets converted to energy; otherwise my solar furnace can't give you any heat or light. $E=mc^2$, you know; you can look it up in my file." The accounting is perfect. Everything is taken care of; there is no wastage. In all these millions, even an ounce is taken into account. That's how I understand those simple words, "He's got the whole world in His hands." He has his eye not only on these millions of tons of hydrogen; he has his eye even on the little micrograms. In Hinduism this is the aspect of the Lord that is called Chitragupta, the "cosmic accountant," where the Lord himself does his own auditing. Sri Krishna is very thrifty; everything must balance. In accounting circles in India there used to be a joke about an auditor looking over some particularly complicated account books where the entry was often GOK—"God only knows." It is like that. At the end of every day he tells the sun, "What about this, *hmm?* Four and a half million. Account for it." And then, smiling to himself, he writes, "GOK."

In other words, there is nothing superfluous in life. Everything is perfectly dovetailed into a delicate balance of matter and energy that extends throughout the universe, and which is just right for maintaining life here on earth. We look at the sun and take all this for granted; we forget the immensity of this miracle that makes life possible. It is not simply a matter of liberating an incomprehensible amount of energy every second; all this has to be tempered to our needs. The amount of energy released at the core of the sun is so vast that if it were released at the surface, there would be a wave of death that would spread throughout the solar system, destroying all life in its wake. Sir James Jeans, the British astronomer, writes that if we could take a bit of the sun no bigger than a pinhead and bring it here to earth, its heat could kill a person standing ninety-four miles away. To keep things from getting too hot for us, the Lord makes a very clever arrangement. The rays created at the core of the sun, astrophysicists tell us, are softened on their journey to the surface by atoms which play no part in the fusion process. They are the sidewalk superintendents who stand around and make comments; their job is to modulate the gamma rays until they leave the sun at just the right temperature to make life possible on earth.

When the astronomer sees all this, he too may feel a sense of awe at how delicately everything is balanced. But where he sees the laws of thermodynamics, the mystic sees the all-pervasive love of the Lord. The mystical poet William Blake declared: "I look through the eye, not with it. When the sun rises, I do not see a round disk of fire somewhat like a guinea; O no, no, I see an innumerable company of the heavenly host crying, *Holy, holy, holy.*"

There is no contradiction at all between Blake's vision and the scientists'. When I say that even the miracle of the sun is an expression of the Lord's love, it is not that I think there is someone waving his flute and saying, "Let these hydrogen nuclei fuse and become one!" The Lord is there in the nucleus of each atom, and the laws by which these transformations of matter and energy come about simply express the unity of his creation. If a star could talk, it wouldn't write poetry about love; it would sing the praises of gravitation. Romantic young stars just a hundred thousand years old or so would be yearning to lose themselves in the immense attraction of a black hole. For them, the unity of life expresses itself in forces like these; for us, it expresses itself in love. The language is different, but the unity is the same.

त्वमक्षरं परमं वेदितव्यं
त्वमस्य विश्वस्य परं निधानम् ।
त्वमव्ययः शाश्वतधर्मगोप्ता
सनातनस्त्वं पुरुषो मतो मे ॥१८॥

अनादिमध्यान्तमनन्तवीर्य-
मनन्तबाहुं शशिसूर्यनेत्रम् ।
पश्यामि त्वां दीप्तहुताशवक्त्रं
स्वतेजसा विश्वमिदं तपन्तम् ॥१९॥

द्यावापृथिव्योरिदमन्तरं हि
व्याप्तं त्वयैकेन दिशश्च सर्वाः ।
दृष्ट्वाद्भुतं रूपमुग्रं तवेदं
लोकत्रयं प्रव्यथितं महात्मन् ॥२०॥

अमी हि त्वां सुरसंघा विशन्ति
केचिद्भीताः प्राञ्जलयो गृणन्ति ।
स्वस्तीत्युक्त्वा महर्षिसिद्धसंघाः
स्तुवन्ति त्वां स्तुतिभिः पुष्कलाभिः ॥२१॥

*18. You are the supreme, changeless Reality, the
only thing to be known. You are the refuge of all
creation, the immortal spirit, the eternal guardian
and support of all.*

*19. You are without beginning, middle, or end; you
touch everything with your infinite power. The sun
and moon are your eyes, and your mouth is fire; your
radiance warms the entire cosmos.*

*20. O Lord, your presence fills the heavens and the
earth and reaches into every corner of the universe.
I see the three worlds trembling before this vision
of your wonderful and terrible form.*

*21. The gods enter your being, some calling out
and greeting you in fear. Great saints sing your
glory, praying, "May all be well!"*

Arjuna tells us over and over again how he is overcome with wonder at this revelation of the infinite power of the Lord. Scientists sometimes are suspicious when they hear all this ascribed to the power of God, but this is simply because they do not understand what the word *God* means to those who have realized him. All of us in the modern world have been conditioned to look upon God as something outside us, something other than us; even in our wildest dreams it is not possible to suspect that he is our real Self. This is the core of the mystical experience, and nowhere has it been more beautifully expressed than in the Sufi tradition, where those great Muslim mystics will say that He whom the vast heavens cannot contain is contained within your heart and mine.

In other words, there is no conflict between the vision of a great scientist and the experience of a great mystic, as we can see in the work of a scientist like Einstein who has access to a higher mode of knowing than the intellect. One such figure in modern astronomy is Abbé Georges Lemaître, a Catholic priest from Belgium, who hit upon a theory about the origin of the universe that shows not only brilliant intellect but the intuition of genius as well. Lemaître suggested that the cosmos was originally packed into an incomprehensibly dense primeval atom, a kind of "cosmic egg" in which there is neither time nor space—perhaps the way matter in a neutron star becomes so dense that it collapses into a black hole, pulling space and time in after it. It is very much the language of the ancient Hindu scriptures, which talk about *Hiranyagarbha* or *Brahmānda,* the 'egg of Brahman,' the germ out of which the cosmos grew. According to Lemaître, this cosmic egg exploded to become our universe, and it is still expanding from the force of this explosion.

Now, the question naturally arises, "What made this primeval egg explode?" The scientist, of course, looks for some cause other than the egg, some external force which struck a big blow at this egg and made it explode. But the mystic will say that the power of the Lord is right there in the egg itself—just as it is within everything, from the hydrogen nuclei in the core of the sun to the seed that will grow into a giant tree. When I look at an acorn, though I don't know much about botany, I know that the power of the Lord is contained in that little seed. That power shows itself not in making a tree appear out of nowhere, but in the seed transforming itself and bursting open to send out a slender shoot that pushes its way upwards to grow into a sturdy tree. Everywhere in that tree there is the expression of the power of the Lord—in the growing branch, in the leaves making food with the energy of the sunlight, in the sap running through every growing part.

Gandhi once said that we may look upon God as *dharma,* the Eternal Law—very much as a scientist would—or as *dharmakartri,* the Lawmaker. Because of our intellectual orientation, many of us today have no trouble accepting it when a mystic like the Buddha talks about an unchanging Law that underlies all existence. It is when we talk about a Lawgiver that many people have reservations. Yet either way, it is the same Reality. Sri Ramakrishna goes straight to the heart of the matter by saying God is both personal and impersonal; the Law and the Lawgiver are two aspects of one supreme Godhead. All laws derive from the same unity of life. The laws of physics or chemistry all express various aspects of the unity underlying the world of change, and though the wording of physical laws will vary as our understanding grows, it is the same unity that is behind both physical and spiritual laws.

In other words, the universe is one. There cannot be a number of unrelated laws; the result would be chaos. If there were no underlying unity in life, there could be no order; we could never know what to expect. We could plant an acorn and poison oak might grow; why not? We could throw a tennis ball into the air and it might never come down. There are laws everywhere, in all the phenomena of existence. The mystic would say that all these laws come from the same source, express the same unity. The law of gravity comes from the same source as the principle of Archimedes; Boyle's Law—it used to plague me as a student—comes from the same source as the law of relativity. How could it be otherwise? One of the most fervent hopes of Einstein was to find an overriding law of nature in which all the laws of matter and energy would be unified. This is very much the driving question in some of the ancient Hindu scriptures, too: "What is That by knowing which all other things may be known?" In samādhi we have direct knowledge of this unity, which is both the source of all laws and the Lawgiver as well.

रुद्रादित्या वसवो ये च साध्या
विश्वेऽश्विनौ मरुतश्चोष्मपाश्च ।
गन्धर्वयक्षासुरसिद्धसंघा
वीक्षन्ते त्वां विस्मिताश्चैव सर्वे ॥२२॥

रूपं महत्ते बहुवक्त्रनेत्रं
महाबाहो बहुबाहूरुपादम् ।
बहूदरं बहुदंष्ट्राकरालं
दृष्ट्वा लोकाः प्रव्यथितास्तथाहम् ॥२३॥

नभःस्पृशं दीप्तमनेकवर्णं
व्यात्ताननं दीप्तविशालनेत्रम् ।
दृष्ट्वा हि त्वां प्रव्यथितान्तरात्मा
धृतिं न विन्दामि शमं च विष्णो ॥२४॥

दंष्ट्राकरालानि च ते मुखानि
दृष्ट्वैव कालानलसन्निभानि ।
दिशो न जाने न लभे च शर्म
प्रसीद देवेश जगन्निवास ॥२५॥

22. *The multitudes of demigods and demons are all overwhelmed by the sight of you.*

23. *O Lord, at the sight of your mighty arms, the multitude of your eyes and mouths, your arms and legs, your stomachs and your fearful teeth, I and the entire universe shake in terror.*

24. *O Vishnu, I can see your eyes shining; your mouths are open, you glitter in an array of colors, and your body touches the sky. I look at you and my heart trembles; I have lost all courage and all peace of mind.*

25. When I see your mouths with their fearful teeth burning like the fires at the end of time, I forget where I am and I have no place to go. O Lord, you are the support of the universe; have mercy on me!

Arjuna has been overcome with awe at the splendor of the Lord; now he describes with horror the grim aspect of the Lord as the destroyer, the power which brings phenomenal existence to an end, whether it is a microbe, a person, or a star. If it is a microbe, the end may come after a few hours; if it is a star, it may not come for billions of years; but sooner or later, as the Buddha puts it, all that has been put together must one day be dissolved.

The Hindu scriptures make this point by drawing a comparison to the monsoon moth, whose life span is only about two and a half hours. After the torrential monsoon rains in South India, thousands of these moths fill the air. They come like the locusts in the biblical plague; you cannot even yawn without running the risk of getting one in your mouth. For just a short while they are everywhere; and then, suddenly, they are gone. Their lives are spent in just a fraction of a day. And the scriptures say, look at the concept these moths must have of time. They don't want a calendar on their wall; they will say, "What's the use? What is this 'month'? We don't believe there *is* a month; life is exhausted in two and a half hours. Give us a calendar for just two and a half hours; give us a watch for one hundred and fifty minutes to last us from birth to death." Every little second would count terribly; every millionth part of a second would be precious to that moth. If we were to try to tell these creatures that a human being lives hundreds of thousands of times longer, they would not even be able to grasp the scope of it. And yet—it is a very grim reminder—our own lives are compared to the lives of these monsoon moths, who come and go in a matter of hours.

At the other end of the scale, there is our own sun—*divākara,* 'Mr. Daymaker.' He was born about six billion years ago, and—poor fellow—he will probably go the way of all suns after about ten billion years of age. Among the galaxies they would all say, "What a premature death; the fellow didn't last long. Here yesterday and gone tomorrow." It is like the day of Brahman and the night of Brahman, measured in units of a million million years. We cannot even grasp these things; for us the universe is eternal. But it is just a difference in scale. Just as fifty years from now not many of us are going to be playing baseball or mowing the front lawn, so after a few more billion years the sun will lose its rugged, youthful vitality. Already our Mr. Sun is middle-aged, and gradually, with the passage of time, he will become a solar Falstaff, big and lethargic. He may pretend to be the same boisterous fellow as before, but we would know otherwise. The fire at his core, his *prāna* or life-breath, now about fifteen million degrees Kelvin, will slowly burn lower and lower, and as his temperature drops, life on earth will become impossible. Then he will shrink into what astronomers call a white dwarf, and finally, when his life span of ten billion years is over, he will no longer be a sun; he will be just a lifeless body no larger than the earth, another dead shell floating in space. One astronomer even says that the phenomenon of the black hole is very much like a giant star digging its own grave, falling in, and pulling the grave after it. It is a terrifying picture. According to the Gita, even the universe itself will come to an end. Estimates of its life span begin at forty billion years and go up from there, but eventually Sri Krishna will come as death and say, "Even for you, time is up."

The wonder of this is that you and I can break out of this terrible cycle to which even the galaxies are subject; you and I can conquer death. This is the promise of all the great religions. We all accept death as inevitable, but there have been spiritual geniuses in every age who dared to challenge death and emerged victorious. Mohammed tells us the secret of this victory in four simple words: "Die before you die." In the Hindu tradition we have a saying that just as a robber does not kill a man who carries no precious gems or gold, death cannot destroy those who no longer wear the jewels of their selfish desires. We go through life decked with such desires: "I must eat this food, wear that dress, travel to this country, own that kind of car." It is these unfulfilled cravings that tie us to our physical and mental condition. Then, when the great robber Death sees us, he cries out, "Here is a rich man. So many desires for me to rob!" If we can learn through the practice of meditation to remove all our selfish desires, we will have cut through the obsessive identification with the body once and for all. After that, though our body will come to an end in the course of time, there will be no rupture in consciousness at the time of death. Instead there will be an unbroken awareness of our real Self, the Lord of Love, who cannot be affected even by the last great change called death.

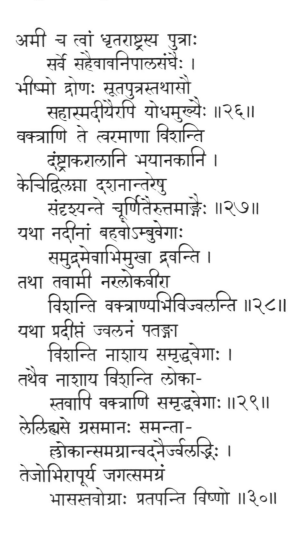

अमी च त्वां धृतराष्ट्रस्य पुत्राः
सर्वे सहैवावनिपालसंघैः ।
भीष्मो द्रोणः सूतपुत्रस्तथासौ
सहास्मदीयैरपि योधमुख्यैः ॥२६॥

वक्त्राणि ते त्वरमाणा विशन्ति
दंष्ट्राकरालानि भयानकानि ।
केचिद्विलग्ना दशनान्तरेषु
संदृश्यन्ते चूर्णितैरुत्तमाङ्गैः ॥२७॥

यथा नदीनां बहवोऽम्बुवेगाः
समुद्रमेवाभिमुखा द्रवन्ति ।
तथा तवामी नरलोकवीरा
विशन्ति वक्त्राण्यभिविज्वलन्ति ॥२८॥

यथा प्रदीप्तं ज्वलनं पतङ्गा
विशन्ति नाशाय समृद्धवेगाः ।
तथैव नाशाय विशन्ति लोका-
स्तवापि वक्त्राणि समृद्धवेगाः ॥२९॥

लेलिह्यसे ग्रसमानः समन्ता-
ल्लोकान्समग्रान्वदनैर्ज्वलद्भिः ।
तेजोभिरापूर्य जगत्समग्रं
भासस्तवोग्राः प्रतपन्ति विष्णो ॥३०॥

*26–27. I see all the sons of Dhritarāshtra; I see
Bhīshma, Drona, and Karna; I see our warriors and
all the kings who are here to fight. All are rushing
into your awful jaws; I see some of them crushed
by your teeth.
28–29. As rivers flow into the ocean, all the
warriors of this world are passing into your fiery jaws;
all creatures rush to their destruction like moths into
a flame.
30. You lap the worlds into your burning mouths and
swallow them. Filled with your terrible radiance,
O Vishnu, the whole of creation bursts into flames.*

This is the Lord in his most terrifying form, the personification of
death. To those who follow the voice of self-will, who pursue their
personal pleasure and profit at the expense of their family and
friends, their community and their world, death often comes in the
awful form of violence.

Because of years of conditioning, particularly by the mass media,
most of us have become caught in a way of life that increases separateness fiercely. Now we find it difficult even to see the connection
between our egocentric lives and the violence which threatens us
today. But on every level, from international warfare to domestic
quarrels, to ignore our unity is to invite social chaos and destruction. Even the ideological differences between two superpowers, for
example, sustain the interest in armaments around the globe. We
have become so accustomed to discussions of nuclear warfare and
its threat to destroy the earth that we hardly raise an eyebrow when
we read that there are enough nuclear weapons on alert around the
world to kill each person on earth twelve times or more.

In 1960, in constant 1983 dollars, world military expenditures
were 344 billion. By 1986 they were approaching 900 billion—$1.7
million dollars every minute. This much buying means a lot of selling, and the big arms sellers are still the United States and the Soviet
Union, who hold roughly half of this highly profitable market. Some
of the biggest customers, ironically, are the developing countries,

who now account for one fifth of the world's arms expenditures. Since 1963, almost half of this trade has come from the United States and its NATO allies; another third came from the Soviet Union. We seldom think how we cripple these emerging nations by encouraging them to buy weapons. But the money they spend on guns means less food, less housing, and poorer medical attention for people who lack these essentials of life.

When we pursue this trade in armaments, profitable though it may be, the Gita reminds us grimly that we are courting death. This courtship embraces more than the immediate buyer and seller. It includes the manufacturers and middlemen and even those of us who fail to raise a voice of protest. The reminder is not pleasant, but the Gita has to shock us into seeing the tragic connection between the petty pursuits we follow with such narrow vision and the death and violence that torment our world today.

Fortunately, we have good reason to believe that even problems like the nuclear arms race can be solved if we set our minds to the task. On December 8, 1987, President Reagan and General Secretary Gorbachev signed the first nuclear arms reduction agreement in history—only a first step, yet a "truly momentous development," as President Rajiv Gandhi of India acclaimed, for it "vividly demonstrated that given the necessary political will," obstacles to peace can be overcome. But we should not expect governments to provide that will. We, the people, must insist on it ourselves.

Violence, of course, is not just an international problem. We Americans kill our own family and friends more frequently than do citizens of any other civilized nation. In the drawers, closets, and glove compartments of the United States are over sixty million handguns—part of an arsenal of private weapons that amounts to nearly two hundred million firearms. People use these guns because they are available. Nearly three out of four murders committed in this country are "crimes of passion": that is, the killing of a family member or a friend in the blind heat of anger, often simply because a weapon was at hand. On the average, 69 persons were murdered by handguns every day in 1980; and in 1981, when President Reagan was shot, one handgun was sold every twelve seconds in the year.

Yet we still can't make up our minds to effect some simple measure to control this gun menace.

This kind of insensitivity to violence will plunge not only you and me into suffering, but our children and grandchildren as well. The Gita compares this to the life of a moth which rushes into a flame. Look at the monsoon moths I mentioned in the preceding verses: only two and a half hours to live, and even that is too long for them; they rush to their extinction in the very first fire they see. After the monsoon rains in Kerala, when the evening sky is so full of those moths that you cannot eat or sleep in peace, people light huge bonfires, and it is a terrifying sight to see thousands on thousands of these creatures throwing themselves into the flames to die. Now, in the depths of his consciousness, Arjuna sees all the warriors who are with him on the battlefield, uncles and cousins, friends and enemies, throwing themselves like moths into the jaws of death.

The more we build our civilization on selfishness and separateness, the Gita is telling us, the more we live like these monsoon moths. When we go on pursuing pleasure and prestige and power, we become blind and deaf to everything around us. Then we forget that the stream of life runs out quickly, as a rain-swollen river runs out to sea. This is why the great spiritual teachers of all religions tell us not to postpone the spiritual life for even one day; every day lost is one we cannot regain. We are moving closer to death with every moment that passes, and once this realization penetrates our hearts, we will begin doing everything we can to go beyond death here and now.

आख्याहि मे को भवानुग्ररूपो
नमोऽस्तु ते देववर प्रसीद ।
विज्ञातुमिच्छामि भवन्तमाद्यं
न हि प्रजानामि तव प्रवृत्तिम् ॥३१॥

31. Tell me who you are, O Lord of terrible form.
I bow before you; have mercy! I want to know
who you are, you who existed before all creation.
Your nature and workings confound me.

Arjuna is shaken to the depths of his being by this vision of the destructive power of the Lord. Just like you and me, he stammers, "I don't understand; you are the Lord of Love, but all I see now is a terrifying vision of birth and death, suffering and destruction. Have mercy upon me." He has glimpsed the central truth of existence—that all life, from the simple virus to the vast galaxy, is marching from birth to death, to birth and death, again and again.

Death is not an event which takes place on a particular day in a particular place. It is a process that starts the day we are conceived in our mother's womb, and every moment that passes brings us that much closer to the day this body will be taken away from us. Even within us the cells of the body are dying every second; it is only the limits of our vision that keep us from seeing that the body we identify with is in a constant state of change. That is why the Book of Common Prayer tells us in haunting words, "In the midst of life we are in death." We can escape this process only when we cure ourselves of the fatal disease of ignorance which makes us identify with the body.

In other words, as Sri Ramakrishna puts it, life is a hospital; the Lord has sent us here so that we may cure ourselves of separateness and become whole. When we encounter violence and hostility, we have an opportunity to improve our condition by remaining steadfast and secure. Unfortunately, we all too often worsen things by retaliating; then we suffer a relapse and have to be readmitted to intensive care. But finally, once we have suffered enough, we realize that retaliation only spreads the highly communicable disease of self-will to everyone around us.

The Compassionate Buddha's Four Noble Truths are a perfect diagnosis of our sickness by a supreme physician. After a careful examination the Buddha gives us the First Noble Truth, that we are seriously ill. Then he gives us the Second Noble Truth, that the cause of the disease is the fierce thirst of self-will. It is a worldwide epidemic, and no one has any immunity against it. At this point, thoroughly shaken, we ask, "What are my chances, doctor? Please give me a straight answer; I can take it." And the Buddha, full of mercy, gives us the Third Noble Truth: "The prognosis is very

bright, if you will follow this eight-course treatment." The Fourth
Noble Truth is the Buddha's prescription for a complete cure, the
Noble Eightfold Path: right knowledge, right purpose, right speech,
right conduct, right occupation, right effort, right attention, and
right meditation. It is a prescription we can follow right in our own
home, by practicing meditation, turning our attention away from
personal desires, and trying constantly to serve the welfare of everyone around us.

श्री भगवानुवाच
कालोऽस्मि लोकक्षयकृत्प्रवृद्धो
    लोकान्समाहर्तुमिह प्रवृत्तः ।
ऋतेऽपि त्वां न भविष्यन्ति सर्वे
    येऽवस्थिताः प्रत्यनीकेषु योधाः ॥३२॥

SRI KRISHNA:
*32. I am time, the destroyer of all; I have come to
consume the world. Even without your participation,
all the warriors gathered here will die.*

These are words that have made the Gita known the world over. It
was this verse that came to Robert Oppenheimer's mind as he
watched the first atomic bomb explode across the desert sky. The
devastating word used here is *kāla,* which has a double-edged meaning—'time' and 'death.' Time *is* death; time is separateness. Its all-
devouring jaws are following us always, closer than our shadow. As
we grow older and our family and friends begin to pass away, we
see how relentlessly time is pursuing all of us; every death should remind us of the imminence of our own. People with whom we played
and laughed—they are no more. Great figures who have walked
across the stage of life—they are no more. Dynasties and empires
have returned to dust. It is only because of the mercy of the Lord
that you and I survive each day. Those who are sensitive to this
have tremendous motivation to take to the spiritual path and slay
this monster of time and death.

Arjuna's experience in this verse is not poetic fancy. It is a realistic vision of what time means, which in a smaller way can come to anyone. A friend of mine in India, a great devotee of Krishna, was once in the midst of a group of people who had gathered on a religious holiday to sing songs in praise of the Lord. At such times her intense devotion used to bring on a deeper state of consciousness. Something must have triggered such a change, because she suddenly looked around in horror; before her eyes, the people there turned into bare skeletons.

The vision lasted several moments. It terrified her so deeply that it haunted her for years. When she confided it to me, she called it the most dreadful thing she had ever experienced. I replied, "It's probably the greatest thing you could have experienced. Instead of blocking it out, try to remember it always." Her whole attitude was changed; instead of a curse, she began to understand it as a blessing.

This is the same service my Grandmother rendered me. Even when I was a boy, just entering my teens, she knew how to open a little window in my consciousness and tell me, "Look carefully. If you can see far enough you'll see Yama waiting for you, just as he is waiting for us all." I have to admit that I did not appreciate this at the time. I could not understand why I, among all the children I knew, should be singled out to be made aware of this dreadful destiny. And Granny seldom tried to explain herself; she planted the seeds of this awareness without ever using words. Though all my cousins were shielded from such experiences, she loved me so passionately that she opened that window onto death for me again and again. More than anything else, she wanted me to understand that nothing is more important than remembering death—not to live in fear, but to make it our first priority to go beyond time and death here and now.

Even now I marvel at the artistry of her teaching. Whenever someone died in our large ancestral family, relatives and friends would gather around a central courtyard in my ancestral home where the grim ceremonies of a funeral are performed. Most of the other boys and girls would not be present on such occasions. But my Grandmother insisted that I stand right in front and watch carefully what was taking place. The body was bathed and taken from the courtyard, and as it was carried away a heartbreaking chorus of hundreds of voices would break out in lamentation. Often it was old people crying, but when it was children my heart would almost stop beating at the sound. Then Granny would tell my uncle, "Now take him to the funeral pyre." I didn't know or guess that this was what great love means. All I knew was that I had to go and stand in the southern courtyard while the body was lowered onto the pyre, to watch the most harrowing scenes I have witnessed in my life.

This fate is waiting for everyone. "I am time, the destroyer of all; I have come to consume the world." For most of us these are only words; for my friend they suddenly became a vivid, shattering experience, burned like Arjuna's into her memory. Far from morbid, I think nothing could be more positive. It is no blessing to be able to forget death, to pretend it does not exist, while we go on playing with the froth and foam of life. It can be the greatest of blessings to remember that every moment is precious, and a lifetime not too long.

My mother is in her late eighties now, a ripe age by any standard. She came to live with us at Ramagiri the same summer we moved in, when work on the first chapter of this book had just begun. Now, in the eleventh chapter, I open the door to her bedroom every morning and stand for a few minutes to watch her sleeping. So much love floods my heart, and so much sorrow. In her younger days she was lissome and graceful, the most beautiful woman in our village. On the Blue Mountain, even in her sixties, she used to walk four, five, six miles a day. Now she can barely walk, scarcely get up or drink her tea. Often it is a great effort for her simply to open her eyes to see that I am there.

If you and I have the good fortune to move so close to ninety, this is the state our bodies are likely to be in too. It is love that makes me say this. It is love that makes me remind myself and those around me to keep this verse in mind every day; it will give a clear goal in every activity, bring complete dedication, strengthen you greatly in the hour of temptation. In my own sādhana, whenever I was tempted by some strong physical urge, the recollection of my Granny's teaching would suddenly well up in my consciousness. I would see death standing by my side, and that temptation would turn to ashes. Similarly, when you feel angry, jealous, hostile, or depressed, remember; this is waiting for us all. There is no time to quarrel, no time to feel resentful or estranged. There is no time to waste on the pursuit of selfish pleasures that are over almost before they begin. Time runs out so soon! In our twenties and thirties we have ample margin to play with the toys life has to offer. But we should find out soon how fleeting they are, no more permanent than writing on water; for the tides of time can ebb away before we know.

Not long ago my mother was reminding me of one of my great-uncles, a contemporary of my Granny. I stood in awe of him as a child because of his immense physical strength and courage. His mother was like that too, and when she shed her body at a very advanced age there was an elaborate funeral, lasting by Kerala tradition for fifteen days. On the fourteenth day the ashes were taken from the funeral pyre and carried to a river about six miles from my village to be immersed. We had a huge procession, including caparisoned elephants. And on the way back this great-uncle of mine, physically so strong, had a heart attack and passed away on the spot.

We couldn't believe it. He had seemed indestructible to us. Here we had just finished fifteen days of mourning, and now there was another fifteen. It made me understand that even when we are healthy and strong and vigorous, in the prime of our lives, death can come at any moment. A venerable monastic friend of mine on the Blue Mountain used to say, "Don't ever put things off until tomorrow. How do you know you will be here tomorrow?" It was not rhetoric for him. It was a simple awareness that we live from moment to moment by God's grace, and that none of us knows when Yama will come to cut the thread of our lives.

"This life of separateness," says the Compassionate Buddha, "may be compared to a dream, a phantasm, a bubble, a shadow, a drop of dew, a flash of lightning." It is good to bear in mind how evanescent life is so that we do not postpone the voyage across this sea of separate existence called *samsāra* in Sanskrit, the ceaseless process of birth and death.

तस्मात्त्वमुत्तिष्ठ यशो लभस्व
    जित्वा शत्रून् भुङ्क्ष्व राज्यं समृद्धम् ।
मयैवैते निहताः पूर्वमेव
    निमित्तमात्रं भव सव्यसाचिन् ॥३३॥
द्रोणं च भीष्मं च जयद्रथं च
    कर्णं तथान्यानपि योधवीरान् ।
मया हतांस्त्वं जहि मा व्यथिष्ठा
    युध्यस्व जेतासि रणे सपत्नान् ॥३४॥

*33. Therefore arise, Arjuna; conquer your enemies
and enjoy the glory of sovereignty. I have already slain
all these warriors; you will only be my instrument.
34. Bhīshma, Drona, Jayadratha, Karna, and many
others are already slain. Kill those whom I have killed.
Do not be afraid. Fight in the battle and you will
conquer your enemies.*

In the *Mahābhārata,* the epic in which the Gita appears, Karna,
Jayadratha, Bhīshma, and Drona are famous heroes among the
forces ranged against Arjuna. For you and me, these forces are the
forces of darkness, destructive powers which we can observe in our
own lives. These particular warriors are mentioned because they
were supposed to be invincible; yet, as the Lord reassures Arjuna,
even the most destructive forces of violence can be brought to an
end, because they violate the unity of life.

   None of us, therefore, can consider himself exempt from the responsibility of joining battle against these forces. I have always had
a great deal of reverence for Mahatma Gandhi because of the way
he chose to take upon himself this gravest of responsibilities. Gandhi taught us that evil has no existence of its own; it is when we con-
nive at evil that it exists. When we all withdraw our support from
the powers of destruction, we discover that they are an enemy
which has already been slain. This is the principle of *satyāgraha,*
'clinging to truth,' which is very inadequately translated as "non-
violent resistance."

Gandhi's discovery of satyāgraha took place when he was still a young, ineffectual lawyer in South Africa, when he was thrown out of a train at night in the high mountain town of Maritzburg because of his brown skin. This must have happened to hundreds before him, but in Gandhi's case it released a tremendous force within him; it whispered in his ear that he could draw upon his deepest resources, through the grace of the Lord, to bring this conflict between races to an end. Many years later, when he was asked what was the most creative experience of his life, Gandhi told the story of that night he spent shivering in the cold of the Maritzburg station, when he dedicated his life to eradicating the barriers which human selfishness has built up.

Gandhi was thrown into prison many times, but he was such a cheerful prisoner that he won the love and affection even of his jailers. While in prison in South Africa he made a pair of sandals especially for General Smuts, the man whose duty it was to oppose him in his struggle for justice. Later General Smuts returned the sandals as a gesture of friendship, saying, "I am not worthy to stand in the shoes of so great a man." Incidents like these, which became commonplace in Gandhi's life, showed us that there is no one who cannot respond to the person who is not trying to manipulate others for his own prestige, profit, or power. When we are with such a person all our defenses are lowered; we relax and begin to trust him, and gradually we too develop the conviction that goodness cannot fail to win and evil cannot fail to lose.

संजय उवाच
एतच्छ्रुत्वा वचनं केशवस्य
कृताञ्जलिर्वेपमानः किरीटी
नमस्कृत्वा भूय एवाह कृष्णं
सगद्गदं भीतभीतः प्रणम्य ॥३५॥

अर्जुन उवाच
स्थाने हृषीकेश तव प्रकीर्त्या
जगत्प्रहृष्यत्यनुरज्यते च ।
रक्षांसि भीतानि दिशो द्रवन्ति
सर्वे नमस्यन्ति च सिद्धसंघाः ॥३६॥

कस्माच्च ते न नमेरन्महात्मन्
गरीयसे ब्रह्मणोऽप्यादिकर्त्रे ।
अनन्त देवेश जगन्निवास
त्वमक्षरं सदसत्तत्परं यत् ॥३७॥

त्वमादिदेवः पुरुषः पुराण-
स्त्वमस्य विश्वस्य परं निधानम् ।
वेत्तासि वेद्यं च परं च धाम
त्वया ततं विश्वमनन्तरूप ॥३८॥

SANJAYA:

35. Having heard these words, Arjuna trembled in fear. With joined palms he bowed before Krishna and addressed him stammering.

ARJUNA:

36. O Krishna, it is right that the world delights and rejoices in your praise, that all the saints and sages bow down to you and all evil flees before you to the far corners of the universe.

37. How could they not worship you, O Lord? You are the eternal spirit, who existed before Brahmā the Creator and who will never cease to be. Lord of the

gods, you are the abode of the universe. Changeless,
you are what is and what is not, and beyond the
duality of existence and nonexistence.
38. You are the first among the gods, the timeless
spirit, the resting place of all beings. You are the
knower and the thing which is known. You are the
home of all; with your infinite form you pervade
the cosmos.

In his joy, Arjuna tells Sri Krishna that he sees the entire cosmos re-
joicing in the sovereignty of the Lord. "You are the refuge of all
creatures," he says; "all beings in the universe can find their rest
only in you. You are everything that has been and will ever be, and
the beginning and end of all creation." This is the experience attained by men and women of God in every age and every tradition
who have dared to tread the razor-edged path that leads from death
to immortality. Saints and sages like Sri Ramakrishna or Shankara,
St. Teresa of Ávila or Jalalu'l-Din Rumi, the Ba'al Shem Tov or
Jacob Boehme, all use very similar words to tell what they have experienced with every cell of their being. The Italian mystic Jaca-
pone da Todi says:

> The doors are flung open. United with the Lord, it possesses
> everything that is in him; it feels that which it never felt; it sees
> that which it never saw; it has that which it never thought could
> be; it tastes that which it never tasted. Being freed from itself,
> it now has attained perfection.

It is such a thrilling vision that even hearing about it makes us long
for it. When we meet somebody who has actually been granted this
awareness, our longing becomes intense; we light our torch from
such a person, for he or she is burning with love for the Lord.

वायुर्यमोऽग्निर्वरुणः शशाङ्कः
प्रजापतिस्त्वं प्रपितामहश्च ।
नमो नमस्तेऽस्तु सहस्रकृत्वः
पुनश्च भूयोऽपि नमो नमस्ते ॥३९॥

39. You are Vāyu, god of wind, Yama, god of death,
Agni, god of fire, and Varuna, god of water. You are
the moon and the creator Prajāpati, and the great-
grandfather of all creatures. I bow before you and
salute you again and again.

Arjuna is prostrating himself at the feet of Sri Krishna, whom he
now sees everywhere, in everyone. His voice is trembling in awe as
he tells the Lord: "You are the whole cosmos, yet you are beyond it;
you are in my grandparents and my parents; you are in every creature and in all the forces of nature." Not only is the Lord in you and
me, he is in the air, in the seas and rivers, in the life-giving power of
heat and light and all the other forces of the universe. Existence is
an unbroken continuum; only the scale of its parts is different. That
is why we suffer so when we damage or exploit anything in nature.
As John Muir, the great naturalist, observed, "When one tugs at a
single thing in nature, he finds it attached to the rest of the world."

Thomas Vaughan, the English mystic, tells us simply: "Have thy
heart in heaven and thy hands upon the earth. Ascend in piety and
descend in charity. For this is the nature of Light and the way of
the children of it." There is much the same image in Jewish mysticism, in which the life of the man or woman of God is said to
be a ladder between heaven and earth. In all creatures, the God-
conscious person sees the presence of the Lord.

Only when we become insensitive to this unity of life do we take
the lives of other creatures wantonly. This is not only in matters
like hunting and fishing; often we do not pay attention even to the
needs of our pets. People take along a dog to entertain them during
their summer vacation and then abandon it when they go back
home, or think nothing of locking up a cat for life within an apartment in the city. Instead of denouncing such people, which will only
alienate them, we can show persuasively how animals need to look
to us as their protectors. My young friend Josh once went about this
in a very winning manner. When he was in the third grade, his Boy
Scout troop was planning a program for Thanksgiving. Josh cham-
pioned the cause of the turkey. Then someone suggested that they

represent the Pilgrim Fathers fishing. The other boys thought this was a harmless pastime, but Josh got up and bravely said, "Fish are God's creatures, too." It speaks very highly of his friends that they could appreciate his point of view, and the Pilgrim Fathers were finally represented as gathering nuts—which, after all, are an excellent source of protein.

नमः पुरस्तादथ पृष्ठतस्ते
नमोऽस्तु ते सर्वत एव सर्व ।
अनन्तवीर्यामितविक्रमस्त्वं
सर्वं समाप्नोषि ततोऽसि सर्वः ॥४०॥

*40. You are behind me and in front of me; I bow
to you on every side. Your power is immeasurable.
You pervade everything; you are everything.*

In Hindu society there is an age-old custom which prescribes the direction in which a person should lie when sleeping. One of the many names for the Lord is Dakshināmurtī, 'he who faces south,' and in this tradition it is considered improper to lie with one's feet towards the north, because that is the abode of the Lord.

Now, some centuries ago in the state of Tamil Nadu there was a great woman mystic named Āndāl, who once had to spend the night in the home of some orthodox devotees. When the woman of the house came to wake her up, she found her guest lying in the wrong direction. The woman was shocked and confused; she didn't know whether to call this great saint's attention to her mistake or not. But Āndāl, seeing her confusion, explained gently: "In what direction shall I point my feet that they not point towards the Lord? If I point them to the north, that is his home, but if I point them to the south, is he not there also? It is the same with east and west. I would sleep standing on my head rather than displease him, but he is above and beneath us also. Where shall I place my feet that they will not point towards the Lord?" It is the same language as in the Koran, in a verse which was a favorite of Mahatma Gandhi's: "Unto Allah belong the East and the West; wherever you turn, there is Allah's countenance."

In the climax of meditation called samādhi, when the mind becomes still and the ego is silenced, we shall see the Lord everywhere around us, enthroned in the heart of every creature. In the Hindu tradition we have countless stories to help us understand this experience. One such story is about Hanumān, an extraordinary monkey who is mentioned in the Hindu scriptures to remind us that the Lord dwells not only in human beings but in monkeys too. Hanumān is completely devoted to Rāma, an incarnation of the Lord. He has to undergo all sorts of trials which test and reveal his love for Rāma. Once, sent on a dangerous mission by Rāma, he is captured and taken before Rāvana, the ten-headed demon who personifies the ego in all its multiplicity. Rāvana's courtiers gather to humiliate Hanumān, but the monkey's devotion to Rāma is so great that he remains undaunted. Personally, he tells the assembly, he doesn't mind being relegated to a seat on the floor, but as Rāma's representative he deserves to sit in a chair. The only response he gets is laughter. But Hanumān prays to Rāma to save his representative from this humiliation, and his faith is so complete that the Lord is able to make his tail longer and longer, until finally it coils up into a tail-throne on which Hanumān sits high above the courtiers.

Rāvana is terribly impressed by Hanumān's devotion to Rāma. To test him further, the demon king takes a pearl necklace from his neck and offers it to Hanumān to try to buy his allegiance. But the monkey only bites one or two pearls and then throws the necklace out the window. The courtiers are outraged, but Hanumān's indifference only makes Rāvana more intrigued. He asks his prisoner, "Don't you know that necklace was worth a king's ransom?"

Hanumān replies, "For me everything is worthless if it doesn't enshrine the Lord. I bit the pearls and saw that the Lord was not there."

Rāvana asks, "Then just where is the Lord?" And Hanumān, in answer, rips open his chest and reveals his heart where Rāma is enshrined in all his splendor. It is a simple story, but it shows in a very vivid way the capacity of all of us to enter into the depths of our consciousness and see there the source of all joy and all security who is the Lord.

सखेति मत्वा प्रसभं यदुक्तं
हे कृष्ण हे यादव हे सखेति ।
अजानता महिमानं तवेदं
मया प्रमादात्प्रणयेन वापि ॥४१॥
यच्चावहासार्थमसत्कृतोऽसि
विहारशय्यासनभोजनेषु ।
एकोऽथवाप्यच्युत तत्समक्षं
तत्क्षामये त्वामहमप्रमेयम् ॥४२॥

41–42. Sometimes, because we were friends, I rashly said, "Oh, Krishna!" "Say, friend!" These things I said casually, openly. Whatever I said lightly—whether we were playing or resting, alone or in company, sitting together or eating—if it was disrespectful, forgive me for it, O Krishna. I did not know the greatness of your nature, unchanging and imperishable.

Now comes a moment of great tenderness, when Arjuna begs Sri Krishna to forgive him for forgetting his friend's divine nature. How perfectly Arjuna represents us, for the instances he mentions in daily living are the very ones in which we too forget that the Lord is within us all. As Jesus says, "Truly I say unto you, as you did it unto one of the least of these, you did it unto me."

   As the supreme source of love, the Lord would never have us beg, "Will you kindly consider my application for forgiveness and arrive at an early decision?" Real love knows no reservations or contracts. Most of us may not find it too difficult to ask the Lord for unreserved forgiveness, but we usually find it hard to forgive others when they have offended us. For me this is the perfect test of love: can I forget my own hurt feelings and ensure their welfare, no matter how he or she has treated me? If I can, my love for that person is secure. My friend, or partner, or son, or daughter will be so certain of my desire to do what is best for them that even if I do something wrong, they will not hold it against me; they will know that I am incapable of doing anything to harm them. This trust is the basis of perfect relationships anywhere, particularly between man and woman.

The marvel of forgiveness is this: when we can completely forgive someone the tantrum they threw this afternoon, loving them even a little more because we see they really need our support, we are at the same time beginning to forgive ourselves for every tantrum we have ever thrown at others. You can see how practical a step it is to take. All those other people may long since have forgotten what we did and said—maybe some of them didn't really care much in the first place. But deep in our own minds, every single storm has left its mark. Every storm has burst a little hole in consciousness through which angry thoughts, angry words, and angry acts gradually seep into our daily life. In this sacred act of forgiveness we are mending thousands of these little holes. It relieves us of part of the tremendous burden that all of us carry within, healing our consciousness and taking the pressure of anxiety off our mind and our nervous system. And it makes us much less likely to get provoked the next time someone rubs us the wrong way. This is the miracle forgiveness works.

St. Francis of Assisi will say that when we have lost this capacity to forgive, we have lost the greatest source of joy in life. Once, in wintertime, it is said that Francis and his disciple Brother Leo were making an arduous journey on foot through the cold, snowy countryside of Italy. They had been walking along in silence for some time—probably repeating their mantram—when Brother Leo turned to St. Francis and asked him, "How can we find perfect joy?"

Francis stopped for a moment and then replied, "Brother Leo, even if all our friars were perfect in their holiness and could work all kinds of miracles for others, we still would not have perfect joy."

He turned to walk on, and Brother Leo ran after him. "Then what is perfect joy?"

St. Francis stopped again. "Even if we knew all the languages of men and of angels, if we could speak with the birds of the air and the beasts of the field and know all the secrets of nature, we still would not have perfect joy."

He started to go on again, but Brother Leo caught at his sleeve. "Then, Father Francis, what is perfect joy?"

"Even if we could cure all the ills on the face of the earth, we would still not have found perfect joy."

Now all Brother Leo's enthusiasm was aroused. "Then please, Father Francis," he pleaded, "what *is* the secret of perfect joy?"

"Brother Leo," St. Francis asked, "aren't you cold and tired and hungry from our day's walk through the snow? Well, suppose we now go to that monastery across the field and tell the gatekeeper how weary and cold we are, and he calls us tramps and thieves, and beats us with his stick, and throws us out into the winter night and slams the gate in our faces. Then, Brother Leo, if we can say with love in our hearts, 'Bless you in the name of Jesus,' then we shall have found perfect joy."

Most of us, of course, do not have to forgive on such a grand scale, but all of us have little resentments which we can forgive every day. Often these resentments are buried so deep in consciousness that we are not aware of the extent to which they undermine our security, drain our vitality, and interfere with our personal relationships. Here it is not very effective to analyze the wrongs we have suffered and then forgive them one by one. If I may say so, often the "wrongs" are not wrongs at all; it is only that our self-will has been violated, not infrequently because we failed to understand what the other person did or said. Instead, it is much more effective not to dwell on the past at all. Whenever a little thought arises and wants to talk over something in the past, don't talk to that thought, don't argue with it; simply repeat the mantram. This is really what forgiveness means, because when we can withdraw our attention completely from the past, it is not possible to be resentful; it is not possible to be oppressed by either past wrongs or past mistakes. All our attention is in the present, which means that every moment is fresh, every relationship is fresh, and there is no possibility of staleness or boredom.

पितासि लोकस्य चराचरस्य
त्वमस्य पूज्यश्च गुरुर्गरीयान् ।
न त्वत्समोऽस्त्यभ्यधिकः कुतोऽन्यो
लोकत्रयेऽप्यप्रतिमप्रभाव ॥४३॥
तस्मात्प्रणम्य प्रणिधाय कायं
प्रसादये त्वामहमीशमीड्यम् ।
पितेव पुत्रस्य सखेव सख्युः
प्रियः प्रियायार्हसि देव सोढुम् ॥४४॥

*43. You are the father of the universe, of the animate
and the inanimate; you are the object of all worship,
greater than the great. There is none to equal you
in the three worlds. Who can match your power?
44. O gracious Lord, I prostrate myself before you
and salute you. As a father forgives his son, or a friend
a friend, or a lover his beloved, so should you
forgive me.*

In the simple, sweet words of a child, Arjuna goes on asking the
Lord to forgive his lapses: "You are my father; doesn't a father forgive his child when he makes a mistake?" It is a beautiful example
of the parent–child relationship which each of us can have with the
Lord.

Sometimes—especially when the neighbors are saying "Report
him to the police" or "Did you hear what your daughter did?"—
parents become insecure and confused. They weigh the pros and
cons of the situation and ask themselves, "Does this deserve forgiveness? Are there special grounds here for giving them a second
chance?" Driving bargains like this does not result in forgiveness.
No child should have to wonder what the chances are that we will
forgive them. If there is love in our relationship, our son or daughter
will be able to come and say, "I've made a lot of mistakes, but I
know you love me so much that you'll keep me from getting into
this trouble again."

My Granny had a unique gift for standing by people when they got themselves in trouble and at the same time teaching them not to get into that trouble again. One of my cousins was much more daring than the rest of us—and who doesn't have a cousin like that? He was always finding situations to put us into where his daring would show itself. Now, all of us used to play soccer until late in the afternoon, and after the game we liked nothing better than to run to the river for a swim. But by the time we started for home it would already be dusk, and dusk is the time when all kinds of snakes love to come out and take their walks. The raised paths between the paddy fields used to be crawling with them. In the fading light it was very difficult to distinguish snake from grass from stick, and without knowing you could easily step on one of these creatures and be bitten before you had a chance to jump. Not only that, some of these snakes are poisonous. Yet this daring cousin of mine loved to lead us home at dusk along these paths, knowing full well we were frightened out of our little wits.

My Grandmother had warned me many times of the extreme danger of doing this, and she had told me repeatedly to come home before dark. Her warnings, unfortunately, fell on deaf ears; I continued to follow after the others. But one evening after our swim, just as we got to a part of the path where snakes loved to make their home, whom should we come upon but my Granny, standing there barefoot by the side of the path just waiting for me. There was no telling how long she had been standing there, and from her expression I understood that she was prepared to wait there for me every night if necessary. She didn't need to say a word. I was cured. I never came home after dark that way again.

अदृष्टपूर्वं हृषितोऽस्मि दृष्ट्वा
    भयेन च प्रव्यथितं मनो मे ।
तदेव मे दर्शय देव रूपं
    प्रसीद देवेश जगन्निवास ॥४५॥
किरीटिनं गदिनं चक्रहस्त-
    मिच्छामि त्वां द्रष्टुमहं तथैव ।
तेनैव रूपेण चतुर्भुजेन
    सहस्रबाहो भव विश्वमूर्ते ॥४६॥

*45. I rejoice in seeing you as you have never been
seen before, yet I am filled with fear by this vision of
you as the abode of the universe. Please let me see
you again as the shining God of gods.*

*46. Though you are the embodiment of all creation,
let me see you again not with a thousand arms but with
four, carrying the mace and disk and wearing a crown.*

The Bible tells us, "Fear of the Lord is the beginning of wisdom."
The image of the Lord with thousands of arms, the embodiment of
all creation, can fill us with awe when we realize that it means he is
everywhere; there is no way we can escape from him. He is in our
parents, our children, our husband or wife or boyfriend or girlfriend, even in our dog or cat. It means that whatever we do, wherever we go, we need to be very vigilant about not causing distress to
any other creature, because the eyes of the Lord are always right
there watching us.

Even when we are alone, we haven't succeeded in escaping those
watchful eyes, because the Lord is within us too. As the Upanishads
put it, he is our real Self. Even when our little self is sleeping, the
Seeing Eye is watching all our thoughts—not because he is a busy-
body, but because he is everywhere and never sleeps. This is the aspect of the Lord which the Sanskrit scriptures call Sākshī, the Internal Witness. The traditional derivation of this word is from *sa,*
'with', and *akshi,* 'eye.' *Sākshī* is 'he who is all eyes,' sitting right in-

side us and everyone else, impartially taking note of everything we say and do and even what we think.

I remember how awestruck I was when I began to grasp the implications of this. As a schoolboy I was under the impression that God was floating about in space, issuing mandates and expecting us to carry them out. Most of us boys reassured ourselves that the Lord's secret service agents were not too efficient, that he would never know about many of the things we did. When we were up to something that he would not have been too pleased about, we would say, "Why bother him with these details?"

Then, one day, a few of us boys got together and made a pact under a particular mango tree to rob a neighbor's mango grove. It wasn't a very malicious plan; we were young, we were all fond of mangoes, and it seemed to us that our neighbor had many more of them than he would ever be able to use. But since we knew he would probably not agree with this conclusion, we all took a solemn oath not to reveal our plans to anyone, and not to speak to anyone among us who let our secret out.

Somehow my Granny managed to find out about all this before I even reached home. When she met me at the gate she asked, "Little Lamp, is there any particularly significant event in which you took part today?"

"Not to the best of my knowledge, Granny."

"Did you happen to see anyone under the mango tree this afternoon?"

"Well, we did walk home that way."

"What happened, Little Lamp?"

Silence.

"Who was with you?"

More silence.

Then she said, "It doesn't matter if you conceal something from me, or your mother, or your aunt and uncle. But there is somebody inside you who is watching everything you do, and who hears everything that you say and think."

Hearing this from her lips made it official. You may be able to hide from your neighbor or keep your dog from following you to the library, but how do you hide from someone who is watching everything you do from the inside? I felt I couldn't do anything without the divine snooper finding out. After that, whenever I was with one of my friends who was prone to mischief, I could always hear her saying, "There's somebody watching. There's somebody listening." If he would wink for just a split second, we could get away with something that he wouldn't like to see. If he would doze off for a moment, we could make a remark without his knowledge. But he is there all the time, and we have no choice but to act in such a way as to win his quiet little nod of approval from within.

Once we begin to realize this, we become extremely alert about everything we say and do. But this does not mean we should always be listening to our own thoughts or thinking about what we are going to do next—quite the opposite. Instead of brooding on ourselves, which is what listening to our thoughts means, we become acutely aware of how the things we think and say and do may affect others. After all, the same Self that is watching us from within is watching in the other person too. If a chance remark of ours happens to hurt someone else, it is not enough to say, "I didn't mean any harm." We should be so fearful of hurting people that even if a clever remark is rushing off our tongue, we can stop it at the gate and take a look at it from the other person's point of view. If it is beneficial—which is not usually the case with clever remarks—we can stamp its visa and let it out. But if there is any chance that the remark will be misunderstood, we should be able to swallow our cleverness and say something else instead. It is better to say something banal but harmless than to be clever at someone else's expense. If worst comes to worst, we can always write the remark down and send it to the *Reader's Digest;* they may publish it and send us five dollars.

In this connection, there is an Arabic proverb that has appealed to me for its practicality. The tongue, the Arabs say, should have three gatekeepers. When words arise, the first gatekeeper asks, "Is this true?" That stops a lot of traffic immediately. But if the words get past the first gatekeeper, there is a second who asks, "Is it kind?" And for those words that qualify here too, the last gatekeeper asks: "Is it necessary?"

Most of us, if these gatekeepers were awake, would find very little to say. Here I think it is necessary to make exceptions in the interests of good company and let the third gatekeeper look the other way now and then. After all, a certain amount of pleasant conversation, when we are sincerely interested in the other person and what he or she has to say, is part of the artistry of living. If we go through life mum as a clam, it doesn't contribute much towards seeing the Lord in those around us. But where the first two gatekeepers are concerned, I think it is very important to keep them alert always—not indulging in gossip of any kind, not speaking ill of anyone, and especially not taking part in arguments or acrimonious discussions, which only agitate everyone involved. If we can learn to be watchful like this about what we say as well as what we do, we are well on the way towards identifying ourselves with our true Self within.

श्री भगवानुवाच
मया प्रसन्नेन तवार्जुनेदं
    रूपं परं दर्शितमात्मयोगात् ।
तेजोमयं विश्वमनन्तमाद्यं
    यन्मे त्वदन्येन न दृष्टपूर्वम् ॥४७॥
न वेदयज्ञाध्ययनैर्न दानै-
    र्न च क्रियाभिर्न तपोभिरुग्रैः ।
एवंरूपः शक्य अहं नृलोके
    द्रष्टुं त्वदन्येन कुरुप्रवीर ॥४८॥

SRI KRISHNA:
47. *Arjuna, through my grace you have been united with Me and received this vision of my radiant, universal form, without beginning or end, which no one else has ever seen.*
48. *Not by knowledge, nor service, nor charity, nor rituals, nor even by severe asceticism has any other mortal seen what you have seen, O heroic Arjuna.*

If we ask any mystic in any of the great religious traditions how the vision of God comes about, they will all give us the same reply: it is not because we are worthy of it, but because the Lord is so merciful. All that we can do is to make our best effort to purify our minds and hearts through the practice of meditation and its allied disciplines. Finally we will reach a point where we can go no further, where we have done everything we can to remove the last impediments of the ego which stand between us and the Lord. Then, with faith that wells up from the very depths of consciousness, we say to the Lord, "It doesn't matter if I don't have a glimpse of you. I want only to love you with all my heart; I expect nothing in return." Rabia, a tremendous woman of God in the Sufi tradition, exclaims:

> Lord, if I love you out of fear of hell,
> Throw me into hell.
> If I love you for the sake of heaven,
> Close its gates to me.
> But if I love you for the sake of loving you,
> Do not deny yourself to me!

When we can say this to the Lord with complete love—whether we call him Sri Krishna or Allah, the Divine Mother or the Buddha or Jesus the Christ—it is only a matter of time before we will be united with him in the form we cherish most. Anyone who has reached this state *is* God-conscious.

In all the annals of mysticism, East and West, there is no finer inspiration than the unanimous testimony to this miracle of grace. *The Imitation of Christ* overflows with it:

> O Lord, how entirely needful is thy grace for me, to begin any good work, to go on with it, and to accomplish it. For without that grace I can do nothing; but in thee I can do all things when thy grace doth strengthen me.

St. Teresa of Ávila puts it in wonderfully practical terms:

> However much we may practice meditation, however much we violate our self-will, however many tears of devotion we

shed, we cannot produce this blessing; it is given only to whom God wills to give it. We are His; may He lead us along whatever way He pleases.

And the Sufi mystic Jalalu'l-Din Rumi sums it up beautifully:

It is not we who shoot the arrow; we are only the bow. The archer is the Lord.

मा ते व्यथा मा च विमूढभावो
     दृष्ट्वा रूपं घोरमीदृङ्ममेदम् ।
व्यपेतभीः प्रीतमनाः पुनस्त्वं
     तदेव मे रूपमिदं प्रपश्य ॥४९॥

49. Do not be troubled; do not fear my terrible form. Let your heart be satisfied and your fears dispelled in looking at Me as I was before.

The Lord is not only love, he is also terror. In the Hindu tradition, this other face of the Lord is expressed by the law of karma, and we can see the fearful effects of its workings all around us today. In the twentieth century, we are reaping all that we have sown. The wars which this century has seen, which have cost so many millions of lives and brought so much sorrow and destruction, have not been inflicted upon us by anybody from outside. The destructive forces in life are not only outside us; they are within us too, in the very depths of our consciousness. All of us are involved in the fearful course our world is taking today. That is why I say so often that just to live is to be responsible—not only for what we do, but for what we fail to do.

To take just one example, there is a saying in my mother tongue that it takes two to get married and two to quarrel. It takes two to trade arms also. If the United States is exporting eight billion dollars worth of armaments, then other countries are importing eight billion dollars worth of arms from us—which means a lot of people who are involved in manufacturing, trading, transporting, stockpiling, and deploying American instruments of war. Every American shares responsibility for this deadly trade. I am not saying that other nations do not share this responsibility; they do. But I live in this country, not in France or the Soviet Union, and I believe it is the stronger party who must take the first step. As our awareness of the unity of life deepens, we see more and more how far-reaching are the consequences of all our actions. You or I may not have put a gun in an angry man's hand, but if we are involved in the manufacture or sale of guns, if we fail to oppose these arms deals or to support gun control legislation, we are implicitly involved when any gun is used.

But there is a very positive aspect to the law of karma too. Just as it is we who have got ourselves into this situation, it is still within our reach to pull ourselves out again. Even though the debit side of our ledger may be red with entries, with scarcely a mark on the credit side at all, there is no need to be despondent. All that is necessary is to stop making entries on the debit side and throw ourselves heart and soul into adding entries to our credit. In this verse, Sri Krishna is reassuring Arjuna by telling him not to be oppressed by the destructive forces he has seen, but to devote his life to revealing the Lord of Love in his own life.

One of the most practical aspects of this is that it does not matter if the entries are large. Most of us do not have occasion to make large sacrifices, and if we wait for the opportunity to make a really big entry on the credit side, we may still be waiting when the cosmic auditor decides to close the books. What is important is to begin where we are and do the best we can. Even on the international level, we do not need to be in a position of fame or power in order to begin making a contribution to world peace. Often I think the world's problems can be solved more effectively by many little people acting together than by presidents or parliaments or corporations.

To begin with, we can begin to make our opinions heard. There is no need to worry about how many people will listen. If our words are true, they have to have an effect; it is only a matter of time. Remember Lincoln's words about government by the people and for the people? They still hold true today. Everyone from Capitol Hill to our local community center is interested in a calm, thoughtful, practical presentation. We can all write letters, and we can talk with our friends and neighbors and encourage them to write letters too. Those with speaking talent can address groups in their communities, and anyone with a flair for writing can put together an article for a magazine or take advantage of one of our biggest forums, the Letters to the Editor page of local and national newspapers. When friends get together for bridge or bowling they can give part of their time for letter-writing; it can be every bit as enjoyable.

Then, second, we can refuse to be a party to violence in any way, no matter how indirect. Many industries and occupations, for example, are involved in the making of arms; many others are involved in their development and sale. If even a small proportion of us withdraw our support from this machinery of violence, these problems could be brought under control.

संजय उवाच
इत्यर्जुनं वासुदेवस्तथोक्त्वा
    स्वकं रूपं दर्शयामास भूयः ।
आश्वासयामास च भीतमेनं
    भूत्वा पुनः सौम्यवपुर्महात्मा ॥५०॥
अर्जुन उवाच
दृष्ट्वेदं मानुषं रूपं तव सौम्यं जनार्दन ।
इदानीमस्मि संवृत्तः सचेताः प्रकृतिं गतः ॥५१॥

SANJAYA:

50. Having spoken these words, the Lord once again assumed the gentle form of Krishna and consoled his devotee, who had been so afraid.

ARJUNA:

51. O Janārdana, having seen your gentle human form my mind is again composed.

In a moment of infinite tenderness, the Lord reveals to Arjuna that He who contains all the galaxies is still none other than Sri Krishna, his beloved companion and guide. Arjuna breathes a sigh of relief, and in his joy he calls Sri Krishna by a very sweet name: Janārdana, 'he who intoxicates people.' Most of us think that intoxication is something that comes through drugs or drinking, but these changes in consciousness are artificial. They are prompted by external circumstances, and when the circumstances change, we are left wide open to depression. The joy Arjuna experiences, the joy of being united with the Lord, is permanent.

After attaining this state of union the mystic lives in the continuous presence of God, seeing and serving Him in all around. John Woolman, the American Quaker, describes in memorable words how this awareness came to him:

> I saw a mass of matter of a dull, gloomy color between the
> North and the East, and was informed that this mass was human
> beings, in as great misery as they could be and live; and that I
> was mixed up with them and henceforth I must not consider
> myself as a distinct or separate being.

Woolman's life reminds us that, when, by the grace of the Lord, we attain this state of illumination, we cannot just tear up our identification cards, sit back, and put our feet up on our desks. The Lord saves his most difficult work for those who have become united with him. It is true that the person who has reached the summit of human consciousness wants nothing more of life than to remain on the spiritual Himālayas, and may be tempted to stay there for eternity. But there are rare men and women who attain these heights and look back upon the plains of the earth to see millions of us crawling through life like ants. They want to live on this Mount Everest of bliss, but every time they close their eyes to the misery below, something in them says, "How can I bask in this happiness when my brothers and sisters are trapped in suffering?" Fortunately for us, these mystics have learned how to make the arduous journey back into the world of change and multiplicity, so that they can show us how we too can put an end to sorrow.

It is said that even the Compassionate Buddha, on the night of his enlightenment, faced this temptation to withdraw from life and its misery. Māra, the tempter, had tried every trick in his book to prevent the Buddha from attaining illumination. Finally, having realized that he could not distract him with sensual temptations, Māra tried a clever psychological ploy. "Blessed One," he said, "I admit that you have found the perfect joy of nirvāna. Why not remain in this state of bliss, instead of going back to a world of selfishness and suffering? When you go back, who is going to understand you? Who is going to strive as you have striven?" It is a heartbreaking question, which comes to every mystic who attains the vision of God. But after a long pause the Compassionate Buddha replied with infinite resolution, "Perhaps there will be a few to listen to me, and believe in me, and follow what I say."

This is all the man or woman of God expects. They do not hope for a meditation revolution sweeping from Alaska to the tip of Chile; when just one person attains Self-realization, the whole world benefits. As the Hindu mystics say, "When the lotus blooms, the bees come looking for it." When the love of God blossoms in anyone's heart, people will be drawn there, for everyone is looking for the permanent joy and security such a person offers.

The trip down from the spiritual summit is fraught with difficulties, for it involves learning how to be in the midst of the world without being of it. In order to reach people and touch their hearts, you must live among them and participate fully in life, yet remain aware every instant of the Lord within you and within all those around you. This is why spiritual living is so challenging. But when the going is rough, you have only to open your heart to be strengthened by the melody of Sri Krishna's flute or the tender image of Jesus. Even though the world outside may be overcast by a pall of violence and suffering, the temple within remains lit in radiance always.

श्री भगवानुवाच
सुदुर्दर्शमिदं रूपं दृष्टवानसि यन्मम ।
देवा अप्यस्य रूपस्य नित्यं दर्शनकाङ्क्षिणः ॥५२॥
नाहं वेदैर्न तपसा न दानेन न चेज्यया ।
शक्य एवंविधो द्रष्टुं दृष्टवानसि मां यथा ॥५३॥
भक्त्या त्वनन्यया शक्य अहमेवंविधोऽर्जुन ।
ज्ञातुं द्रष्टुं च तत्त्वेन प्रवेष्टुं च परंतप ॥५४॥

SRI KRISHNA:

52. It is extremely difficult to obtain the vision you have had; even the gods are always longing to see Me in this aspect.

53. Neither knowledge, nor austerity, nor charity, nor sacrifice can bring the vision you have seen.

54. But through unfailing devotion, Arjuna, you can know Me, and see Me, and attain union with Me.

As Jesus reminds us, it is only the pure in heart who see God. It is only the pure in heart who are capable of complete faith, which is what it takes to see the Lord everywhere around us always.

In the Hindu tradition we have beautiful stories showing the power of such faith, which is often dramatized as characteristic of a simple child. One of these stories is about a boy named Haridās, whose mother was a great devotee of Gopāla, the youthful Krishna. Every day Haridās had to walk to school through a forest inhabited by all kinds of wild animals. The journey frightened him so much that he asked his mother what to do. "Don't be afraid, Hari," she replied. "You have a big brother, Gopāla, who lives in the forest. All you have to do when you pass that way is call his name and he will come and escort you to school."

Haridās had never heard about this older brother before, but he believed his mother's words completely. The next time he entered the woods he called out, "Gopāla! Gopāla!" At first no one appeared, but the boy's faith was so great that he just went on calling and calling. After a while, out from behind a tree stepped a handsome young man in a yellow silk dhoti, wearing a peacock feather jauntily in his rich black hair. "What's all the shouting about?" he teased. The two became good friends, and from that day on Krishna appeared every time the boy called, and went with him as far as the edge of the forest. Haridās was never afraid in the woods again.

One day, however, the boy came walking home from school very slowly, with his head drooping. "There's a feast tomorrow," he told his mother, "and the teacher asked us all to bring something to eat. But we're so poor that I don't think I'll have anything to take."

But Hari's mother was unperturbed. "Don't worry," she said; "just ask your brother tomorrow for some yogurt for you to take."

The next day Hari arrived at school with a little bowl of yogurt, and when they all sat down to eat, Hari's yogurt was passed around with all the other dishes. It was just a small bowl, and there should have been scarcely enough for three or four. But no matter how much was taken from it, the bowl was never empty.

Naturally, the teacher became quite interested in this phenomenon. "Hari," he asked, "where did you get this bottomless bowl?"

"From my older brother, Gopāla, who lives in the woods."

"But you don't have an older brother," his teacher objected. "Come on, now, tell me the truth."

But Hari, of course, only stuck to his story.

Finally the teacher decided to accompany the boy home that afternoon and meet this mysterious "older brother" Gopāla, who handed out miraculous, unending bowls of food. But in his heart he still thought the boy was lying. They reached the woods and Hari called out, "Gopāla! Gopāla!" Sure enough, Krishna appeared around the bend of the path, looking quite natty in his silk dhoti and peacock feather. Hari waved and cried, "Hi, Gopāl!" Then he turned to his teacher and said, "See, *there* is my older brother. Now will you please excuse me so I can run home to tell my mother about the feast?" And without waiting for a reply, he hurried off into the forest. But the schoolteacher was left standing there feeling rather ridiculous, because he could not see anyone at all.

It is a simple story, but it illustrates the power of complete faith.

When we come to have this kind of unquestioning trust in the Lord within us, without any kind of selfish reservation for ourselves, there is no end to the inner resources that will flow into our lives.

Most of us, of course, do not begin the spiritual life with this kind of devotion. But love for the Lord is not something that descends miraculously from the skies; it can be fostered and deepened immensely through our own effort. At present, very little of our love is likely to be flowing to the Lord. Most of it is flowing to all sorts of other things down other channels—towards money, or pleasure, or a new sports car or quadraphonic stereo set. In some cases, our vital capacity has been flowing down these channels for so long that they have been cut very deep. Then, when the time comes to dam them up and divert the love in them to flow towards the Lord, we feel we are standing there throwing pebbles into the Grand Canyon.

Here it is necessary not to become depressed by the immensity of the task, but just keep on throwing in the pebbles. They may not seem like much, but after a while they all add up. Take the problem of overeating. A handful of Brazil nuts may be a small thing, and no one would deny that once in a while they are not likely to do anyone any harm. But every time we pass up a snack, our will becomes a little stronger; we have thrown one more rock into the canyon. After a while, when we learn to do this freely, every rock we throw in will precipitate an avalanche, and soon—often before we even realize it—the Grand Canyon of that particular craving may be completely filled.

But there is another very practical suggestion I can make here. It *is* necessary to dam up the old channels down which our love is flowing, but if we do nothing but block the flow, there is always the danger that the dam may break or the water may overflow. So instead of giving all our attention to the rather negative work of throwing rocks, we can do our best throughout the day to dig a new channel straight to the Lord in those around us—by being patient, by being loyal, by always keeping our eyes on their welfare rather than our own. For a long, long time this new channel may seem terribly dry, but if we just keep digging, it will soon begin to drain off a little of the love that is now flowing down other channels. Finally it will become so deep that all our desires will be unified in a vast flood of love for the Lord.

मत्कर्मकृन्मत्परमो मद्भक्तः सङ्गवर्जितः ।
निर्वैरः सर्वभूतेषु यः स मामेति पाण्डव ॥५५॥

55. Whoever makes Me the supreme goal of all his work and acts without selfish attachment, who devotes himself to Me completely and is free from ill will for any creature, enters into Me.

For a few great men and women of God, who are capable of total devotion to a divine incarnation, seeing God may mean an actual vision. In the Christian tradition, for example, St. Francis of Assisi was blessed with visions of Jesus the Christ, and in India Sri Ramakrishna saw the Lord as the Divine Mother. But while the idea of seeing visions and hearing angelic voices may capture our imagination, I would like to present a much more practical interpretation of what it means to see God. As Sri Krishna tells us in these magnificent verses, the man or woman who performs all actions as an offering to the Lord, without a trace of selfish attachment or ill will, is aware of the Lord always. In our own age, Mahatma Gandhi is a perfect example of what this kind of awareness means. With his characteristic candor, Gandhi once said that he had seen no lights, heard no voices, and witnessed no visions. But Gandhi was nonetheless a man of immense spiritual awareness. He was able to work tirelessly for the welfare of all those around him—not just of those who were for him, but of those who were opposed to him also—without any thought of his own comfort or prestige, disarming his opposition not through force but through the power of his love.

This is the vision of the Lord which we can cultivate everywhere, all the time. Whenever we are able to forget our own petty satisfactions in working for the welfare of the whole, whether it is for our family, our community, or our world, we are becoming a little more aware of the Lord. Whenever we are able to remember that what hurts us hurts others too, and are able to refrain from unkind words and deeds and even thoughts, we are becoming a little more aware of the Lord. Whenever we are able to respond patiently and positively to others even if they are hostile to us or rub us the wrong way, we are becoming a little more aware of the Lord. So when Sri Krishna tells us about devotion, he doesn't mean a private relationship between us and the Lord; he means the whole of our relationships with every living creature.

When you are always aware of the unity of life, you see the Lord in every living creature. Then you welcome every opportunity to serve others, and you become incapable of doing anything at their expense. To put it more personally, you see everyone as dear to you; every child is your child, and every dog is your dog. I don't think anyone has ever put it more beautifully than the Compassionate Buddha, when he tells us that we should love and protect every man, every woman, every child, every creature on earth, the way a mother loves and protects her only child.

In this final verse of chapter eleven, the Lord gives us his promise that if we devote ourselves to him completely—whether we call him Krishna or Christ, the Buddha or Allah or the Divine Mother—we will be united with him without fail, entering into his wholeness to become one with the indivisible unity he has revealed. As Jesus says, "I am the true vine, and my Father is the husbandman. Abide in me, and I in you. As the branch cannot bear fruit of itself, except it abide in the vine, no more can ye except ye abide in me."

If we keep our eyes on this supreme goal all the time, our life will be full of meaning; every decision we make will be significant to the whole. Every morning we will renew our decision not to live for ourselves but to do what adds to the welfare of everyone, and once we have learned to make this decision we can live in any country or any society and give a good account of our lives. Of course, everyone does not make the same kind of contribution. Some are doctors or nurses, some are teachers, some are mothers or fathers. But whatever our place in life, each of us has a contribution to make that can be made by no one else. Each of us can learn to apply the changeless values of selfless living to his or her own life, and because the Lord dwells in every one of us, none of us need ever be diffident about our capacity to leave the world a little better than we found it.

There is a story from the folklore of India that illustrates this point effectively. On the first day of the sun's creation, people expected to see it shining in the sky forever. No one knew that the sun had to dip into the water in the evening for a twelve-hour bath so that it could rise refreshed in the morning. So on the first evening of creation, everyone was terrified to see the sun about to set and the darkness beginning to spread across the world. They didn't know what to do. Then one little person stood up and said, "I'll light a candle." Someone else added, "I will too." Here, there, everywhere, millions of people started lighting candles, and soon the whole world was filled with light again.

This simple little story shows the importance of every person on earth, no matter how insignificant our lives may appear to be. Ordinary though we may be on the surface, within the heart of each of us lie tremendous capacities for love and service, and if we can keep our eyes always on the Lord of Love, there is no problem on earth too dire for ordinary people like you and me to solve.

इति विश्वरूपदर्शनं नामैकादशोऽध्यायः ॥११॥

CHAPTER TWELVE

The Way of Love

अर्जुन उवाच
एवं सततयुक्ता ये भक्तास्त्वां पर्युपासते ।
ये चाप्यक्षरमव्यक्तं तेषां के योगवित्तमाः ॥१॥

ARJUNA:

1. Of those who love you as the Lord of Love, ever present in all, and those who seek you as the nameless, formless Reality, which way is sure and swift, love or knowledge?

Arjuna has just been granted the vision of the Lord's universal form. Now, overwhelmed by love for Sri Krishna, he is ready to do anything to be united with him forever.

This intense longing is the keynote of any genuine mystical experience, and we hear it echoed in the writings of the men and women of God in all ages and all traditions. In Hinduism it is beautifully expressed in a scene between Sri Krishna and the lovely village girl named Rādhā. Rādhā is passionately in love with Sri Krishna, and her intense passion represents the heart's longing for union with the Lord.

The scene opens with Rādhā entering the glade where she and Sri Krishna had often wandered lost in love. Now he has gone, and tormented, she searches everywhere for him until finally all her other desires are consumed in the intensity of her love.

Then, from far off, she hears the haunting notes of Sri Krishna's flute. Slowly the music comes closer. At last she sees him, and Rādhā is transported with joy. But only for a moment: just as quickly as he came, her Beloved disappears again, leaving her alone once more in the renewed anguish of desolation.

In the Western tradition, St. Teresa of Ávila uses almost the same image to explain her own experience:

> We can compare this kind of union to a tryst, because it is over in the very shortest time. All giving and taking have now come to an end, and in a secret way the soul sees who this Spouse is that she is to take. By means of the senses and faculties she could not understand in a thousand years what she understands in this way in the briefest space of time. But in that one short visit her Spouse, being who he is, leaves her worthier than before to join hands with him in union; and the soul, for her part, becomes so fired with love that she will do anything not to thwart this divine betrothal.

It is to deepen our love, to unify our desires, that the Lord gives us this fleeting taste of the joy of union. Once we taste this joy, all we want is to be permanently aware of him in everyone, everywhere, every minute. And here Arjuna, fresh from his experience of unity, asks a very practical question: "How can I best attain this state, through knowledge or through love?" It is a question with far-reaching implications, because it involves a very basic issue: what are we, as human beings, and what can we become?

This is not just a philosophical issue; it affects every aspect of our lives. Our upbringing, our relationships, our attitudes towards the environment, our physical and emotional well-being are all conditioned by the assumption that the basis of human personality is physical. In scientific language, personality is a product of our genetic makeup, shaped in part by the environment we encounter as we grow up. Deep in our consciousness, whether we think about it or not, this is the picture to which all of us subscribe: our character has already been determined, and we have no choice but to accept ourselves the way we are.

This belief has tragic consequences; it limits our outlook everywhere to the lowest common factor of existence. As William James says, it is like having the whole human body at our disposal and going through life moving only our little finger. We don't even suspect that there *is* a body; we think this one little finger is all we have.

Here I like to remember the example of Albert Einstein, whose theories revolutionized the physical sciences. When he was asked how he discovered relativity, Einstein replied simply, "By questioning an established axiom." In the same way, this chapter of the Gita is going to question our concept of the human personality, and therefore the basis of our civilization.

The challenge is simple: *we* are not what our genes are; the body is. We are what we think. Conditioned behavior may be dictated by our genetic makeup, but when we get below the surface level of consciousness and get hold of the thinking process itself, we can go beyond conditioning and change our personality completely.

Up to now, in previous chapters, I have been trying to show that there is no conflict between scientific knowledge and spiritual wisdom. There can be no conflict, because any investigation of nature *is* an inquiry into the unity of life. There is no better example than Einstein's theories of relativity, which—to use the words of C. P. Snow—"quietly amalgamated space, time, and matter" in the search for the underlying unity of nature. But no matter how far its investigations proceed, science can never go beyond the physical world of finite objects and passing events, which is just the surface of reality. As Spinoza puts it, "The finite rests upon the bosom of the Infinite."

This applies not only to the world of space and time, matter and energy; it is equally true of the human personality. There too, with our physical orientation, we see only the surface and mistake it for reality. But unfortunately, very few of the important problems in life—those which threaten our health, our happiness, our relationships, our very survival—can ever be solved on the physical level. More than that, when we try to apply a physical solution we are all too likely to make such problems more acute, because we are usually dealing not with the cause but with the symptoms.

The other day, for example, I was reading about how physicians sometimes deal with compulsive overeating by making a surgical detour around some of the organs of digestion. The underlying assumption is that there is nothing else that can be done. From the mystic's perspective, there is always something more that can be done—in this case, actually to go beneath the surface of consciousness and undo the compulsion to overeat. But even to understand that this is possible, we need a wholly different concept of human nature. To use Spinoza's image, the biochemical level is only the surface of personality. Our real Self, the Ātman, is at the very core of consciousness; and if we can get below the surface, we can change our personality at will.

This is in full accord with the principles of genetics; it is simply a larger picture. Recently I saw a physiology textbook that compared the genetic code to a movie film, unrolling through our lives with every interior event predetermined. The rationale is that brain neurons, like other cells, have their special properties coded by our genes. From this, many scientists conclude that the patterns of thought and personality are written into our genetic code. As long as we identify ourselves with the body and are subject to biological conditioning, this may be valid. But to repeat, we are *not* what our DNA is. Genetics may limit how tall we can be, but it can't limit the stature to which we can grow spiritually. If we can change our way of thinking, many processes of the brain can be modified—not only the production of the behavior-related neurotransmitters and hormones, but perhaps even which portions of the DNA are expressed in certain cells. It is as if each DNA molecule had a secret key of its own: "You can change the expression of these genes through the practice of meditation."

If our lives were on film, the genes would only be stagehands; the ego is the director. The mind and senses get the supporting roles, and thousands of distractions run about as extras to make up for the lack of plot. This is the first reel, and if we could see it clearly, most of us would walk out.

In meditation, however, we get hold of the camera and turn the directing over to the Ātman. The supporting cast is the same, the makeup artist and set designer are the same, but we get a new script and a new star. Even biologically, it means that we have become a different person: the genetic material is the same, but the person is wholly transformed. In the language of mysticism both East and West, we have been born again. As Eckhart says, "The old man is dead and the new man is born; the pauper is dead and the prince is born."

श्री भगवानुवाच
मय्यावेश्य मनो ये मां नित्ययुक्ता उपासते ।
श्रद्धया परयोपेतास्ते मे युक्तमा मताः ॥२॥

SRI KRISHNA:
2. For those who set their hearts on Me and worship Me with unfailing devotion and faith, the way of love leads sure and swift to Me.

In India there is a story about a villager who wanted to learn to meditate. For several weeks, following his teacher's instructions, he repeated the mantram *Om* and tried to fix his mind on the formless Absolute. But his mind did nothing but wander. Finally he went back to his teacher and complained, "Sir, I just can't keep my mind on the Absolute. I don't know what it's like."

The teacher got the hint and decided to take a more practical approach. "All right," he said, "what is it that appeals to you most deeply?"

With some embarrassment the villager replied, "My cow."

"Very well," said the teacher, "go and meditate on your cow." That is one of the skills of a good spiritual teacher; he always knows how to begin where you are.

A few days later the teacher decided to look in on his new student. To his surprise, the man hadn't come out of his meditation room for three days. His teacher pounded on the door. "Open up!" he commanded. "What are you doing in there?"

There came a faint answer, a little like a bellow: "Meditating."

"Come out at once," the teacher repeated. "I have some instructions to give you about moderation."

"Sir," came the reply, "I *can't* come out. My horns are too big to fit through the door."

This is the basis of meditation: we become what we meditate on.

Whatever we constantly dwell on shapes our desires, our decisions, and finally our destiny. And the mystics of both East and West draw the same conclusion: then we become what we love.

In this sense, every one of us has been meditating for a long time. The problem is that we have no control over what we meditate on. To take a negative example, look at what happens over a period of years to someone whose love has been captured by money. At first he may show only a tendency to be greedy. But if he dwells on making money, that desire starts to condition his ways of thinking. Making a profit comes easily to such a person, for the simple reason that he doesn't really see anything else. As the Buddha would remind us, we don't see with our eyes. We see with our mind, and here the mind is always thinking about money. If he sees a redwood grove, he thinks, "That's a dollar a board foot!" If he sees the Grand Canyon, he wants to dam it up and turn it into a resort. And the tragedy is this: after many years, he won't be able to think of anything else. He will be so preoccupied with profit that he won't be aware of the needs of family or friends or society. He may even be willing to work at jobs that are harmful to others, such as manufacturing cigarettes or armaments, just to make a few more dollars. In a sense, it is no longer realistic to expect him to be otherwise; he just can't *see* any other way. This is the immense power of thoughts, which few of us even suspect.

But all this has a positive side too. Just as we stunt ourselves by dwelling on some private, personal satisfaction, we can grow to our full stature by giving our love to an ideal that embodies the perfection of human nature.

The annals of mysticism are full of examples of this, but I know of none more appealing, more human, than that of St. Francis of Assisi. He was born into a well-to-do merchant family, and though he must have been a sweet-tempered young man, his mind seems to have been full of no more than poetry and music and the romance of the Crusades. But when his heart turned to Jesus, his desire to become like Him was so passionate that it transformed and transfigured him completely. As G. K. Chesterton has said, if you find the Jesus of the Gospels unapproachable, if you find it hard to believe that the Sermon on the Mount can actually be practiced by a human being, you have only to look at Francis, the perfect image of his Master.

If this is difficult to understand, it is because most of us have no idea of what love really means. Look at how the word *love* is used today, not only in the mass media but by some of the most respected people in every profession. It shows how unreal our world has become; everything is a matter of biology. If someone says, "Two people are embracing each other; they are making love," we consider that an intelligent statement. But if I were to see someone being patient in the face of provocation and say, "*That* person is making love," people would think it was a quaint example of a professor from India mixing up his English idioms. How thoroughly we have turned life upside down! What is untrue is universally accepted, and what is true cannot even be understood.

When I first came to this country, I gave a talk on the spiritual life to a group of teenage girls. In those days practically no one had heard of meditation, so I centered my remarks around something in which girls of that age are always interested: personal relationships. The young president of the club listened very carefully, and when I had finished she said, "You have used the word *love* a lot, but not the way we are used to hearing it. Will you please tell us what love means to you?"

I like that kind of direct question very much, and I told her: "When I say I love a person, it means only one thing: that person's happiness, that person's welfare, means more to me than my own."

She looked around at the others. "Well, girls," she confessed, "I guess that means none of us has ever been in love."

It was a thoughtful observation, for this is a concept of love that does not even occur to most of us today. To the mystics, love has very little to do with sentimental or physical attraction. I don't think anyone has described it better than St. Paul:

Love suffereth long, and is kind; love envieth not; love
vaunteth not itself, is not puffed up, doth not behave itself
unseemly, seeketh not its own, is not easily provoked, thinketh

no evil; rejoiceth not in iniquity, but rejoiceth in the truth;
beareth all things, believeth all things, hopeth all things,
endureth all things. Love never faileth. . . .

Now, in the traditional interpretation, the message of this chapter
of the Gita is to love the Lord. But I don't think it is any exaggera-
tion to say that the meaning is simply to love. The reason is simple:
even to love another person completely, consciousness has to be
united.

Look at the universality of mystical language East and West. In
Hinduism, the relationship between God and creation is said to be
advaita, 'not two'. In Christianity, all mystics would concur with
St. Paul's eloquent exclamation: "Not I, not I, but Christ liveth in
me." In other words, lover and Beloved are one. And if we can cast
our eyes to the summit of human nature, isn't it the same even between individuals? "Here are my duties, here are yours. This is the
boundary line. If you stay on your side, I'll respect you; but if you
cross over, you're an invader." Wherever people go their separate
ways like this, there can be no love; there is scarcely a relationship.
The very nature of love is not to have qualifications or reservations
at all.

When I talk like this people sometimes object, "I've never spent
a day like that, much less a lifetime! If that's what love means, I
don't think I'm capable of it." I have never accepted this statement
from anybody. Every one of us can learn to love. Naturally, we all
start with imperfections: self-will, self-centeredness, demands and
opinions of our own. But there is no need to throw up our hands as
so many are doing today and say, "Let us be separate *and* have a
relationship"; it is not possible to do both. Instead, we start where
we are—somewhat selfish, somewhat self-willed—but with a deep
desire to relate lovingly to each other, to move closer and closer
together. It requires a lot of stamina and many years of hard work,
and there will be anguish in it as well as joy. But immediate consolation: we don't have to wait until our love is perfect to reap the
benefits of it. Even with a little progress, everyone benefits—not
only those we live with, but ourselves as well.

This is what the Gita means by the way of love. It can be practiced in all relationships, but a loving relationship between man and woman provides a particularly good context. There the desire for union is already present. It needs only to be nurtured, so that every day you love each other a little more.

The Sufis have a vivid image to illustrate this, which I can elaborate from my own experience. In some parts of Muslim society, it is still not uncommon to see women wearing the veil. I first saw this at close quarters when I was teaching on a campus in Central India, where the women students would sometimes sit together behind a common veil on one side of the room. This veil aroused great curiosity: all the boys wanted to see who was behind it. You could hear the girls' bangles jingling and now and then a soft ripple of laughter, and none of my best quotes from Shakespeare could compete with those delicate sounds.

At first the veil looked quite opaque. But as I looked with more concentration, I began to make out silhouettes behind it. Then I could see some of the features, and finally, as I learned what to look for, I was able to recognize the faces on the other side.

This is what happens in personal relationships on the way of love. At first there is just an opaque curtain between us and the one we love. The Lord *is* there, but we cannot see him—in fact, at the beginning we scarcely know what to look for. Gradually, however, our concentration deepens. Now we sense that there really is someone behind the curtain, and every once in a while we glimpse a silhouette. As vision becomes clearer, we seem to see the beautiful eyes of Sri Krishna or Jesus or the Divine Mother behind our partner's eyes—and the more we see, the deeper is our desire to see more.

In the end, all our other desires merge in the immense longing to have no barrier between us and our real Beloved. Only one veil remains, and it is so thin that every morning we go to meditation knowing that this may be the day that we are united with the Lord at last. We may wait like this for years, but finally, without warning, the veil falls at last. Then, in the rapturous language of St. John of the Cross, we merge in the Beloved and are transformed: *"Amado con amada, amada en el amado transformada."*

Most of us think of love as a one-to-one relationship, which is all it can be on the physical level. But there is no limit to our capacity to love. We can never be satisfied by loving just one person here, another there. Our need is to love completely, universally, without any reservations—in other words, to become love itself. It can take our breath away to glimpse the vastness of such love, which Dostoevsky describes beautifully in *The Brothers Karamazov:*

> Love all that has been created by God, both the whole and
> every grain of sand. Love every leaf and every ray of light.
> Love the beasts and the birds, love the plants, love every separate
> fragment. If you love each separate fragment, you will under-
> stand the mystery of the whole resting in God. When you per-
> ceive this, your understanding of this mystery will grow from
> day to day until you come to love the whole world with a love
> that includes everything and excludes nothing.

This is what it means to realize the unity of life, and in these troubled times, when turmoil has invaded our society, our homes, and even our hearts, I don't think there is any more precious attainment. That is why this chapter of the Gita is so acutely relevant today. As one Hasidic rabbi put it, the community of the living is the carriage of the Lord. Where there is so little love that the carriage is torn asunder, we must love more, and the less love there is around us, the more we need to love to make up the lack.

A man once came to Rabbi Israel Ba'al Shem and said, "My son is estranged from God; what shall I do?" The Ba'al Shem replied simply, "Love him more." This was my Granny's approach to every problem, and I know of no more effective or artistic or satisfying way to realize the unity of life in the world today. It is an approach to life in which everything blossoms, everything comes to fruition. As Sri Krishna will go on to explain, Arjuna's question about love and knowledge is really unnecessary. Where there is love, everything follows. To love *is* to know, *is* to act; all other paths to the Lord are united in the way of love.

ये त्वक्षरमनिर्देश्यमव्यक्तं पर्युपासते ।
सर्वत्रगमचिन्त्यं च कूटस्थमचलं ध्रुवम् ॥३॥
संनियम्येन्द्रियग्रामं सर्वत्र समबुद्धयः ।
ते प्राप्नुवन्ति मामेव सर्वभूतहिते रताः ॥४॥

*3–4. As for those who seek the transcendental
Reality, without name, without form, contemplating
the Unmanifested, beyond the reach of thought and
of feeling, with their senses subdued and mind serene
and striving for the good of all beings—they too
will verily come unto Me.*

This is the other concept of God: not a personal ideal that can be
loved, but the formless, impersonal Ground of existence. It is an
idea that many people subscribe to intellectually today, in the belief
that faith in a personal God is either superstition or intellectual
weakness. But jnāna yoga, the 'way of knowledge,' has nothing to
do with the intellect. The intellect can operate only in a world of
duality, where there is subject and object, knower and known. Here
we must soar beyond all divisions into a realm of absolute unity,
where the separate personality merges completely in this formless,
infinite Reality and all distinction between knower and known disappears. In this supreme state, called *nirvikalpa samādhi* in Sanskrit, there is no one present to take notes. Sri Ramakrishna used to
tell about a doll made of salt who went to measure the depth of the
ocean. As soon as she waded into the water, she dissolved—and then,
Ramakrishna asks, who was left to tell of the ocean's vastness?

In this realm all trace of distinction disappears, so it is not surprising that we find mystics of all epochs and all traditions struggling to describe their experience in nearly identical language. Meister Eckhart in thirteenth-century Germany and Shankara in eighth-
century India often sound interchangeable; and Dionysius the Are-
opagite, probably a Christian monk writing at the end of the fifth
century, uses terms reminiscent of this very verse:

> Then, beyond all distinction between knower and known, . . .
> the aspirant becomes merged in the nameless, formless Reality,
> wholly absorbed in That which is beyond all things and in
> nothing else. . . . Having stilled his intellect and his mind, he is
> united by his highest faculty with That which is beyond
> all knowing.

To the intellect, which *has* to classify, the different traditional
approaches to God—called, in Hinduism, jnāna, bhakti, karma, and
rāja—are watertight compartments. But in fact, these are not separate paths. They are different aspects of the same spiritual experience, which flow together in life and practice.

To see this, all we have to do is look at those men and women
who have followed the path of knowledge—not at their philosophy,
but at their lives. Historians, for example, like to remember Shankara as a towering intellectual, the architect of an imposing philosophical structure that expounds his direct experience of the transcendent, impersonal Brahman, "One without a second." But this
same uncompromising nondualist was also an ardent lover of the
personal God who poured out his devotion to Shiva and the Divine
Mother in magnificent poetry, sometimes as a simple child of the
Lord:

> You are the Mother of the universe;
> Why should I wonder at your love for me?
> Even if his faults cannot be counted,
> A mother never abandons her child.

Shankara died at the age of thirty-two, but in that short lifetime
he traveled all over India, tirelessly revitalizing its spiritual heritage—founding monastic orders, establishing monasteries, teaching
successors, and leaving behind a great body of writing to pass on the
fruit of his spiritual experience. In such a life, love, selfless service,
and spiritual wisdom all fuse; each path comes to perfection in the
same soul.

In the language of Hinduism this underlying Reality, called Brahman, is said to be *advaita,* 'not two.' It cannot be described, because

there is nothing from which It can be distinguished. It is "what is and what is not," from which, as Shankara says, both "words and thought recoil." Still, to inspire us, the first part of these verses tries to convey a little of the stark majesty of this infinite, eternal Reality. *Aksharam:* it is inexhaustible, imperishable, without either beginning or end. *Anirdeshyam:* we cannot point to it or define it, because it is neither outside nor inside; subject and object are one. *Avyaktam:* it is unmanifest; it cannot be seen. Who could be the seer? Yet, *sarvatragam:* it is everywhere; it is Existence itself. And finally, *acalam:* unshakable, beyond all change.

These are inspiring words, because as the Upanishads say, *"Tat tvam asi"*: this is our real nature. We were never born; we shall never die. But at the same time, it gives us some idea of the awesome challenges of jnāna yoga, which I do not hesitate to say is beyond the capacity of all but a handful of people in any age. It is all very well to go about saying, "I am not my body, I am not my mind," but for most of us, how much effect would this have on consciousness? We would still get angry, still harbor resentments, still be subject to doubt and vacillation. As long as it is only an intellectual effort, this sort of exercise has nothing to do with jnāna. In fact, there is a danger to it. Far from shrinking the ego, it can actually swell it and make us more acutely aware of ourselves.

In the second half of these verses we get the qualifications we need to practice jnāna yoga. They are really stiff. *Samniyamy 'endriyagrāmam:* first, there has to be complete self-control. There should be no clamor from the senses at all, and if they do happen to ask for something that is not beneficial, we should be able to withdraw our desires without a hint of protest. *Sarvatra samabuddhayah:* no likes and dislikes, no personal entanglement in the world of sense objects. Friend and enemy should be equally respected. *Sarvabhūtahite ratāh:* our only joy should be in serving the welfare of others, without any thought of our own individual satisfaction. To me, it is all very much like the escape clauses you find in small print on the back of a contract: "If you can practice this yoga, you don't need it; if you need it, you won't be able to practice it."

In this connection, Sri Ramakrishna tells a story about the *gopīs* or cowherd girls who were Sri Krishna's companions in Vrindāvana. In these stories the gopīs represent all of us, the aspiring human soul; and they are passionately in love with Sri Krishna, the Lord of Love.

One day, Ramakrishna says, a jnāna yogi came to Vrindāvana. Seeing that the gopīs were completely devoted to an incarnation of God, the man began to teach them about Brahman, eternal and immutable. One by one, the girls fell asleep. When they woke up again they explained gently, "Holy one, we don't understand any of this. All we know about is our Krishna, whom we can see and enjoy and love."

Ask any young man whether he would rather have a date with Miss Principle of Femininity or with his girlfriend. Miss Femininity is perfect, but she is also formless—in fact, she doesn't have any attributes at all. If I know anything about men, that chap will tell you candidly to keep your Miss Perfection for yourself; he would rather go out with the girl he loves. She may have freckles and an unpredictable temper, but she has a hand he can hold, eyes he can gaze into, and a smile that lightens his heart. And Sri Krishna says now gently, though we may pride ourselves on our intellect, it is the same with us. With our physical conditioning, how is it possible for people like us to aspire to disembodied consciousness? It is not enough that the Ātman be eternal and immutable; it must also be packaged attractively in a human form. This is the miracle of divine incarnation, and when the Lord comes to life like this in a human being, it can capture our imagination and unify our dedication completely. St. Bernard gives the same explanation within the Catholic tradition: "The main reason for the invisible God incarnating himself physically in the midst of human beings was to lead them who can only love physically to the healthy love of his physical appearance, and then, little by little, to spiritual love."

क्लेशोऽधिकतरस्तेषामव्यक्तासक्तचेतसाम् ।
अव्यक्ता हि गतिर्दुःखं देहवद्भिरवाप्यते ॥५॥

*5. Yet hazardous and slow is the path to the
Unrevealed, difficult for physical man to tread.*

A few centuries ago, a mystic from Kerala summarized the problem
of jnāna yoga perfectly: "Jnāna is for those whose senses have come
under control."

That is the rub. For those who meet the qualifications—giants
like Meister Eckhart, Shankara, or Anandamayi Ma—jnāna yoga is
a perfectly adequate way to Self-realization. These are people who
are already free from the clamor of the senses, so they scarcely identify with their bodies at all. But if you believe in your heart that you
are essentially physical, Sri Krishna says dryly, you are going to find
this path very tough going.

Unfortunately, there are very few in the world today who do not
fall into this category. Virtually all of us believe that we are the
body, and if you doubt it, all you have to do is look around and ask
a very simple question: how do we spend our time? When we want
to celebrate, do we meditate or do we eat? When we get a vacation,
what do we choose to do? What are the usual themes in the books
and magazines we read, the songs we listen to, the movies and television shows we watch? We may protest, "This is the age of science.
The path of knowledge *has* to be right for us." But Sri Krishna
would only smile. "Do your senses listen to you? If they do, you
might be on the right track. But if they do not, you'd better consider
the way of love instead."

This is not a comment on the effectiveness of jnāna yoga. It is a
comment on the physical conditioning with which all of us have
grown up. Ours *is* a physically-oriented world, so we should not be
embarrassed to discover that we have learned to look on life with
wholly physical eyes. But it is equally important to understand
that we need not resign ourselves to this conditioning. We can
change our thinking completely—and if we do not, we will find it

very difficult to maintain any lasting relationship with those around us. The fiercer our physical conditioning is, the more separate we will feel, and the more we will be prey to all the problems of a divided mind: vacillation, depression, jealousy, and alienation. These problems *can* be solved, but not on the physical level where they arise. We need access to much deeper levels of consciousness.

Take, for example, a Don Juan who is all involved in a "meaningful relationship" with a young lady named Dulcinea. Juan is a very passionate fellow and intensely jealous. His mother will tell you that is his nature; he cannot change. Unfortunately, since Dulcinea is attractive, Juan's life is an agony of suspicion. The minute she is out of his sight he can't concentrate on anything, he can't enjoy anything, he can't stop worrying about what she is doing.

Now, according to one school of thought, if Don Juan can exchange his Dulcinea for a Juanita, as loyal as she is lovely, this uncertainty can be dispelled. "Change the environment, change the response"—isn't it axiomatic? But unfortunately, as most of us know from our own experience, this simply doesn't work. Juan has a jealous mind. He *has* to be jealous of somebody, and if Dulcinea is not around, he will be jealous of her maid. The problem is not with Dulcinea or Juanita or anything else in the outside world; the problem is the uncertainty in the mind of Don Juan. As long as he is living on the physical level, he cannot help being possessive. But it *is* possible for Juan to overcome his jealousy: not by reasoning with it, not by suppressing it, not by taking security hormones, but by learning to be master of his mind. When that is done, all insecurity goes—not only insecurity over Dulcinea, but insecurity over anything. Then he can take Dulcinea out to the Alhambra café, where her former boyfriend plays flamenco, and not be apprehensive at all. His face may look the same, his fingerprints may be the same, but Dulcinea will testify that he has become a different person.

Unless we can get beneath the physical level of consciousness, however, the conditioning of this level cannot be undone. Abraham Maslow, I think, says that if the only tool you have is a hammer, you treat every problem as if it were a nail. That is what we do when we try to deal with human problems from within a physical orientation. All we can look for is physical solutions, which cannot be effective because the problems are not physical in origin. Worse, such attempts can have dangerous consequences.

Recently, for example, I have been reading about the biochemical approach to personality. It is a fascinating area for research. Just as in our galaxy there are about one hundred billion stars, there is a galaxy within us too: the ten billion cells of the human brain. When Galileo is looking through his telescope at the stars, he is seeing them through those stars inside. And just as the Milky Way contains all kinds of little worlds, each seemingly self-contained but part of an integral whole, there are biochemical island-worlds within the galaxy of the brain—the cerebral cortex, the hippocampus, the thalamus, the amygdala—each with its histories of growth and commerce in which whole dynasties of proteins rise and fall.

This is not merely figurative language. I'm trying to show not only the fascination, but also the unity of these realms. Just as it is all one universe, for all those billions of apparently separate stars, it is all one head. It sounds elementary, but look at current research. Scientists have managed to probe into the molecules in the cells of the brain and are able to trace neurotransmitters like dopamine and serotonin which seem to trigger changes in mood. It is an amazing achievement. But when they suggest that by manipulating neurotransmitters we can help the brain to achieve its maximum potential, we have to raise our eyebrows. The brain is not conscious; it is an instrument of consciousness. When consciousness is changed, of course there will be correlated changes in brain biochemistry and in behavior. But by changing brain biochemistry, we can never change consciousness itself. All we can do is suppress particular symptoms, which is like trying to solve an electrical problem in a car by removing the little red light on the dash.

To take a particular example, neuroscientists tell us that there is an "appestat" in the hypothalamus that tells us when to eat or drink. When we feel hungry, we *have* to eat. Sometimes, in fact, even when we don't feel hungry we have to eat. The appestat has gone off, the juices are flowing, and even if the refrigerator has been locked up we will find some way to get inside. In other words, we have very little choice.

Now, as long as we are completely identified with the body this is an accurate picture, and all of us know people who are victims of compulsive eating. But in meditation, we can learn to reset the appestat—not to turn our backs on it or stifle it, but to change our appetite at will. In fact, for those who are meditating, the problem of overeating is one of the easiest problems to solve. It means that even the hypothalamus can be put in its place.

Now take another very practical application: hyperactivity. Researchers have learned that certain drugs can have a quieting effect on children whose learning problems have been ascribed to their "hyperactive" behavior. These are children with uncontrollable energy—which, from the biochemical perspective, is a serious liability. To me, however, this kind of behavior is often the expression of tremendous vital capacity which is crying out to be harnessed. Often such children have the potential for great achievements, and quieting their behavior with drugs, while it may be necessary in extreme cases, is going to suppress their capacity for achievement as well as their capacity for running amuck. It is the same capacity: that is the key. The capacity to cause trouble is the capacity to solve the problem of causing trouble—just as the capacity to be selfish is the capacity to become loving. In sedation, what happens is that the medication blunts the cutting edge of consciousness. After some time of this, we don't even have the blade of consciousness any more; we have only the handle. This is the danger of manipulation on the physical level. There may be a temporary relief of symptoms, but there is often a worsening of the problem.

The real issue with manipulating personality like this is the damage to human growth. In all these so-called solutions on the physical or chemical level, the will is forgotten or even undermined—and without the will there is no capacity for choice, no capacity for growth, no capacity for love. That is what physical conditioning leads to when it is taken to extremes. To overcome this conditioning we need to get to a deeper level of consciousness, where we can deepen our will and make the choices which enable us to grow.

ये तु सर्वाणि कर्माणि मयि संन्यस्य मत्परः ।
अनन्येनैव योगेन मां ध्यायन्त उपासते ॥६॥
तेषामहं समुद्धर्ता मृत्युसंसारसागरात् ।
भवामि नचिरात्पार्थ मय्यावेशितचेतसाम् ॥७॥

*6–7. But they for whom I am the supreme goal,
who do all work renouncing self for Me and meditate
on Me with single-hearted devotion—these will I
swiftly rescue from the fragment's cycle of birth
and death to fullness of eternal life in Me.*

When my wife and I were living on the Blue Mountain, we had a visit from a young American who had been living in India as a spiritual aspirant for a number of years. He was dressed just like a traditional Indian *sādhu,* but when he spoke, his English still had its old Harvard accent.

We talked about the spiritual life for some time, and when evening came he offered to come with us to our little meditation center and give the inspirational talk. Our group consisted mostly of simple villagers, and I was afraid his words might be too sophisticated. But there was no cause for worry. He spoke their native Tamil without stumbling, and the story he told was one that anyone could understand.

"Look," he said, stretching out his hands with open palms. "Sri Krishna is saying to every one of us, 'Here, I have a very special gift for you—the gift of immortality. Won't you reach out and take it?'

"'Thank you,' we say, 'but can't you see? Our hands are full of these sweet mangoes.'

"Sri Krishna smiles. 'Let go of the mangoes,' he explains patiently. 'Then your hands will be free.'

"'But Lord,' we protest, 'we *like* mangoes. Why don't you give us your present first? Then we promise we'll throw away the mangoes.'"

This is the essential conflict in every human heart. Part of us wants to reach out for the highest, part cannot let go of our little personal desires. Consciousness is split in two—between our higher and our lower natures, between the selfless and the selfish. And the Lord says simply, "Make yourselves whole." *Matparāh:* "Make Me your only goal." Don't do anything just to please yourself; don't do anything just to please Tom, Dick, and Harry. Everything should be for the sake of the Lord, the Self, in you and in those around you.

In this—and here the mystics of all traditions are unanimous—there is no room for doubts or reservations. The other day I read a remark that the Ten Commandments are rapidly becoming the Five Suggestions. This is the contemporary approach: we just don't like to be told what to do. So why not have Moses say, "Here are Five Suggestions for your careful consideration, for those who have the time"? But Sri Krishna says, *Sarvāni karmāni:* "No exceptions. Give Me everything: not only the big things, even the trifles." Moses and Jesus use the same language: "Thou shalt love the Lord with *all* thy heart and all thy spirit and all thy strength."

For the most part, this is not something we do on the surface level of awareness. We need to get into the very depths of our personality, where the fierce desires for personal satisfaction arise. Meditation enables us to enter these levels, but meditation by itself is not enough. Once we break through the surface of consciousness, we come to places where we can neither go forward nor withdraw. We see the doors to deeper awareness there in front of us, but we don't know how to open them. At such times, no amount of exertion on our part is going to make it through those doors. It takes both hands, and one hand is still hanging on to something personal, something private, that we don't want to leave behind. Until we let go, we are saying in effect, "Yes, Lord, I *would* like to go forward—just as long as I can stay here too."

No one has described this more vividly than Augustine. At the time of which he is writing, in his *Confessions,* Augustine is thirty-one. The storm within him has been going on for over twelve years. Now it is almost resolved, but he does not realize it: on the surface of personality, the conflict has grown so fierce that he feels torn in two. "I was bound," he exclaims—

not by another man's chains, but by my own iron self-will.
My capacity to desire was in enemy hands, and he had made a
chain of it to hold me down. For a will that is bent awry becomes
selfish desire, desire yielded to becomes habit, and habit not re-
sisted becomes compulsion. With these links joined one to the
other . . . a hard, hard servitude had me in its grip. The new will
being born in me . . . was not yet strong enough to overcome
the old will that had been strengthened by so much use. Thus
two wills warred against each other within me—one old, one
new; one physical, the other spiritual—and in their conflict
they wasted my spirit.

Then, with penetrating insight, he gives us the clue to victory:

I was in both camps, but there was a little more of me on the
side I approved than on the side I disapproved . . . for it had
become more a matter of unwillingly experiencing [my desires]
than of doing something that I actively wanted. . . .

It was I who willed and I who was unwilling: it was *I*. I did
not wholly will; I was not wholly unwilling. Therefore I strove
with myself and was distracted by myself. . . .

The analysis is perfect. It is not two selves in conflict; it is one
self—sometimes on one side, sometimes on the other. And to win,
all we have to do is put more and more of ourselves in the other
camp. Every time we withdraw our desires from some self-centered
activity, a little more of us has defected from the side of darkness
to join the side of light.

The dynamics are simple; but to do this, especially at the deeper
levels of personality, is terribly, terribly hard. For a long time we
cannot even see our choices clearly; we cannot bring our will to
bear. In the latter stages of spiritual development, even the greatest
mystics have cried out from the depths of their heart when they see
how far off the goal is and how frail their strength, how limited their
capacity. As Augustine says, it is like trying to wake up out of the
seductive torpor of a dream—knowing it is time to wake up, longing

to see, but unwilling to open our eyes. If we could watch our dreams, we would see that there is no freedom in the unconscious; our dream actions are all compulsive. And Augustine says, it is the same in waking life: our will is not our own.

> By this time I was certain that it would be better to give myself to Your grace than to yield to my own desires. But though the former appealed to me and convinced me intellectually, the latter still ruled my wishes and bound me. I was still stuck for an answer to Him who said, *Wake up, sleeper, and rise from the dead, and the Christ will give you light.*

In these verses Sri Krishna is answering a practical, penetrating question: when we are immersed in this dream, how is it possible to wake up simply by willing it? We may see our choices clearly enough on the surface, but deep in the unconscious our will is fast asleep, and we want to go on dreaming. Here knowledge is not enough. "We require," says St. John of the Cross, "a more ardent fire and a nobler love"—something that means more to us than the petty, passing satisfactions of the senses; something we desire so deeply that we are willing, in the end, to give up every self-centered attachment to obtain it. This is the supreme purpose of an incarnation of God: to draw us forward with such "burning fervor," as St. John says, that when the time comes to leave some personal desire behind us, we let go so eagerly that we do not even look back.

The French mystic Blaise Pascal brings this out beautifully in a little note he wrote towards the end of his life, after an experience of the unitive state. His language bears the unmistakable stamp of personal experience. For about two hours, it seems, his individual personality has been consumed in the intense fire of union with the Lord. Then the fire subsides; the experience comes to an end. But the proof of its reality is that now he is prepared to pay any price for making that experience permanent.

He puts it very movingly: *"Mon Dieu me quitterez vous?"* My Lord, are you going to leave me? You come and fill my heart with joy and then you abandon me; what kind of cruelty is that? *"Que je n'en sois pas séparé éternellement"*: shall we then be separated forever? I know now what it is like to be united with you, and I cannot bear to be separate again. How can I possess this joy forever? . . . And then he answers himself with words that could have come right out of the Upanishads: *"Renonciation totalle et douce"*; renunciation, complete and sweet. When we finally want to be united with the Lord more than anything else, there is no longer any bitterness in giving up our attachments. It is sweet—not because there is no pain in it, but because it takes us closer to the object of our love. The Sufi epigram is perfect: "When the heart grieves over what it has lost, the spirit rejoices over what it has found."

In the final stages of meditation we need such dedication, such total trust, to let go, that in my own small experience I have no doubt I would have found it impossible without the all-consuming love I developed for Sri Krishna. I was not born with this kind of love. I learned it, through the long, hard process of withdrawing all my personal desires from every selfish channel and redirecting them to flow towards Sri Krishna. In every tradition, we have the testimony of men and women who have learned to do this and crossed the chasm of separateness into the unitive state. And Augustine's words can strengthen all of us when he exhorts himself, "Can you not do what these men and women have done? Or could they have done it by themselves, without the Lord their God? . . . Cast yourself upon him and do not be afraid; he will not draw away and let you fall."

This is not blind faith. It is tested continually as spiritual experience deepens, and those who have made their faith unshakable—great saints like Sri Ramakrishna, Francis of Assisi, Teresa of Ávila—tell us pointedly from their own experience that Jesus the Christ or the Divine Mother is much more real than we are. Physical reality is superficial: it is all a matter of physics and chemistry, a world of constant change. And the mystics say with one voice, "That alone is real which never changes." The body will perish, the universe itself is transient; but the Self in each of us will never pass away.

With infinite tenderness, Sri Krishna is leading us in these verses to the theme of death and immortality. As long as we hold on to the passing pleasures of the physical world, we cannot avoid the suffering that overtakes the body in the course of time. In the first half of life, we have a certain margin for learning this—a certain amount of time to assess the value of physical satisfactions and weigh what they promise against what they actually give. But as we grow older, if we fail to assess wisely, life is not going to ask us if we are ready to give up our attachments. It is going to take them from us, and in that taking is most of the suffering of old age and death.

Here, I think, my Granny was at her best. "Little Lamp," she used to ask, "don't you have a sense of self-respect? Why do you have to be forced to make choices that you can make voluntarily? Don't let life back you into a corner and rob you. Give these things up now, when you are strong; that is the way to be free." On the spiritual path we let go of all our selfish attachments little by little, according to our capacity—not under duress, but of our own free will—until finally we no longer need to hang on to anything else for support. To be forced to surrender is bitter. But to give up something for one we love, though at first it may seem a cup of sorrow, is found at last to be immortal wine.

"Wake up, sleeper, and rise from the dead, and the Christ will give you light." This is the promise of all the great religions: when we unify our consciousness completely, we pass beyond the reach of change and death into eternity. East and West, the language is the same. "Wake up!" says the Compassionate Buddha. "It is time to wake up. You are strong and young in heart; why do you waver?" The alarm is ringing, and no one can sleep forever; it doesn't behoove us to pull the blankets over our heads. And when we're awake, all we can do for a while is rub our eyes. What once seemed day is now the night of ignorance. We have been living in our sleep, and now, as St. Teresa says, we live in "the light that knows no night," in a day that never ends.

मय्येव मन आधत्स्व मयि बुद्धिं निवेशय ।
निवसिष्यसि मय्येव अत ऊर्ध्वं न संशयः ॥८॥

8. Still your mind in Me, still yourself in Me, and without doubt you will be united with Me, Lord of Love, dwelling in your heart.

In my classes in India, I had two brothers who were excellent soccer players. They knew each other so well that they seemed to communicate at another level of consciousness; they played as one man.

Once, after a particularly good game, I suggested, "Look, why don't you use that same concentration in my class? That's all you need to get an A."

They just laughed. "To tell the truth," one replied, "we don't know how we do these things. We don't even think about it. Our feet do everything; we just watch."

Ask any champion athlete. With some self knowledge, he or she will tell you the same thing: "When we're playing, our mind doesn't play a part." If the mind does step in, the consequences can be disastrous. You worry about losing; you remember something your boyfriend said or a remark some newscaster made about your game. Concentration goes, and you begin to make mistakes. I think any good athlete will understand and agree when I say that if you reason while you're playing, you're lost. You can't afford to stand there deciding what to do: "Shall I kick it or head it—or try to dribble? And if I decide to kick, where shall I kick it?" By the time you have made up your mind, you will be in the middle of the next play.

All of us understand this when it comes to physical skills, but when you talk about having a still mind in life, people think you mean becoming a zombie. It is quite the opposite. Just as an athlete comes to life on the playing field when he or she can play without thinking, we come to our full stature as human beings only when the mind becomes still. The reason is simple: the only source of mental agitation is the ego. A still mind means a still ego—and when the ego is still we can see clearly, we are free from compulsions, and there are no barriers to interfere with our personal relationships.

I have said this many times, but here let us look at the dynamics of self-will and love. The more self-will we have, the harder it is to love. So in order to love, we have to reduce self-will—and if we are not reducing self-will, no matter what else we are doing, we are not learning to love. If you look at the rest of the verses in this chapter, you will see that they all have one unifying theme: making the mind steady, especially in relationships, by rising above self-will.

The less self-willed we are, the more detached we become—not from others, but from ourselves. You can see the mechanics of it. Without detachment from yourself, you get easily caught up in your own reactions. Then it is easy to become jealous, or to lose interest in a person, or to become resentful when you don't get your own way. On the other hand, the more detached you are from yourself, the easier it is to remember the needs of others, without which you cannot love.

Most of the time we can think of the mind as a see-saw, constantly going up when things are the way we like and down when they are not. And gradually, as self-will subsides and detachment rises, this see-saw motion becomes less and less erratic. When motion ceases completely, the mind is still. There is no self-will, no separateness, no sense of compulsion. We live in unity always, and the natural expression of unity is love—not just love for one person or another, but love for all people, all life. This is our native state. It is not necessary to acquire anything to become loving: when all self-will is removed from the personality, what is left *is* love.

This is an inspiring picture, but more than that, it can be practiced—by all of us, even those whose minds are far from calm. For one, "Still your mind in Me." In practice, the meaning is simple: if you want to rest your mind in the Lord, the Self, don't try to rest it on the ego. In other words, don't brood on yourself. This kind of brooding can come up in many ways. It may be self-righteous reflection on the past: "Why doesn't so-and-so behave the way I want?" It may be a fear of what somebody will say, or a bewitching memory, or a fantasy of MGM Studios calling on the phone, or a thousand and one other things. The content of these thoughts varies endlessly, but the focus is always the same: *I, I, I.* Whenever you dwell on yourself like this, you are trying to rest your mind on the ego. And the answer is quite straightforward: the minute you catch yourself doing this, start repeating the mantram.

In the beginning, it will take some time to recognize these thoughts for what they are. As detachment increases, however, you discover that there are only a few basic themes, with innumerable variations. One of the most popular themes with everybody is "I

Don't Like It." Whether the "it" is breakfast cereal or the way your friend laughs, the emphasis is always on the "I." So as soon as you catch yourself thinking "I don't like this"—or especially "I don't like you"—don't stop to ask whether the opinion is legitimate or not; just repeat the mantram. Gradually, as you become more vigilant, the mantram will come to your rescue more quickly and more often.

There was a good illustration of this the other day in our back yard. Our nonviolent ways must have given us a reputation in animal circles, because we have attracted a number of gophers who are completely unintimidated by our presence. If they put their heads up and see me standing nearby, they don't hesitate; they come right up and go about eating whatever they like. But when they pop their heads out of the ground and see that our cat Charles is around, Charles has only to give one little smile and the gophers disappear.

That is how the mantram should be. In the early days, a self-centered thought will come up and nibble away at our attention until it is full. Then, after retiring for a nap, it comes back out of its hole again for more nibbling, all in its own sweet time. That is what agitation is: a thought burrowing in and out of consciousness as it likes, eating whatever it wants. But once we remember to bring the mantram on the scene, the thought will disappear. As we become more alert, the gap between the gopher popping up and Charles smiling—between the thought and the mantram—will narrow, until the response is immediate. That is a very promising state, because it means that soon all our negative thoughts will go looking for quieter turf.

Next, "Still yourself in Me." The word used here is *buddhi:* the intellect, discrimination. Not only the mind, but the intellect too has to rest completely in the Lord. Otherwise there is still the possibility of turmoil. This doesn't mean that the intellect should be put to sleep forever. But to function well, it needs to rest securely under the direction of the Self. Its job is to make discriminating judgments: "What are the implications of this particular action? What will follow if I do this or do not do that?" To do this, it needs an overriding goal against which to compare and evaluate. Without a goal, on its own, it is liable to stay in its own little closet splitting hairs while the mind makes all the decisions, mostly on the basis of "I like this" and "I don't like that." So "still your intellect in Me" means to look at life not from the narrow perspective of the ego, but from the perspective of the Ātman. In practical terms, don't judge things only by your own interests; look at the needs of the whole.

People sometimes ask me, "How can we know what the perspective of the Ātman is? Let alone identify with it, we don't even know where to look." It's a fair question: after all, most of us seldom look at life from any perspective other than our own. Here there are a number of questions you can ask. For one, whenever you are about to do something—or are already in the middle of doing something—that you like very much or that is getting your mind all excited, ask yourself, "Whom will this really benefit?" You may get some rather partial testimony from the ego: it's all for the other person's benefit in the long run, simply a coincidence that it's what you really want too, and so on. But that is the purpose of the intellect, to be a good judge—listen very carefully, ask penetrating and embarrassing questions, and finally render a sternly worded judgment: "This doesn't benefit anybody, not even yourself."

This isn't to say that you shouldn't care about your own personal benefit. But don't go *exclusively* after your personal benefit. Keep the needs of the whole in view; then your own needs are included automatically. When you can do this always, continuously, you won't even have to think about personal needs; they are taken for granted in the overall picture.

Second, take a long view of everything. The ego is short-sighted. It can't see past the end of its nose, because it is all caught up in what it can get for itself right now. But the Ātman is detached, which means that it can look far down the chain of cause and effect to see the long-term result of every action—not only the result on the doer, but on others too.

Once we get past our early twenties, for example, I think most of us will have burned our fingers enough to draw the conclusion that if we see a flame, we can be reasonably certain that it will burn. Especially where pleasure is concerned, it can be very helpful to ask simply: "What does this promise and what has it actually delivered, to the best of my knowledge?" You can make a ledger and draw your own balance: "One German chocolate cake. Promise: gourmet ecstasy. Delivered: fifteen minutes of sweetness, stomachache, surrealistic dreams, and two pounds of extra weight." It can help, even with a powerful desire like sex. But it's not enough simply to analyze on the surface. You have to look deep within yourself and take a long view to see the total picture: what it promised and what it actually gave, not simply the next day but two years, ten years later.

Third, remember the injunction of the previous verse: *Matpurāh,* "Make Me your only goal." Everything can be referred to that. "Will this deepen my meditation, improve my concentration, make my mind more even, make me less self-centered?" If it will, I will do it; if it won't, I will not. "Will this divide my attention, isolate me from others, make me more speeded up, activate an old memory or desire?" If it will, I won't do it, no matter how pleasant or how innocent it may seem. Keep the words of the Katha Upanishad always in mind: "What is pleasant is one thing; what is wise is another. The first leads to sorrow, though pleasant at the time. The latter, though at first unpleasant, leads to lasting joy."

Then, more subtly, don't allow yourself to be caught in anything. The moment you get caught in a particular activity, detachment goes. Worse, you are that much more cut off from the whole. One small part of life becomes blown up out of proportion, and all the rest shrinks into the background without your even realizing it. It is not possible to see this clearly without an overriding goal, but when you have such a goal, you can measure all your priorities against it.

Look, for example, at the question of physical fitness. Currently everyone seems to be running—not just jogging, but running for several miles every day. Not long ago there was a cross-city competition announced in San Francisco, a distance of some seven and a half miles, and almost fourteen thousand people showed up to take part. Now, I am all for physical fitness; who isn't? It is important for everyone, and it is especially important for those who are meditating seriously. But after all is said and done, running can be only a part of the spiritual life. If this is forgotten, there is the danger of filling your life with running—at the expense of meditation.

Let me make myself clear: I am all for running. But I would apply the same criterion to it as to every other human endeavor: "How much does this help me to realize the goal of life?" That is the measure of its value and the index of its priority.

"Still yourself in Me." Next to the entrance to a bridge in San Francisco there used to be a sign with a short message from an Indian mystic of this century, Meher Baba: "Do your best. Don't worry. Be happy." I suppose many of the businessmen crossing that bridge at rush hour thought Meher Baba was playing Pollyanna. He was not; he was being supremely practical. Worry is usually no more than self-will in one of its more subtle disguises: everything is either "Am I up to this?" or "Is so-and-so going to manage to do this the way I want?" When you really *are* doing your best—in your meditation, in the other spiritual disciplines, at work, at home— there is no attention left over for worrying. Then you are beginning to rest yourself in the Lord, the Ātman, at the very core of your being.

All this can be effectively practiced in personal relationships, which is the central theme of this chapter. Wherever there is agitation in a relationship—vacillation, estrangement, doubt, reservation—the capacity to love is divided; love is not yet complete. "How much did you do for me today? How much did you put into the emotional till? Six cents? I'm going to count. If it is six cents, I'll give you six cents back. But if it's five, I'm not going to give you more than five." This is what we are accustomed to call love, even in some of the great romantic affairs of literature and history. But the mystics say, "That's not love; that's a commercial contract." It divides two people, and it divides consciousness. If you want to love, all these reservations have to go.

When your mind is still always—twenty-four hours a day, seven days a week, not only in waking life, but even in your dreams—then, says Sri Krishna, "You will live in Me continuously, absorbed in Me, beyond any shadow of a doubt." It is a state that is almost impossible to describe in words, but there are certain signs. For one, your awareness of the Lord will be unbroken. In a sense you will be meditating wherever you go, even if you are at your office or caught in the downtown shopping. Brother Lawrence's words are perfect:

> The time of business does not with me differ from the time of prayer, and in the noise and clatter of my kitchen, while several persons are at the same time calling for different things, I possess God in as great tranquility as if I were upon my knees at the blessed sacrament.

To put it another way, the well of your love will be always full and always flowing. It will be natural for you to love; it will be impossible for you *not* to love. You won't have to stop to think about how to respond to others. You will respond naturally, spontaneously, however is most appropriate for that person's long-term welfare. And in your personal relationships there will be no conflict, no doubts, no reservations, no irritation. You will not need to prompt or force your love, and you will need no reason for loving or trusting or forgiving. As St. Bernard says, love is its own reason: "Love seeks no cause beyond itself and no fruit; it is its own fruit, its own enjoyment. I love because I love; I love in order that I may love."

अथ चित्तं समाधातुं न शक्नोषि मयि स्थिरम् ।
अभ्यासयोगेन ततो मामिच्छाप्तुं धनंजय ॥९॥

9. If you cannot still your mind in Me, learn to do so through the regular practice of meditation.

Here I imagine Arjuna, so much like us, complaining, "I'd like to still my mind, but it just keeps jumping around. Don't you know some shortcut?"

Sri Krishna says, "Of course. I'll give you a way that has worked for spiritual aspirants all over the world."

Arjuna, expecting some great secret, leans forward eagerly. And Sri Krishna whispers in his ear: *"Try*—and keep on trying until you succeed."

It sounds hard—it *is* hard—but there is no other way. Nothing about meditation is easy; nothing takes place overnight. Even a giant like the Buddha is said to have taken seven years to attain nirvāna—and if someone of his stature requires seven years, I think it is only reasonable for people like you and me to be patient with ourselves and admit that even a lifetime would not be too long for this stupendous achievement.

Recently I read an advertisement for an "enlightenment workshop" that promised illumination in a weekend. Being taken in by claims like these is like thinking you can put on a pair of toe shoes and make a guest appearance with the Bolshoi Ballet without any practice or preparation. I saw some sequences from Bolshoi performances in a film the other day, with shots of great dancers like Rudolf Nureyev and Margot Fonteyn. When Nureyev took one of his famous leaps, he seemed to be suspended in midair. It looked so effortless that I could almost imagine myself out there on the stage, making wonderful leaps and breathtaking glissades. But the shots of the training that young dancers receive at the Bolshoi School brought me back to earth. What torture! Standing at the practice bar all day long, kicking your legs up while the ballet master stands there like a galley slave driver counting "One, two, three! One, two, three!" It wasn't anybody's idea of effortless grace; it was just hard work.

That training, I understand, goes on for ten years or more. Often it starts at a very tender age. And once you make your professional debut, the work only becomes more arduous. Nureyev doesn't say, "I don't feel like it today." Whether he feels like it or not, he goes to the bar and practices—four, five, six hours every day. As I watched, I understood: this is the secret of excellence in anything. Spontaneity, effortless grace, comes only after years of practice. Dancers like Nureyev and Fonteyn *are* gifted, but the gift is not gracefulness; it is dedication.

Now, meditation is training the mind, which in many ways is like training the body. When you start jogging or doing sit-ups, at first you hear nothing from the muscles but complaints. It isn't because they are being overused, but because they have never been used.

Similarly, when you try to concentrate in meditation, there are going to be taut tendons in your mind. If you are impatient and start trying to be patient, your mind is going to ache all over; by the end of the day it will be begging you to stop. But I have never seen anybody who sincerely wanted better health say, "My tendons ache today, so I'm not going to run. I'm going to stay here in bed and give them a rest." Everybody knows that you just keep on running; soon the muscles become stronger and stop complaining. That is how it is with meditation. You keep working at it every day with the same enthusiasm and determination I saw in the faces of those students at the Bolshoi. There is no easy way.

Now, I have to confess that I have developed a rather personal interpretation of these verses. If you look at the text of this verse and the two that follow, it is quite explicit: "If you cannot still your mind, learn to meditate; if you can't meditate, serve Me in those around you," and so on. But when it comes to something as important as Self-realization, I am the kind of person who won't leave any stone unturned. Even if it is only a little pebble, I have to turn it over. If I am going to devote so many years of my life to extinguishing the ego, I want to make sure it is extinguished once and for all. So even if Sri Krishna himself assures me that meditation, for example, is enough by itself, I will still say, "Excuse me, Lord. It may be enough for the Compassionate Buddha, but a little person like me can't afford to take chances. I'm going to do everything I possibly can: meditate *and* put others first *and* learn to be detached from the results of action, all together." It is a very practical attitude, which I must have absorbed from my Grandmother's example: there is always something more that you can do.

Let me illustrate from my own life how I began to apply this. When I started meditating, just like every beginning meditator, by the end of an arduous day I would have used up most of the power that had been released in my morning meditation. But for some time, it never occurred to me that I could meditate again in the evening. I had a very full work load, and often, even when the day was over, I would go back to campus again after dinner to attend faculty meetings or other college functions and try to make a contribution there. So naturally, when I did have a little time to myself in the evening, I liked to relax: read some of my favorite authors, listen to classical music or the All India news, attend a play or lecture.

Then I began to realize that there was more I could do about my meditation, and immediately my priorities underwent a change. To begin with, I told All India Radio it would have to miss me, and I began to meditate regularly every evening too. I didn't understand it at first, but I was beginning to make my day whole, which meant that I was making my consciousness whole as well. Now instead of a sometimes slender thread connecting one morning's meditation with the next, there was a thread connecting morning and evening—and then a new thread connecting evening with the following morning. I could see the benefit almost immediately—not only in my morning meditation, but in the quality of my life during the day. And to strengthen that new thread, instead of falling asleep in a Dickens novel or in classical Indian music, I started to read the great classics of world mysticism, beginning with the *Gospel of Sri Ramakrishna*. It wasn't always easy, because I enjoyed literature and music very much. But soon I discovered that though my liking for these was still present, I got much more from the words of a great saint like Ramakrishna—simple, powerful, profound words, which went straight to my heart. It wasn't long before I was looking forward to my reading and my meditation every evening. After that, even if a favorite play came to campus, unless there was a matinee I would just tell my friends, "I'm sorry, I have some other engagement."

That gave me the key: put meditation first. Make it the first priority; everything else can be second. Nothing important will ever suffer by this. And once I realized that, I began putting it into practice everywhere. I even used to meditate at noon when I could—right in the faculty room, seated quietly in a chair with my eyes closed, so that people must have thought I had been up all night reading Shakespeare and now was catching forty winks. I wasn't; I was practicing the refrain of the Bhagavad Gita: *Matparāh,* "Make Me your only goal." In ways like this I discovered that everybody has time for meditation, and every day is full of odds and ends of time that can be used for spiritual growth.

The key word in this verse is *abhyāsa*, 'practice': trying to keep the mind focused on a single point by bringing it back gently but firmly whenever it strays. I have translated *abhyāsa* here as "the practice of meditation." But after some experience, I began to see that *abhyāsa* is essentially a matter of training attention. It throws light on every minute of daily living, because it means we don't need to confine our practice to a half hour or so in the morning and evening. We can train our attention wherever we are, whatever we are doing. The dynamics are twofold: we unify consciousness by making the mind one-pointed, and by keeping it focused on what we choose, we keep it from dwelling on itself.

In practical terms, this means gaining control over the thinking process itself. When we can finally put our attention wherever we choose, we can think whatever we choose. The implications are tremendous: we can *become* whatever we choose. As Ruysbroeck put it, we can be as holy as we want to be—or as secure, or as loving.

Eventually—this is the ideal to be aimed at—the mind should not wander at all. Only then can it become still. When the mind wanders, consciousness is divided; attention is weaving all over the road. Everybody knows what it is like to share the highway with a bad driver. He is driving along in the lane next to you and suddenly, without warning, he wanders into your lane. Perhaps his eye has been caught by a sign, perhaps he has remembered an errand; his mind may even be in a different county. Then, with equal abruptness, he realizes what he has done and overreacts—first with the brake, then with the accelerator—and darts back into his own lane.

If we could only see it, everything in life suffers like this when attention wanders. A mind that darts from subject to subject is out of control, and the person who responds to it weaves through life oblivious to others, running into difficult situations and colliding with other people. But the mind that is steady stays in its own lane. It cannot be swept away by an impulsive desire or fear, and because it stays completely in the present, it cannot be haunted by an unpleasant memory or by anxiety about the future. Most of our problems in life are caused by the mind weaving out of the here-and-now into a Never-Never Land of what was, or might be, or might have been, and that is why I have come to the conclusion that there is no skill more worth learning that the art of directing attention as we choose.

In principle, the practice of this is simple: when the mind wanders, bring it back to what it should be doing. The problem arises when the distraction is not stray but compulsive: resentment, irritation, apprehension, craving. The power of such thoughts is that they are egocentric. There is nothing the ego likes to do more than to think about itself, and when a self-centered thought comes up, everything in our conditioning screams, "Hey, look at that! Pay attention to that!"

Here again, our greatest ally is the mantram. Whenever a selfish thought comes up, repeat the mantram. When the mantram takes hold, the connection between the thought and your attention is broken. A compulsive thought, whether it is anger or depression or a powerful sense-craving, does not really have any power of its own. Thoughts, in this sense, are very much the same; none of them has any more muscle than the others. All the power is in the attention we give—and when we can withdraw our attention, the thought or desire will be helpless to compel us into action.

Now, attention is very much like a searchlight, which is mounted in such a way that it can be trained on any subject freely. When we are caught up in ourselves—in other words, when attention becomes compulsive—this searchlight has become stuck. After many years of this, it is hard to believe that the light *can* turn: we think, in other words, that that compulsion has become a permanent part of our personality. But gradually, all of us can learn to work our attention loose. Once we do this, we can redirect our attention freely.

This can be practiced. For one, try to work cheerfully at jobs you dislike. It has nothing to do with the job; you are freeing your attention. Second, whatever you do, give it your best concentration—and, when necessary, learn to drop what you are doing and shift your attention immediately to something else. When you leave your office, for example, leave your work there too. Don't bring it home in a briefcase or, just as bad, in your mind. And finally, the moment you take up something that does not require attention—doing the dishes, for example—start repeating the mantram. All this is the spiritual equivalent of those kicking exercises in the Bolshoi School. By practicing these things, anybody can learn to direct attention freely. And when you can do this, you will never again direct it at yourself: not only because it brings such suffering, but because the ego, by its very nature, is such a crashing bore.

I like to illustrate all this by comparing the mind to a theater. Thoughts are the actors, and getting into the unconscious, if you like, is like going backstage into the green room, where everybody is getting made up. Anger is there putting on his long fangs, fear is rattling his chains, jealousy is admiring herself in the mirror and smearing on green mascara. And attention is the audience.

Now, these actors are like actors everywhere: they thrive on a responsive audience. When jealousy comes out on stage and we sit forward on our seats, all eyes, she really puts on a show—if you want to see how much of a show, look at what happens in *Othello*. But on the other hand, what happens if nobody comes to see the performance? No actor likes to play to an empty house. If they're real professionals they might give their best for a couple of nights, but after that they're bound to get a little slack. Jealousy doesn't bother with her makeup any more; who's going to admire it? Anger throws away his fangs, fear puts away his chains; whom can they impress? And finally, the whole cast gives it up as a bad job and goes out for a midnight cup of hot chocolate.

In other words, when you can direct attention, problems will never be compulsive again. I wish I could convey what freedom this brings. No matter how severe the problem, how painful the experience, how powerful the craving, you will be able to go to your meditation room and get up again after an hour or so with all sense of oppression gone and your mind refreshed. That is the beginning of freedom in life. There may still be shackles on your hands, but now you know from your own experience that though it may take a long time and a lot of effort, every one of them can be removed through the practice of meditation and the allied disciplines.

अभ्यासेऽप्यसमर्थोऽसि मत्कर्मपरमो भव ।
मदर्थमपि कर्माणि कुर्वन्सिद्धिमवाप्स्यसि ॥१०॥

10. If you lack the will for such self-discipline,
engage yourself in selfless service of all around you,
for selfless service can lead you at last to Me.

Here again, my application of this verse is personal but practical. Even in the early days, I have to confess, my capacity for concentrating in meditation was rather good. If I had taken this verse literally, I could easily have concluded that these words were not addressed to me. Instead, I tried to practice this verse too. It helped my meditation greatly, and that is why today I never talk only about meditation; I always say "meditation *and* the allied disciplines." Meditation is essential, but for the vast majority of us today, meditation by itself is not enough. The task of training the mind is so difficult that we need the support of a comprehensive program of spiritual disciplines which work together to strengthen each other.

Again, let me illustrate this from my own experience. When I began meditating morning and night, I could have been excused if I had decided not to try to squeeze any more into my day. But as I said, I don't like to leave any stone unturned. So when I saw an occasion when I could be of help to someone around me—by taking time to be with a student, for example, when he was in the hospital—I took a close look at my schedule and told myself, "Well, you don't have to go to that movie on Saturday. You don't have to attend this concert on Friday night." I don't say that there wasn't a pang or two, especially when I had to miss an event I had been looking forward to. But the rewards more than made up for any momentary sense of loss. For one, my meditation deepened. Often I would notice the difference the very next morning. But more than that, there was a fierce joy in turning my back on myself to help people. I know that in a sense I was not doing it for them personally; I was doing it for the Lord in them.

Gradually, I began to understand that "serve Me in all around you" didn't mean merely reading to the sick or feeding the poor. It meant, in the simple words my Grandmother used, putting other people first. Once my eyes were opened, I didn't need special occasions to practice this. There were opportunities every day—on a busy day, many times every hour. And the dynamics of it is this: whenever you are mindful of somebody else's needs, you forget yourself. Forget yourself completely, and you are united with the Lord.

The more I read in world mysticism, the more I appreciate the penetrating practicality of this approach. When all is said and done, I doubt very much if any of us in the modern world is able to extinguish the fierce fire of self-will without the benefit of personal relationships. In many traditions, the approach is what has been called the Via Negativa: you try to destroy the ego by a direct assault. It has worked for many great mystics, but for most of us, there is no motivation that we can grasp—and where there *is* motivation, the mechanisms are absent, for it is almost impossible to forget yourself when you are living in a world of one. But in a close relationship between man and woman, parent and child, or friend and friend, it is natural to want to put the other person first at least part of the time. I don't say it is easy. But it *is* natural and fulfilling, because the desire for unity is already there. You have something in common with the other person, so you can identify with him and find joy in contributing to his welfare. This is the Via Affirmativa, the positive way, to emphasize not what is lost but what is gained.

There are some important things to remember when trying to put this into practice. To begin with, putting other people first does not mean saying yes to everything they say and do. I repeat this often, because it has a vital place in love. In fact, saying yes to everything can be the opposite of love, because it is not always in the other person's real interests. To love, we have to learn the art of saying no tenderly but resolutely when those we love are about to do something that can only bring them sorrow.

Most of us fall short of this, even in our most intimate relationships. Often instead of saying no we remark casually, "When you have time, will you turn this suggestion over in your mind?" Or we write a little note: "This passage from Corinthians may be of interest to you." This is called dropping a tactful hint, but unfortunately nobody notices these hints and nobody picks them up.

To me vague remarks like this show lack of love, because they are made out of fear of how the other person might respond. If someone we love is about to do something harmful to himself or others, we should have the security to say, "Even if you don't speak to me for a month I'm going to stand in your way, lovingly but firmly, until you change your mind." At the time it may be a source of irritation. But after that person has a chance to cool off, he will know he has a friend who really cares about his lasting welfare.

This doesn't apply only to relationships between man and woman. It can be practiced everywhere: between friends, between parents and children, even between doctors and their patients. I learned this in my early days as a college teacher. Boys and girls used to come to our town fresh with the simplicity of Indian village ways, and sometimes, after a little exposure, they would get caught in activities that could only bring them sorrow in the long run. Some of my colleagues insisted that it was not my responsibility to intrude into my students' lives. "You're not their father," they said. "You're here to teach them Shakespeare and syntax." For a while I accepted this as the voice of experience. But I had a deep love for those students, and in turn they came to love me and trust me. It hurt me to see them hurt, and quite naturally, without doubt or vacillation, when I saw that they were about to get into trouble I would take them out for a walk, talk to them, and help them to see more clearly the consequences of what they were about to do. It wasn't always easy for them to accept this kind of loving criticism, but I don't think any of my relationships suffered. On the contrary, my students and their families came to appreciate me for it. "He's not just trying to please us," they would say. "He really cares what happens."

People sometimes ask me, "How can we tell how to put somebody else first?" I don't think there is any special secret to this. The same answer is given in all the world's great religions, but I especially like the phrasing of the Compassionate Buddha: "Remember—what hurts you, hurts others too. What irritates you, irritates others too." To take just a few examples, people may differ in their preferences for salad dressing, but nobody likes a joke at his expense. No one likes to be talked about behind her back. No one likes to be ignored when he says hello, or to be talked down to, or to be interrupted in what she is saying or doing. Everybody is hurt by rudeness, irritated by an angry word, agitated by being rushed or pressured. One Western mystic sums it up in a simple phrase: "Be kind, be kind, be kind." That is the sum and substance of putting others first.

What keeps us from doing this? In one word: *samskāras*. Put simply, a samskāra is a compulsion, a rigid, automatic response to life which we think of as a permanent part of someone's character. But the samskāra itself is not rigid; it is a process. A samskāra is nothing more than a thought repeated over and over a thousand times, leading to words repeated a thousand times, resulting in action repeated a thousand times. A person with an anger samskāra, for example, is prone to anger over anything. His behavior has very little to do with external events; by conditioning, anger has simply become the way his mind responds to life. By thinking angry thoughts, saying unkind things, and finally indulging in hostile behavior, he has made himself an angry person. A kind of neurological shortcut has been dug in his mind, down which consciousness flows automatically to the same conditioned response.

What we call personality is nothing more than a collection of samskāras. In other words, we are what our samskāras are. It is a revealing but hopeful analysis. On the one hand, it means that there is very little freedom in what we do or even when we think. But on the other hand, it means that personality is not really rigid; it too is a process. Though we think of ourselves as always the same, we are remaking ourselves every moment by what we think, just as every tissue in the body is in a constant state of repair and change.

Usually, because of our samskāras, we go on repairing the same old shaky structure. But actually, every thought is an opportunity for choice. Just as a samskāra is built up through repeated thought and word and action, it can be unbuilt through repeated thought and word and action of the opposite kind.

Now see what this means in practice. If someone provokes you and you respond with anger, you are actually making your anger samskāra stronger. Even if you avoid that person afterwards, you are making the samskāra stronger. It will be that much more disruptive in all your relationships in the future, and that much more difficult to overcome. But look at the mystic's attitude: when you feel angry towards someone, that is all the more reason to be kind. It's not simply being kind to that particular person. You're being even kinder to yourself, because you are undoing a compulsion, taking one more step towards being free.

There is a particularly vivid way to illustrate this. Until we are free from our compulsions, we are like hand puppets; the samskāras are the puppeteers. We may think we choose to get angry—I have actually had somebody tell me this. But more accurately, the anger samskāra is doing everything: putting its fingers up into our arms and head—say, where the amygdala is—and making us throw crockery about, slam the door, and use words that are anything but kind. It is an apt illustration, because it is the nervous system itself that has been conditioned. But it can be deconditioned, and when it is, we are free.

The deconditioning process is straightforward enough: when a samskāra comes up, don't act on it. When it tries to tell you what to do, say no. Repeat the mantram, go out for a long, brisk walk if possible, and throw yourself into hard, concentrated work, preferably for the benefit of someone other than yourself. When you can shift your attention to your work or to the mantram, you have shifted it away from the samskāra. Immediately the samskāra is weakened a little, and the will to resist is strengthened.

Conversely—this can provide motivation—if you do act on the samskāra it is strengthened, and you have struck a blow at your own will. To put it another way, you can't choose not to fight. When you act on a samskāra, you *have* joined the battle. The trouble is, you have joined the wrong side.

If you really want to land a blow at a samskāra, go against it. Do just the opposite of what it says. It is a daring approach which appeals to me very much. If somebody has been unkind to you, go out of your way to be kind to him. It can require a lot of endurance simply to be patient with such a person, but I'm talking about more than endurance now; I'm talking about daring. Try it: there is an exhilaration in it, and a special delight in seeing the other person rub his eyes in disbelief. "I was just rude to that chap, and now he's being thoughtful. Is he out of his mind?" Few people can go so far, but there is the same keynote in those marvelous words of Jesus: "If someone takes your coat, give him your cloak as well; if he makes you go a mile with him, go with him two."

Samskāras go deep into consciousness, and the will and intellect usually operate only on the surface. We may say in all sincerity, "I'll never get angry again!" But the samskāra asks smugly, "Says who?" We don't even see these forces lurking in the unconscious, and if we do get a glimpse of them, we don't recognize them for what they are. It is only below the surface of consciousness in meditation that we begin to encounter samskāras without their makeup on. For a long time, vision is blurred in those depths. But when you get close to a samskāra in meditation, there are certain external signs.

For one, there is a period of expectancy. You are about to get into trouble, about to repeat some conditioned pattern of behavior which you will later regret, and your subconscious is on the lookout for an opportunity. Second, concentration will be more difficult. Your attention will be scattered; it will be hard to keep your mind on a job, and you will find all sorts of excuses for putting off jobs that you don't want to do. And in meditation, it will be especially difficult to keep your mind on the passage. Attention will wander, and if you are not vigilant you may follow a distraction for a long time or even fall asleep.

Like road signs, all these signs have an explicit meaning: "Go Slow. Drive Carefully. Samskāras At Work." That is the time to be especially vigilant about all your spiritual disciplines. Be regular in meditation, use the mantram as much as possible, and work hard during the day, giving everything your one-pointed attention and enthusiasm. Be careful not to get speeded up or to allow your senses too much license. And especially, don't get caught in brooding on yourself. When you do that, you are inviting the samskāra to come in and stay as long as it likes.

Undoing a samskāra is the most challenging battle a human being can face. If you have been impatient for many years, for example, learning patience can be excruciating. At the end of the day, if you've really been trying hard, every cell in your nervous system will be crying out for rest. Samskāras can erupt anywhere, everywhere, and they don't pay attention to the rules of Queensberry. They'll hit you from behind, below the belt, in your sleep; they'll gang up on you; it's all open street fighting. The fight can be terribly dispiriting, especially when you get below the surface level and see how powerful these forces really are. But there is a positive side too: this is the opportunity you have been waiting for. Every time you come face to face with a samskāra, it is an opportunity to change yourself. The reversal in outlook is revolutionary. When you're tired, when people are provoking you, when your patience has worn thin and your morale is turning blue at the edges, you can rub your hands together with anticipation: you're in the ring at last, and the bell is about to go off. Previously you might have said, "I don't want to go home now. The minute I walk through the door, I know I'm going to blow up." Instead of going home, you'd be off to Sonoma Joe's for a few rounds of bitter ale. But now you say, "Sure—one partner, two children; three people to irritate me. That's just the odds: three chances to learn to be more patient. Even if I miss one, I'm sure to have another."

The samskāra may knock you around a few times, but as long as you keep on fighting like this, you're training. Your muscles are getting stronger, and the samskāra, though it may not look any weaker at first, is taking the beating of its life. You are beginning to change your personality, and though the bigger samskāras are going to be in the ring for a good, long time, every round of the fight is bringing you closer to your goal.

अथैतदप्यशक्तोऽसि कर्तुं मद्योगमाश्रितः ।
सर्वकर्मफलत्यागं ततः कुरु यतात्मवान् ॥११॥

*11. If you are unable to do even this, surrender
yourself to Me in love, receiving success and failure
with equal calmness as granted by Me.*

This verse, which sounds so simple, is probably one of the hardest
verses in the Gita to put into practice. If it seems easy to follow, it
is because the idea of surrender has been so often misinterpreted.
Surrender has nothing to do with doing nothing—and as for "just
letting things flow," that is a state that is achieved only after years
of almost superhuman effort. The Gita is essentially a call to action.
But it is a call to *selfless* action, that is, action without any selfish attachment to the results. In other words, it is not action or effort that
we must surrender; it is self-will—and this is something that is terribly difficult to do. You must do your best constantly, yet never
allow yourself to become involved in whether things work out the
way you want.

It takes many years of practice to learn this skill, but once you
have it, as Gandhi says, you will never lose your nerve. All sense of
inadequacy goes—in fact, the question of "Am I equal to this job?"
cannot even arise. It is enough that the job needs to be done, and
that you are doing your absolute best to do it. Then, no matter how
stiff the challenges or how bleak the prospects, you can throw yourself into selfless action without conflict or diffidence or fatigue.

This is an elusive concept, and sometimes people ask me incredu-
lously, "You mean you're not interested in the results of what you
do?" Of course I am interested. I doubt that there is anybody more
interested in his work than I am, because I know how much people
can benefit from what we are doing at the Blue Mountain Center of
Meditation. But after many years of practice, I have learned to do
my best and then not worry about whether things will work out my
way.

Worrying about results not only makes us less effective, it is futile. By our very nature we see only a small part of the total picture,

and we make our plans on an appropriately narrow and egocentric scale. The result is usually about D minus, barely passing—unless, of course, somebody else is trying to get things *his* way too, in which case everybody runs the risk of getting an F. But when we learn simply to do our best and leave the question of success or failure to the Lord, the result can really be spectacular. Where we had something barely passing in mind, the Lord turns up with results that rate an A.

One of the most moving episodes in the *Rāmāyana* illustrates this vividly. In just twenty-four hours, young Prince Rāma's life is turned upside down. He goes to sleep expecting on the following day to be crowned heir to his father's kingdom; the whole city is celebrating. But he wakes up to find that his stepmother has turned against him, and instead of receiving his birthright, he is sent into exile in a forest for fourteen years. Rāma's brother Lakshmana wants to take matters into his own hands. But Rāma pacifies him with a very simple question. "Lakshmana," he asks, "haven't you ever planned something down to the last detail—done everything you could to make sure nothing goes wrong—and then had the whole affair turn out completely differently? Doesn't that show you that there is a power in the universe that encompasses us all, that it is not possible to ordain our lives the way we will?"

If we could but stand back from our lives and take a much longer view, even the smallest events would be seen to fit into a vast picture in which, as Jesus says, every hair of our heads is numbered. There is no contradiction between this idea and free will. The power Rāma speaks of is the law of karma: we are shaping our lives continuously by what we think and say and do. To Lakshmana, Rāma's banishment seems nothing less than a disaster. But it is all part of a much larger drama. Many years earlier, by accident, Rāma's father killed the son of an old sage. When Rāma is banished, King Dashāratha loses *his* son: and that same exile, which seems so cruel, is actually the door through which Rāma enters into his own glorious destiny. Shakespeare's words go deeper than he may have known: "There's a divinity that shapes our ends, rough-hew them how we will."

If I may say so, the Lord is a very thorough teacher. When necessary, he will see to it that those who love him are tested from every quarter—as my Granny would say, not any more severely than they can bear, but never any less severely either. For most of us, there is no other way to learn to remove the last vestige of selfish attachment from our work. When you are taking refuge under one corner and it caves in, you can always hide under another. If all four corners fall in, you can at least stand in the center. But when you are standing in the center, about to breathe a sigh of relief, and the roof falls in, you have nowhere left to look for help but inwards. And the amazing thing is that when you trust in this completely—*and* do your best—help always comes. It may not be in the way you expect it, it will not be at the time you expect it, but it *will* come; of that there is no doubt.

In a small way, this is the history of our own meditation center too. There were times in the early days when we faced nothing but obstacles—not only relevant obstacles, the kind one expects at the outset of spiritual work, but sometimes unnecessary, even silly difficulties too, which I think the Lord must have placed before us only out of a Puckish sense of humor. At such times, I kept on reminding myself that it was not *my* work. From the assurances in the Gita, I knew that all I had to do was empty myself of all self-will and put myself in the hands of the Lord—how he used my life after that was not for me to worry over. And today, after many years of practicing this, I do not get upset over anything where the work of our Center is concerned. I have no doubt now that work that is free from all self-seeking *has* to prosper in the long run—though it calls for resourcefulness, discrimination, and a lot of dedicated effort.

This is not blind faith; it is acquired after many years of trial. When I first took to meditation, though I had the example of my Granny to guide me, I had no experience of these truths myself. As my meditation deepened, I had to face some difficult decisions about the conduct of my life. At such times, I usually made the best choice I knew how, even when it was not particularly pleasant—and, like most ordinary people, I sometimes made wrong decisions that carried painful consequences. But after a while I began to notice that even when the decision was not the wisest, if I had really done my best in deciding, the painful consequences would not be too painful. Either I would surmount the difficulty through some turn of events, or the difficulty would prove to be an opportunity. It was not at all clear at the time, but now I can look back and see that all these difficulties were training me to do my best and leave the rest to the Lord. When you do this, you can be sure that things will work out for the best of all concerned. "After all," Sri Krishna asks simply, "don't you trust me? I who am responsible for the rhythms of the galaxies, if you are really trying to serve me, don't you think I can be trusted to give you all that you need for spiritual growth?"

श्रेयो हि ज्ञानमभ्यासाज्ज्ञानाद्ध्यानं विशिष्यते ।
ध्यानात्कर्मफलत्यागस्त्यागाच्छान्तिरनन्तरम् ॥१२॥

12. Better indeed is knowledge than mechanical practice. Better than knowledge is meditation. But better still is surrender in love, because there follows immediate peace.

This beautiful verse wraps up the four which precede it. On the intellectual level, it may seem obscure. But after some years of practicing these disciplines, the meaning becomes clear if we remember that here, words like "knowledge" and "surrender" are not watertight categories. After all, where there is knowledge of the unity of life, there *is* love. Where there is love, there is a direct apprehension of unity. And unless the mind is stilled through meditation, it is not accurate to talk about either transcendental knowledge or love. All these are categories of the intellect, which cannot help dividing. But in practice they flow together, which is why I have no hesitation about recommending the approach I have found effective in my own life: to practice all of them together.

"Better indeed is knowledge than mechanical practice." This is not to deprecate mechanical practice: after all, at the beginning, the practice of any spiritual discipline is bound to be mechanical. If somebody comes to me and asks, "You want me to repeat the mantram *mechanically*?" I say simply, "Of course." How else can we

repeat it at the start? To be able to repeat the mantram with devotion, self-will has to be very small. But—and this is the very heart of
this chapter of the Gita—devotion can grow. We begin repeating
the mantram with as much enthusiasm as we can, whenever we can,
and after a lot of practice, it slowly begins to penetrate to a deeper
level of consciousness.

Similarly with meditation. At the beginning, though it should
never be mechanical, meditation is only on the surface. It takes a
lot of regular, enthusiastic work to break through the surface and
open up a channel into our deeper consciousness.

Gradually, however, as we practice these disciplines, insight
grows. We begin to see that living for ourselves has certain inescapable consequences for which we hadn't bargained: alienation, loneliness, deteriorating relationships, a sense of desolation. The more
we grab for our own happiness, the faster it recedes. And conversely, we discover that when we go after the happiness of others,
relationships improve, depression disappears, and it is easier to face
the challenges of life with resourcefulness and peace of mind. This
is the advent of jnāna. We are beginning to see beneath the surface
of life, through the bewitching illusion of separateness called Māyā,
and everything benefits from it: meditation, relationships, security,
love.

But understanding life is not enough. These insights need to be
practiced. And for translating insight into daily living, we need
meditation—not meditation on the surface now, but one-pointed
concentration that drives spiritual ideals deep into consciousness
and releases the power to act selflessly during the day.

As we practice this, the barrier of the ego is lowered and love
grows. We ask less and less "What can I get?" and more and more
"What can I give?" At last, after many years, if our practice of these
disciplines has been sincere and systematic, we may reach a stage
when we can truly say "I love." All barriers are gone; every trace
of self-seeking has been removed. We no longer want anything only
for ourselves; we live in all. Then, and only then, the heart is flooded
with utter peace—the "peace that passeth understanding." The ego
has been stilled forever, so there can be no more turmoil in the

mind, no more vacillation, no more depression. It is not a temporary experience; every corner of the personality is bathed in peace that cannot be taken away. Jesus says, "Peace I leave with you; my peace I give unto you: not as the world giveth, give I unto you." And St. Catherine of Genoa explains out of the fullness of her own experience:

> . . . when the soul is naughted and transformed, then of herself she neither works nor speaks nor wills, nor feels nor hears nor understands; neither has she of herself the feeling of outward or inward, where she may move. And in all things it is God who rules and guides her, without the mediation of any creature. And the state of this soul is then a feeling of such utter peace and tranquility that it seems to her that her heart, and her bodily being, and all both within and without, is immersed in an ocean of utmost peace. . . . And she is so full of peace that though she press her flesh, her nerves, her bones, no other thing comes forth from them than peace.

अद्वेष्टा सर्वभूतानां मैत्रः करुण एव च ।
निर्ममो निरहंकारः समदुःखसुखः क्षमी ॥१३॥
संतुष्टः सततं योगी यतात्मा दृढनिश्चयः ।
मय्यर्पितमनोबुद्धिर्यो मद्भक्तः स मे प्रियः ॥१४॥

13–14. That one I love who is incapable of ill will and returns love for hatred. Living beyond the reach of 'I and mine,' and of pleasure and pain, full of mercy, contented, self-controlled, firm in faith, with all his heart and all his mind given to Me—with such a one I am in love.

Now we are entering one of the most beautiful, precise, and practical descriptions of the man or woman of God that I have seen. The purpose of such descriptions is not merely to inspire us, but to show us our real evolutionary potential: what kind of person you and I can actually become, in a marvelous transformation, through the practice of meditation and the allied disciplines.

In a sense, the words of an inspirational passage like this are not just words. They are more like depth charges, which are set to go off when they reach a certain level of consciousness. In meditation, by the concentration we give, we drive each word deep into consciousness so that it can release its potential. But when these words explode, instead of causing damage, they heal. Internal conflicts are resolved, doubts and reservations fall away, and we get the certitude that we are equal to challenges from which we used to run away.

This does not happen overnight, and like most people who are meditating sincerely, I used to wonder at times if this explosion was ever going to take place in my own consciousness. After all, I reasoned, the words of the Gita are thousands of years old; even the best of ammunition can fizzle after the passage of time. But I went on giving my best every day, and eventually I reached a stage in meditation where I could almost feel these words trembling deep in my consciousness, ready to go off. I didn't know what was happening, but for a long time there was a strange air of expectancy. Then, one by one, each word released its potential, and I realized that the passage had become an integral part of my consciousness.

When translated literally, many of the words in these two verses sound negative: "without ill will for any creature, without any sense of *I* or *mine*." But in this case, what is a negative construction in grammar has a wholly positive meaning in life. By *not* acting selfishly, speaking harshly, thinking negatively, we finally arrive at our native state, which is love itself.

In other words, this transformation does not take place by meditation alone. Meditation gives the power, but we then have to draw on this power to check every self-willed impulse during the day. Unless there are changes in our day-to-day behavior, even if they are modest and slow, we cannot talk about the transformation of personality.

You can see that this puts personal relationships in a wholly different light. From the spiritual perspective, if we are resentful towards a particular person, it is a much more serious problem than just one impaired relationship. That resentment is preventing us from attaining our native state. These verses do lead to deeper relationships, but their real purpose is much more: to enable us, *through* personal relationships, to realize the unity of life. If only in terms of our own spiritual progress, we need to learn to relate with kindness and consideration not only to a little clique of people whom we happen to like, but to everybody: at home, at work, in the store, on the bus, wherever we are.

It is easy to write this, or to read it and nod approval. But to practice it, day in and day out, is a constant battle. The other day an acquaintance was telling me he had been a soldier for twenty-five years. I wanted to reply, "Me, too." The person who tries to live in accord with verses like these has been drafted into the toughest battle that life has to offer, and sent to the front lines without even a drop of rum.

Sometimes, riding my bicycle home from the university after a day of crossfire between department difficulties and student problems and all the university red tape, I used to think with a sigh of the spiritual aspirants in their caves on the Himālayas, watching the deer come to drink at a nearby brook and listening to the wind in the trees. I wouldn't really have traded places with them, because it is only the rarest of individuals in any age who can extinguish self-will in the solitude of a cave. But there is nothing easy about realizing the Lord in the midst of society either. From first to last, it is a battle—and in a sense, every word in these verses is a battle strategy.

The very first phrase gives the key to all the others: *Adveshtā sarvabhūtānām,* 'incapable of ill will towards any creature.' Look at the daring of these two simple words! It is not enough not to express ill will; we must become incapable of it. Who even considers it possible today? Ill will is probably the most insidious enemy anyone could face. It doesn't conquer us overnight, so that we wake up the next day with a different personality. It infiltrates consciousness with a few well-trained paratroopers: dislikes, resentments, petty, personal grudges. Paratroopers, as you know, wear camouflage,

and the moment they land, they pretend they are part of the shrub-
bery. That is exactly what resentment does. It has all kinds of disguises, such as rationalization and righteous indignation. And like
a good commando, it doesn't stay hiding in the bushes; it immediately tries to occupy the strategic centers of the mind. Judgment is
one of the first to fall, and once judgment has been occupied by resentment, we do not see things as they are. We feel threatened where
there is no danger, and where there *is* danger we don't see anything
at all. After some time of this, the final occupation is easy. We welcome the enemy forces as liberators, and our loyal friends—equanimity, unselfishness, good will, trust—we treat with suspicion as
traitors.

Even at this stage, I would say, it is possible to resist and win.
But any strategist from Hannibal to Ho Chi Minh will say that if you
intend to drive an enemy out, the least you can do is not first invite
him in. In other words, don't wait until the mind is teeming with
invading resentments. As soon as you see a hostile thought, shoot it
down with the mantram. It doesn't matter if the thought seems jus-
tified or not; that is part of the camouflage. Don't stop to ask questions; don't wait for it to land and give you a password—shoot. At
the beginning there may be a number of wild shots, but keep repeating the mantram until the thought drops out of sight. After a while,
with a lot of practice, you will be able to pick off an invading resentment with just one shot.

At the heart of problems like this is our compulsive attachment
to two narrow concepts: *I* and *mine*. This is the ego's vocabulary.
It goes around with a little mental stamp like those you pick up in
a stationer's, stamping everything and everybody it fancies: *Mine,
Mine, Mine*. What it really means is *Me, Me, Me*.

Look at how people identify with their cars, or their clothes, or
even their hair styles. I have a close friend, for example, who is devoted to her Volkswagen "bug." If I compliment her on it, she is
pleased; if I tell her what Ralph Nader says about VWs, she feels in-
sulted. Where is the connection? *She* is not a bug.

Or take the way some people feel about their hair. If you make a
remark about my hair—or lack of it—my hair might have reason to

bristle, but why should I? I am not my hair; and if I start identifying with my hair, or with anything else external, my ego would swell to such a size that it couldn't help bumping into other egos and taking offense.

This can be extended even to opinions, which is where many difficulties in personal relationships arise. Most of us identify ourselves with our opinions. Then, when we are contradicted, we take it personally and get upset. If we could look at ourselves with some detachment, we would see how absurd this is. There is scarcely any more connection between me and my opinions than there is between me and my car, and once we realize this at a deeper level of consciousness, most of the resentment in differences of opinion disappears.

This kind of detachment does not come easily, but it can be cultivated. Again, it may be helpful if I illustrate from my own life. In my earlier days—to change a few names—if Henry Ford, say, objected to my opinions on history and told me point-blank, "History is bunk," I used to get upset. After a few times, I would begin to think of Henry Ford not as the man who made Detroit, but as the man with irritating views on history. In other words, I began to make a simple, common, but disastrous equation: "Henry Ford *is* the opinion that history is bunk." Once the equation is drawn, it follows that if you dislike the idea, you have to dislike Henry Ford: and that is exactly what I used to do, except, of course, that I am using Mr. Ford here only as an illustration. After a while I would even block out his name; I would think, "Oh, you know, what's-his-name: the man who thinks history is bunk."

Now, I am not denying that there are people who are disagreeable about their opinions. There are such people in every walk of life, and it is only normal to avoid them. But the Gita is not talking about being normal; it is talking about living in freedom. And when I began to understand this, I said to myself, "Why not try sitting back from your opinions with a little detachment? After all, it doesn't mean you have to give up your opinions. You don't have to agree that history is bunk in order to like Henry Ford." The real issue is not opinions at all; it is how to lower the barrier of self-will that keeps us from relating freely to everyone.

My desire to learn this was so great that if no one was around to contradict me, I used to seek out somebody whose ideas made my hair stand on end and say, "Hello, Henry, why don't you explain to me your views on history?" And instead of arguing, I would sit and listen carefully and draw him out with the utmost courtesy. It had several surprising consequences. For one, I discovered I didn't really mind the man after all. In fact, once I got my prejudices out of the way, I began to like him, simply as a human being. Second— which I hadn't expected—I began to understand his point of view. I didn't always agree with it, but I began to understand it: and that enabled me to listen with real interest, because it helped me to understand my own position better too. And third, even more un-expected, he began to listen with respect to me.

In other words, there is nothing wrong with disagreement. In fact, where relationships are concerned, it is a necessary part of love to disagree when the other person is about to do something he or she will later regret. What upsets us in such situations is simply lack of detachment: we don't know how to disagree with complete respect.

Though I have been in this country for many years now, there are still many American expressions that I don't understand. I remember trying to explain about meditation to a young fellow in Berkeley who kept shaking his head and saying, "Man, I just don't hear you." In all innocence, I started over again a little louder. Finally it dawned on me what he really meant: "I just don't *want* to hear you. I don't like what you're saying, so I'm going to plug my ears until you're finished."

This is what most of us do when there is disagreement. We carry around a pair of earplugs, and the minute somebody starts saying something we don't like, we stuff them in our ears until he or she is through. Watch with some detachment the next time you find your-self quarreling with someone you love. It won't look like a melo-drama. A detached reviewer would write, "First-rate comedy! Two people trying to reach an understanding by not listening to each other." One is saying, "What did you do the other day when I said such-and-such?" And the other replies, "What about you?" Can you imagine anything more comical? They are not trying to settle their differences; they are trying to make sure that they will never forget them.

If we could ask the mind on such occasions why it doesn't listen, it would answer candidly, "Why should I? I already know I'm right." We may not put it into words, but the other person gets the message: "You're not worth listening to." It is this lack of respect that offends people in an argument, much more than any difference of opinion.

But respect can be learned—again, by acting as if we had respect. And one of the most effective ways to do this is simply to listen with complete attention, even if we don't care for what the other person is saying. Try it and see: the action is very much like that of a classical drama. For a while there is the "rising action," just as I used to draw it for my students on the blackboard. The other person's temper keeps going up, language becomes more and more vivid; everything is heading for a climax. But then comes the denouement. The other person begins to quiet down: his voice becomes gentler, his language kinder, all because you have not retaliated or lost your respect for him.

When detachment has deepened considerably, you can actually see the mental states behind a person's behavior. It is an extraordinary leap in human perception. Just as a physician makes a diagnosis from X-rays of a patient's lungs, you gain the capacity to read a kind of X-ray of a person's mind and understand why he or she is behaving in a particular way. When this comes with detachment, you stop judging others. Then you can begin uprooting ill will not only from your words and behavior, but from your very thoughts.

Fortunately, this capacity does not ordinarily come without considerable detachment from oneself. The reason is simple: without detachment, there is too much of the ego in the way for vision to be clear. It is a precious safety clause, because sometimes even behind

pleasant words, the mental state is anything but pleasant. But when
you look at a person's behavior with detachment, it's almost like
seeing the inner mechanisms of a clock. Most of us, when we have
a problem with an alarm clock, don't throw it out the window. We
turn it around and try to find out what has gone wrong. Here it is
much the same. You still see the face of the clock—the dial, the
hands, the pendulum swinging back and forth, the little bird sticking out its beak at you and saying "Cuckoo!" But now, instead of
taking all this personally and getting angry, you can look behind the
face to the mechanisms inside and see what has gone wrong. It releases great compassion, for as Voltaire says, "To understand all is
to forgive all."

The words Sri Krishna uses here are among the most beautiful
in the Sanskrit language. *Karuna:* there is a continous flow of love
and sympathy, which comes when you see yourself in all and all
in you. *Kshami:* 'full of mercy,' ready to forgive everybody no
matter who they are or what they may have done. This is much
more than simply shaking hands and saying, "I forgive you." Real
forgiveness flows automatically, and with it comes the desire and
the capacity to move closer to those who offend you, and to help.
Maitrah: this is real friendship, where you never withdraw your respect, never retaliate, but always see the best in people and help
them to live up to the highest of which they are capable. Then, says
Sri Krishna, *"Yo madbhaktah sa me priyah."* This *is* loving the Lord;
and when we try to live like this, we not only benefit those around
us, we are helping to unite ourselves with the Lord once and for all.

यस्मान्नोद्विजते लोको लोकान्नोद्विजते च यः ।
हर्षामर्षभयोद्वेगैर्मुक्तो यः स च मे प्रियः ॥१५॥

15. Not agitating the world or by it agitated, he
stands above the sway of elation, competition, and
fear, accepting life, good and bad, as it comes.

"Wherever you go," my Granny used to tell me, "you are going to
encounter ups and downs—pleasure and pain, fortune and misfor-

tune, people who like you and people who don't care for you at all."
The nature of life *is* up today and down tomorrow, and the Gita says
simply, let it go up and down; you don't have to go up and down
with it.

Recently there has been a lot of popular interest in "biorhythms."
According to the current theory, each of us has built-in cycles of
emotional ups and downs. For two weeks I can be cheerful, but
then for the next two weeks I have to go into a slump. If I'm irritable
in those two weeks, I'm sorry, but I *have* to be irritable; that's just
the way my cycles go.

The idea, of course, is that if you can plot all these cycles, you
can pursue your goals when you're at your best and stay at home
in bed when you are not. Unfortunately, the demands of life pay
very little attention to anybody's cycles. If they did, I doubt that we
would ever learn to grow up, which in the Gita means being at our
best always—loving when life is for us, equally loving when life is
against us. This is just the opposite of a colorless existence. It means
going beyond the conditioned cycles of elation and depression to
live in an abiding sense of joy.

Most of us do not think of elation as a problem. After all, doesn't
everybody like to be on cloud number nine? I agree: if we could
stay on cloud number nine, life might be very pleasant. But as all
of us know, the cloud eventually evaporates. Then we not only
come abruptly back to earth, we usually burrow right into its depths
and hide—that is, we go into a depression.

In other words, the problem with elation is depression. "What
goes up must come down" is true of moods as well as of Newton's
apple. Elation and depression are inseparable aspects of the same
phenomenon, the erratic swinging of the mind: up with what it
likes, down with what it doesn't like. Because of our conditioning,
we like to make a distinction: when the mind swings up, we say that
the swinging is pleasant; when the mind swings down, we say it's
unpleasant. But a good spiritual scientist like the Buddha would say,
"No. Swinging is swinging." In both elation and depression the
mind is in agitated motion, and if we let it get agitated over what it

likes, it will stay agitated when it encounters—as it must—something it does not like. The agitation is the same; the focus of attention has simply changed.

This is an important point, because depression today has become literally epidemic. By more than a few doctors' appraisal it is the most serious mental health problem in this country, the condition most frequently encountered in a doctor's office today. Perhaps as many as twenty million people a year suffer from depression acutely enough to require medical attention, and no one can guess at how many more cases have not been recognized and counted.

In an important sense, however, depression is not a medical problem. There are drug approaches that can be effective first aid, but they do not get at the mechanisms of depression; they only affect its symptoms. When Dr. Paul Dudley White, the distinguished American heart specialist, was asked what he considered the best treatment for heart disease, he answered simply, "Prevention." That is the best treatment for depression too, and it is entirely possible. Until we understand the connection between excitement and depression, we are not likely to be able to keep depression from recurring. But once we understand the mechanisms of the mind, the picture becomes very reassuring: no matter how severely we may have been subject to depression in the past, we need never be depressed again.

There are a number of ways to illustrate how excitement and depression work. One way that throws light on the role of the senses here is to think of the senses as windows. In my old state of Kerala, houses are mostly one-story buildings with large wooden windows, which open out onto verandas when weather is pleasant and which close securely during heavy rains or the oppressive heat of the afternoon. Windows made from good wood can function well for centuries, but those made from cheap wood pose a constant problem: after a little exposure to tropical heat and monsoon storms, they warp. Then they open only with difficulty, and there is always the danger of forcing them open so wide that they get stuck and can't be closed again. When that happens, you are at the mercy of all kinds of weather—until finally a good strong storm comes along and slams the windows stuck with a vengeance. After that, you can't easily get them open again. One minute you're wide open to the world, everything outside is blown right in; the next minute you're sealed inside.

The senses behave in a very similar way. They are windows into the mind, meant to open smoothly when we are interacting with the outside world and to close securely when they are not in use. But in a person who gets easily excited, the windows of the senses are not just opened gently. They are thrown open as far as they can go, because of the intense desire to take in all the stimulation of the outside world.

We are not usually aware of this when it happens, because all our attention is turned outwards; there is no attention left for reflection and self-knowledge. But what happens is that the senses are thrown open with such force that they get stuck that way, leaving us completely at the mercy of the weather. We take in everything without discrimination; and just as we tried to take in what we thought was pleasant, we have to take in what is unpleasant too.

Then, eventually, there comes a storm. Something unpleasant comes along and slams the senses closed with a bang, locking us inside. That is depression.

What follows then is really tragic: we cannot help brooding on ourselves. In a mechanical sense, the senses continue to receive impressions—sights, sounds, and so on—but attention has turned completely inwards. If you look at a depressed person's eyes, you will see a little sign: "Closed. Nobody Home." There *is* somebody home, but he or she isn't answering any calls. You can take him to a movie and he won't respond; you can talk to her and she may not even hear: their attention is all caught inside, in brooding on themselves. There is even a characteristic expression, like the look on the face of somebody listening to the hi fi with a big set of earphones, slumped down in a chair all absorbed in a world of his own. But depression is listening to an "in-fi": the ears are covered to the outside world, and the person is hearing nothing, listening to nothing, except his or her own thoughts. And the tragedy is that the program is never positive. Everything is in negative mode: "Nobody likes me, I don't like anybody, I can't stand myself."

In personal relationships, the tragedy is at its worst. In a sense, while we are in a depression, we are not aware of any relationship with those around us—which means, among other things, that we are cut off from the major source of joy and meaning in life. To relate to people, attention has to flow outwards to them, so that we can identify with them and include them in our world. But if the windows of the senses are closed, there is no connection with others at all. We can be in the midst of a jolly crowd and still feel utterly alone.

There is an interesting comparison here with meditation. There too the senses are closed down, and the mind is trained upon itself. But in meditation, this is done freely. You choose a time and place for going inwards, and coax the eyes and ears and other senses to sit still while your higher mind takes a close look at your lower mind and concludes, with compassion, "What a clown!" All this is done in free choice, and after meditation you can turn your attention outwards again with the same freedom. But in depression, when the senses are slammed shut without your consent and the mind is turned in on itself compulsively, what happens is not a matter for joking. Everything is distorted, the way it is in a house of mirrors. Your partner looks as big as an elephant, you look like a little mouse; one side of you seems twisted and deformed. Smiles look like grimaces, and every gesture is threatening. If the bout of depression is prolonged, or if such bouts come frequently, you can even come to think that's how you and those around you really are.

Here, as usual, the approach of the Gita is very practical. Don't expect such people to be able to love, to be steadfast or patient or to work consistently at their jobs; show them how to get the windows open. Once that has been accomplished, you can teach them how to open and close their senses gently and with discrimination, so that they can guard themselves against depression coming again.

Essentially, the biochemical approach to depression is to force the windows open again, very much in the way in which they were slammed shut—that is, involuntarily. This approach can save lives, but it cannot do much to change the habit of oscillation in the mind. This is the real problem, and unless this habit is changed, depression is bound to recur. But to change the habit, we have to learn to open and close the windows of the senses for ourselves.

There are innumerable ways to do this, but here let me suggest just a few that are most effective in first aid. For one, don't isolate yourself; be with people. When you are in a depression, all your conditioning is crying out for you to lock yourself in your room, put on your headphones, and brood over how depressed you are. This may be natural, but it is probably the worst thing you could do. To open the sense-windows you need to come out, be with people, and give them your full attention. It is especially good if you can throw yourself into hard, selfless work with other people. Activity, especially hard physical activity, helps to keep your mind off yourself. And don't act depressed; act normal. Your mind may complain about the company—"a lot of crashing bores"—but you can still pretend to be interested. You don't have to talk, but you can at least listen with interest—and smile, even if you have to pull the corners of your mouth up with your fingers. *You* know you're really depressed, other people may know it too, but what does it matter? By acting normal you are becoming normal, freeing your attention from where it has been compulsively caught. The moment will come when you forget that you are acting. Then you are not acting any longer; the depression has lost its hold on you.

In all these approaches, the key is the same. A depressed person has lost the capacity to direct his attention. To get out of a depression, it is necessary to go against your conditioning and turn attention outwards again. When you can keep attention focused outwards, depression is gone; the windows are open again.

But there is another way to look on the mechanics of depression, and that is in terms of vital capacity: in Sanskrit, *prāna*. This is an extremely useful approach, because it connects directly with the cause of depression: excitement.

For purposes of this discussion, prāna is very much like gas in a car. It is the energy of life, not only on the physical level but on the emotional level as well. Now, in terms of energy, being excited consumes a lot of gas. It shows in many ways. There are people who, as soon as they get excited about something, begin to talk and talk. Excitement means that the mind is a bit out of control, and the lack of control overflows into their speech. Other people simply get speeded up, trying to fit more and more into their day, their sentences, even their thoughts. All this burns a lot of fuel, not only on the physical level but on the emotional level as well. If you could monitor your body when you're excited, you would see all sorts of signs that energy is being burned excessively. The heart beats faster, muscles become tense, breathing is rapid and irregular. It is like punching holes in your gas tank: in all these ways, vitality is draining out. That is why excitable people often feel harassed and tired as the day wears on, always busy but accomplishing comparatively little.

Then, after prāna drops to a certain level, the capacity for excitement drops too. We may still be in the same surroundings—on the same cruise, with the same people, visiting the same Caribbean island—but what seemed so exciting earlier now seems dull or irritating. This is depression. We have opened the petcock on our gas tank, and after a while we find that there is no more fuel with which to generate attention. In general, unless we can reverse the conditioning of depression, it takes as long for the tank to fill up again as it took to drain it through our excitement.

Actually, to me, this is a precious safety mechanism. The conditioning of excitement is so powerful that without some kind of cutoff, most of us would go on getting excited and drain a lifetime of prāna before it occurred to us that we were throwing away our capacity to live. In this sense it is possible to think of depression as a friend, very much like indigestion. Without indigestion, many of us would overeat until it was difficult to reverse the damage. Similarly, depression is a friend that is sending us an urgent reminder, special delivery: "You haven't been using your senses very well; you haven't been taking care of your mind. No more prāna until you give your mind and body a rest." It isn't pleasant, but depression gives a kind of recuperative period in which the senses close down so that our tank can fill up again.

One of the clearest illustrations of this is that in severe depression, sexual desire is often absent. There is a direct connection, because there is no more powerful stimulus to excitement than sex—not simply sex on the physical level but especially in the mind, where the desire arises. Dwelling on sex, anticipating it, longing for it, all takes up a lot of prāna. Then the tank is depleted, and when sexual desire is absent for a while in depression, we are getting a little breathing spell in which to consolidate vitality again and to learn to protect ourselves against undue excitement in the future.

But let me be clear on this point: it is not sexual desire that is the problem. It is elation, the mind going out of control. Prāna is drained by any kind of excitement, and today, everything is supposed to be exciting: vacations, restaurants, music, cars, even breakfast cereals and lipstick. There is a general attitude of seeking excitement that is in the air, and to me it bodes very ill for our civilization if we do not learn how to change. Where people are looking for excitement everywhere, epidemic depression *has* to follow: and as I said earlier, this is what we are beginning to see today.

Recently, for example, I saw a newspaper story about what was billed as one of the most exciting events of the season: a "Look Like Greta Garbo" party. Imagine—five hundred women paying a small fortune to come to a party all looking alike, not only in their costumes but in their wigs, their accents, even their gestures. There must have been weeks of feverish anticipation, planning, rehearsing, fantasizing, talking, dwelling on the pleasure that party would bring. With the Gita's perspective, I had only to read that article to know that before long the offices of practitioners all over that city would be full of five hundred look-alike depressives.

Ultimately, it is not overindulging the senses that is the problem in depression; it is indulging our self-will. Whenever we dwell on ourselves—rehearsing pleasure, replaying the past, worrying about getting our way—we are indulging self-will. And the result, as far as vitality goes, is like letting your car sit in the garage all night with the engine idling: you go out in the morning and find that there is no more gas.

The critical message here is that all this can be prevented—by not wasting prāna. Depression, put simply, is an energy crisis. With conservation there is no crisis. Your tank is always full, so there is always plenty of vitality with which to weather life's ups and downs. In terms of the mind, there is no more erratic motion; the waves of agitation have been stilled. The exhilaration of this state is conveyed in precise, simple language by St. Teresa of Ávila in one of her rare little poems, stamped with her own experience:

> Her heart is full of joy with love,
> For in the Lord her mind is stilled.
> Having renounced all selfish attachments,
> She draws abiding strength from the One within.
> She lives not for herself, but lives
> To serve the Lord of Love in all,
> And swims across the sea of life
> Breasting its rough waves joyfully.

अनपेक्षः शुचिर्दक्ष उदासीनो गतव्यथः ।
सर्वारम्भपरित्यागी यो मद्भक्तः स मे प्रियः ॥१६॥

16. He is pure, efficient, detached, ready to meet every demand I make on him as a humble instrument of my work.

I once knew a chap who was an expert at card games, who had a quiet way of making the most of every hand. "A good player," he explained, "can't afford to depend on chance. He's got to be able to play whatever he's dealt." Then he would add, with understandable pride, "Let anybody you like set up the cards—some good, all bad, I don't care. At the end of the evening, I'll still come out on top."

He was talking about cards, but I was thinking, "That's the way to live in freedom too." The word the Gita uses here is *anapekshah*, for which "detached" is a very pale translation. Literally, *anapekshah* means 'without expectations.' It sounds negative, even passive, but it is just the opposite. *Anapekshah* means always ready for the unexpected—in other words, ready for anything. It is a very daring attitude, because it means telling life, "I'm not concerned with what you send me. Good or bad, pleasant or unpleasant, it doesn't matter; I can make the best of whatever comes."

The opposite of this is not preparedness; it is rigidity. Most of us are subject to this, and it comes to the surface when we have to deal with unexpected problems. From what I have seen of life, problems are a repertory theater. We may see all sorts of characters, but only a very few problems are playing all the roles. Self-will, of course, is one of the most versatile. Now, give us a problem that we recognize—dressed in a particular costume, cast in a particular role, appearing at a particular place and time—and we know how to deal with it. But the moment the same problem appears in a way we do not expect—say, wearing a false moustache and a fez—we go to pieces. The mind looks through its catalog and throws up its hands: "Boss, this isn't supposed to happen! I don't know what to do."

In other words, to live without expectations is the secret of freedom, especially in personal relationships. There is a song from *My Fair Lady* in which Rex Harrison sings in exasperation:

> Why can't a woman be more like a man? . . .
> Why can't a woman be like *me*?

It did not surprise me to learn that this was a very popular song. In every emotional relationship, even if we don't know how to put it into words, each of us has a rigid set of expectations which require the other person to act and think in a particular way. Interestingly enough, it is not *that* person's way; it is our own. Then, when he or she acts differently, we get surprised and feel irritated or disappointed. If we could see behind the scenes, in the mind, this sort of encounter would make a rather good comedy. Here I am, relating not to you but to my idea of you, and I get irritated because you insist on acting your own way instead!

In the end, this is the basis of most difficulties in personal relationships. It is really no more than stimulus and response. If you behave the way I expect, the way I want, I'll be kind. If you behave otherwise, I'll act otherwise too: rude or irritated or disappointed or depressed, depending on my personality, but always something in reaction to you. It means, very simply, that none of us has much freedom; our behavior is dependent on what other people say and do.

When I first began to observe this in myself, I was astonished. Imagine going through life with handcuffs on and thinking that you're free! Being a college professor, I had always assumed that my intellect did a rather good job. But when I saw that my behavior was nothing but stimulus and response, I looked my intellect in the face and it hung its head. "Look at you," I said, "so well trained, so clever! How is it that you couldn't see that my daily living isn't being done by me but by Tom and Dick and Harry?" It was a shocking discovery, but on the other hand, it was a hopeful one. With that discovery came a deep desire for freedom to take my life away from that dubious trio and bring it into my own hands.

There is a simple but effective way to do this: give your best everywhere, without reference to anybody else. It frees you from all the vagaries of stimulus and response. On the one hand, by using verses like these in meditation, you set yourself very high standards of conduct—perhaps the highest that can be imagined. Then you try to apply these standards to everything you do and say and even think throughout the day, without being swayed by anybody else's reaction. If things go your way, you can give your best; if they don't go your way, you can still give your best. All the choices are yours.

In practice, this means that we become the same person always. Most of us *think* we are the same always, but if we could make objective observations at certain critical times of the day, we would have to conclude that the similarities are on the surface. A mother may say of her pediatrician, "Oh, Dr. Jekyll! He's always so kind, never loses his temper with little Jamie." But ask his wife or his medical assistant; they may tell you a very different story. "Come see the doctor at home; he's a regular Mr. Hyde." It's like people being meticulous about how they look when they go out, but going about unshaven or with their hair up in curlers when they're at home. To me, it's a curious reversal of perspective. I don't want to be at my best only with the mail carrier or the checkout clerk; I want to be at my best always, with everyone, beginning with those who are nearest and dearest.

Now, I will be the first to admit that this takes a lot of endurance. When you start giving another person your best, especially in an emotionally entangled relationship, he may not notice it for weeks. This kind of indifference can really sting. You want to go up to him, tap him on the shoulder, and say, "Hello, George, I've just been kind to you." George would say, "Oh, thank you, I didn't even know it"—not because he was trying to be rude, but because he was preoccupied with himself. To be patient and go on giving your best, you can't have expectations about how other people are going to respond. You can't afford to ask, "Does he *like* me? I've been putting him first for two whole weeks, and I don't think he even cares." What does it matter? If you go on putting him first, never mind that he benefits from it too; you're growing.

Especially in a loving relationship, this question of "Does he love me in return?" should not be asked at all. Give the person you love your very best and don't ask about the response. It frees you in your relationship, but more than that, it strengthens the other person. In one-to-one relationships, most of us tend to lean on each other. If one person wobbles, the other person wobbles too, and sometimes even falls. When you are always at your best, you become a real source of strength to those around you. No matter how much they may vacillate, they know they can always lean on you and trust you to stand firm.

If it takes patience to do this in even the best of relationships, it requires real courage in the face of hostile opposition. Here I can make some practical suggestions. For one, concentrate on your own personal conduct. Don't allow your attention to wander to how rude the other person is; concentrate on not being rude yourself. It is terribly difficult, but it frees you to choose your response.

In a sense, this is like the attitude a good athlete has in competition. When the going gets rough, there are some players who get rattled and lose their capacity to concentrate on their own game. I have seen a well-known tennis champion lose to a chap who didn't

have half his skill, simply because he lost his concentration whenever his challenger got ahead. But there are other players who are
at their best when they're behind. They don't start thinking about
the other player and get all rattled. They dig in and concentrate
even harder on their own game, and some of the most brilliant tennis I have seen comes when a fellow like Bjorn Borg fights his way
out of a hole against heavy odds to win.

Another suggestion I can offer that used to help me greatly when
I caught on to it is this: in an emotionally charged situation, when
you find it difficult to concentrate on giving the other person your
best, pretend you're an actor on the stage. Play the role of someone
who is detached—and give your best to your performance.

Let me give a personal example. In earlier years, as a professor,
I often had to attend faculty meetings, where sparks can really fly.
Naturally, when the issue was important to me, I used to express
my opinion at those meetings—and as often as not, somebody who
felt just as strongly about the opposite view would stand up and
take to pieces everything I had said. Certain people did this with
such regularity that the minute they stood up, my adrenal glands
would start working overtime, simply because I was about to be
contradicted.

Then I began to pretend that instead of being a professor, I was
playing the part of a professor: using learned, professorial words,
striking certain intellectual attitudes, but all as if it were a role in
an off-Broadway performance. If somebody contradicted me, my
mind could just sit back and watch; it was all part of the play. I
even came to enjoy practicing, and when my opinions came under
fire, I would pretend to be Laurence Olivier: take my time to reply,
bring the fire of righteous indignation into my eyes, and then state
my position in forceful but courteous Victorian English.

Remarkably enough, my colleagues seemed to appreciate this
too. Two or three even went so far as to say, "You know, you've
really been making a contribution to these meetings." After all, I
felt the same responsibilities, held the same educational concerns; I
was simply learning to hold my opinions without rancor in the face
of opposition. And where I used to go home after a heated meeting

feeling irritated, I now felt like a critic going home after a show. *"Much Ado About Nothing* again—same cast, modern dress. But not a bad performance from E. E."

People sometimes object, "Isn't this being hypocritical?" Not at all. If anything is hypocritical, it is being angry, behaving rudely, using words that are calculated to hurt another person. Any kind of negative behavior is untrue to our real Self, and when we try to play the role of someone who is kind, we are really learning to be ourselves. There is no need to be afraid of past performances. After all, some of Hollywood's best known "good guys" aren't always such good guys off the screen. Similarly, no matter what you have been like, you can always play a better part, which you will gradually assimilate.

When we quarrel, when we act resentful, that too is a play. It seems natural only because we have rehearsed it so many times. In acting with respect towards others, we are still taking part in the same play, but we have chosen a different role.

Naturally, it is difficult to remember this in the heat of the moment, let alone to do it. Even good actors sometimes forget their lines, drop out of character for a moment, and whisper, "What do I say next?" You can do the same—repeat the mantram and recall these beautiful verses, which meditation will drive deep into your heart: "Pure, efficient, detached, ready to meet every demand I make on him as a humble instrument of my work." And then go back to the play. You may not feel the epitome of compassion, but I promise you, you can learn to play the part to perfection.

The marvel of this is that the more often you practice it, the more easily the lines and actions come. After a while they become an integral part of your consciousness. Some time ago in India there was a play about a great saint which must have been performed all over the country for a number of years. The actor who played the title role, by his own account, was not at all saintly when he took the job. But after so many years of speaking those inspired lines, taken mostly from the saint's own words, and acting like a saint night after night, the man's consciousness began to change. He began to want to *be* a saint. Finally, after the run of the play was over, he gave up acting and devoted himself entirely to the spiritual life.

Ultimately, to give up expectations is to lay aside all the absurd impositions of self-will. Then there is nothing that you require of life; all you want is to give. You have thrown away your defenses: they serve no purpose, for there is nothing that life can take from you. As the Upanishads put it, you are always full—"Take away from fullness and it is still full, give to fullness and it is still full." And the rest of us, in the presence of such a person, lay down all our defenses too.

Some time ago I took my wife and some friends to see the film version of *Camelot*. One of the younger members of the party was just entering the age when the promises of romance seem eternal, so after the film I asked her what she thought of all those knights.

"Oh," she said, "they must have had a very thrilling life. But imagine having to carry around those silly shields!"

Unfortunately, it's not only in Camelot that people carry shields. Virtually all of us labor under defenses that are much more rigid and cumbersome: our expectations. Whenever we feel challenged, we shove these shields up in front of us—and then, when we have trouble relating to others, we complain about bad communication! Even when two people say they are in love with each other, though each may be trying to embrace with one arm, the other arm is still holding on to the same old shield, ready to bring it up again the moment he or she feels a little insecure.

How much vitality is wasted in life by carrying around these shields! They don't even protect us; and as far as relationships go, they constitute most of our problems. And the Gita says simply, "Throw all your shields away." Then you have both arms free to embrace with—in the end, to embrace all life. When you can really embrace with both your arms, the message is clear to anyone: "There is nothing I want from you; all I want is to give." This is what all of us are looking for: not only to receive such love but to offer it, freely and consistently, so that our lives will be cherished by everyone around us.

यो न हृष्यति न द्वेष्टि न शोचति न काङ्क्षति ।
शुभाशुभपरित्यागी भक्तिमान्यः स मे प्रियः ॥१७॥

*17. He is dear to Me who runs not after the
pleasant or away from the painful, grieves not over
the past, lusts not today, but lets things come and
go as they happen.*

A friend of mine once asked her eight-year-old son what he wanted
for Christmas. She was expecting him to say a bicycle or some
Beatles records, or perhaps an electric guitar. His answer took her
completely by surprise: "A pair of handcuffs."

When we go through life running after what we like and away
from what we dislike, this is just what we are asking for: handcuffs
to inhibit every chance of relating to others in freedom. I have met
people who were as proud of their handcuffs as that eight-year-old
boy. "I'm a man of strong opinions," they say. "I'm a woman who
knows what she likes. I'm spontaneous; I'm free." But someone like
St. Francis just gives them a curious smile. "Free, is it? What are
those things on your wrists?"

With rare exceptions like St. Francis, this is the conditioning that
all of us share: to run after the pleasant and to avoid the unpleasant.
It is the old story of stimulus and response. The other day I was
reading that certain microorganisms, which ordinarily go about in
random motion, become intentional when particular substances
are introduced into their environment. If the substance is pleasant,
they move towards it; if it is obnoxious, they move away. I said to
myself, "How human!" But there is a crucial difference between us
and the rest of creation. All of us, as human beings, have the capacity to decondition ourselves, to train the mind to make the choices
that take us beyond conditioned behavior.

The villain here is not actually the mind; it is the ego. The ego
has an obsession with taking everything personally. It can't let anything go by without putting in its opinion: "I like this, I don't like
that." We may not be aware of it; but if we could listen in on our
thoughts, this is the incessant refrain behind all our experience.

When I was living in Oakland I used to go for long walks around
the park, and on Sunday afternoons during the summer I would encounter a band concert. After a while, I began to take my walks at
a different hour. It wasn't that I didn't like the music. What I objected to was that there wasn't any choice about listening to it;
wherever you went, you had to be accompanied by John Philip
Sousa.

That is the way the ego is. He has a large repertoire of songs and
dances, but they all have the same chorus: "I like this, I don't like
that." Isn't there a famous choir in which all the singers are boys?
Here all the voices are our *samskāras*, our compulsions. They take
every part from soprano to bass, and if they are sometimes squeaky
or raucous, they make up for it in enthusiasm. They're willing to
practice seven days a week, twenty-four hours a day, as long as
we're willing to listen. And the ego is the conductor, standing there
with his baton and making sure that everybody comes in on cue.

It is absurd how flimsy likes and dislikes can be. Often, when we
meet someone, all it takes to set us off is one little personal characteristic—his nose, her voice, the way he laughs, the way she shows
her teeth. Immediately the chorus will set in. And the ego is a good
conductor. He doesn't have to saw the air; he just lifts his baton and
cocks his eyebrows and everybody starts right up: "I don't like it,
I don't like it, I don't like it!"

It is pointless to blame the ego for this; it is his nature. If the ego
had to declare his identity going through customs, he would say
proudly, "I'm a conductor." And if the officials asked, "Is there
anybody accompanying you?" I am sure that he would trot out his
whole band. "Come on up, boys!" And they would start up right
there in the customs shed: "I like this, I don't like that." That is
the ego's show, and to paraphrase the Compassionate Buddha, if
we hire the ego, we hire the show too.

To put it into practical language, underneath all our liking and
disliking is one and the same samskāra. A samskāra, remember, is
a habit of mind that operates independently of external circumstances. I sometimes compare it to a searchlight: once a searchlight
is on, it *has* to shine, no matter where it is pointing. In this case, we

may think we have all sorts of unrelated likes and dislikes—peppermint chip ice cream, hang gliding, names that begin with *A*—but underneath all of them is the same old samskāra: "I like this, I don't like that."

To take an example, look at procrastination. "I don't like" puts on a fancy costume and calls itself "I have postponed." The disguise can be quite elaborate: "I have all this urgent work to do," "My other responsibilities just don't leave me time," "I still haven't cleaned out the garage." There may be all sorts of complicating reasons, but underneath, it is often no more than "This isn't pleasant, so I'm not about to do it." That is why Jesus says so often, "Forthwith." If something needs to be done, do it now, without even asking whether it is pleasant or unpleasant. Then you are undoing the samskāra, getting rid of your handcuffs.

Now, for a bigger surprise, look at vacillation. Who would think that there is a connection between finding it difficult to make decisions and not being able to love? But as we begin to see the mental states behind behavior, it becomes clear that vacillation has very little to do with external circumstances. The mind has simply learned to wobble, and it will wobble back and forth over anything whenever its security is upset.

There is a good word for vacillation in Sanskrit: *cancala*. It almost sounds like the bangles on a dancer's ankles, and in Sanskrit poetry, a girl with dancing eyes is called *cancalākshī:* 'she whose pupils are always darting back and forth.' In the days of classical Indian drama, this was considered a rare attribute. But I see eyes like this every time I go into a supermarket—trying to decide whether to get mint toothpaste or regular, weighing the pros and cons of two brands of soap, wondering whether herbal essence or musk best suits their personalities. People of both sexes are subject to this. They may think they are making independent decisions, but underneath, they are asking the same question over and over again: *Do I like this?* It can lead to taking half an hour to decide what kind of toothbrush to buy. "Do I like this? It says it's soft, but there are only two rows of bristles. Or do I like this? It has three rows, but there's no recommendation by the ADA." We aren't satisfied any more with liking one thing and sticking to it; we have to keep asking about it more and more often, so that our attention is dancing all over the store.

Now, here is the Gita's revelation: this has very little to do with shopping. It is a habit of mind, and the person who has trouble making decisions in any part of life is going to have trouble making decisions everywhere. In the end, that person will vacillate even in personal relationships. The underlying question is still the same: *Do I like this?* "Do I like him or don't I? He has a nice nose, and I think he likes me, but sometimes I don't care for the way he walks." When we think this way, every time the other person does something we don't like we stagger a little in our stance. Then he staggers too—we're uncertain, so he's uncertain. It can come to such a state that neither person is able to stand firm; and when that happens in a relationship, life can really be miserable.

That is how far this samskāra can go: in the end, "I don't like" becomes "I can't love." This is why I put so much emphasis on going against likes and dislikes in little things like food. It has really very little to do with food; you're working on the samskāra. Enjoying something nourishing which you detest—say, broccoli—may not seem like much of a challenge. But when you learn to eat without rigid attachments, you are really undoing the conditioning of liking and disliking in everything, opening up the handcuffs that keep you from being free.

The problem here, the Gita says, is that our relationships are upside down. We try to build relationships on what is pleasing to us, on physical or emotional attraction. But if there is anything sure about physical attraction, it is that it *has* to change. We cannot build on it; its very nature is to come and go. To build on a firm foundation, we have to stop asking this question of "What do I like?" and ask only, "What can I give?"

Physical attraction, in other words, is a sensation—here one minute, gone the next. Love is a relationship. It *is* pleasant to be with someone who is physically attractive, but how long can you enjoy an aquiline nose? How long can you thrill to the timbre of a voice when it doesn't say what you like? It's very much like eating: no

matter how much you are attracted to chocolate pie, there is a limit
to how much you can enjoy. Beyond that limit, if somebody merely
mentions chocolate, your stomach stages a revolt.

That is the most tragic truth about the satisfactions of the senses:
they cannot last. It is their nature to come and go, and when the initial attraction begins to wane, the very things that seemed so pleasant now begin to irritate you. He had such a nice sense of humor
when you first met; how is it that his jokes seem corny now? Her
smile used to dazzle you; why does she now seem to be all teeth?
The wave of passion has risen, now it has to fall: that is all. Pleasure
cannot last, any more than the tide can rise without falling again.
If you want to build a relationship, don't build it on what changes.
Build it on what endures, where the question "Do I like this?"
doesn't even arise. Then there is joy in everything, because there is
joy in the relationship itself—in ups *and* downs, through the pleasant
and the unpleasant, in sickness and in health.

In Sanskrit, physical attraction is called *kāma:* selfish desire, in
which I ask only what pleasure I will receive. It is a tremendous
force, as we can see from the lives of those with strong passions who
are hurled in and out of relationships even against their will. But
kāma can be transformed—not negated or repressed, but made a
matter of free choice, by gradually changing the focus from *me, me,
me* to *you, you, you.* Then we say in Sanskrit, *kāma* becomes
prema: pure love, where my attention is not on my own pleasure
but on the happiness and welfare of those around me.

One of the difficulties in talking about this is that our English
word "love" has become almost impossible to use. We talk about a
mother's love for her children and mean one thing; we talk about
"making love" and mean another. We even talk about loving
cheesecake, and we use the phrase "falling in love" as if it were
something that could happen every day, like falling into a manhole.
Is it so easy to fall in love? We have to learn to love, and it takes a
lot of time and a lot of effort.

Listen to our popular songs; look at our magazines and newspapers. When they say "I love you," that's not what I hear; I hear
"I love me." If we could listen in on a marriage proposal with the

ears of St. Francis, this is what we would hear. The man gets down on bended knee and says, "Sibyl dear, I love me; will you marry me?" Isn't it an accurate translation? *You'll make me happy, so won't you marry me?* And Sibyl, who is nobody's fool, says, "I love me too—and you'll make *me* happy. So I will."

To be honest, there is a little undertone of this in the relationships of almost all of us. There is no need to be ashamed of it: this is how we have been conditioned, to put ourselves first at least some of the time. But where I like to place emphasis is on the fact that all of us can change. Every relationship begins like this to some extent: some passionate *I love you*'s and some undertones of *I love me*. But if you want your relationship to blossom, you won't dwell on each other's weaknesses; you'll set to work to correct them and really learn how to love.

I wish I could convey what unending artistry there is in this challenge—artistry and satisfaction and lasting joy. Every day we should be able to love more than the day before. Otherwise there is no growth, which means that things are getting pretty dull. Every day the same old story, "I love you with all my heart"? It may be enough for the romance magazines, but it's not enough for a mystic.

Look at our travel ads—"Experience the Bahamas." How gullible we can be! They show us a couple of swaying palms, some azure waters lapping at white sands, and then they ask innocently, "Wouldn't you like to sit beneath these coconut palms and fall in love?" I come from Kerala, the "land of the coconut palm," and you can take it from me: never try to pursue your dreams beneath a coconut tree. Coconuts have a way of falling on romantic heads, and even the smallest nut, if it drops from a height of fifty feet, can put an end to your romance before it starts. What do swaying palms and azure waters have to do with love? Love doesn't need an exotic setting; it can flourish in the kitchen, in the garden, wherever two people are putting each other first.

If you want to know what love is, look at a woman who knows how to be patient when her husband is irritated. Instead of fanning his mood, she strengthens him by bearing with him until his mind quiets down. In my book, that woman is a great lover. Or look at a man who comes home after work instead of going to a bar, who plays with his children even though he's tired, stays and talks with his wife while they do the dishes instead of flopping down in front of the TV. He is a great lover, even if you never see his name on the Hollywood marquees.

When you live with a person like this, the time will come when you find it impossible even to think a harsh thought about each other. You may not completely understand each other, you may not always see eye to eye, but each of you will know without doubt that the other's loyalty will never waver. When this happens, you are no longer living in Berkeley or San Francisco. It is paradise, "Jerusalem's green land," right here on earth. There may be differences on the surface, but underneath the surface there is only pure, selfless love.

Two people like this are no longer two; they are one. When things are sunny, you may not notice how their relationship shines. But wait until the storms begin to blow outside, when everything is going wrong: you will see unfailing support between them, unfaltering loyalty, tenderness that never ends. "Call it not love that changes": it is wise advice. This is the pinnacle of love, and nothing less can ever satisfy us.

समः शत्रौ च मित्रे च तथा मानापमानयोः ।
शीतोष्णसुखदुःखेषु समः सङ्गविवर्जितः ॥१८॥
तुल्यनिन्दास्तुतिर्मौनी संतुष्टो येन केनचित् ।
अनिकेतः स्थिरमतिर्भक्तिमान्मे प्रियो नरः ॥१९॥

18–19. Who serves both friend and foe with equal love, not buoyed up by praise or cast down by blame, alike in heat and cold, pleasure and pain, free from selfish attachments and self-will, ever full, in harmony everywhere, firm in faith—such a one is dear to Me.

I don't think anyone illustrates these verses better than Gandhiji, for whom love and selfless action were one. "I don't want to be at home only with my friends," he said; "I want to be at home with my enemies too." It wasn't a manner of speaking; he lived it out through forty years of solid opposition.

The other day I saw some newsreel footage of Gandhi with a prominent political figure who opposed him so relentlessly that people said he had a problem for every solution Gandhi offered. These scenes were shot in 1944, when the two leaders met for a series of talks in which literally millions of lives were hanging in the balance. It took my breath away to see Gandhi treating his opponent with the affection one shows an intimate friend. At the beginning of each day's discussions the man's face would be a mask of hostility; at the end of the day both men would come out together smiling and joking. Then by the next morning the man would have frozen over again, and Gandhi would start all over with the same cheerful patience, trying to find some common ground.

That is how the mystic approaches conflict, and it pulls the rug out from under all the traditional theories. There is a lot being written these days about conflict resolution, which I am glad to see. But no matter what you read, they will always say in effect, "This is how you deal with your opponent." Gandhi, St. Francis, St. Teresa, would all say, "No. The moment you start thinking about the other person as an opponent, you make it impossible to find a solution." There are no opponents in a disagreement; there are simply two people facing a common problem. In other words, they are not in opposite camps. They are in the same camp: the real opponent is the problem.

To apply this, you have to set aside the question of who is to blame. We have a saying in my mother tongue: "It takes two to get married and two to quarrel." No matter what the circumstances, neither person bears sole responsibility for a quarrel. It is an encouraging outlook, because if both are responsible, both together can find a solution—not merely a compromise, but a way actually to resolve the quarrel peacefully.

To do this, however, it is necessary to listen—and listen with respect. Don't be afraid if the other person is angry. An angry person is blind. He is so absorbed in his own point of view that he cannot see what is happening around him, including what is happening to himself. We don't get angry with those who are blind; we help them: after all, unless they have taught themselves to be extraordinarily sensitive with their other faculties, blind people can bump into things and hurt themselves and others. That is just how an angry person is; and when we have to face such people, we need to listen with patience and respect and help them not to rush off blindly into a lamp post. Whether the other person is polite or not, the objective is still the same: how can we find the common point of view?

Here the mystics ask a simple but subtle question: how can you end a quarrel if you do not even hear what the quarrel is about? How can you solve a problem with two sides if you never hear what the other side is? More than that, if you can't listen to the other person with detachment, you will not have the detachment to understand your own position objectively either. It's not just one side of the problem you can't see; it's both. So listen with respect: it may hurt you, it may irritate you, but it is a healing process.

Gradually, if you can bear with this, you will find that you are no longer thinking about "my point of view" and "your point of view." Instead you say, "There is a point of view that is common to you *and* me, which we can discover together." Once you can do this, the quarrel is over. You may not have arrived at a solution—usually, in fact, there is a lot of hard work left to do. But the quarrel itself is over, because now you know that there are two of you playing on the same side against the problem.

Not long ago I was watching the Brazilian athlete Pelé play his last game of soccer. He is retiring now at the peak of his career, one of the best soccer players the world has seen, and in this last game he was playing with the New York Cosmos against a team for which he had scored his most memorable goals: Santos of Brazil. For the first half of the game, Pelé played his best for the Cosmos. But the second half had a brilliant touch: he joined his opponents and played his best for *them*. This is what we should do in a disagreement: play half-time for the other side, half-time for our own. It is not a question of sacrificing principles; this is the only way to see the whole.

If we could only see the game more clearly—and the results were not so tragic—the spectacle of a quarrel would make us laugh. When we played soccer in my village, one of my cousins used to get so excited that he would shoot the ball into his own goal. We used to say, "Never mind the other side; watch out for Mandan." But when two people quarrel, that's just what they are doing—scoring against their own side. Whatever the disagreement, *we* are the Home Team, the Cosmos—all of us. Our problems, whether personal or national or environmental, are the Visitors. And the mystics say simply, "Support your team. *There* is the opponent, down at the other end of the field. Unite against the problem; don't go scrapping among yourselves."

Otherwise, if I may say so, there are no winners in this game. Once we divide against ourselves, whether at home or between races or nations, there can only be losers. On the other hand, there is no disagreement so serious that it cannot be set right if both sides can join hands and work hard for a common solution. It is not at all easy, and the results will not be immediate. But wherever there is hatred, complete love can be established; wherever there is conflict, complete unity can be established. The choice is up to us.

Jesus puts it perfectly: *Love your enemies.* You will never see any loftier words, but never any more practical either, for he is telling us how to rise to our highest stature. Look at the sun, he says; does it shine only on those it likes? It shines on all, it gives to all; and we should learn to love the way the sun shines, without favor or interruption. *Bless them that curse you; do good to them that hate you.* In time they may learn to love you, but that is not the point. What we are called on to do is to be at our best always.

There is room for great artistry in this—especially when it is not on a grand scale, as it was for Gandhi, but in the everyday life of home and work. Here, I think, there is no better example than St. Thérèse of Lisieux:

> In our community there is a Sister who has a talent for displeasing me in everything—her ways, her words, her character seem to me *very* disagreeable. However, she is a holy Sister whom the good Lord must find quite agreeable. So, not

wanting to give in to the natural antipathy I was feeling, I
told myself that charity must consist not in sentiments but
in action. Then I applied myself to do for this Sister just what
I would do for the person I love most. . . . I tried to render
her every possible service, and when I was tempted to answer
her in a disagreeable way, I contented myself with giving her
my friendliest smile and tried to change the subject. . . .

As she was absolutely ignorant of how I felt for her, . . .
she told me one day with a contented air, almost in these
very words: "Would you tell me, Sister Thérèse, what attracts
you so much towards me? Each time you see me I see you
smiling." Ah! What attracts me is Jesus, hidden in the depths
of her soul—Jesus who makes sweet that which is most bitter.
. . . I answered that I was smiling because I was pleased to see
her. (Of course, I didn't add that it was from the spiritual
point of view!)

In a small way, this is something that every sincere spiritual aspirant must go through in order to learn to love. In my own life, I too
had to deal with people who disliked me—and I have to confess, I
did not care for them either. But as meditation deepened, I began
to understand: *that* was the challenge of it. As Jesus asks, "Where
is the achievement in loving those who like you? Anybody can do
that." If you're daring, it is a challenge that can appeal deeply.
After all, if you really want to play championship tennis, you won't
want to play against people like me. You'll say, "Put me across the
net from Chris Evert or Jimmy Connors. Even if I lose, the game
is going to be worthwhile."

Once I got that perspective, I really joined battle with my likes
and dislikes where relationships were concerned. If there was someone I had always avoided, who always avoided me, I gritted my
teeth and began to try to win him over. The first few times, my knees
were shaking as if somebody had given me a pair of boxing gloves
and put me in the ring with Muhammad Ali. And sometimes, at the
beginning, I *was* knocked down. But I wasn't depressed: even if I
hadn't laid a glove on my samskāra, I had made it through the first

round. That itself was a triumph and a revelation. I wanted to cheer, to pat my mind on the back and say, "Never mind about winning or losing. At least we know that now we can make a fight of it; we don't have to give up and be knocked out by the very first blow." I felt as if all my chains had been broken, and if I had been the uninhibited kind, I would have got up and danced like Zorba the Greek. And after that, if a desire to retaliate or speak harshly came up, I would fight it with all I had.

It hurt. After all, I was a professor of the English language. I knew how to use words, I had a large vocabulary at my disposal, and sometimes all sorts of choice remarks would rush to my tongue and pile up behind my teeth, clamoring to get out. But no matter how much pain it caused, I wouldn't speak until I could make my point in calm, courteous language that would not hurt the person who had hurt me.

Sometimes, after a lot of patient effort, I was successful in winning over such people. But sometimes, though I tried my level best, I was not. It was terribly disheartening. At times I was tempted to ask myself, "Wasn't all that effort wasted? All that time you spent with that person, listening to him, walking with him, playing tennis with him, when you could have been reading the Gita?" But then I looked again. I hadn't lost a thing—and I had made myself so secure that I could flourish in any relationship and never be let down.

Be ye therefore perfect, Jesus says, *even as thy Father in heaven.* That *is* the goal, nothing less. Why ask if it is possible? It doesn't matter; we can always move towards perfection. In India—I imagine the same is true all over the world—children like to measure their height each year with a little mark on a wall. We can do the same: take a few minutes to take stock of our day and see how we can improve. Don't psychologize or dwell on major failures. Two or three minutes morning or evening should be enough to take a bird's-eye view of landmark events and look for ways in which you can do better on the next day. When you came to breakfast, were you a little abrupt? Did you get caught up in a silent dialogue with your oatmeal? Make a point of being especially attentive the following day. Was there somebody at work to whom—perhaps unintentionally—you gave a cold shoulder? Next day make it warm. That is all—little things. Life consists of these little things, and it is by putting other people first every day in a thousand little acts of kindness that we make ourselves perfect in love.

There are people, I am told, who examine their faces every evening for signs of advancing age. I would say, don't look for crow's-feet on the surface; turn the mirror inwards. Take a detached look, shake your finger at the mirror, and tell yourself, "Watch out! You think you did pretty well today—but tomorrow I'm going to be even more patient; I'm going to love even more."

If you want to love with all your heart, this is the key: don't ever ask how much you can get. Ask how much you can give. It is applicable everywhere. Last week I saw a very accomplished actor, Paul Scofield, in a film of one of Shakespeare's finest plays: *King Lear*. The tragedy is relentless; and when you watch it from the perspective of the scriptures, it can tear your heart to hear old Lear, in the twilight of his life, trying to bolster himself with attestations of his daughters' love: "Regan, how much do you love me? Goneril, how much do you love me?" For me, I had only to hear those lines to foresee that terrible moment when Lear cries out to the gathering storm,

> You see me here, you gods, a poor old man,
> As full of grief as age. . . .

I am no longer an English professor; my whole life is devoted to teaching meditation. But if I could make a sally back into the world of letters, I could write a very different version of that play. I wouldn't write a tragedy. Lear would learn to change his whole way of thinking: it would all be "Goneril, how much can I love you? Regan, how can I love you more?" And at the end of the play, instead of huddling on the moors all buffeted by the winter weather, he would stand erect and tell the sky, "Look upon a man as full of love as he is of age." *That* is King Lear; the other was a pauper. It can be true of all of us: the power to rewrite is in our hands.

"If you want to know how good a person is," the mystics say, "ask how much he loves." It is a perfect epigram, but I like to turn it around. If you want to test the depth of someone's love, look at how kind he is, how patient she is—not when things are going smoothly, but in their hours of trial. A ship isn't tested in a harbor; it's tested on the high seas. There are great scientists, artists, philosophers, soldiers, who function well enough when life is with them but go to pieces when the storms begin to blow. And the mystics say, "Set aside the goal of life, set aside meditation; what good is a ship that's only seaworthy in port?" Look at the daring of a great lover like Gandhiji or St. Teresa. When somebody opposes them, instead of running away, they move closer; when someone is angry with them, they try all the harder to be kind.

Love "has no errors," says William Law, "for all errors are the want of love." When we have problems in our relationships, it is not that love has failed; these are defects in our ability to love. In our contemporary climate of separateness, it has become almost impossible for a man and woman to remain together for more than a short period of time. But to throw up our hands and say that love won't work, that lasting relationships are no longer possible, simply betrays our ignorance of what love means.

I read a lot these days about the decline in literacy. But when it comes to love, virtually all of us are illiterate. It is not a condemnation. When you were two, did you know how to read? And even when you began to learn, wasn't it mostly things like "See Spot run"? There is no need to be embarrassed about it; that is how all of us began. To read a writer like Shakespeare with real understanding takes most of us twenty years—and even then we may not be able to follow the simple words of John of the Cross when he soars into realms where we have never been. It is the same with love. At the outset, it is wise to admit freely that this is an art that we do not know. But we can put ourselves to school; and if we are willing to put in at least the time it takes to understand Shakespeare, all of us can become perfect in love.

When two people love each other, there is one sure sign: they want to lose themselves in their unity. The words are simple; but the more you reflect on them and try to practice them, the more you will see how profound a concept this is, how difficult to practice. It is just the opposite of what we hear around us: "Maintain your individuality, maintain your own little separate personality, and then try to get along together as best you can." In the Gita's terms, this is the denial of love. Each person is drawing a little circle around himself or herself and saying, "I will function freely in my circle; you can function freely in yours." The circles do not even overlap, which means that there is no real relationship between those people at all.

This is how we begin. Most of us, if we could see objectively, stand inside virtually separate circles, which we ourselves have drawn. That is what self-will does; and to move closer, we need to reduce self-will. It is difficult, distressing, even dangerous; that is its challenge. But gradually, as self-will decreases, the circles you and your partner have drawn around yourselves move closer together, until at last they touch.

After that, the work is equally strenuous. Now you try to make the circles overlap, so that each intersects a little arc. During eight hours together, you try to preserve at least one hour when there is no acrimony, no competition, no selfishness. For the other seven hours, your mind may have been complaining bitterly. It's quite all right: there is now an arc in common. There are still vast areas that need to come together, but you can concentrate on that little area of unity and say, "Yes, it *is* possible. Even if it takes years, these circles can become one."

If we could but see it, there are not many separate circles; there is only one. All have the same center and the same radius; nobody's area is different from anybody else's. You may have been born in Rhodesia and your partner in Rhode Island—two different environments, different languages, different cultures—but there is not the slightest difference between the Self in you and the Self in him or her. This is the realization that comes in samādhi. All circles merge, and afterwards you don't see separate circles at all. Love is playing like a perpetual fountain in your heart: love not for only one person but for all people, all creatures, all forms of life.

The closer two people grow, the deeper is the longing to become closer still. But nothing short of absolute unity is going to fulfill the deep, driving need in the heart of every one of us to be one and indivisible. Even in the most passionate Romeo-and-Juliet relationship there will always be a void, a hunger that can be satisfied only for a short while. Pick up the paper almost any morning and you will find somebody complaining that this satisfaction has come to an end. "We're together all week long; I need a vacation from him." "She's always there when I come home; I need one evening a week all to myself." I read recently about two people trying to preserve their relationship by seeing each other only on weekends. I wanted to ask, "What relationship is there to preserve?" If the object is to keep life from becoming humdrum, why not just have a breathless encounter once a year when your paths cross in the air terminal at St. Paul?

When two people really love each other, they will want to be together always. It is one of the surest tests of love. It doesn't mean becoming dependent on each other, or sitting together on a love seat writing sonnets. It means working together in a selfless cause, merging two lives into a single, beneficial force. When you have a relationship like that, even a hundred years together would not satisfy you. If you can be satisfied by anything that is limited, your love is not complete. When your two circles come together you will cry, with the daring of the mystic, "Let there be no separation."

In the spiritual tradition of India, we have a story that illustrates this beautifully. There was a girl who was born of highly spiritual parents. She went to school, where she had many friends among the other girls; and gradually, as they reached the age for marriage, she began to come home with wonderful news. "Mummy," she would say, "Nalini is going to get married! You know Nalini, the one who wears jasmine in her hair. She is going to get married, and her mother is getting her a beautiful new sari, and she'll be exchanging garlands and wearing new jewelry..."

And her mother, who knew how to read the mixed look of joy and longing in her daughter's eyes, would smile and say, "Be happy for her."

This happened many times, year after year, until at last our little girl had grown well into her teens. Finally, on the day of her graduation, she came home crying as if her heart would break. "Mummy," she said, "all the girls in my class are married now! I saw their faces shining at the wedding, and now I don't see them any more. Their lives are joyful—and look at me; I don't think I'm going to be married at all."

The mother, who was a woman of great spiritual stature, did not try to answer immediately. She took her daughter into the meditation room, sat down with her, and taught her how to meditate. Then she explained, "These marriages you have seen were good; but in life, the sunshine is always mixed with shadow. There are days that are sweet, but there are also days that are bitter: and after this play of light and shadow, sweet and bitter, has gone on for many years, time itself is going to bring the relationship to an end."

"Is there no marriage that is perfect?" the daughter asked. "Is there no relationship that lasts, that has no end?"

"There is," her mother said. "It *is* possible to love for ever; but it is terribly, terribly hard."

"That's what I want," the girl pleaded. "That is what I have been longing for all these years, and to love like that, I am prepared to give up everything else."

"Then give all your love, your heart, your time, your life, to serve the Lord of Love. Offer him everything: 'whatever you do, whatever you give, whatever you enjoy, even what you suffer'; do it only for him. Make your whole life a gift to him, and you will be united with him by a love that time can never bring to an end." She looks at her daughter, so eager and so strong, and asks: "Are you able to do all this?"

And the girl, now gone far beyond her years, answers simply, "I am." Like the other great teenagers of the Hindu scriptures—Nachiketa, Mārkandeya—she devotes herself completely to the overriding goal of going beyond change and death. And the story tells beautifully—almost in the same language that Catholic mystics use—that at last, in the supreme experience of samādhi, Sri Krishna comes to her in the depths of her consciousness and takes her as his eternal bride. *"Amado con amada,"* writes John of the Cross,

"Amada en el amado transformada"—lover with the Beloved, united, transfigured, transformed.

ये तु धर्म्यामृतमिदं यथोक्तं पर्युपासते ।
श्रद्धाना मत्परमा भक्तास्तेऽतीव मे प्रियाः ॥२०॥

20. But even dearer are the devotees who seek Me in faith and love as life's goal. They go beyond death to eternal life.

In the Rig Veda, one of the most ancient of the Hindu scriptures, there is a prayer that must still find a response in every heart:

> Lead me from the unreal to the real,
> Lead me from darkness to light,
> Lead me from death to immortality.

This is the central theme of mysticism in all religions: the quest for deathlessness, for everlasting life.

Until I took to the practice of meditation, it never occurred to me that immortality could be any more than a figure of speech—a rhetorical device that can strengthen and inspire us, but nothing that could be literally true. It was only by observing my Granny's attitude towards death that I began to understand that the quest for deathlessness was real—a living search that any person with drive and enthusiasm could undertake, not after death but in this very life. In both East and West there have been rare men and women who have been enabled through spiritual disciplines to transcend the conditioning of time, place, and the physical body. For people like this, there *is* no death. The body dies, of course; but there is no interruption of consciousness when the body falls away, because their identification with the body has already been severed.

In deep meditation, when consciousness is withdrawn from the body and senses, there actually come a few moments when you go beyond the body. The five buttons of the body-jacket—the senses—are undone, and for a short while you are able to slip your arms out, hang up your jacket in the meditation room, and rest in your real nature. That is a taste of immortality right on earth, and there is such joy in it, such a deep sense of peacefulness and rest, that afterwards you will be willing to give everything to extend those moments into the full twenty-four hours of the day.

Once that is done, the ties of identification with the body are severed once and for all. You know at the deepest level that you are not the body but the Self, and when death comes, it is simply a matter of hanging up this particular jacket for the last time. As al-Ghazzali asks, where is the cause for grief in this? Is consciousness ruptured when you take off your shirt at night?

There are no words to describe this state, but the mystics of all religions say quietly, "It's like waking up." Before the realization of God, we are living in our sleep—dreaming that we are separate fragments of life, small enough to be satisfied with wisps of experience that come and go. Aren't the experiences of a dream real while we are dreaming? In a vivid dream, there is at best only a hazy memory of another state of consciousness to which we can wake up. Yet when we *do* wake up again, the dream falls away. And the mystics ask a very simple question: when you have been dreaming that you are Marco Polo, ranging all over the world into distant lands, and you wake up, are you a different person? Do you grieve that Marco Polo is gone? He isn't gone: you were dreaming that you were he; now you wake up, the dream is forgotten, and you remember who you really are.

In the Katha Upanishad, there is a daring teenager named Nachiketa who goes straight to the King of Death for the secret of immortality. "I have heard," he tells Death, "from the illumined sages that there is a kingdom where you never come, where one lives free from death in everlasting joy." There *is* such a kingdom, but it is not outside us. In the early part of our lives, most of us are off on an external journey, looking for Shangri-la in the lands of the senses. But to those who are sensitive, there comes more and more insistently a sense of homesickness, of being wanderers on the earth; and finally there comes a point where we throw aside all the travel brochures of the sense-world and turn inwards to find our real home. Then the quest for deathlessness begins in earnest.

This is a demanding, arduous, challenging journey. As meditation deepens and we get beneath the surface level, we see a wholly different world within us: the world of the unconscious, as vast as the world outside us, without boundaries in time or space. Gerard Manley Hopkins gives a glimpse of these realms in a tortuous poem:

> O the mind, mind has mountains; cliffs of fall
> Frightful, sheer, no-man-fathomed. Hold them cheap
> May who ne'er hung there. . . .

To those who live on the surface of life, the dangers of this world seem "cheap," insignificant. But once we glimpse the scope of the unconscious, it can take our breath away. Hopkins is not exercising poetic license; these mountains and cliffs and gorges are as real as those beneath the surface of the sea. To make a journey like this, it is not enough to have courage and determination. We should also have some idea of where we are going.

I saw an intriguing book title the other day: *If You Don't Know Where You're Going, You'll Probably End Up Somewhere Else.* We are already somewhere else; our need now is to get back home. If you have a goal in life, it is like a polestar: you can guide your whole journey by it. You may have taken detours, but if you keep your eyes on the goal, you will always be able to know when you are off course and what to do to get back again. Without a goal there can only be wandering; with a goal you can never get lost. And Sri Krishna says here, *Matparamā:* "Don't settle for anything outside you; make Me your only goal."

A few weeks ago my little friend Rama received a picture puzzle of an elephant, and last night I came into the living room and found pieces strewn all over the floor. I grew up among elephants, so I thought I would be able to recognize an elephant from any conceivable angle. But no amount of looking at those pieces enabled me to distinguish head from tail. Then Rama showed me the picture on the box. After that, even though it might take a long time and a lot of trial and error, I knew I would be able to make those pieces into an elephant if I tried.

This is what we do in meditation. I would suggest memorizing this chapter of the Gita, "The Way of Love," and using it regularly in meditation; there is no more inspiring portrait by which to arrange the pieces of our lives. As you travel deeper into consciousness, these verses will shape your daily living; even in your sleep you will want to realize them. "Free from selfish attachments and self-will, ever full, in harmony everywhere..." At the beginning they are only inspiring words, describing someone like Mahatma Gandhi or St. Teresa. But after many years of meditation and the allied disciplines, when this ideal has been completely integrated into your consciousness, it will be in a small way a portrait of yourself: not the little self with which you identified when you began this journey, but a person who has been transformed, reborn, remade in the image of this all-consuming ideal.

In the final stages of this journey, it is necessary to use all kinds of contradictions to describe what is happening within you. Everything is coming together, your desires are almost unified; and when you sit down for meditation, you drop like a plummet into the very depths of consciousness. In some strange way, you expect without expecting. You wait impatiently, yet you are prepared to wait a hundred years. Every day you give your very best in your meditation, your work, your personal relationships, so that nothing will delay this tremendous climax. And in the evening too you stay vigilant, keeping the mantram going ceaselessly; for as Jesus warns, "Ye know not what hour thy Lord may come"; he may come like a thief in the night. In these final stages there can be deep experiences in your sleep, experiences which are preparing the way for samādhi. You may hear the mantram reverberating through your consciousness, or the words of a passage you have been using in meditation. You may see one of the great spiritual figures you love deeply, or even have a vision of Jesus or Sri Krishna or the Compassionate Buddha. It is like the curtain trying to go up on a play you have been waiting for all your life. You can see the feet of the stagehands, you know that the sets are being moved into place, but that is all;

and it so inflames your eagerness that you exclaim, like India's
great saint and poet Mīrā,

> Oh, how I long to see my Lord!
> At dawn I search for Him
> Every day in my meditation;
>   I cannot sleep until my eyes behold Him.
> Ages have I been separated from you, Beloved!
> When will you come?

This is not the experience of a few days. It can go on for months,
even years, and it is the most deliciously difficult time in sādhana.
No mystic would ever be spared that agony. There is such joy in it
that the Sufis ask, how much more joy must there be in the final
union, when all separateness comes to an end? Then, says Abu Said
in rapture, "I am lover, Beloved, and love in one; beauty and mirror
and the eyes that see." Jāfar exclaims:

> I have joined my heart to Thee: all that exists art Thou.
> O Lord, beloved of my heart, Thou art the home of all;
> Where indeed is the heart in which Thou dost not dwell? . . .
> From earth below to the highest heaven, from heaven
>   to deepest earth,
> I see Thee wherever I look: all that exists art Thou.

When we are united with the Lord, every created thing, from
the farthest star to the atoms in our bodies, is our kith and kin. Remember William Blake looking at the sun and seeing a choir of
angels singing *holy, holy, holy*? The whole of creation is singing;
if we cannot hear it, it is simply because we are asleep.

When I was growing up at the feet of my Grandmother, though
I loved her passionately, I understood very little of her perspective.
My attention was elsewhere, on Shakespeare and Dickens and the
"Ode to a Nightingale"; I couldn't hear what her life was proclaim-
ing every instant—in the simple words of St. Angela, almost the
same as those of the Gita, "the whole world is full of God."

There is no barrier between us and this realization except self-
will. That is all that keeps us thinking that we are separate from the

whole. The more we love, the less our self-will—and the less subject we are to time and death. All of us have moments when we forget ourselves in helping others. In those moments of self-forgetfulness, we step out of ourselves: we really cease, if only for an instant, to be a separate person. Those are moments of immortality, right on earth. Stretch them out until they fill the day and you will no longer be living in yourself alone; you will live in everyone. And St. John of the Cross reminds us, "We live in what we love." If you love the Lord in all, if you *live* in the Lord in all, what is there to die when the body dies?

On her deathbed, St. Thérèse of Lisieux was asked what she thought heaven would be like. Thérèse replied in her gentle way that she couldn't imagine it would be so very different. "Oh, I know I'll *see* God. But as for being in his presence, I couldn't be more so there than I am here."

Perfect words. When the little prison of the ego has been left behind, there is no longer any real difference between "there" and "here." We no longer live in a separate body, a separate little personality. As Shankara says, the whole universe is our home.

Sri Sarada Devi, mourning for Sri Ramakrishna on the evening after he died, heard him ask in the depths of her consciousness: "Am I dead, that you are acting like a widow? I have only moved from one room to another." And the Compassionate Buddha, in one of the most magnificent passages in mystical literature anywhere, chooses almost the same image:

> In vain have I gone around these countless cycles of birth and death, looking for the builder of this house. How wearisome is the suffering of being born again and again! But now I have seen you, housebuilder; you shall not build this house of separateness again. The rafters are broken, the ridgepole has been destroyed: I have gone beyond all selfish craving; I have attained nirvāna, in which all sorrows end.

इति भक्तियोगो नाम द्वादशोऽध्यायः ॥१२॥

The Way of Love

ARJUNA:

Of those who love you as the Lord of Love,
Ever present in all, and those who seek you
As the nameless, formless Reality,
Which way is sure and swift, love or knowledge?

SRI KRISHNA:

For those who set their hearts on Me
And worship Me with unfailing devotion and faith,
The way of love leads sure and swift to Me.

Those who seek the transcendent Reality,
Unmanifested, without name or form,
Beyond the reach of feeling and of thought,
With their senses subdued and mind serene
And striving for the good of all beings,
They too will verily come unto Me.

Yet hazardous and slow is the path to the Unrevealed,
Difficult for physical man to tread.
But they for whom I am the goal supreme,
Who do all work renouncing self for Me
And meditate on Me with single-hearted devotion,
These will I swiftly rescue
From the fragment's cycle of birth and death
To fullness of eternal life in Me.

Still your mind in Me, still yourself in Me,
And without doubt you shall be united with Me,
Lord of Love, dwelling in your heart.
But if you cannot still your mind in Me,
Learn to do so through the practice of meditation.
If you lack the will for such self-discipline,
Engage yourself in selfless service of all around you,
For selfless service can lead you at last to Me.
If you are unable to do even this,
Surrender yourself to Me in love,
Receiving success and failure with equal calmness
As granted by Me.

Better indeed is knowledge than mechanical practice.
Better than knowledge is meditation.
But better still is surrender in love,
Because there follows immediate peace.

That one I love who is incapable of ill will,
And returns love for hatred.
Living beyond the reach of 'I and mine'
And of pleasure and pain, full of mercy,
Contented, self-controlled, firm in faith,
With all his heart and all his mind given to Me—
With such a one I am in love.

Not agitating the world or by it agitated,
He stands above the sway of elation,
Competition, and fear, accepting life
Good and bad as it comes. He is pure,
Efficient, detached, ready to meet every demand
I make on him as a humble instrument of My work.

He is dear to Me who runs not after the pleasant
Or away from the painful, grieves not
Over the past, lusts not today,
But lets things come and go as they happen.

Who serves both friend and foe with equal love,
Not buoyed up by praise or cast down by blame,
Alike in heat and cold, pleasure and pain,
Free from selfish attachments and self-will,
Ever full, in harmony everywhere,
Firm in faith—such a one is dear to Me.

But dearest to Me are those who seek Me
In faith and love as life's eternal goal.
They go beyond death to immortality.

Glossary & Guide
to Sanskrit Pronunciation

This is a glossary of the Sanskrit and other Indian terms in this book. For a more complete guide, see A Glossary of Sanskrit from the Spiritual Tradition of India *(Nilgiri Press, 1977).*

GUIDE TO THE PRONUNCIATION OF SANSKRIT WORDS
Consonants. Consonants are generally pronounced as in English, but there are some differences. Sanskrit has many so-called aspirated consonants, that is, consonants pronounced with a slight *h* sound. For example, the consonant *ph* is pronounced as English *p* followed by an *h* as in ha*ph*azard. The *bh* is as in a*bh*or. The aspirated consonants are *kh, gh, ch, jh, th, dh, ph, bh*.

c as in *ch*urch	*g* as in *g*old
h " " *h*ome	*j* " " June

The other consonants are approximately as in English.

Vowels. Every Sanskrit vowel has two forms, one short and one long. The long form is pronounced twice as long as the short. In the English transliteration the long vowels are marked with a bar (¯). The diphthongs—*e, ai, o, au*—are also pronounced twice as long as the short vowels. Thus, in the words *nīla* 'blue' and *gopa* 'cowherd,' the first syllable is held twice as long as the second.

a as in *u*p	*ri* as in *wri*tten
ā " " f*a*ther	*e* " " th*ey*
i " " g*i*ve	*ai* " " *ai*sle
ī " " s*ee*	*o* " " g*o*
u " " p*u*t	*au* " " c*ow*
ū " " r*u*le	

SPELLING OF SANSKRIT WORDS
To simplify the spelling of Sanskrit words we have used a minimum of diacritical marks, retaining only the long mark (¯) for the long vowels. Some subtleties of Sanskrit pronunciation, such as the difference between retroflex and dental consonants, are therefore lost. The gain in simplicity, however, seems to outweigh this loss.

abhyāsa Regular practice.

adhyāropa [or *adhyāsa*] Shankara's theory of superimposition; the process of ascribing the qualities of one thing to something else of a different nature.

advaita ['not two'] Having no duality; the supreme Reality, which is the "One without a second." The word *advaita* is especially used in Vedānta philosophy, which stresses the unity of the Self (Ātman) and Brahman.

ajapajapa The Holy Name (*mantram*) repeating itself in the consciousness of the devotee without effort on his part.

akshara The eternal; the syllable *Om*.

Ananta The cosmic serpent on which Vishnu reclines in rest.

Ardhanārīshvara "The Lord who is half female (and half male)," name of a form of Shiva.

Arjuna One of the five Pāndava brothers, and an important figure in Indian epic and legend. He is Sri Krishna's beloved disciple and friend in the Bhagavad Gita.

āshram [Skt. *āshrama*, from *shram* 'to exert oneself'] A spiritual community, where meditation and spiritual disciplines are practiced.

Ātman 'The Self'; the innermost soul in every creature, which is divine.

avatāra [*ava* 'down'; *tri* 'to cross'] The descent of God to earth; the incarnation of the Lord on earth; the birth of the Lord, of divine consciousness, in the heart of man.

Bardo [Tibetan *bar* 'between'; *do* 'two'] In Tibetan mysticism, the state between two lives in which the soul awaits a proper body and context for rebirth.

Bhagavad Gītā [*Bhagavat* 'Lord'; *gītā* 'song'] "The Song of the Lord," name of a Hindu scripture which contains the instructions of Sri Krishna.

bhakti [*bhaj* 'to serve, worship, love'] Devotion, worship, love.

bhakti yoga The Way of Love.

Bhārata India; a native of India; a descendant of King Bharata.

Bhīshma A revered elder of the Kaurava dynasty who allows himself to be killed by Arjuna in the *Mahābhārata* battle.

Brahmā The god of creation. Brahmā, the Creator, Vishnu, the Preserver, and Shiva, the Dissolver, make up the Hindu Trinity. *Brahmā*, a word with masculine gender, should not be confused with *Brahman*, which has neuter gender. (See next entry.)

Brahman The supreme Reality underlying all life, the Divine Ground of existence, the impersonal Godhead.

Brahmānda "The egg of Brahman," the primordial atom from which the cosmos evolves.

Brahmavidyā The science of knowing Brahman.

Buddha [from *budh* 'to wake up'] "The Awakened One." An enlightened being; the title given to the sage Siddhārtha Gautama Shākyamuni after he obtained complete illumination. The Buddha lived and taught in North India during the sixth century B.C.

buddhi Understanding, intelligence; correct view, idea, purpose.

deva A divine being, a god.

Dhammapada [Pāli, from Skt. *Dharmapada*] An important early Buddhist scripture.

dhārana The first stage in meditation.

dharma Law, duty; the universal Law which holds all life together in unity.

dhyāna Meditation; specifically, in Patanjali's yoga, the second stage in meditation.

dvāpara yuga See *yuga*.

Ganges [Skt. *gangā*] A great river of northern India, looked upon as a sacred symbol.

Gītā "The Song," a shorter title for the Bhagavad Gita.

gopī Cowherd girl, milkmaid, especially the companions of Krishna as a young man in Vrindāvana.

guna Quality; specifically, the three qualities which make up the phenomenal world: *sattva*, law; *rajas*, energy; and *tamas*, inertia.

Hanumān The monkey devotee of Rāma.

Hari [*hri* 'to steal'] "He who has stolen our hearts," name of Vishnu or Krishna.

Himālaya [*hima* 'snow'; *ālaya* 'abode'] The great mountain range which stretches across the northern border of India, important in mythology as the home of Shiva and other gods.

jnāna [*jnā* 'to know'] Wisdom; higher knowledge derived from spiritual disciplines.

jnāna yoga The Way of Wisdom.

Kali "The dark one," name of the Divine Mother as the consort of Shiva.

Kālidāsa "Servant of *Kālī*," name of a celebrated poet of ancient India.

kali yuga See *yuga*.

kalpa A period in cosmic time equaling one day of Brahmā or 1,000 "great yugas"–a total of 4,320 million years. See also *yuga*.

kalpa tree A wish-fulfilling tree said to grow in paradise.

Kāma Selfish desire, greed; sexual desire, sometimes personified as Kāmadeva, "god of desire."

karma [*kri* 'to do'] Action; former actions which will lead to certain results in a cause and effect relationship.

karma yoga The Way of Action; the path of selfless service.

Kauravas "The sons of Kuru," usually referring to Duryodhana and his brothers, who are the enemies of the Pāndava brothers.

Keshava "He who has long, beautiful hair," name of Krishna.

Krishna ['black'; or from *krish* 'to draw,' 'to attract to oneself'] "The Dark One" or "He who draws us to Himself," name of an incarnation of Vishnu. Krishna was born in response to Mother Earth's plea to Vishnu to save her from the evils threatening her. Many stories are told of his childhood in a small, simple village, and he is often worshipped in the form of a child. As a young man he was adored by all the village girls, especially Rādhā, and their romance symbolizes the lover–Beloved relationship which the devotee may have with the Lord. Later on Krishna became the friend and advisor of the Pāndava brothers, especially Arjuna, to whom he reveals the teachings of the Bhagavad Gita. He is the Lord of Love who dwells in the hearts of all.

kundalinī "The serpent power," spiritual or evolutionary energy.

līlā Game; the divine play of the Lord disguising himself as many.

Mahābhārata Name of a great epic composed from two to three thousand years ago, traditionally attributed to the sage Vyāsa. It relates the conflict between the descendants of Pāndu (the forces of light) and those of Dhritarāshtra (the forces of darkness).

mahātma "Great soul."

manas The mind; specifically, the faculty which registers and stores sensory impressions.

mantram [or *mantra*] A Holy Name or phrase; a spiritual formula.

Māra "The Striker"; in Buddhism, the Tempter, the Evil One who tries to prevent the Buddha's enlightenment.

Māyā Illusion; appearance, as contrasted with Reality; the creative power of the Lord.

muni A sage.

Nārada The divine musician and sage who is a devotee of Sri Krishna.

nirvāna [*nir* 'out'; *vāna* 'to blow'] Complete extinction of self-will and separateness; realization of the unity of all life.

nirvikalpa samādhi A state of spiritual awareness in which there is no perception of duality, of inside or outside, of subject and object; merger in the impersonal Godhead.

Om [or *Aum*] The cosmic sound, which can be heard in deep meditation; the Holy Word, taught in the Upanishads, which signifies Brahman, the Divine Ground of existence.

Pāndavas "The sons of Pāndu," a collective name for Arjuna and his four brothers, Yudhishthira, Bhīma, Nakula, and Sahadeva.

Patanjali The author of the *Yogasūtras,* a concise description of the way to Self-realization through meditation. He lived around the second century B.C., and his method is sometimes referred to as *rāja yoga.*

prakriti The basic energy from which the mental and physical worlds take shape; nature.

prāna Breath; vital force.

prema Intense divine love.

preya (opposite of *shreya*) That which seems pleasing to the senses; passing pleasure.

Purusha ['person'] The inner soul, the spiritual core of man. In the Gita, the terms *Ātman* and *Purusha* are virtually interchangeable.

Rādhā The milkmaid who is Sri Krishna's beloved while he sojourns in Vrindāvana. She represents the human soul seeking the divine Beloved.

rāja yoga The Royal Path; the path of meditation taught especially by Patanjali in the *Yogasūtras*.

rajas Passion, energy; the second of the three qualities (*gunas*).

Rāma [from *ram* 'to rejoice'] The Lord of Joy; the principle of joy within.

sādhana A body of disciplines or way of life which leads to the supreme goal of Self-realization.

sādhu A holy man, sage.

samādhi Union with the Lord; a state of intense concentration in which consciousness is completely unified.

samsāra The world of flux; the round of birth, decay, death, and rebirth.

samskāra A personality trait conditioned over many lives or one life: a mental and behavioral pattern; a latency or tendency within the mind which will manifest itself if given the proper environment and stimulus.

Sanjaya The sage who divinely perceives the narrative of the Gita and reports it to the blind king Dhritarāshtra.

Sānkhya One of the six branches of traditional Hindu philosophy. Sānkhya seeks to liberate the individual *Purusha* (spirit) from *prakriti* (mind and matter) through the knowledge of the ultimate separation of these two realities.

sattva Goodness, purity, law; the highest of the three qualities (*gunas*).

satyāgraha [*satya* 'truth'; *āgraha* 'grasping'] Gandhi's term for a moral struggle as opposed to a violent opposition.

satya yuga See *yuga*.

savikalpa samādhi [*sa-vikalpa* 'having distinctions' or 'admitting separateness'] Samādhi in which some duality of subject and object remains, the devotee being absorbed in his meditation upon the Lord without becoming completely one with Him; union with the personal God.

Shankara "Bringing about eternal welfare," name of Shiva. Also name of a Hindu saint of the sixth or seventh century A.D., born in Kerala, who is the author of many devotional hymns and philosophical works, including a commentary on the Gita. He is the leading teacher of the doctrine of nondualism or Advaita Vedānta.

Shiva Third in the Hindu Trinity; he who destroys the ego and conquers death.

shraddhā Faith.

shreya The Good, that which is permanently beneficial.

Sītā The wife of Rāma and the ideal for womanly love and loyalty.

soma A drink used in Vedic ritual in ancient India; the drink of the gods.

Srī [pronounced *shrī*] A title of respect originally meaning "Lord" or "holy"; in modern India, simply a respectful form of address.

sthūlasharīra The physical body.

sūkshmasharīra The subtle body, made up of *samskāras*.

tamas Inertia, ignorance; the lowest of the three qualities or *gunas*.

tanhā [Prākrit, from Skt. *trishnā* 'thirst'] The thirst for selfish satisfaction, the craving of the senses and the ego.

tapas Austerity, control of the senses; the spiritual power acquired through self-control.

Tat tvam asi "That thou art." Quoted from a verse in the Chāndogya Upanishad: "That subtle essence which is the Self of this entire world, *That* is the Real, That is the Self, That thou art."

tejas Brightness; spiritual energy and power.

tretā yuga See *yuga*.

turīya "The Fourth," the highest state of consciousness, union with Brahman. The other three states are waking, dreaming, and dreamless sleep.

Upanishads Ancient mystical documents found at the end of each of the four Vedas.

Vaikuntha Vishnu's heavenly realm.

Veda [*vid* 'to know'] "Knowledge"; the name of the most ancient Sanskrit scriptures. Orthodox Hindus regard them as the direct revelation of truth from God to the first sages.

vīnā An ancient South Indian stringed instrument used in classical music.

Vishnu Second in the Hindu Trinity; the Preserver who incarnates himself in age after age for the establishment of dharma and for the welfare of all creatures.

Vrindāvana Name of a village on the Yamunā River where the historic Krishna spent his youth as a cowherd, befriending the local cowherds and milkmaids. Today it is an important place of pilgrimage.

yoga [from *yuj* 'to unite'] Union with the Lord, realization of the unity of all life; a path or discipline which leads to such a state of total integration or unity.

yogī A man who practices spiritual disciplines.

Yudhishthira Arjuna's elder brother, who is famous for his adherence to dharma at all times.

yuga An age, eon. In Hindu cosmology there are four yugas, representing a steady deterioration in the state of the world from age to age. Satya yuga is the age of perfection, followed by tretā yuga. The incarnation of Sri Krishna is said to mark the end of the third yuga, dvāpara. We are living in the fourth and final yuga, kali, in which the decline of creation reaches its lowest point. Together the four yugas equal a *mahayuga* ('great yuga') or *kalpa,* a period of 4,320,000 years. One thousand *mahayugas* equals one day of Brahmā. At the end of one such day the cosmos is recalled into the Lord, and for an equal period—one night of Brahmā—there is a cosmic rest. At the dawn of the next day of Brahmā, the whole process of creation begins anew.

Index

Meditation *(cont.)*

accelerates evolution, 50, 149; allied disciplines and, 14–18, 21–22, 58, 141–142, 175–177, 194, 195, 237, 315, 359, 363, 364, 377, 418; attention in, 15, 142–143, 158, 182–183, 188–189, 361, 369, 387;

brain and, 138, 330; by itself is not enough, 359, 364, 377;

capacity for, 34, 58, 100–101, 198; centers of consciousness and, 129–130; climax of, 29, 86, 110, 138, 146, 163, 305, 418–421; compared to physical training, 141, 145, 358–359; concentration in, 14–15, 142–143, 188–189, 273, 359, 369, 375, 377; criticism of, 213;

daily living and, 129, 134, 218, 249, 375, 377; death is motivation for, 242–243; death process and, 110; deepening, 165–166, 218, 369, 375, 417–418; defusing a memory in, 188; difficulties in, 34–35, 159; distractions in, 15, 142–143, 172, 188–189, 330, 369; dynamics of, *see* Meditation, principle of;

early days of E.'s, 364, 373; early stages of, 23, 140, 174, *see also* Dhārana; effect of, *see* Effect of meditation; effort in, 27, 97, 159–162, 315, 418; ends boredom, 97–98; enthusiasm for, 91, 134, 140, 359–360; expectancy in, 335, 369, 377; experiences in, 129, 172, 418–419;

fruits of, 136–137;

genetics and, 330; going beyond body in, 23–24, 330, 415–416; guidance in, 34–35;

importance of, 134–135, 154, 199, 355–356, 359–360; in the evening, 359–360; incentives for, 63–65, 124, 128; inspirational passage in, *see* Inspirational passage; insight grows in, 375; instructions in, 14–15; is climbing Himālayas of consciousness, 232–

Meditation *(cont.)*

233; is dangerous if selfish, 175–177; is *devayāna*, 130; is diving into sea of the mind, 238; is education for living, 249; is hard work, 33, 134, 140, 174, 358; is assuming responsibility, 114; is journey to real home, 123; is like amla fruit, 144; is like drawing water from well, 173; is like skiing up slope, 145; is rāja yoga, 136, 257; is training the mind, 358–361, 364;

kundalinī released through, 50, 138;

later stages of, 24–26, 110, 165, 171–172, 198, 251, 315–316, 349, 418; light in, 129–130, 171; longing for union in, 180, 327–328, 335, 348–349, 419;

mantram and, 143, 167; mind in, 62, 143, 158, 245, 251, 253, 356–357, 361; misunderstandings about, 140;

Om in, 46–47, 109;

passage for, *see* Inspirational passage; Patanjali on, 22, 236; physical exercise and, 38, 141–142, 355–356; picture of spiritual figure in, 143; place for, 141; power released in, 50, 141, 157, 189–190, 219, 377; postponing, 123–124; posture for, 143; prāna controlled through, 210; precautions for, 142–144; principle of, 15, 25–26, 180–181, 194–199, 330–331; problems in, 160, 165; problems solved through, 124, 145, 166, 363, *see also* Effect of meditation; progress in, 129, 140–144, 160–161, 165–166, 171–172, 211–214, 346, 358; purifies, 230, 247, 315; purpose of, 62, 175–177, 180–181, 194;

reaching deeper consciousness in, 160–161, 165–166, 236–237, 417, 418; recalls mental energy, 188; regular practice of, 91, 100–101, 141, 179, 180, 369; reincarnation and, 111–112; required for

Library of Congress Cataloging in Publication Data:

Easwaran, Eknath.

    The Bhagavad Gita for daily living.

    Includes indexes.
    CONTENTS: v. 1. The end of sorrow. —v. 2.
Like a thousand suns.
       1. Mahābhārata.   Bhagavadgītā.   I.   Mahābhārata.
Bhagavadgītā.   English & Sanskrit.   1979–
II.   Title.
BL1130.E2   1979   294.5 924   79–1448

ISBN 0–915132–03–6   v. 1.
ISBN 0–915132–17–6   v. 1. pbk.

ISBN 0–915132–04–4   v. 2.
ISBN 0–915132–18–4   v. 2. pbk.